Prospects of Legal Semiotics

Anne Wagner · Jan M. Broekman
Editors

Prospects of Legal Semiotics

Springer

Editors
Prof. Anne Wagner
Université du Littoral Côte d'Opale
Dépt. Droit
Rue Saint Louis 21
62327 Boulogne sur Mer
France
valwagnerfr@yahoo.com

Prof. Jan M. Broekman
Penn State University
Dickinson School of Law
S. College Street 150
17013 Carlisle Pennsylvania
USA
jmb56@dsl.psu.edu

ISBN 978-90-481-9342-4 e-ISBN 978-90-481-9343-1
DOI 10.1007/978-90-481-9343-1
Springer Dordrecht Heidelberg London New York

Library of Congress Control Number: 2010936281

Printed on acid-free paper

Springer is part of Springer Science+Business Media (www.springer.com)

Promises and Prospects of Legal Semiotics—An Introduction

Anne Wagner and Jan M. Broekman

1 Promise and Prospect

This book's title alludes evidently to J. Balkin's "The Promise of Legal Semiotics", an essay in 1990/1991 that was path breaking at the beginning of that last decade of the twentieth century (Balkin 1990). Its text was conceived in the wane of the Critical Legal Studies Movement and showed undoubtedly new ways to understand law's need for enduring intellectual work that would provide new techniques of hermeneutic nature and lawyers' self-understanding. The critical attitude inherent to the CLSM was transferred to a reinforced responsible social critique pertaining to the roles of law in society (Unger 1983). Both, interpretation and critique were eagerly received and supported the basic ideas of what then was called "a new school of legal semiotics". This movement-in-spe should broaden the perspectives of legal rhetoric whilst covering ideas of post-structuralism, legal feminism and post-modern multiculturalism in law and legal studies (Wagner et al. 2005). Balkin's text belongs to a short-living but highly profiled conglomerate of articles in well-established legal journals which promised to become a hinge for semiotics in legal studies. The cluster was originated by remarks in Jeremy Paul's 1990 "The Politics of Legal Semiotics" and concluded in Duncan Kennedy's 2000 study "Semiotics of Critique". All this was object of reflection in Balkin's recent essay "Critical Legal Theory Today" (Paul 1990, Kennedy 2000).

It interests how some strong feeling of "promise" forms an almost seamless connection between CLSM and semiotics of law (Balkin 2008). The first focused on undermining the claims of coherence that characterized legal scholarship, especially as developed in Civil Law scholarship and practice, especially in the emerging European Union Law (Broekman 1999). That opened a promising road to understand and accept the idea of a radical indeterminacy of legal doctrine. The semiotic appreciation of contrasts—so elegantly adapted in the construction of Greimasian squares which put in-depth legal viewpoints in perspective (Greimas

A. Wagner (✉)
Université du Littoral Côte d'Opale, Dunkirk, France
e-mail: valwagnerfr@yahoo.com

1968, 1983)—played a role in understanding legal doctrines as a series of principles and counter-principles, rules and exceptions, profiled policies and contrasting policies. Why were these never effective in legal resolutions of social conflicts? (Greimas 1970) The idea has fit the social and intellectual drives of the CLSM and also attracted legal semiotics. A dominant question remains, however: is the downfall of the coherence-idea in legal thought formation an issue of legal theory and jurisprudence, or is this idea rooted in the unbreakable and close ties between law and politics? The decay of coherence in legal conceptualization could never be performed in theory alone; it relates with necessity to political situations and their analysis. The Paul–Balkin conversation had this theme as a repeatedly profiled question: is the outcome of semiotics that "law is with necessity politics"—also in a society with post-modern principles at the horizon, and with multiculturalism as its forthcoming feature? (Balkin 1990; Paul 1990). Emphasis on the attitude engrained in the expression "promise" is evident here!

Balkin suggests in the tradition of the most far-sighted authors in CLSM context (Balkin 1990):

> When people speak of the relationship between law and "politics," they mean law's relationship to the many different forms of power—economic, social, cultural, political, military and technological—that law constrains, enables or propagates. They also mean the ideals, ideologies and arguments that people use to justify these forms of power. "Politics" refers to people's contrasting visions and to the values that they want to realize or recognize in public life. But it also refers to the power to realize or recognize those values and visions. So when one considers the relationship between "law and politics" one is also interested in the question of law and power—how people justify and legitimate power directly or indirectly through law. And one must also account for law's own methods of proliferating its own power, whether it be through legal concepts, legal institutions, legal culture, legal education, legal officers, or the legal profession as such. In any case, law is not simply politics; rather it is a surprisingly plastic medium of discourse about power and for the exercise of power.

The relation between law and politics, and certainly the question whether law is politics, is not definitively clarified with these reformulations about law as a social power. Law is in semiotic perspective *a discourse of power*, and that formula opens new dimensions (Wagner and Pencak 2006). Once citizens become aware of the fact that they are speakers of a specific discourse, they are indeed empowered *to speak differently*—to each other as well as to their respective social institutions. The different speech could be seen as the result of *legal semiotics as criticism*. This is far more than a harmonious image of society speaking a newly transformed language! To take the language of law in one's own mouth is a dubious gesture, as history has demonstrated clearly. Balkin formulates:

> (...) by choosing to speak in the language of law, powerful people and interests can sometimes be called to account because they try to legitimate what they are doing in those terms. The people they take advantage of can argue that this is a misuse of law, an illegitimate attempt at mystifying rhetoric. They can appeal to the values that law seeks to protect to promote better, more just, and more humane practices and forms of human association.

No wonder, that at the end of the first decade of the twenty-first century, the Balkin "promise" formula is still remembered as a strong sign given by legal semiotics. This is well documented by the 2009 Special Issue of the International Journal for the Semiotics of Law that offers papers from the 2008 International Roundtable in Boulogne-sur-Mer, France, bearing that wording as its title (IJSL Vol. 22, No. 4). Some chapters of this book go back to ideas exchanged and intuitions given a textual character during the conference. Does it mean that lawyers and students of semiotics are still under the spell of the "promise" of legal semiotics? *Quod non,* as this book clearly demonstrates. "Promise" has conscientiously been changed in "Prospect". What does that mean?

Promise and *Prospect* differ importantly; with the consequence that contemporary legal semiotics does not unfold its major ideas and practices in the spirit of promises but rather be represented under the heading of *prospects*. Is a *promise* an expression of hope, of future development, of suggestions beforehand, a *prospect* is rather the anticipation of emerging powers and activities, a well delineated work that could be joined, a project unfolding, a view of things within the reach of eyes. The latter is exactly what this book is about: it shows multiple thoughts, projects and perspectives to readers who are witness of unfolding ideas and realizations. With Umberto Eco, one should keep in mind that readers play always an active part in the interpretation of texts—lawyers as readers are therefore outstanding forces in the unfolding generative process of legal texts (as Eco's *Role of the Reader*, 1979 shows). The change from promise to prospect appears to be a sign in its own right: semiotics of law as offered here, is a sign in reach of what (Sebeok 2001) once called "global semiotics". Various issues are important in what is within the reach of our eyes.

2 Fundamentals, Criticism and Communication

Among the variety of issues included in a prospect on legal semiotics are three outstanding themes. Many of them have historically important ties with preceding developments in legal theory and legal thinking in general. Three are selected to represent those general developments most prominently: fundamentals, criticism and communication. The *first* pertain to a sophisticated and often differentiated scrutiny of the foundations of legal semiotics, mostly circling around the age-old question about what law is in essence. The *second* was definitively at home in the critical considerations of the CLSM, which developed in the US, and European Critical Theory with in particular the so-called "Frankfurter Schule" and its "Institut für Sozialforschung" established shortly after World War II. The critical dimensions focused the relation between law and politics, in particular the dimensions of social justice. These dimensions transformed in contemporary legal semiotics into a multicultural critical theory of law. It is thus understandable how a *third* development in legal semiotics pertains to communication as an issue in its own right. The influence of mixed legal systems and law integrating non-formal legal views in society became provoked by for instance social movements, citizen participation and migratory movements. Those occurrences emphasized again and anew how law functions only on the basis of communication between citizens and legal subjects. A closer look at those three themes enables the reader to understand the design of this book and its various contributions.

2.1 A Changing Concept of Law

A constant interest in a different understanding of law and legal expressiveness is widely awakened by the stronger global coherence of legal systems—a development, which was in the last decades of the twentieth century primarily understood as forces that merge the Common Law and the Civil Law legal systems. Today's semiotics no longer focuses this particular merge but understands how legal semiotics must refer to mixed legal systems, which merge continuously during the process of global cooperation. Thus Boaventura de Sousa Santos points out already in 1995 (Santos 1995) what he later calls "interlegality":

> Rather than being ordered by a single legal order, modern societies are ordered by a plurality of legal orders, interrelated and socially distributed in different ways.

This process has become most challenging in so far as classical definitions or circumscriptions of law and legal discourse, at its minimum the idea that law can bedelineated as a specific discourse (a point debated in Hart's positivist mood and vehemently disputed by Judith Shklar (1986), are now put in perspective and need a new global expressiveness. "Global" is here not only a geographical index, but also an index for social meanings of what law is and should be. Legal semiotics refers to Roberta Kevelson's slogan and book title "Law as a System of Signs" (Kevelson 1988), which indicated a point of interest and of fundamental insight into the basic features of modern law, which with the idea of a peculiar systemic character shows the dynamics that law and semiotics share:

> Semiotics in law attempts to show the process of legal procedure as it develops in each case, and as the system of cases constitutes the moving parts of that moving and developing whole.

In general one could say that modern legal semiotics questions the traditional definitions or circumscriptions of law, and underline how there is no legal semiotics without an elaborated theory and philosophy of law (Kevelson 1996). That conclusion is often problematic for legal students and practitioners who want to become active in a field of legal practice without considering its non-practical implications, and thus qualify semiotics in law as a form of legal philosophy—rather a hobby than a necessity for lawyers! So the change of the concept of law from the days legal semiotics was projected under the heading of promises has consequences for today's understanding. Merging, mixing and provoking the dynamism of law (Wagner 2005a) as a social component of life within global dimensions means that the law-politics relation is no longer on the foreground of considering law in the light of semiotics and does no longer create harsh contrasts between the two discourses. This changed situation strengthens the critique as coloured by multicultural dimensions and weakens the role of oppositions between left- and right winged viewpoints in legal discourse and the necessary foundations of law. It also influences a vision on the communicative effects of legal speech acts and of law in its entirety (Wagner 2005c).

2.2 *Critique, Multicultural*

Balkin's "Promise"-article (Balkin 1990) confirms a fundamental connection between critique and semiotics in saying that

> ... historical deconstruction, and the associated phenomenon of ideological drift, shows the contextual nature of the political valences of legal, moral, and political ideas over time. Yet ... it is often possible to see how existing legal, moral, and political ideas can be "flipped" to serve radically different political ends at one and the same time. This deconstructive "flip" is a synchronic function of the sign, while historical deconstruction and ideological drift are diachronic functions of the sign. The recurring debate in the Critical Legal Studies movement over whether legal doctrines are always "flippable" (and thus never have a determinate political valence), or whether they have a particular "tilt" which is a function of their historical situation (and thus can meaningfully be said to be progressive or conservative at a particular time) is a manifestation of these two different ways of looking at the signs that constitute legal doctrine. The former view is synchronic, the latter diachronic.

That critical function could, however, be expanded when we conclude that semiotics has in itself no political basis to unfold critique of any sort, but solely an epistemological basis (epistemology meaning "concerning dimensions of knowledge") so that the epistemological dimensions of law considered in semiotics, determine the multiple meanings of the concept (Wagner 2005b). This is the most important where a *plurality* of orders determines the modern world. The latter plurality forms a whole scale of viewpoints for future political experiences and legal consequences, becoming visible in changes in legal education, in lawyers never completely fulfilling promises but rather developing visions on cases and problems so that their task—even including the many decisions to be made—seems a new form of looking forwards and unfolding a new "view with the mind". The latter descriptions form the semiotic attitude, which is required to perform the change from promises to prospects. The critical dimension in semiotics, inherited from the CLSM, is rather a guiding principle in the confusing multicultural reality than a set of commands or the fixation of orders. In that regard, one should say, is the expression "a progressive legal semiotician" a pleonasm, because all semiotic projects and attitudes include progressive ideas initiated by new epistemological perspectives.

The latter perspectives show at least three presuppositions at work, which form the background of all contributions to this book. One is *that all semiotic work contributing to the construction of legal discourse has to operate on the basis of law understood as a language*. Next, and closely connected with the first, is the Peirce's idea that *law is continuously in parallel with systems of signs* (Peirce 1931). That was also intended when Kevelson choose the title of her 1988 book on Law as a System of Signs—both "system" and the plurality of signs pertain to the language metaphor. A third is, *that law has always to be conceived as a cultural phenomenon*. This seems formulated under the influence of a certain melancholy of postmodernism as well as the correlated fascination for multicultural determinants of the modern world. Critique is here inherent to the semiotic unfolding of those three presuppositions; human individuals (even in the garment of being a subject of law) embrace a critical attitude when they acknowledge that culture and ideology just are what allow individuals to know how to follow rules or conventions. Law is thus not a discourse of norms, commands or related social signs but rather an all-embracing language to conceive such entities, which leads to the construction of social institutions (Wagner 2005b). This fits Balkin's remark that the purpose of any semiotic activity is in the understanding of *sign systems, which create meanings* in the heart of every pattern of culture. One should underline in this context that each individual in each cultural setting is born to unfold its personal properties *within* an already existing system of law—as a language: an observation that reinforces the influence of language as a cultural data for the engenderment of human individuals in a society. It is remarkable how the semiotic approach to law explores the limits of language in this context, focusing visual semiotics in order to understand the moves from word to visual sign and vice versa.

2.3 Communication

This peculiar change in legal criticism and its emphasis on language are features of nearly all contributions in the book. They put the normative and behavioursrestricting task of law in perspective and find even in these legal epiphenomena an element of a creation of meaning and sense that has to be based on communication between human individuals. This embraces an attitude, which is not the traditional legal one with its emphasis on a first-class performance of the vocation, but rather a holistic stance that requires thinking broadly and decides moral issues as cultural components (in contrast to playing blame-games). As a consequence, legal performance in semiotic perspective includes a growing awareness about the always-implied question in legal cases: "in whose interest are the various decisions at hand made?" This acquired thought-pattern explores and communicates problems that require value judgments and value-laden trade-offs.

It is often difficult for lawyers to notice how the dichotomy of decision-making is replaced with a communicative practicing of insights in the fact that everything does not have to embrace an either/or solution. To distance oneself as a lawyer from these dichotomy patterns is often difficult and frustrating. It is difficult because the communicating power of this pattern touches the very identity of lawyers' activity; and it is frustrating because of feelings like: "for what other purpose did I spend all those years in a Law School?" It shows under the heading of a concept of communication, that lawyers have a fixed understanding about the world around them as well as their own identity and that they are not educated to use this or alternative sets of insights for being creative.

Such lawyers' creativity focuses widely held artifacts, symbols, beliefs and myths, and provokes oftentimes various forms of direct participation as a viewer, reader, listener or other sensory responses to aspects of general culture. Rosen (Rosen 1990, p. 517) noted that:

> the legal process incorporates, shapes, and transforms cultural behaviors and attitudes. That there is a complex dependency between law and culture is not just a consequence of citizens bringing to the law their cultural baggage and the law seeking a legitimacy that speaks to citizens. Social justice (or at least a morally rich pluralism) depends not only on the autonomy of law but also on the interdependencies of law and culture. Interdependence is normatively required, at least in part, because not only must the law morally matter to a culturally heterogeneous population, but also the law ought to be able to speak to those whose claims it does not currently recognize.

It should, however, remain in the forefront that each sign-activity needs what Peirce evoked as a social world, so that semiotic activities in general need to keep a relation with any form of understanding and interpreting communication. Although, as Bergman underlines (Bergman 2009), communication is not a primary factor in Peirce's philosophy (Peirce 1958), there is absolutely a need for semioticians to keep in mind that there cannot be any sign-activity without communication. Whether semiotics is *grounded* in any concept of communication is another question and not a subject of reflection in the context of this publication.

3 Deconstruction and the Legal Semiotic Attitude

The deconstruction mode is by no means a following of Derrida or a symbol of post-modernism; it rather forms a substantial part of the semiotic approach towards or in law. All chapters of this book demonstrate that approach clearly, and in particular the first four chapters who focus on foundational issues.

3.1 Philosophical Dimensions

The following chapters analyze law as "legisigns" (Kevelson's variation on a Peircean expression), which she described as

> ... provisional judgments, held and acted on as if they were truths, although they are in fact the product of an ad hoc community that comes together out of common purpose so long as it is certifiable, verifiable, useful, and is not a bulwark against open, free inquiry and discover. Once the framework for consent is clearly seen as inadequate in the light of new discovery, new significant knowledge, *new Reality* in short, this referential complex legisign must then be either reinterpreted if possible or de-composed if reformation and modification is not possible without totally deranging and disfiguring in procrustean fashion the original (that is, currently established leading principle) (Kevelson 1996, p. 51).

Jackson explores in this context the *basic differences in the identification of the nature of legal semiotics*. Is law a phenomenon of logic, discourse, or experience? A widespread agreement forwards the idea that law embraces a grammar of modalities expressed through different logical and semiotic systems—but are those modalities to be understood as logical relationships external to but expressed by legal discourse, or are they simply particular forms of legal discourse? Notice, how the deconstructive approach refers to the presupposition that law is a discursive phenomenon and hence has to be treated as a language. This does, however, not do away with the fast that legal discourse also expresses an *experiential* dimension (Jackson 1985). Law has not only the task to be effective, but also show affective dimensions, which come more and more to the fore if one considers law's inter-legality and its multicultural dimensions in mixed legal systems. Whereas criminal law adopts for instance a "penal" model—prohibition backed up by a negative sanction (fine, imprisonment, etc.) imposed by the State, private law deploys powers as were they parties to a contract by mutual agreement, which underline obligations towards each other. In so far as states are still able to format a legal system, a "promotional" function is widely used to further particular activities by the promise of a reward (e.g. tax incentives). A recent fundamental discussion pertains to the question whether the traditional deontic operators successfully account for this "promotional" function. The logic of legal expressiveness is remarkably researched and they engender important philosophical questions, which lead to the foundations of legal semiotics.

Broekman notices in his chapter on "Firstness and Phenomenology" how close encounters between Peirce and Husserl show strong ties between semiotics, law and philosophy. Peirce's idea of *firstness* (consequently followed by *secondness* and *thirdness*) has been widely discussed in many Peirce interpretations (Peirce 1958). The idea is a key concept that inspired semiotics. One concludes in hindsight that not *thirdness,* but *firstness* needs full attention in philosophy and semiotics. Explaining *firstness* as an attitude inherent to the sign, one refers to phenomenology as a major field of semiotics, so that semiotics can in its turn reveal the structure of legal thinking.

There is a remarkable parallel to this *firstness* in twentieth century philosophy, the "instellungsänderung"(attitude change, or change of approach) in Edmund Husserl's phenomenology (Husserl 1952, 1954). This makes us understand the complex structure of transcendental phenomenology in its close relationship with semiosis and semiotics. Peirce and Husserl accompany and even foreshadow the linguistic turn of modern philosophy and its implicit phenomenology of social relations.

But is semiotics only to be *applied* in legal practice and legal scholarship, or should the link with application as the basis for legal practice becomes transcended in approaches to legal semiotics? Should a semiotic approach towards law for instance lead to a total *re-engineering* of law and legal practice? The character of *firstness* changes and highlights the relevance of semiotics.

de Ville focuses on Derrida's book *Given Time I. Counterfeit Money*, with the gift as its main theme as a meaning-giving subject. Such philosophical considerations have many forms, which altogether express the three presuppositions mentioned as characteristic for a prospect of legal semiotics. They focus the concept of law in a new light; renew critical dimensions and search for new meanings in the concept of communication. In his definition of justice in *Force of Law*, Derrida refers specifically to justice as a "gift without exchange". It seems essential in order to understand what justice entails that the (perfect) gift be understood beyond our epistemological dimensions of meaning and sense. Derrida's analysis of the gift is essential for politico-legal decision-making. To understand the "place" and "nature" of the gift, we see with Heidegger how to rethink Being and Time in its relevance for semiotics. Marcel Mauss's *The Gift* inspired Derrida in detail. The exchange of gifts lies at the origin of law, morality and economy, Mauss suggests—also in our modern society.

Derrida agrees, but shows that the gift does not fit any terms of exchange. A gift can only qualify as a gift if it expects no return. Heidegger's *On Time and Being* shows that the gift (involving no return) is "situated" beyond the ontological difference, beyond the difference between Being and beings. The gift is in close association with *différance*. This leads to "psychoanalytical" themes: forgetting, sexual difference, repression, mourning and the death drive, which are analysed in the essay with reference to Freud, Abraham, Torok and Heidegger, as well as Derrida. De Ville concludes about the impossibility of a gift in all politico-legal meaning and decision-making.

Salter discusses the key role of semiotic issues, whilst combining theoretical and methodological analyses. Those considerations focusing Derrida and his possible approach to semiotics, come close to dialectical approaches towards law from Hegel to Adorno. He argues that any interpretation and application of legal signs and symbols remains hitherto an underdeveloped area in contemporary dialectical approaches focusing law. He thus discusses the possibilities for developing a model of legal semiotics based upon the distinctly dialectical theories of language, culture and society contained in the writings of Hegel and Theodor Adorno. It builds upon, and contributes to, a growing interest in Hegel's theory of language more generally. For both Hegel and Adorno, it is not possible to develop a viable theory of culture, social integration and cultural / intellectual development occurring over various transitional stages without considering how the semiotic dimensions of human experience operate. The routine employment of various signs associated with for example "law", "legality", "legal procedure" and the relations between them, help generate, sustain and modify an overall and collectively shared interpretative framework. Focuses is thus on only three of the host of possible themes that a Hegelian semiotics of law could address. They are: the interpretation of core semiotics distinctions; the implications of the mediating role played by signs; and, thirdly, the application to our lived-experience of legal signs of a semiotically informed methodology of "immanent criticism". The latter approaches advanced research into contextual aspects of semiotic themes. A self-critical view on "law and semiotics" has yet to be achieved. The Hegelian tradition rejects the idea that the relationship between legal signs and the signified is *essentially* arbitrary. That tradition treats such an interpretation as an arbitrary and ideologically-loaded construct, which articulates specific pathologies of late modern social, cultural and political relations. Instead, one should seek to expose remnants of the mutual implication of these two strata from within our concrete life experiences of signs. Its critical methodology aims to analyze contradictions between the implications of law's normative expressions, and the impact of the actions of legal institutions upon specific groups of human subjects. Such a critical approach contrasts actual institutional outcomes with the implications of the norms they continue to rely upon in order to secure their legitimacy. That is, however, only possible if we grasp the significance of the potentially in a dialectical manner, mutually defining the nature of the sign / signified relationship. This confrontation leads to a practical reasoning about the sciences in which, generally spoken, phenomena of language and interaction become complementary, and emerge as sources of mutual enrichment.

3.2 Communicative Dimensions

Although Peirce's philosophy has no clear theory or circumscription of communication as a subject for semiotics, it plays a major role. The pragmatic fact that there is no sign-activity without communication is a strong point, which several authors of this book agree upon in the choice of their subject and/or their theoretical background. For Peirce it was a more or less foundational idea that could serve pragmatic approaches pertaining to the question of social cohesion and human togetherness in social patterns. This becomes an issue of further consideration when Kevelson brings law and semiotics together. Legal discourse and social cohesion appear to be most effective for her if both are understood in terms of social contract (Kevelson 1988; Kennedy 2000):

> Peirce's pragmatism is grounded on the conviction that value in thought and in reality accumulates through a process of transacting and exchanging ideas by persons who contract to accomplish a mutually agreed-upon purpose.

Habermas highlights, in contrast to Kevelson correlative and non-contractual aspects of the same issue (Habermas 1995, p. 131). He states, that in a multicultural society the inclusion of every form of life that has rights consists of the recognition for everybody to have

> the opportunity to grow up in the world of cultural heritage and to have his or her children grown up in it without suffering discrimination because of it. It means the opportunity to confront this and every culture and to perpetuate it in its conventional form or to transform it.

Both opinions show another issue: signs thus relate to deep structures of social reality whilst creating a space for sharing among participants. The signs, which are contours of a legal system, imply multiple dependencies upon the needs of various communities of inquirers in their diverse guises and settings.

Mapping the contours of a legal system equals an interpretation of a system of legal signs. That interpretation of law is apt to contribute to the changing needs of institutionally anchored functions, like those of judges, lawyers, legislators or citizens. So it is not necessary to unfold a coherent theory of communication in legal semiotics, but it is essential to highlight that communication is a prerequisite of sign-activity in general. This insight has, however, many facets.

Wolcher reminds us that Nietzsche once underlined how the great danger of direct questioning a subject *about* the subject is in the fact that it could be useful and important to interpret oneself *falsely*. Wittgenstein generalised Nietzsche's warning in saying "Nothing is so difficult as not-deceiving oneself". One should try to heed both warnings. It shows that the idea of the grounding subject represents a desperate and ultimately futile attempt to repress awareness of (and evade personal responsibility for) the essential sadness and tragedy of the world. It alleges that the most thought and reason can ever do is provide the human body with a thin tissue of grounding statements made up of symbols and images. These symbols and images will never span the existential distance between the grounding subject and the causal subject, ends from means, words from deeds, and, more generally, human suffering and all of the seemingly endless casuistries that we offer to justify it. Go ahead and dream your dreams and plan your plans—but do not *ever* try to convince yourself that "they" (the dreams and principles) genuinely underlie and justify what you do in the world! *Using* principles of justice is natural if not inevitable. *Feeling* principled and just, on the other hand, makes for a hell on earth that can be just as horrible as the hell made by those who give unbridled license to a ravening will to power.

Lippens explores the works of the painters Pollock and Rothko, thus expanding the reach of semiotic analysis. Continuing Francis Haskell's exploration of prophetic painting, he sets out to illustrate how emerging, diagrammatic "forms of life", and the codes of law and governance that reside in them, tend to materialize first in the visual sensory sphere before they do so conceptually. Using "Deleuzoguattarian" thought—Deleuze's work on painting in particular—he shows how Pollock's and Rothko's work, painted between 1945 and 1950, harbours traces of an emerging late-modern "form of life" where vitality and radical freedom are inextricably linked with precautionary tension (and vice versa).

Bainbridge examines how law is "a powerful (legal) fiction... crucial to the exercise of political power and legal authority across many different fields, especially the 'cultural'" (Redhead 1995; Husserl 1913) and connect it to popular culture—namely the impact of popular culture on public perceptions of law (the signifiers) and justice. He examines the context in which the study of popular culture in relation to law has developed and its principal goals and working assumptions of those engaged in this work. He thus focuses what been carried out in view of perceptions of law and justice as affected by popular culture.

The term "law" has many meanings, not just in legal institutions (where it can refer to positivist law, natural law, indigenous law or police powers) but also in the wider culture. Law seems to be a malleable concept, its definition often depending upon the context in which it is found. Despite this, legal and cultural theorist Steve Redhead notes 1995 that conventionally "in jurisprudential and political theory" law is taken as a given—"we assume that we know what it is and where to find it, and also what it does" (Redhead 1995; Husserl 1913). Redhead goes on to suggest that this is in fact "a powerful (legal) fiction which may be crucial to the exercise of political power and legal authority across many different fields, especially the 'cultural'".

Exploring Ferdinand de Saussure's notion of *semiotics* as the study of communication, one is witness of how communication practices can be broken down into a series of units called *signs*. A relation between the signifier and the signified is called *signification,* the process by which meaning is made. When we are confronted with images, such as a statue of justice, an image of a courtroom, or the figure of a lawyer or a policeman, we can understand them all as the physical *signifiers* of the *signified*, called law.

Massimo shows how "semiotic landscapes" are patterns of perceptible elements that individuals come across in *public* space. "Semiotic scenes" are patterns of perceptible elements that individuals come across in *private* space. Whereas semiotic scenes are mostly controlled by individual agencies, and are therefore relatively stable and transparent, semiotic landscapes are mostly controlled by collective agencies, and are therefore relatively unstable and opaque. Large migratory phenomena usually modify the semiotic landscapes of contemporary cities. New somatic features, new kinds of cloths, new gestures, postures, and movements, new feelings of distance and proximity, new music, new food, new sounds and smells, new buildings, new ways of experiencing the body in space and time, new conceptions of private and public, individuality and collectiveness become increasingly conspicuous. Individuals and groups react to these changes by either semiotic engagement (modifying their semiotic habits) or by semiotic disengagement (contrasting changes so that semiotic habits are not modified). The point of equilibrium that a certain society reaches between semiotic engagement and semiotic disengagement manifests itself also in legal sources.

Legal controversies about the establishment of new mosques in Australia are analysed in order to investigate the nature of this point of equilibrium in the Australian society. The semio-cultural analysis of one of these controversies shows the existence of a gap between the way in which multiculturalism is conceived by the political, legal, administrative, and bureaucratic discourse at the federal and state level, and how it is embodied in local reactions toward difference. Suggestions are made about policies that might help filling such gap. The semiotic engagement of the Australian society is compared with that of the Italian one. The semio-cultural analysis of a recent project of law concerning the establishment of new mosques in Italy shows that the leading socio-political framework in Italy is still relatively monocultural. A vicious circle between the religious majority and its mediatic and political referents shows discriminatory attitudes toward religious minorities. These attitudes might become different if Italy would adopt policies already proved successful in other societies, like the Australian. The latter has a long experience in managing cultural and religious differences.

4 Our Prospects

Both series of contributions presented in this book—those who lead to the foundations of legal semiotics and philosophy as well as those who offer a semiotic analysis of concrete social and communal developments in the modern world, show a surprising multiplicity of perspectives. Whilst offering this prospect, they also operate with a constantly changing concept of law and legal discourse. The book in its totality shows that such changes do not prevent a certain unity in outlining the relevance of legal semiotics. The two components are very different indeed:

changing *law* differs from changing *sign-activities*. Both have, however, the *seme*, the sign as a common property. The future of our system of societies on a global scale is in *plurality*. That is a challenge of hitherto unknown anthropological dimensions. The human mind is in our days a learning mind: learning about its proper capacities, brain functions, life prospects, and its social constructions (Wagner et al. 2005; Wagner 2005b). Kevelson thus highlighted how a semiotics of law should be capable of accounting for inter-systemic communication between systems that are culturally, historically, and ideologically differently located on the map of the globe, and different on the global map of legal systems (Kevelson 1988). It is this plurality, which forms a challenge for our future, is the inspiration of this book when it offers a prospect of semiotics' contribution to legal and social developments.

References

Balkin J.M. 1990. The Hohfeldian Approach to Law and Semiotics. *University of Miami Law Review*, 44, 5.

Balkin J.M. 1990/1991. The Promise of Legal Semiotics. *University of Texas Law Review*, 69, 1831.

Balkin J. M. 2008. Critical Legal Theory Today. In ed. Francis J. Mootz III, *Philosophy In American Law*. Oxford: Oxford University Press.

Bergman, Mats. 2009. *Peirce's Philosphy of Communication*. London and New York, NY: Continuum IP.

Broekman J.M. 1999. *A Philosophy of European Union Law*. Paris/Leuven: Peeters.

Greimas, Algirdas J. 1968. The Interaction of Semiotic Constraints. *Yale French Studies*, 41, 86–105.

Greimas, Algirdas J. 1970. *Du Sens. Essais Sémiotiques*. Paris: Ed. Du Seuil.

Greimas, Algirdas J. 1983. *Du Sens II. Essais Sémiotiques*. Paris: Ed. Du Seuil.

Habermas, J. 1995. In ed. Stephen K. White, *The Cambridge Companion to Habermas* (Cambridge Companions to Philosophy). Cambridge: Cambridge University Press.

Husserl, Edmund. 1913. *Logische Untersuchungen Band II*, 2 vols. Hall a.d.S: Max Niemeyer.

Husserl, Edmund. 1952. *Ideen zu einer Reinen Phänomenologie und Phänomenologischen Philosophie Bd. II: Phänomenologische Untersuchungen zur Konstitution. Husserliana*, vol. IV. Den Haag: Martinus Nijhoff.

Husserl, Edmund. 1954. *Die Krisis der Europäischen Wissenschaften und die Transzendentale Phänomenologie. Husserliana*, vol. VI. Den Haag: Martinus Nijhoff.

Jackson Bernard S. 1985, 1997. *Semiotics and Legal Theory*. London: Kegan Paul. Reprint Deborah Charles Publications.

Kennedy, Duncan. 2000–2002. Semiotics of Critique. *Cardozo Law Review*, 22, 1147.

Kevelson Roberta. 1988. *The Law as a System of Signs*. New York, NY: Plenum Press.

Kevelson, Roberta. 1996. *Peirce, Science, Signs*. New York, NY: Peter Lang.

Paul, Jeremy. 1990–1991. The Politics of Legal Semiotics. *Texas Law Review*, 69, 1779–1829.

Peirce, Ch. S. 1931–1935. In eds. Charles Hartshorne and Paul Weiss, *Ed. The Collected Papers of Charles Sanders Pierce*, vols I–VI. Cambridge, MA: Harvard University Press.

Peirce, Ch. S. 1958. In ed. Arthur W. Burks, *Ed. The Collected Papers of Charles Sanders Pierce*, vols VII–VIII. Cambridge, MA: Harvard University Press.

Redhead, Steve. 1995. *Unpopular Cultures: The Birth of Law and Popular Culture*. Manchester: Manchester University Press.

Rosen, R. 1990. Liberal Battle Zones and the Study of Law and the Media. *Law and Human Behavior*, 14(5), 511–521.

Santos, Boaventura de Sousa. 1995. Three Metaphors for a New Conception of Law: The Frontier, the Baroque, and the South. *Law and Society Review*, 29(4), 569–584.
Sebeok Thomas, A. 2001. *Global Semiotics*. Bloomington: Indiana University Press.
Shklar, J. 1986. *Legalism. Law, Morals, and Political Trials*, 2nd edn. Cambridge: Harvard University Press.
Unger, Roberto Mangabeira. 1983, 1986. *The Critical Legal Studies Movement*. Cambridge: Harvard University Press.
Wagner, Anne. 2005a. Semiotic Analysis of the Multistage Dynamics at the Core of Indeterminacy in Legal Language. In eds. V. Bhatia et al., *Vagueness in Normative Texts*. Bern: Peter Lang.
Wagner Anne. 2005b. Le diagnostic de la pluralité en droit médical – 'The Human Fertilisation and Embryology Act 1990' et ses implications. *Semiotica*, 151-1/4, 183–200.
Wagner, Anne. 2005c. Les apports de l'analyse linguistique dans la conception du flou et de la sécurité juridique. *La Semaine Juridique, Edition Générale*, 51, 2355–2359.
Wagner, Anne et al. 2005. *Contemporary Issues in the Semiotics of Law: Cultural and Symbolic Analyses of Law in a Global Context* (Oñati Series in International Law and Society). London: Hart.
Wagner, Anne and Pencak, William. 2006. *Images in Law*. Aldershot and Burlington, VT: Ashgate.

Contents

Contributors

Jason Bainbridge Swinburne University, Boston, MA, USA; Swinburne University of Technology, Melbourne, VIC, Australia, jbainbridge@swin.edu.au

Jan M. Broekman Dickinson School of Law, Penn State University, Pennsylvania, PA, USA, jmb56@dsl.psu.edu

Jacques de Ville University of the Western Cape, Cape Town, South Africa, jdeville@uwc.ac.za

Bernard S. Jackson Liverpool Hope University, Liverpool, UK, jacksob@hope.ac.uk

Massimo Leone University of Torino, Turin, Italy; Monash University, Melbourne, VIC, Australia, massimo.leone@unito.it

Ronnie Lippens Keele University, Newcastle-under-Lyme, UK, r.lippens@keele.ac.uk

Michael Salter University of Central Lancashire, Preston, UK, msalter@uclan.ac.uk; msalter1@aol.com

Louis E. Wolcher Charles I. Stone Professor of Law, University of Washington School of Law, Seattle, WA, USA, wolcher@u.washington.edu

About the Authors

Jason Bainbridge is Senior Lecturer in Media, Journalism and Communications at Swinburne University of Technology, Australia. He has published widely on popular media representations of law, social media and current issues with journalism and is the co-author of *Media and Journalism: New Approaches to Theory and Practice* (Oxford, 2008).

Jan M. Broekman studied Law and Social Sciences in Leiden (Neth.) and Philosophy in Göttingen (Germ.) (PhD.1961). He was 1961–1966 Vice-Director of The Hague Social Academy, 1966–1968 Associate Professor Contemporary Philosophy and Aesthetics at the University of Amsterdam, 1968–1996 Professor Philosophy of Law, Legal Theory and EU Law as well as Professor Contemporary Philosophy at the KULeuven Belgium. Broekman was 1988–1994 Dean and Pro-Dean of the Leuven Law Faculty and 1980–1995 Professor Philosophy of Medicine and Medical Ethics at the Free University, Amsterdam, He co-directed 1975–1979 Courses "Marxism and Phenomenology" at the Yugoslave Interuniversity Center, Dubrovnik. He is since 2006 Distinguished Visiting Professor of Law at the Penn State University Dickinson School of Law where he established in 2008 "he Roberta Kevelson Seminar on Law and Semiotics" which he directs since that date, and guest edited the IJSL 2009 and 2010 Special Issues related to the Seminar. Broekman authored 25 books and more than 400 scientific articles on Law and Legal Theory, Philosophy of Medicine, Contemporary Philosophy, Semiotics, Education, Culture and Politics in 13 languages, among them his 1971 *Structuralism* in English, Dutch, German, French, Spanish and Chinese.

Jacques de Ville is Professor and Head of the Department of Public Law and Jurisprudence at the University of the Western Cape, South Africa. His early publications were in the fields of constitutional law, administrative law and legal interpretation, and include two monographs: *Constitutional and Statutory Interpretation* (2000) and *Judicial Review of Administrative Action in South Africa* (2003). His research and publications currently focus on deconstruction, psychoanalysis, and legal philosophy. This includes a number of publications on Jacques Derrida and his relation to law. He is the holder of an Alexander von Humboldt fellowship, and the English book-review editor of the *International Journal for the Semiotics of Law*.

Bernard Stuart Jackson, b. 1944, holds degrees from Liverpool (LL.B. (Hons), 1965), Oxford (D. Phil., 1969), Edinburgh (LL.D., 1987) and Hebrew Union College, Cincinnati (D.H.L., *honoris causa,* 1998). He has held posts at the Universities of Georgia (USA), Edinburgh, Kent, Liverpool (Queen Victoria Professor of Law, 1989–1997) and Manchester (Co-Director of the Centre for Jewish Studies, 1997–2009; Director of the Agunah Research Unit, 2004–2009), and Visiting Appointments in Jerusalem, Oxford, Harvard, Paris, Bologna and Brussels. He now teaches part-time at Liverpool Hope University. His research interests are in the semiotics of law and the history and philosophy of Jewish law: he was a founder member of the International Association for the Semiotics of Law and of its journal, the *IJSL*; founder editor of *The Jewish Law Annual*; past President and currently Chairman of The Jewish Law Association. He is the author of nine single-authored books, including *Essays in Jewish and Comparative Legal History,* E.J. Brill, 1975; *Semiotics and Legal Theory*, Routledge & Kegan Paul, 1985; *Making Sense in Law*, Liverpool: Deborah Charles Publications, 1995; *Making Sense in Jurisprudence*, Deborah Charles Publications, 1996; *Studies in the Semiotics of Biblical Law*, Sheffield Academic Press, 2000; *Wisdom-Laws: A Study of the Mishpatim of Exodus 21:1-22:16*, Oxford University Press, 2006; *Essays on Halakhah in the New Testament,* E.J. Brill, 2008. Full publications list at http://www.legaltheory.demon.co.uk/lib_biblioBSJ1.html.

Massimo Leone is Research Professor of Semiotics and Cultural Semiotics at the Department of Philosophy, University of Torino, Italy. He graduated in Communication Studies from the University of Siena, and holds a DEA in History and Semiotics of Texts and Documents from Paris VII, an MPhil in Word and Image Studies from Trinity College Dublin, a PhD in Religious Studies from the Sorbonne, a PhD in Art History from the University of Fribourg (CH). He was visiting scholar at the CNRS in Paris and at the CSIC in Madrid, Fulbright Visiting Professor at the Graduate Theological Union, Berkeley (USA), and Endeavour Research Visiting Scholar at the School of English, Performance, and Communication Studies at Monash University, Melbourne (AUS). His work focuses on the role of religion in modern and contemporary societies. Massimo Leone has authored two books and numerous papers in semiotics and religious studies. He has lectured in Africa, America, Asia, Australia, and Europe.

Ronnie Lippens was educated at Kortrijk Polytechnic, Universiteit Leuven, and Universiteit Gent (all in Belgium), obtaining a PhD in Criminology from the last named. He then moved to Keele in 1999 where, since 2006, he is a Professor of Criminology. Ronnie's research interests include critical criminology, organizational criminology, and, more recently, also the imaginary of justice, law and order, as expressed in e.g. novels and paintings. He has published numerous contributions on these topics in a wide variety of venues, and is currently working on the emergence of forms of governance in what could be called prophetic painting.

Michael Salter is a Professor of Law at the University of Central Lancashire, Preston, UK, PhD Sheffield 1988. He formerly held academic posts at the

Universities of Birmingham, Ulster and Lancaster. He has published numerous articles and books on various aspects of legal theory, including Hegel and Law, critical methodologies and the involvement of intelligence agencies in war crimes trials.

Anne Wagner (Ph.D.) is Assistant Professor at the Université du Littoral Côte d'Opale (France) and Research Professor at China University of Political Science and Law (Beijing, China) in Legal Semiotics and Legal Discourse Analyses. Anne Wagner is an expert in Legal Semiotics and Legal Discourse Analyses. She has extensively published research papers in the area of law and semiotics, legal discourse analyses, law and culture, and legal translation. Her main edited volumes include *Contemporary Issues in the Semiotics of Law: Cultural and Symbolic Analyses in a Global Context* (2005, Hart), *Images in Law* (2006, Ashgate), *Legal Language and the Search for Clarity* (2006, Peter Lang), *Interpretation, Law and the Construction of Meaning* (2006, Springer), *Obscurity and Clarity in the Law* (2008, Ashgate), *Diversity and Tolerance in Socio-Legal Context* (2009, Ashgate). She is the Editor-in-Chief of the *International Journal for the Semiotics of Law* (http://www.springer.com/law/journal/11196). She is a new editorial board member of SemiotiX (www.semioticon.com). She is the President of the *International Roundtables for the Semiotics of Law*. She has launched a website dedicated to the study of Law, Semiotics and Visual Culture (http://www.semioticsoflaw.com). She is co-editing with Richard K. Sherwin the *Treatise on Law, Culture and Visual Studies*, 2 volumes (Forthcoming Springer, 2011). This project will aim to promote an international, interdisciplinary debate on the nature and scope of the law, semiotics and visuality movement by bringing together diverse research traditions ranging from cultural studies, communication theory, rhetoric, popular culture, law and film studies, the cultural history of law, and visual jurisprudence, among other fields. She is a Permanent Member of the *Instituto Subalpino per l'analisi e l'insegnamento del diritto della attività transanzionali—ISAIDAT* led by Professor Rodolfo Sacco. She is one of the founding members of the International Language and Law Association initiated by Lawrence Solan, Dieter Stein and Peter Tiersma (http://www.illa.org/).

Louis E. Wolcher is the Charles I. Stone Professor of Law at the University of Washington School of Law, in Seattle, Washington (USA). Holding degrees from both Stanford University and Harvard Law School, he has written extensively in various fields of philosophy and law, including philosophy of language, philosophy of law, critical legal theory and human rights. One of his essays, "Time's Language", was awarded Second Prize by the final jury of the Millennial International Essay Competition in 2000, and his most recent book, *Law's Task: The Tragic Circle of Law, Justice and Human Suffering*, was published in 2008 by Ashgate Publishing. He has also given and published numerous lectures abroad, including at the European Court of Human Rights in Strasbourg, France, at the Institute of Political Science in Tashkent, Uzbekistan, at the University of Ljubljana Faculty of Law in Ljubljana, Slovenia, at Kobe University and Osaka University in Japan, at Birkbeck Laws School in London, and at Mofid University in Iran. He lives with his partner Susan Haluk Wolcher on Mercer Island in the state of Washington.

Part I
Deconstructing Legal Semiotics

Chapter 1
Legal Semiotics and Semiotic Aspects of Jurisprudence

Bernard S. Jackson

1.1 Introduction

1.1.1 Problematics

Any account of legal semiotics must necessarily take stances upon three very debatable issues: the nature of "law", the nature of "semiotics", and the nature of the relationship between them. Each one presents the scholar with many options. While describing here a wide range of approaches found within the field (in what is necessarily, through constraints on space, no more than an outline account of the subject), I make no claim that what follows represents more than a set of personal choices and interpretations.

1.1.2 Law as Logic, Discourse, or Experience?

Within the literature of the semiotics of law, we find reflections of basic differences in the identification of the nature of the subject-matter: is law a phenomenon of logic, discourse, or experience? There is widespread agreement, though expressed through different logical and semiotic systems, that law has recourse to a basic grammar of modalities (Greimas 1976; Kalinowski 1976; Jackson 1985a, Section 4.4). But are these modalities logical relationships external to but expressed by discourse (Kalinowski) or simply particular forms of discourse (Greimas)?

B.S. Jackson (✉)
Liverpool Hope University, Liverpool, UK
e-mail: jacksob@hope.ac.uk

This article was written in 1990 as a (rather ethnocentric, as I have increasingly come to realise) review of the state of the art in legal semiotics. It may now be viewed as a contribution to the history of the discipline. I am indebted to a number of friends and colleagues for assistance, of a variety of kinds, in the preparation of this article, especially Takanori Kitamura (who directed my attention to the work of Sudnow), Eric Landowski, François Paychère, Carol Prescott, Roland Posner and Thomas-M. Seibert.

A. Wagner, J.M. Broekman (eds.), *Prospects of Legal Semiotics*,
DOI 10.1007/978-90-481-9343-1_1, © Springer Science+Business Media B.V. 2010

But there is also a further dimension of legal sense: the experiential dimension. Whereas criminal law adopts a "penal" model—prohibition backed up by a negative sanction (fine, imprisonment, etc.) imposed by the State—and private law deploys private powers (as where parties to a contract change, by mutual agreement, their obligations towards each other), the "promotional" function is one widely used by the State to promote particular activities, by the promise of a reward (e.g. tax incentives). Recently, there has been discussion as to whether the traditional deontic operators successfully account for this "promotional" function (Gonzalez Ruiz 1989; Paychère 1989).

1.1.3 The Unity of the Legal System and the Problem of Reference

Much writing within legal semiotics seems to presuppose that which is most problematic in legal studies, namely the unity of the legal system: the claim that a law, its written expression, the legal structure of a particular state, and indeed the ideological manifestations of the concept, all somehow belong to a single system, "the legal system" (sometimes, "the law"). To make that presupposition is to indicate the continuing predominance of the basic *positivist* paradigm within legal studies.

One common feature of the different forms of "legal semiotics" resides in their capacity to problematise this notion of the unity of law—whether it be through an analysis of the different sign-types involved in legal activity (which Landowski 1988a, has called *sémiologie juridique*); or the study of the signifying structures of particular forms of discourse ("*sémiotique juridique*", in Landowski's terms); or the Peircian-inspired notion that every act of signification involves an open-ended process of interpretation (Kevelson 1988b).

The (transnational) lexeme "Jurisprudence" is also polysemic. In the Anglo-Saxon world, "Jurisprudence" is normally (at least in academe) taken to mean legal philosophy; in the Francophone world, the same lexeme means "case law". From the viewpoint of positivist legal philosophy, we have here two quite different referents, since "case law" is part of the "primary" sources of the law (the law itself), while legal philosophy (at best) is a secondary source, a discourse *about* law. But from a semiotic viewpoint, "jurisprudence" in the sense of "legal philosophy" is not a secondary or meta-discourse in the sense that it *refers to* or is *about* some entity (the law), the meaning of which is defined externally to the discourse of legal philosophy itself. While "Jurisprudence", in this sense, certainly makes *claims* to refer to something outside itself, the meaning of that to which it claims to refer is constructed internally within legal philosophy itself. If we adopt such a view, "jurisprudence" in the sense of legal philosophy and "jurisprudence" in the sense of case-law are *parallel* discourses which belong to that family of discourses which *claim* to refer to the same external referent. They are, by this token, equal partners in the construction of the legal culture.

1.2 Semiotic Presuppositions of Traditional Jurisprudence

Though legal philosophy still takes inspiration from the teachings of Locke and Bentham, only rarely, and relatively recently (e.g. Scarpelli 1988) have legal philosophers sought to relate the general semiotic theories of Locke and Bentham to their contributions of the philosophy of law. But linguistic considerations have proved important in the English analytical tradition stemming from Bentham. I briefly consider here the different approaches to the language of Jurisprudence employed by Bentham's contemporary and follower, John (not J.L.) Austin, and by the leading English legal philosopher of the post-war generation, H.L.A. Hart.

1.2.1 Austin

The jurist, John Austin (1790–1859, not to be confused with the twentieth century linguistic philosopher, J.L. Austin), like Bentham, had a *penchant* for clear definitions. His attention to language forms part of his methodology—it is needed in order to create the possibility of a "scientific" approach to law. He sought to distinguish the "proper" from the "improper" uses of the word "law" (Morris 1960): "every *law* or *rule* (taken with the largest signification which can be given to the term *properly)* is a *command*." "If you express or intimate a wish that I shall do or forbear from some act, and if you will visit me with an evil in case I comply not with your wish, the *expression* or *intimation* of your wish is a *command*" (1954, 13 f.). Within the category of law properly so-called, Austin finds two main species: "laws set by God to his human creatures, and laws set by men to men." But the latter category, human law, is itself divided into two: laws set by men as political superiors (in a relationship of sovereignty), and laws set by men not in that capacity (1954, p. 10).

The reason for such differentiations is a matter, quite simply, of accurate description. For Austin, it appears to be a goal in itself that language should accurately reflect differences in the world. The criterion of "accurate" description is a quasi-logical one. Things "resemble" each other in the "strict" sense when "they both belong to some determinate genus or species expressly or tacitly referred to; when they both have every property, which belongs to all the subjects included in the class" (1954, p. 119).

Yet Austin also offers a second, substantive category, of "positive morality"—which spans the linguistic categories of that which is "properly" and "improperly" termed law: it includes both "commands" issued by non-sovereigns and rules emanating from non-determinate sources (thus, not commands) such as customary law. The reason for this is that the categories of accurate description do not correspond exactly to those of proper scientific method. Even once the categories of accurate description are established, one may find that different scientific methodologies are applicable to different species within a single *genus* and conversely that the same scientific methodology may be applicable across different *genera*. Thus positive law is that species within the *genus* of law properly so-called to which (alone) the science of law is applicable, while a different methodology, that applicable to "positive morality", may apply to some phenomena properly called law (e.g. some forms of constitutional law) and to some phenomena not properly called law (e.g. customary law).

1.2.2 Hart

Unlike Austin, Hart has explicitly eschewed attempts to construct a theory of law on the back of definitions of terms. He has preferred to adopt a version of the Wittgensteinian notion of "family resemblance", in exploring the relations between different uses of the expressions "law" and "legal system". For Hart, therefore, the structure of language is important for the methodology of jurisprudence. While he has paid only passing attention to the nature of signs (Jackson 1985a, pp. 149–152), it is clear from his account of the workings of legal language—including the "penumbra of doubt" which attaches to the interpretation of general terms—that (even while abandoning the command theory of law) he continues to see the legal sytem in terms of a *communicational* (rather than *significatory*) system.

Hart's categories of description are linguistic: social phenomena as identified by ordinary language. But Hart is not content merely to record what he observes. He is concerned to subject these observations to critical analysis: to determine whether our everyday experience can be justified in analytical terms.

Hart's epistemology is succinctly stated in the Preface to his *Concept of Law*: "Many important distinctions which are not immediately obvious, between types of social situation or relationships may best be brought to light by an examination of the standard uses of the relevant expressions and of the way in which these depend on a social context, itself often left unstated. In this field of study it is particularly true that we may use, as Professor J.L. Austin said, " 'A sharpened awareness of words to sharpen our perception of the phenomena' " (1961, p. vii; see also Jori 1979; Jackson 1985a, 152 ff.). But Hart clearly wishes to go beyond this. He is looking for "important" distinctions, and the criterion of importance does not consist purely in the fact that these distinctions are socially accepted. "The lawyer will regard the book as an essay in analytical jurisprudence, for it is concerned with the clarification of the general framework of legal thought." An example of linguistic distinctions which evidence our social experience is used by Hart to criticise Austin's version of positivism. Our use of modal verbs shows that we regard as significant the distinction between two types of rule: "power-conferring" rules and "duty-imposing rules".

"Law" itself is a concept embedded in our social knowledge through linguistic usage, but that linguistic usage is multi-faceted. We should consider the relations between the different usages of the concept "law", and decide upon the significance of the similarities and differences which we observe. Such relations are best captured by Wittgenstein's notion of "family resemblance". It has been argued, however, that Hart's method is closer to Hilary Putnam's notion of a "cluster concept" (Sartorius 1966, pp. 171–72).

1.2.3 Kelsen

The leading exponent of pure positivism, or "normativism", is Hans Kelsen. He proposes a theory of law as a system of "norms", in which his notion of "legal meaning" *(Bedeutung)* assumes a central place. A "norm", for Kelsen, is neither the act of a human being (e.g. a command), nor is it a textual or linguistic phenomenon—a particular form of words. Rather, it is a particular form of meaning attributed to human action: "'Norm' is the meaning of an act by which a certain behaviour is commanded, permitted or authorized." (1967, p. 5). "For example: People assemble in a large room, make speeches, some raise their hands, others do not—this is the external happening. Its meaning is that a statute is being passed, that law is created."

Kelsen adds to this conception a distinction between "subjective" and "objective" meaning. An act has a particular legal meaning only when such legal significance is *objectively,* not subjectively attributed to it. Thus: "Somebody makes some disposition, stating in writing what is to happen to his belongings when he dies. The subjective meaning of this act is a testament. Objectively, however, it is not, because some legal formalities were not observed" (1967, p. 3). Passages like this make it reasonably clear that by "meaning"—whether subjective or objective—he really means something like "illocutionary force", a matter of the significance of the utterance or the act, rather than its signification.

In order for this system to work, Kelsen had to attribute to the "norm" a dual function, one which presupposed a hierarchy (or cycle) of legal acts and meanings. On the one hand, the "norm" was the meaning attributed (in terms of the constitution) to the acts of individual legal subjects; on the other, it is used as a frame of interpretation for the behaviour of others, to which its text "refers". As Kelsen puts it: "To say that a norm 'refers' to actual behaviour is to say that the norm can be applied to actual behaviour, that actual behaviour can be confronted with it, that this behaviour can be interpreted according to it and judged as conforming to or departing from it" (1960, p. 181).

This, perhaps, is not a technical application of the notion of "reference"—certainly not as it might be understood by an analytical philosopher like Strawson (1950; Jackson 1988b, Chapter 2). Clearly, the legislators have no communicational intention in respect of future actions of which they have no knowledge. Kelsen is here merely saying that future behaviour "can be interpreted" according to the norm. In this particular passage, he begs the vital question of who is authorised so to interpret the norms.

1.2.4 Law as Interpretation: Ronald Dworkin

Dworkin has suggested that the reasoning of judges in "hard cases" presents significant parallels with the practices of a different group of professional interpreters, the literary critics (1978, 1986; Jackson 1985a, Chapter 9; 1988b, Chapter 5). The development of the law is like the activity of literary critics, or even the writing of a "chain novel". Legal reasoning employs a form of coherence which is not a purely legal construct: it is a "holistic" form of meaning, which depends upon semiotic processes similar to those found in literature. But the discretion of the judge is limited in particular ways. There exist, for example, two different types of legal sign, which the judge must distinguish: "principles" and "policies". Increasingly, Dworkin has seen his interpretation theory as akin to that of the hermeneutician Gadamer (Dworkin 1986, pp. 55–62 and 419–420 n. 2).

Dworkin claims (contrary to the positivists in general and Hart in particular) that the judge, even in "hard cases", does not create law but gives effect to the existing rights of the parties. The issue has been debated in terms of the presence or absence of "logical spaces" in the legal system (Dworkin 1977; Jackson 1985b). In claiming that law exists only when legal institutions have said so, Hart must inevitably argue that when legal institutions have not endorsed the existence of a rule, that rule does not exist in law. The closure rules implicit in this argument are a form of propositional logic: the propositions: "the legal institutions have endorsed rule x" and "the legal institutions have not endorsed rule x" are contradictories: the denial of either one entails the affirmation of the other. With the affirmation of either one, there must follow the consequences which attach to it. If it is not the case that the legal institutions have endorsed rule x, then rule x cannot be part of the law. We can represent this argument in the form of a logical square, the contraries of which are (A) the affirmation that the legal institutions have endorsed rule x and (E) the internal negation of that affirmation (viz., that the legal institutions have endorsed the negation of rule x). The contradictories are the respective external negations of the two contraries: the denial that the legal institutions have endorsed rule x (O, the contradictory of A) and the denial that the legal institutions have endorsed the negation of rule x (I, the contradictory of E). According to the elaboration of the logical square by modern logicians such as Blanché (1966) and Kalinowski (1972, 165 f.), we arrive at a fifth point (Y), which is that the legal institutions have endorsed neither rule x nor the negation of rule x. This fifth point stands in a triadic relationship to the two contraries, in the sense that the affirmation of any one point in the triad entails the denial of the other two (although the denial of any one does not indicate which of the other two should be affirmed—an extension of the logic of contraries).

The judge has to give a decision, and this decision, for Dworkin, must be based upon his knowledge of the rights of the parties. The adoption of this closure rule results in a quite different semiotic structure from that underlying Hart's model. The contradictory positions (points O and I in the square) of the two contraries (points A and E) are excluded in practice; they function only as the bases of presuppositions leading to adoption of the opposite contrary. If the judge does not know that x has a right to succeed (O), he must act as if he does know that x has no right to succeed (E); if the judge does not know that x has no right to succeed (I), he must act as if he knows that x has a right to succeed (A). In other words, the two contraries are treated in practice as if they were contradictories: not only does the affirmation of one entail the denial of the other; the denial of one entails the affirmation of the other. We have here an example of the semiotic square of Greimas (1970, 136 ff.; cf. Greimas and Rastier 1968), rather than the square of classical logic, and its modern extensions.

1.2.5 Legal Realisms

"Legal Realism" is a term applied within Jurisprudence to those who see law as a species of fact, describable as a set of practices determined in terms of causal relations, rather than as a body of rules which inhabits a separate normative universe.

American legal theorists have been influenced by behaviourist versions of legal realism, and by a pragmatism which, it has been argued, manifests the influence of C.S. Peirce (Kevelson 1988a, Chapter 17). An approach to the understanding of law as discourse which seeks inspiration from *gestalt* psychology is made by the noted "fact sceptic" Jerome Frank in his *Courts on Trial* (1949), in explanation of the judge's intuitive judgment on questions of fact.

Amongst some neo-Marxist legal philosophers, one finds sensitivity to the importance of language as a means for the construction and transmission of ideology. But attention here tends to be placed more on the ownership or control of the media for the production and transmission of messages, rather than upon the signifying structures which they use (Edelman 1979). At the same time, some radical lawyers have shown particular interest in the structure (Arnaud 1973; Kennedy 1979) and rhetorical tropes (Goodrich 1986, 1987) of legal discourse, both as indicants of the real values of the authors of such discourse, and as subversive of the formalist legal argument which such discourse purports to convey. The "Critical Legal Studies" movement in the United States—a group of radical theorists influenced by European social theory, particularly that of the Frankfurt school—has also paid lip-service, on occasion, to structuralism or semiotics as a source of inspiration (see Hunt 1986, p. 36), but even such radical semioticians as Barthes have largely been supplanted for these scholars by a post-modernist/deconstructionist trend represented especially by Derrida (Douzinas and Warrington 1987; Douzinas et al. 1991; Balkin 1987; Kramer 1988, 1991; Norris 1988, see further Jackson 1986a, 1988b, Chapter 7). Here, systems of signification, as well as any other form of ordering, are seen principally as instruments of their own subversion. A Lacanian/Foucaultian approach is being developed by Milovanovic (1986, 1988; see also Casanovas I Romeu 1988 on Foucault).

"Command theories" of law are found not only within legal positivism (Section 1.2.1, above) but also in Scandinavian legal realism. For Olivecrona, the language of the law is a part and parcel of the object of study ("law") itself, and not merely an important element in the methodology of its description. It is by attending to some of its linguistic features that we are able to construct a "command" theory which avoids some of the weaknesses found in Austin's version. For language is the principal means by which feelings of coercion (with which they identify "law"), are created. Olivecrona (1971, Chapter 5; see also Harris 1981) distinguished between the semantic content (the *ideatum)* of legal rules—the behaviour patterns *(requisitum)* they seek to promote together with the modality requiring or permitting such behaviour (the *agendum),* and the communication of the coercive character of such rules (the *imperantum).* The latter was created and conveyed by the historic associations of the uttering of the word "law", through which feelings of coercion had been internalised. He provides a similar account of legal transactions, which ultimately he came to view in terms of the speech act theory of J.L. Austin: a sentence containing a performative is viewed as a "veiled imperative" (1971, 217 f.). Words for legal concepts "actually denote nothing, not even imaginary entities" (1971, p. 252). They are "hollow". Their function in our language is primarily to serve as guides to action, [...] as points of reference for consequential ideas concerning correct and obligatory behaviour [...]."

1.3 Legal Philosophies Explicitly Employing Forms of Semiotics

In many of the jurisprudential theories sketched above, semiotic issues play an important, though not always central, role, though frequently without any explicit reference to (or even, in some cases, familiarity with) the semiotic literature. But the last 20 years have also witnessed the development of a body of jurisprudence in conscious and explicit relation to one or another of the major streams within semiotics (Carrión-Wam 1985; Jackson 1986b). The following general approaches may be distinguished.

1.3.1 Logical Analysis of Legal Languages: Georges Kalinowski

For some, the semiotics of law is synonymous with the logic (or metalogic) of law and of its linguistic expressions. A pioneer of this approach was F. Oppenheim (1944); in recent times, Wróblewski has made substantial contributions (1983, 1989, 1990a, b). Here, attention is drawn particularly to the work of Georges Kalinowski.

Kalinowski (1965, 1980, 1985, 1988, 1990; cf. Carrión-Wam 1985) has offered a systematic account of "sémiotique juridique", modelled explicitly on the traditions of Frege (1879); Carnap (1942–1943, 1956) and Morris (1938). Kalinowski's major contribution lies in his distinction between different forms of legal language—legislative language, adjudicatory language, and doctrinal language (all of them distinct from the "language of norms" itself)—for each one of which he systematically investigates the syntactic, semantic and pragmatic components. Amongst the distinctions which may be made between legal languages is one between the language of the law (meaning here legislation) and the language of lawyers. This form of legal semiotics is close to philosophical logic, even where Kalinowski—developing work of Martin (1959) and Montague (1974, 1976)—deals with pragmatic aspects.

The dominant motifs of Kalinowski's work are truth and logic, not claims and signification. The law consists of a series of different languages, each with its particular forms of logic, in accordance with which truth-claims may be made. There is the logic of norms themselves, independent of the expression of those norms in either legislative or judicial language. This is the place of deontic logic.

Kalinowski sees reference as part and parcel of semantics, even though the meaning of expressions derives in part from their relationship to other expressions in the language. Thus a normative proposition, being descriptive of a state of affairs in the normative universe, together with a claim that this state of affairs does indeed exist in that normative universe, does make a truth-claim which is in principle verifiable.

1.3.2 The Italian Analytical School

The most systematic early work of the Italian analytical school is that of Scarpelli (1959/1985), which sought to provide an empirical theory of definitions of legal concepts. For definitions were conceived as rules of use of linguistic expressions based on the correlation of linguistic primitives to the basic data of experience (1985, p. 37). Scarpelli (1976, 1985, p. 39) places his analysis of legal language within the tradition of Morris (1938) and Carnap (1942–1943, 1956), and particularly the division of Morris of semiotics into syntactics, semantics and pragmatics. Definitions determine meaning (only) in the semantic and syntactic senses. Scarpelli claims a greater affinity to the English analytical tradition rather than the logical positivist tradition of the Vienna Circle (1985, p. 40), and within the school of Scarpelli in particular the work of Hart has enjoyed a considerable popularity (e.g. Jori 1979).

Other members of the Italian analytical school have pursued in a variety of directions the agenda mapped out by Bobbio (1950) and Scarpelli. Definitions have remained an abiding interest (Martino 1975; Belvedere et al., 1981). Interest in the classification of the functions of legal rules, and further exploration of the relationships with the work of the Scandinavian realists, are found in the works of Pattaro (1985, 1986–1987, 1986a), who has also addressed the relationship between linguistic function and linguistic rules (Pattaro and Gonzalez Ruiz 1988). The formal analysis of the typology of legal rules has provided the focus for Conte (1983, 1985a, 1985b, 1988), Guastini (1983) and Azzoni (1987), and this has often been allied to an interest in the theory of institutions associated with Searle (Carcaterra 1974). Tarello (1950/1976) has sought to marry the analytical approach with "critical" perspectives which relate legal language to the functioning of ideology and power. Recent contributions include an analysis of vagueness in legal language by Luzzati (1990), and a semiotically-informed account of the analytical theory of legal concepts (with chapters on Hart, Ross 1968, Scarpelli, Dworkin, MacCormick and Goodrich) by Pintore (1990). A systematic account of penological theory by Luigi Ferrajoli also proceeds from the linguistic premises of the Italian school (1988; 1989, Chapter 3).

The closest interest in mainstream semiotic theory is found in the works of Mario Jori, a jurist who has contributed the articles on "semiotics", "meaning", "communication", "sign", and "referent", to a major Italian philosophical encyclopedia (1985), and has been a major protagonist in current debates in legal semiotics regarding the nature and role of "reference" (1987, 1989; see further Section 1.4.1). Jori addresses for legal semiotics many of the central theoretical issues of general semiotics, e.g. the choice between diadic and triadic models, "performance oriented" versus "competence oriented" semiotics (1989), and the problem of reference (1987). In general, the Italian school is closer to the logicians, and to truth-conditional semantics, than to structural semiotics in the Saussurian tradition. Nevertheless, Jori in some of his recent work attempts to accommodate aspects of the intensionalist position.

1.3.3 Rhetorical and Pragmatic Approaches to Legal Semiotics

Modern interest in legal rhetoric derives largely from the work of the Brussels school founded by Chaim Perelman (e.g. 1976), which revived the study by lawyers of classical rhetoric, linking it to a theory of practical reasoning. More recent work is more sceptical about the reality of the attainment of such rationality, and often views the rhetoric as significatory rather than reflective of a strategy of argumentation. Within the diverse group of approaches to the rhetoric of law, we may distinguish at least two broad attitudes towards the relationships between rhetoric and semiotics. For some, the study of legal rhetoric is the study of the pragmatics of law, manifesting a set of interactional rules (albeit situationally negotiable—Sbisà and Fabbri 1980). For example, Bourcier (1984) studies the use of connectives within legal argument, in the spirit of Ducrot (1972, 1980). Speech act theory in the tradition of Austin and Searle has also proved a major influence within the Italian school (e.g. Carcaterra 1974, Section 1.3.2 above), and elsewhere (e.g. MacCormick 1973; Amselek 1986). The linguistic characteristics of legal speech acts in general have been explored in a recent monograph by Dennis Kurzon (1986). A number of scholars have sought to apply it to particular legal phenomena (see Kurzon 1988 on hearsay evidence, van Alphen 1988 on contract, van den Hoven 1988 on justification).

German approaches to the semiotics of law appear to have commenced with the objective of facilitating formalisation for computer analysis (stressing the syntactical relations between legal signs), but soon developed towards the pragmatics of law, through co-operation with text-linguists, rhetoricians, and analysts of argumentation (Posner and Krampen 1981; Seibert 1979). This latter trend is particularly associated with the Mainz school (esp. Schreckenberger 1978, Ballweg, Seibert), influenced by Viehweg. This has generated both empirical studies of legal communication in its interactional context (e.g. Seibert 1981, 1989), and the development of a theory of analytical rhetoric and its application to examples of legal argumentation (Ballweg and Seibert 1982; Ballweg 1987). Building upon Nietzsche and Morris, Ballweg (1987) offers a comprehensive set of relations between interpreter, object and sign which incorporates not only the pragmatics, semantics and syntactics of Morris, but also a set of "holistic" relations, classified as ontotactical, axiotactical and teleotactical, plus a set of "phronetic" relations (agontics, ergontics, and pithaneutics). A recent, substantial contribution from the Mainz School is that of Sobota (1990), a study of "matter-of-factness" in the rhetorical art of the jurist.

A different approach to "legal rhetoric" views rhetoric as the absence of rules or regularities, the conscious manipulation of language in a sometimes anarchic fashion, often for ideological purposes. This approach to rhetoric is to be found particularly amongst some deconstructionists and adherents of critical legal studies (Section 1.2.5, above). One may wonder how any meaning (even ideological meaning) is conveyed on the basis of this concept of rhetoric. On the other hand, Goodrich has made a substantial contribution to our knowledge of the history of legal rhetoric (1986, Chapter 6, 1990b, Pt. 1), and the use of rhetorical analysis to make manifest the ideological assumptions of legal texts has been widespread.

1.3.4 Sociological and Socio-Linguistic Approaches to Legal Semiotics

Semiotics has been viewed by some as providing a major way forward for the sociology of law. The most notable contributions have been made by André-Jean Arnaud (1981, 1985; see also Carrión-Wam 1985), Domenico Carzo (1981, 1985, 1986) and Peter Manning (1977, 1980, 1988). This section also notes, more briefly, two parallel trends within socio-legal studies—socio-linguistics and the autopoietic approach—both of which may be expected to engage increasingly with the semiotics of law.

Carzo (1985) seeks

> [t]o pick out and to define (a) who it is that makes use of the grammatical and lexical properties that are typical of the legal code, and what their structural features are; (b) what are the messages that can be transmitted; (c) what are the rules that allow the transmission and exchange of messages [. . .].

In the context of a study of the Italian Civil Code on Succession he distinguishes communicational and significatory structures and emphasizes the ideological aspects of interaction between individual and society, arguing that the whole system of succession is based on this opposition. He also offers a two-level communicational analysis of the code:

> We can speak of 'successional communication' on two distinct levels [. . .]: the issuer-donor and the receiver-beneficiary of the property or services which are communicated *by means of* the discourse on succession are totally different from. . . the sender (donor = author = legislator) and the receiver (beneficiary = judge = notary) of the story as a whole.

But these two levels of communication are not separate, the first being dependent on the existence of the second:

> "the communicative action of the sender or receiver of property or services is legitimised by the person who has organised the whole discourse (author = legislator); the communicative action of the latter is legitimised by the communicative (normative) code to which the discourse on succession belongs."

Arnaud devotes a major section of his analysis of francophone sociology of law to semiotic approaches (1981, Pt. III). In them, he stresses the plurality of "legal systems", from the official to those of the "*droit vécu*". Elsewhere, he applies this to the notion of juridicity itself (1985):

> The most important thing is to be able, at any particular moment, to establish a matrix of 'possible' juridical systems, and to be able to associate each one of them with the appropriate legal conflict, whether it be a scholarly conflict (as represented by legal doctrine or precedent) or a conflict involving popular opinion or pressure groups. It is by this method that we can reconcile the formal aspect of law and its day-to-day realities.

Manning is concerned with impact of organizational context on the production of meaning. He states as his aim "to clarify the role of information and rationality in modern life and to identify some limits on rational discourse". He seeks to provide a combination of "organisational and communicational theory and semiotics", i.e. a semiotically sensitive version of ethnomethodological and interactionist sociology, one of whose principal inspirations is the work of Goffman (1981). He calls for a science of signs, invoking Saussure, Peirce, Culler, Hawkes, and Eco. He endorses the Saussurian view of meaning being constituted by contrast, opposition, transformation and marking of differences: "signs are a function of difference and similarity in context". From Peirce he takes the view that every sign is incomplete because it requires an "interpretant," something that links the expression (the signifier) and the content (the signified). Because interpretants change, signs change meaning. There is no reality behind a sign, no "real world" against which the sign can be checked. The interpretant of a sign is another sign, and that sign is validated by yet another sign, and so on (1988, p. 4). He describes the claim that "a meaningful connection between the expression and the content must be socially constructed" as a "primitive phenomenology". Such connections

> [a]re shared and collective and provide an important source of ideas, rules, practices, codes, and recipe knowledge called culture (Culler 1975) [...]. The arrangement of signs that is meaningful can be syntactic (based on order), syntagmatic (based on proximity), or metaphoric (based on similarity in meaning). Several domains of meaning, when collected, constitute a field.

Meaning in organizational communications is produced by four inter-related social factors: the technology which drives the informationally based communication system, the coding of requests, interpretations made of communication units at various points in the organization, and the roles and tasks of members of the organization.

Manning is sceptical of the simple communicational model, as applied to organizations. Such a model

> [o]mits the questions of how general knowledge of the language, issues of context, and the metalinguistic marking of communicational units, what Goffman (1974) calls framing, operate within linguistically defined settings. The limitations of the linguistic model, in short, are severe when analysis of organizational functioning is combined with analysis of the process by which communication is accomplished (Jameson 1972). The analysis of the communication (and understanding) of transmission of units larger than the sentence, communicational units seen as messages, texts, records and the like, requires an ethnography of speaking (Hymes 1974).

Manning stresses that rules within organisations may function as justifications of action rather than as causes of decision-making. "Individuals do not look to rules to guide practice but act and at times refer to a rule or written conventional justification for their actions" (1988, p. 5). He approves Giddens' concept of "knowledgeability" (Giddens 1984, p. 4) as an account of the "sense of events for [...] organisational actors. Knowledgeability can only be partially captured by the sociologist's concept of rule-based action". Manning synthesises the roles of rule and commonsense typifications of behaviour by stressing that "the concept of a rule indicates actors' sense of rules rather than official rules or even the officialisation of discourse discussed by Bourdieu" (1977, Chapter 1).

An influential new trend in the sociology of law is the application of the theory of autopoiesis, inspired partly by the work of Luhmann, for whom (1984, 1985) society is a system of communications, in which the individual communicative act is itself self-referential (H.-G. Deggau 1988, pp. 132–134). The basic units of a legal system are neither legal norms nor actors and organizations, but rather communicative events which change legal structures.

> "Here we find the basic circularity that defines the legal system: the circular relationship between legal acts and legal norms. Circularity replaces extra-legal foundations of law as does Kelsen's fictitious *Grundnorm*"

(Teubner 1988, p. 4). In short, law is here viewed as a self-reproductive system of communication, taking its models from systems theory rather than linguistics or semiotics, though agreeing that no such system has access to reality outside itself (Teubner 1988, p. 10). Unlike the semiotic approach here advocated, autopoietic theory argues for the autonomy of law, that autonomy itself being defined in communicative terms. Thus "Luhmann (1988) insists on the strictly system-specific and exclusively internal character of information processing" (Teubner 1988, p. 10). On the other hand, the simultaneous presence of events in several meaning processing systems is said to allow for the interpenetration of autonomously operating mechanisms.

Following the pioneering monograph of Mellinkoff (1963), socio-linguistic approaches to legal texts, in America under the banner of the "law and language" movement, have developed very rapidly in recent years, as reflected in a substantial special issue of the journal *Text* (Danet 1984). Their progress has been documented in two major "state-of-the-art" surveys by Brenda Danet (1980, 1990), rendering further summary here superfluous. In France, Sourioux and Lerat (1976) have examined the characteristics of the French legal lexicon, while Mimin (1978) has studied the style of judgments. Amongst socio-linguists, Coulon (1988a, b) has been one of the first to seek a rapprochment with semiotic approaches.

A 1990 Workshop held at the International Institute for the Sociology of Law at Oñati sought to explore the relations between the semiotics and the sociology of law, with contributions by Bogoch (1994), Carzo (1994a, b), Casanovas I Romeu (1994), Danet (1994), Danet and Bogoch (1994), Jackson (1994), Kevelson (1994), Kurzon (1994), Landowski (1994), Nelken (1994), and Sheleff (1994).

1.3.5 Peircian Legal Semiotics

Though the work of Peirce has been taken into account in the more logically-oriented approaches noted above, it is in the United States that Peircian influence has been most prominent. Peirce forms the focus for the entire work of Roberta Kevelson. Indeed, in much of it the law is seen as a means to exemplify, and sometimes to refine, the Peircian concepts themselves. The emphasis here is philosophical, upon the open-ended reasoning processes involved in the law—one of several Peircian themes stressed by a number of American commentators (e.g. Benson 1988; Brion 1987, 1988; Cornell 1987; Lachs 1988; Pencak 1987; Price 1987; in Kevelson, ed., 1987, 1988a, 1988b). For example, Cornell relates contemporary jurisprudential discussion (and particularly the debate between Dworkin and Fish (Fish 1980, 1989) on legal interpretation) to Peircian philosophy.

For Kevelson, law is seen as an entity which manifests Peircian claims about epistemology in general. Semiotics is here viewed as "a method of inquiry into the process of inquiry" and "assumes that inquiry, always dialogic, is a process of communication or message exchange by means of signs and sign systems" (1988b, p. 3). Kevelson regards law as "a prototype of intersubjective social exchange of value as a whole" (1988b, p. 4). For her,

> [t]he legal argument is not a formal argument. Its premises are neither true nor false, but hypothetical. Therefore it was believed for a long time that analysis of legal discourse must necessarily be much looser and less conclusive than discourse proceeding from true propositions. Yet it was Peirce's genius to recognize that at bottom all propositions are hypothetical and all arguments are enthymemic [. . .]. *Enthymeme* is a term known from classical rhetoric which describes an argument that presupposes, that is, does not make explicit, either the major or minor premise or the conclusion. Peirce convincingly shows that all argument is based on unexpressed presuppositions (1988b, p. 5).

Questioning and defining are particularly important procedures of discovery, in this context. We have to consider what combination of logics, erotetic, deontic and nonmodal, are applicable in each of the prototypical types of verbal legal act: rules, commands and decisions (1988b, p. 7). Kevelson claims that Peirce "had enormous influence on continental legal theory at the turn of the century" (1988b, p. 6).

Amongst the topics considered by Kevelson from a Peircian standpoint are: legal decisions, rules of law and rules of conduct, limits of authority in law, contract, law and morality, economic justice, hermeneutics of law, American realism, the constitution as interpretant sign, property, conflict of laws, and inquiry and discovery procedures. Amongst her major themes are: the relationship between legal systems and their referent, social institutions; the argumentative function of the relationship between the judicial decision and social customs/values; the application of iconic, indexical and symbolic sign functions to codes of law and other legal phenomena, in accordance with context and purpose; the structures of legal reasoning—syllogistic and dialogistic, the latter yielding two or more alternative conclusions and forming an open-ended but yet complete structure of argument; the relations between logic, ethics and value (aesthetics), the three parts of the normative sciences in Peircian semiotic theory; the roles of fictions in legal procedures; and the conflict between Holmesian and Austinian concepts of law (1988b, pp. 11–12).

1.3.6 Greimasian Legal Semiotics

In collaboration with Greimas and other members of the Paris group, and later independently, Eric Landowski has sought systematically to apply the insights of Greimasian semiotics to legal discourse. Commencing with a "pilot" study of a French commercial law statute (Greimas and Landowski 1976, see also Jackson 1985a, Pt.II), and in later work which develops a semio-narrative approach to the underlying significatory structures of legal discourse and its enunciation (Landowski 1985, 1988b, 1989, 1994; see also Stockinger 1988), including a study of the process of legal proof, which narrativises the production of verification in court (Landowski 1988/1989), Landowski has exhibited not only those vast areas in which law depends upon structures of signification no different from those present in other forms of discourse, but also has given a semiotic account of some aspects of the specificity of legal institutions.

Greimas and Landowski call the performance of the legislator "*production juridique*", and identify it with the act of naming within legislation. But whether "naming in legislation" will be the only method of "*production juridique*" will depend upon the rules of the particular legal system concerned. Where (as in Common Law systems) the decisions of the courts are accorded the status of a direct source of law, naming in legislation will not be the only means of "*production juridique*", although there will still remain a difference between the "force" or "sense" of that which is produced in legislative discourse on the one hand, judicial or doctrinal discourse on the other, since only the words of the statute will be recognised as "canonical".

Unlike the grammar of social semiotic systems, which normally remain implicit (as in the example of the code of table manners), Greimas and Landowski note, in the context their study of a particular legislative text (the French 1966 *Loi* on *Sociétés Commerciales)* that "legal grammar" seeks to be explicit and to make its rules public (1976, pp. 87 f.). By contrast, the fact that the grammar of non-legislative forms of legal discourse may well be non-explicit is at the root of the contemporary debate amongst legal philosophers concerning the possibility of the existence of "logical gaps" in legal discourse. That jurisprudential discussion fails to take account of precisely these differences in the underlying structure of semiosis of different forms of legal discourse: explicit statement in the law is *not* the criterion of existence of rights (Dworkin, Section 1.2.4 above), nor indeed of *doctrinal* propositions arrived at through the interpretation of explicit legislative enactment.

The "recognition" of *production juridique* is not contained within legislative discourse itself. It remains, for the purposes of this particular discourse, "virtual". It is within a different form of legal discourse—that of adjudication—that such recognition is expected to be given. That recognition will take the form of explicit citation of statements made in legislation by way of justification of conclusions drawn within this different discursive system.

The less technical work of Jackson is closely associated with this approach to legal semiotics, but argues also for attention to issues highlighted in interactional sociology and psychology, within an overall semiotic framework. That framework consists in taking into account the psychological processes involved in the use of signs within the legal system. These psychological processes themselves involve the deployment of socially-constructed knowledge. Using as an overall framework the Greimasian notion of the semio-narrative deep structure of signification, he seeks to identify social knowledge as a particular stock of narratively-constructed themes, against which the individual perceives (encodes), memorises (stores), recalls (retrieves) and enunciates (communicates) individual events (Jackson 1994). In an account of the processes of legal adjudication (1988b, 1988c, 1988e), he argues for the application of narrative models (including narrative typifications of professional behaviour) to the pragmatics as well as the semantics of both fact and law construction in the courtroom.

1.3.7 Aesthetic/Symbolic Approaches

Legal semiotics has also taken an interest in non-verbal symbols, as used in the legal system. A monograph by Garapon (1985; see also 1988) considers many aspects of courtroom ritual, notably space, time and dress, within a primarily sociological framework (Bourdieu, Carbonnier, Durkheim, Lévy-Bruhl, Mauss). "Deictic signs" (such as traffic signals) have been considered by Beck (1988), viewing them as a metaphor for legal rules in general. The influence of Lévi-Strauss (see Jackson 1980, 1982, 1987, 1988d), and particularly the distinction between the savage and the domesticated, has been apparent in the work of Lachmayer (1988), Robertshaw (1975, 1985), Arnaud (1973) and Hermann (1975). A systematic study of the iconography of the Common Law has recently been initiated by Goodrich (1990). The study of non-verbal symbolism in law manifests a major concern amongst practitioners of legal semiotics, to show how the text conceals, yet at the same time reveals, its underlying messages.

1.4 Some Hypotheses for Legal Semiotics

In this section I suggest four central hypotheses for legal semiotics: (1) "Reference" within the legal system is intra-discursive, and incapable of verification on the basis of correspondence; (2) A parallel account of the pragmatic dimension of legal discourse to that of the semantic dimension of legal discourse is both possible and necessary: a model is at hand in the "narrativisation of pragmatics"; (3) No satisfactory account of legal semiotics can be given without full attention to the diversity of "semiotic groups" operating within "the legal system" and to the particularities of the "legal culture" of each one; (4) The concepts of "normativity" and "truth" as deployed within the legal system are merely claims; their meaningfulness and plausibility can only be described by semiotics, but no special onotological status can be ascribed to them.

1.4.1 The Problem of Reference

The problem of reference in the semiotics of law has been most directly addressed in debates between Jackson (1985a, 1990), Jori (1987, 1989) and Landowski (1989). The problem goes beyond that of the structure of semiosis—whether diadic or triadic—since it is far from clear that a triadic scheme (such as that of Peirce) necessarily claims, in any of its parts, a direct correspondence between language and outside reality. The issue is fundamentally epistemological: whether the claims to refer (and to refer truly), made by the users of a discursive system from within that system, can be verified. Jori argues for a triadic, referential semiotics on the grounds of its greater adherence to empiricism (1987, p. 44), and its necessity for the purpose of explaining recourse to authority as legal justification (1987, p. 10). It should be noted, however, that adherents to a Saussurian-based diadic structure of the sign do not deny that language is regularly used with a referential function. In common with some analytical philosophers (such as Strawson 1950; see Jackson 1988b, Chapter 2), they claim that reference belongs to the pragmatic, not the semantic dimension of language: it is something done with language by its users, not part of the meaning (or sense) of the language itself. A non-referential semiotics substitutes for the question of verifiability that of the construction of the plausibility (or appearance of verifiability) of the referential claim.

If referential claims cannot be verified within language, since the verificatory language itself continually reconstitutes the referent, major problems arise for the claim to the unity of the legal system, since this unity is continually constituted by internal reference to "the law". For normativists, on the other hand, different legal discourses refer (some of them indirectly) to the same external referent. From a semiotic viewpoint, we have here a phenomenon of co-referentiality from different discourses, each one of which *claims* to refer to a single external referent (see further Section 1.4.4).

1.4.2 Semantic and Pragmatic Levels

The relationship between the semantic and pragmatic dimensions of legal discourse may be exemplified through an analysis of the process in the Common Law courtroom. Conventionally, the "battle" which occurs there is assumed to be between the two parties to the litigation: plaintiff and defendant in civil cases, prosecutor and accused in criminal. But it does not take long to observe the fact that the two parties to the dispute very rarely engage in the combat. There will be no occasion in the trial during which the parties confront each other, as speaking subjects. Rather, the judge or jury observes a series of polemic interactions, between each witness and cross-examining counsel, between the two counsel themselves, sometimes between judge and counsel. Each of these interactions may be analysed in semio-narrative terms, the participants taking on different actantial functions (sender, subject, helper, etc.) according to their place in the particular syntagm concerned. It is this story—that of the pragmatics of the trial—which the judge or jury observes; it is only through this process that they have access to the facts whose truth or otherwise is to be established; and the possibility of this latter objective is contingent upon the intelligibility of that through which it is mediated (Jackson 1988b).

The above analysis encompasses a vitally important theoretical claim as to the structure of semiotics, quite apart from its potential for providing an explanatory model of judicial discourse. Its theoretical claim is that we cannot separate the semantic and pragmatic dimensions of a text, or (to use different terminology) its semiotic and rhetorical features. The two are inexplicably intertwined. Purpose and audience affect discursive structure. To many, this will appear obvious, commonplace and banal. But in current debates regarding legal semiotics, it is a theoretical position not to be taken for granted. For there are many who portray the viewpoint of the Greimasian school as excluding pragmatics from semiotics entirely.

Rhetoric does not here provide a model antithetical to the role of narrative coherence in the construction of truth—as Bennett and Feldman (1981) appear to fear. Rhetorical practices simply manifest a second level of narrative, that of "the story of the trial" in contrast to "the story (told) in the trial". That "story of the trial" is as much subject to the constraints of narrative coherence as is "the story (told) in the trial". For the "story of the trial" is at root just another piece of human action, no different in kind from "the story (told) in the trial". We have conventional narrative frameworks for the understanding of the former no less than for the latter. We know what it takes—who, how, etc.,—to persuade. Any theory of narrative coherence must take due account of the narrativisation of pragmatics.

1.4.3 Semiotic Groups and "The Legal Culture"

As argued above (Sections 1.1.3 and 1.4.1), one important theoretical issue which the semiotic analysis of law raises is that of the unity of the legal system. On the one hand, that unity is proclaimed by many different semiotic processes; on the other, these processes, as used by different participants in legal activities, are so diverse as to cast doubt upon that unity. For these purposes, it is useful to develop the notion of a "semiotic group"—a group of people using one particular system of signification, that system not being shared with others. From this point of view, one may identify a diversity of semiotic groups within the legal system, such as (hypothetically), legislators, superior court judges, inferior court judges, doctrinal writers, big city solicitors, high street solicitors, police, court administrators, clients of different types, etc. The systems of signification used by each of these semiotic groups reinforce their self-identity in relation to other semiotic groups within the legal system. Legal dress, for example, often has more to do with hierarchical structures *within* the legal system than with connotations for the outside world. Equally, conventions of speech—both inside and outside the courtroom—confirm and apply internal legal notions of hierarchy and role (Atkinson and Drew 1979; O'Barr 1982).

Yet despite all this, the appearance of the unity of the legal system is powerfully conveyed. Semioticians need to investigate how this is done. In part, it is through the use of unifying symbols, often of a visual kind. The scales of justice, for example, claim not only the impartiality of the legal system, but also the sense that it is universal cross-culturally: that law really is justice.

1.4.4 Normativity and Justification

One of the primary tasks of legal semiotics is to provide an alternative account of the lawyer's concepts of normativity and justification. For all non-realist jurisprudence insists that normativity exists and that some form of objective justification of legal decision-making is possible. In recent times, this argument has been advanced most forcefully by MacCormick (1978, Chapter 2, etc.), who regards deductive syllogistic reasoning as playing an essential role in judicial argument, and who attributes to such argument the function of justification of decisions. Since the major premise of such a syllogism is a proposition about the current state of the law, the conventional view may be described as a theory of normative justification.

Realists of various types would want to deny the reality of any such justificatory process. Semiotics (at least in the Saussurean tradition) would deny it except insofar as it forms part of a particular discourse. Justification would there fall to be described (as an empirical phenomenon) as part of the communication process of the law. In short, while MacCormick embraces a normative theory of justification, semiotics views it as a communicative fact. The ascription of justification here parallels the ascription to facts of the quality of truth: as Landowski (1988/1989) has argued, we can describe the process of *vérédiction*, and that which plausibly creates its appearance (Jackson 1988b, Chapter 6), even if the rejection of a correspondence theory of reference prevents us from speaking of verifiable truth.

A semiotic approach to "normative justification" may be based upon two claims: first, that "normativity" means the ascription (in discourse) of a particular modal value (that of normative validity) to a particular proposition; secondly, that "justification" means the act of ascribing such a quality, and that such an act resides in performance of an act regarded as sufficiently close to the conventional narrative typification of justificatory behaviour. We may thus construct a theory of normative justification which views the construction and transmission of modalities within the context of the narrativisation of pragmatics.

If justification is a communicative fact, we have to distinguish the different modes in which it may be communicated and the different semiotic groups to whom it may be directed. We do not have to search very far for material. The judgment of a court may comprise within it a combination of discourses, corresponding to the different audiences which the judge (in fact, if not in intention) is addressing. It may contain the justification directed at the parties to the litigation. It may contain the justification which the judge would have *the legal profession* understand to lie behind it. At the same time, it may include other forms of justificatory discourse, directed to other kinds of audience. I doubt not, for example, that some judges are looking over their shoulders (even subconsciously, if one can do that) at the media, and providing levels of justification more appropriate for a popular audience. The normative syllogism, in which deduction is used as a logical operation to justify a legal conclusion, once the elements in both the major and minor premises have been determined, is the form of justification accepted by a particular (I maintain, primarily professional) audience; it is the form of argument most calculated to persuade that audience, for whom the use of such formal argument represents the narrative typification of good justificatory behaviour. (See further, Section 1.5.7 on justification of judicial decisions.)

1.5 Semiotic Analyses of Particular Legal Phenomena

1.5.1 Legal System

One of the most basic cultural assumptions of modern Western civilisation is that the National State has a single "legal system" (thus, a single external referent of all legal discourse); indeed some theorists have come close to identifying the State with the legal system itself (Kelsen). Two questions arise: the first, how recognition is accorded to the existence of such a single legal system within a State; the second, how recognition is given to the identity of particular rules and other legal phenomena, as belonging to that system. The criteria for recognition in both cases are, according to many theorists, heavy, since the "public" character of "the law", combined with the severity of the coercive measures it is capable of bringing to bear, make it important (from the perspective of the ideology of the "Rule of Law") that both the existence of the legal system and the identity of particular phenomena as belonging to it, should be not only recognisable, but indeed *demonstrable.* (For the "demonstrability" thesis see Dworkin 1977.)

Perrott (1980) has suggested that legal systems have a "deep structure" which, following a Chomskyan model, makes the legal system recognisable as such, and allows us both to generate and recognise well-formed legal rules. He adapts parts of the legal philosophy of Hart (Section 1.2.2 above) for this purpose. However, the analogy has been criticised (Jackson, 1988a), on the grounds that laws are not like natural language, faces, or music—for all of which there may be good psychological reasons to suppose that there is some level of innate human ability required for their recognition. Nevertheless, legal phenomena do present themselves as "demonstrable" as such, in ways which must attract the interest of the semiotician.

1.5.2 Legal Institutions

MacCormick (1973; MacCormick and Weinberger 1986) has modified the legal positivism of Hart by re-phrasing it in terms of the speech act theory of Searle (1969): law thus becomes a form of "institutional fact". The "institutions" which he analyses are such legal concepts as marriage, ownership, adoption, succession by will, contract (but see van Alphen 1988 on debate within the Netherlands as to the appropriateness of the speech act approach here). MacCormick notes that it is a characteristic of such institutions that they possess a life-history, the structure of the institution being the combination of institutive, consequential and terminative rules. There are rules which govern the creation of an instance of the institution, rules which state the consequences of such creation, and rules which govern its termination. MacCormick (1988) has recently stressed the temporal quality of the legal institution, in order to sustain the view that a temporal state of affairs is brought about by the creation of an instance of an institution, such that true or false statements regarding entitlement may be made of it. Comparison has been made with the syntagmatic axis of Greimasian analysis (Jackson 1985a, Chapter 8), and recent discussion (Jackson and Paychère 1989) has suggested that the legal institution cannot be viewed in the abstract, but only in the context of the behaviour of different semiotic groups which refer to it.

1.5.3 Legal Codes

By "legal code" I here refer to that genre of legal document which is called a "code", generally understood as a comprehensive statement of the rules of the legal system as a whole, or of a major area within it. This is a "code" in the legal, rather than the semiotic sense. Internally, the question arises as to the signification of the choice of material within the code (quite apart from the meaning of the individual rules), and the way in which it is arranged. Is it based upon some arbitrary principle of arrangement, some serial basis (alphabetic, chronological, etc.) or on some principled basis, and if so what? Structural analysis has been used by Arnaud (1973) to explore the concealed (perhaps even to the authors) surviving pre-revolutionary ideology within the French Code Civil, and by Kennedy (1979) to similar effect in relation to the (private) codification of English law by William Blackstone. But the semiotician needs to pose questions external to the text also, questions of pragmatics concerning the identity of the users, and nature of the use of the Code. There is considerable evidence that in the ancient Near East, these documents were not designed for use in court, in the manner of modern statutory interpretation, but rather were symbols of the claims of the ruler to have established peace and justice (Jackson 1975; 1989). There is evidence, too, of a didactic use according to which the code was taught, discussed and interpreted, the lead being taken by those who possessed the written texts, and who took them for this purpose into the wider community. It was only later that the code acquired a primarily adjudicatory function. Yet even in modern times, the populist ideology of codification—that of rendering the whole law accessible to the people—survives in iconic form, through the publication each year of an edition of the French Civil Code in pocket-book size, capable of being carried around by any citizen. But possession of this "code" is by no means, nowadays, equivalent to possession of (knowledge of) the law.

1.5.4 Legal Rules

To the layman, and perhaps also to many lawyers, the individual legal rule is regarded as the basic unit of the legal system. How such rules are recognised is one of the principal questions posed by contemporary legal philosophy. Positivists answer this question in terms of legal pedigree: a rule is legal if it has been created in accordance with what the legal system itself regards as a source of law. The question of the status of normativity (Section 1.4.4 above) bears heavily upon this question: do there exist autonomous legal sources and rules, or merely the claim, made in discourse, that a particular behaviour pattern is obligatory because of the ascription to it of the quality (semioticians may say: the modal value) of normativity? According to the latter view, the proposition: "rule X is valid" is of the same order as the proposition: "rule X is useful", or indeed "this picture is beautiful". But of course, the manner in which such validity is communicated tends to be far more subtle than is the case in the ascription of other, overtly evaluative modalities.

For those who believe in the existence of a separate, normative universe, it makes sense to conceive of the existence of a legal rule in the abstract. From the semiotic viewpoint, however, a legal rule is to be equated with some discursive manifestation, whether in writing or behaviour. Whatever the form such manifestation takes, we have to ask to whom the rule is intelligible as such, and how, within that semiotic group, its obligatory character is constructed and communicated.

1.5.5 Rights

Few items within the lexicon of jurisprudence have provoked as much controversy as the notion of "rights". It would be simple for the semiotician simply to adhere to a (jurisprudentially) realist view of rights (such as that of the Scandinavian Realists, Section 1.2.5 above) and to see the use of the term as no more than a particular type of rhetorical assertion of a claim—an assertion whose effectiveness is aided by the use of the term in moral as well as legal discourse. More interesting, perhaps, is the linguistic disambiguation of the concept of "a right", as used in judicial discourse, by the American scholar Hohfeld (1923). Hohfeld distinguishes four different senses of the term, and claimed that the four different relationships so revealed amounted to a set of fundamental legal conceptions, a kind of grammar of legal relationships: rights as (a) claims, (b) liberties (or privileges), (c) powers and (d) immunities.

Diagram A: Hohfeld's "Fundamental Legal Conceptions"

right privilege power immunity
Jural Opposites
no-right duty disability liability
right privilege power immunity
Jural Correlatives
duty no-right liability disability

Each one of these concepts has a correlative, reflecting the fact that Hohfeld defined the different forms of right in inter-personal terms, assuming in each case a legal relationship between two persons. Thus, if X has a right against Y in sense (a), this means that X may claim that Y must perform or abstain from a certain act, and Y correlatively has a duty so to perform or abstain. Hohfeld's scheme thus generated eight concepts, which he grouped in two sets, according to whether they were relationships under the present law or potential relationships which took account of capacities (or incapacities) to change the current legal position. Hohfeld showed that the two sets of four were each characterised by a logical relationship: right (a) was the contradictory (he called it the jural "opposite") of the correlative of right (b), while right (b) was the "opposite" of the correlative of right (a), etc. Thus, Hohfeld's sets could be represented as a square, the diagonals of which were contradictories. Attempts have been made, thus far without success, to compare Hohfeld's scheme with either the semiotic or the logical square, but the attempt fails because the horizontal relationships are not logical contraries, but rather inter-personal correlatives (further: Paychère 1991). But Hohfeld has presented a problem of considerable semiotic interest: the logical structure of the basic (in his view, a restricted set of) interrelationships recognised by the legal system between two subjects. He thus invites us to construct a grammar of legal relationships. The fact that important analytic distinctions can be drawn between different uses of the single lexeme, a "right", also calls for explanation.

1.5.6 Courtroom Behaviour: Witness and Counsel

Both the giving of testimony by a witness and the arguments of counsel on points of law may be analysed in terms of the narrativisation of pragmatics (Section 1.4.2 above).

A provisional schematisation of this process, together with the different types of narrative analysis which have been applied to it, might be divided into four sections: (1) internal psychological processes, prior to any particular act of enunciation; (2) the act of enunciation itself, viewed strategically from the viewpoint of the enunciator; (3) the meaning of the act of enunciation, as perceived by its addressees/perceivers; (4) negotiation of the outcome of the act of enunciation between the parties concerned. Of these, (1) has been addressed by story grammarians and cognitive psychologists; (2) has been largely neglected by proponents of narrative theories, though it has been considered by social psychologists in the context of particular forms and contexts of enunciation; (3) is the level addressed both by Bennett and Feldman (1981) and some semiotic theories; (4) is the concern of some sociologists, including ethnomethodologists, but forms part also of an overall narrative conceptualisation when we take full account of the narrativisation of pragmatics.

The behaviour of counsel in court is susceptible to a fundamentally similar analysis, but what (s)he perceives, stores, recalls and enunciates is not past "facts" but rather models of effective courtroom behaviour. A formalisation of this process has been offered by Jackson (1988b, Chapter 4) for the procedure of courtroom "objection" by counsel.

1.5.7 The Judge: Justification of Decisions on Law

The distinction between (judicial) decision-making and justification of decisions has now been widely accepted, even amongst positivists (MacCormick 1987). However, the positivist seeks to claim that, whatever the social and psychological influences on the judge in arriving at a particular decision, that decision either is or is not justified in terms of the legal system, and the decision is legally justified only if the judge is able so to justify it. But clearly, justification belongs to the pragmatics of the legal system: it is something done by participants in it, for a particular purpose. Van den Hoven (1988) has systematically explored the formalisation of the pragmatic features of justification, as a legal speech act. One may suspect that MacCormick would not dissent too far from this type of analysis, given his own use of speech act theory as the basis of the legal institution. That being so, there may be agreement between positivists, legal philosophers and semioticians as to the conventionality of justification: justification is contingent upon both the norms of a particular legal system (which the positivist fully accepts to be conventional) and upon conventional judgments as to what is reasonable. The point at which those who assert the reality of justification depart from a semiotic view is through their linguistic usages which, in their significatory effect, convert such conventional judgments into something more, an apparently autonomous realm of (natural?) rationality or justification. Analytically, they may agree that the proposition "X is reasonable" or "Y is justified" really implies "X is reasonable according to the conventions of a particular society or group" or "Y is justified according to such conventions". But the fact that the full analytical statement is regularly suppressed creates the significatory effect (not least for the speaker) that the reasoning and justification has a reality of its own. This phenomenon brings into play each one of the four central hypotheses of legal semiotics, identified in Section 1.4 above. The *appearance of normativity* is created through a *false reference*: an implicit claim that the reasonableness of the speaker's proposition corresponds to something outside that discourse. But the suppression of conventionality is itself a function of the *behaviour* of the *particular semiotic group* within which the enunciation takes place. The fact that the enunciation "X is reasonable" may go without challenge within a particular semiotic group does not mean that it will go unchallenged elsewhere. The construction of even legal reasonableness is not necessarily the same for different types of legal practitioner, not to speak of different types of official and layperson.

1.5.8 The Criminal Justice Process

Criminal justice is the area of law where we are closest to an overview of the semiotic processes through a succession of organisational contexts. We start with the first call to the police and conclude with the criminal trial (or appeal). The main stages in the process may be characterised as (police) investigation, the exercise of prosecutorial discretion by public officials, and the trial. The attention of legal philosophers and semioticians has been directed primarily towards this last. However, it is important to draw attention also to the earlier stages, and to the possibilities which exist of fitting them within a single semiotic framework of analysis.

A member of the public first observes some incident in the outside world; later, he telephones the police to tell them about it. He does that with the object of getting the police to launch an investigation. Manning (1988) has studied the routinization of the calls from the public to the police as mediated through the institutionalised structures of the police, which themselves develop "images, techniques, and shorthand interpretations and indexes" (1988, p. 6). In Greimasian terms, recognition of performance of the caller's goal may be provided within the telephone call itself, in the manner in which the information is processed, and perhaps in some final message from the operator: "we are looking into it", or something similar. That is the narrativised pragmatics of the call: whether the caller succeeded in getting the police to do what he wants them to do (investigate). There is clearly also a parallel to the narrativised semantic level: that which the caller tells the police—which in principle bears the same relationship to the original perception as does the story of the witness in court to the witness's own perception. The caller is telling the police not only what he perceived but also the story of his perception of it (cf. Section 1.5.6, above). For the police to be persuaded into action, credibility must attach to three things: the content of the story perceived, the circumstances of its perception, and the present enunciation of those two past narratives. We start with an incident: stimuli in the outside world which operate as a "sender" (in the actantial sense) to an observer, and which institutes that observer as the subject of a performance.

The general pattern of the relationship between the semantic and pragmatic levels becomes especially clear in the case of the interaction between the caller to the police and the operator (though it should be equally clear in the case of the trial itself): through success in the performance of a particular act of enunciation (success being judged in terms of the perceived plausibility of the semantic level, the *énoncé*, itself) the speaker seeks to manipulate the receiver into some further action, which may well consist in a further step within the communicational chain itself. Thus, by persuading the operator of the intelligibility/credibility etc. of the complaint (*that* the caller observed *that* a certain event took place), the caller seeks to get the operator not only to accord recognition to the caller's successful performance of that particular act of enunciation, but to do so by agreeing to be instituted as subject in a further act in the communicational chain—conceived narrowly, to pass on the message to the controller, who will then instruct the officers on the beat, etc.; more widely, that the police (conceived as a collective *actant)* should agree (accept the "contract") to investigate the "crime".

Let us now move to a later stage in the negotiation of the criminal process. The police have investigated the incident, and now present the result of their investigation to an official, the District Attorney (US) or Crown Prosecutor (England), seeking his recognition in the form of a decision to prosecute. We are faced with differences in semiotic groups between the original initiator of the complaint (the member of the public), the police, and the prosecutor. We need to develop a methodological model for the empirical investigation of the interaction between the police and the District Attorney, taking account of the different semiotic groups to which the police and the prosecutor belong. There is bound to be an interactional process here, with some degree of negotiation of the typifications of good investigation work on the one hand, good prosecutorial discretion on the other hand.

Proceeding a stage further, we may draw upon the work of Sudnow (1965) for observations on the relationship between the District Attorney (DA) and the Public Defender (PD), as observed in some US courts. The two of them—Sudnow claims—effectively form a "team" for the processing of (minor?) criminal matters before the court, in such a way as to arrive at a plea bargain which will represent the defendant "getting his due". The implication is that even the public defender has this motivation, rather than (as one might assume in an adversarial system) the objective of producing the smallest possible sentence. Conversely, the DA is not out to secure the maximum sentence, but rather to process the case efficiently through a plea bargain, and thereby to get through a workload; we may compare here the work of H.L. Ross (1960), in the civil context, on the processing of insurance claims. The DA and the PD develop shared understandings, through day-to-day contact, which in semiotic terms might be regarded as the construction of a code, but a code which is constrained by the pressures of the occupational structures to which they belong (in the same way as occurred with the insurance adjuster). This code is certainly different from that of the complainant to the police, and of the police in producing the file.

In Greimasian terms, these processes manifest the transfer of different modal values. The delivery of the police file represents a transfer by the police of an "obligation-to-do" (*devoir faire*) to the District Attorney. Yet there is more than one "sender" here, which institutes the DA as a "subject". On the one hand, the police file does represent the transfer to the DA of "knowledge of facts" (*savoir être*), and also of a capacity to select from those facts, to use them for his purpose (a *pouvoir faire*). But the difference in the code represented by the shared understandings of the "team" of the DA/PD derives from the fact that the *devoir faire* received by the DA comes not from the police, but rather from the occupational structures to which the DA/PD actually belong. It is these structures (themselves, perhaps, conceived as syntagmatic *actants collectifs*) which impose upon the "team" the obligation to process these cases in as efficient a way as possible, thus leading to the pressure for plea bargains—though subject to conventional standards as to "due desserts". The distinction in the modal values which are transferred to the DA/PD from the different sources explains more specifically than otherwise how it comes to be that the "code" employed by the "team" differs in practice from that represented by the "file" which is sent to them.

To explain the effectiveness of negotiation between the PA and PD, Sudnow introduces a conception of "normal crime", which we might understand as comparison with narrative typifications of crime. But these are narrative typifications of crime internalised from daily interaction within the group of the DA/PD, and internalisation of the facts as filtered through the pressures of the occupational structures concerned (thus constrained, one might argue, by *both* the file sent by the police *and* the occupational structures, ethic and interaction of the professional negotiators here involved).

1.6 On the Status of Legal Semiotics

Beyond the sociological and institutional links between scholars in legal semiotics (which fall far short of constituting a discipline "via profession"), the writings of legal semioticians would seem to form a single corpus only at the level of inter-discursivity: many cite each other—but the significance of that fact will depend upon the status one attributes to "reference". But if such scepticism is suspended, one might hazard the following conclusions. Legal semiotics is hardly a discipline, since it does not follow a common set of methods. For some (notably, Landowski) it is a sub-discipline (of general semiotics), but this cannot be said of the vast majority of practitioners of legal semiotics. To many, it functions inter alia as a meta-discipline, providing a language within which to study the traditional methods of "legal science". This, I suggest, represents a common point between the Greimasians and Peircians, notwithstanding the immense differences between them. For others (the Italian analytical school, perhaps, and for some sociologists of law), semiotics provides an auxiliary discipline: their objectives, framework and basic presuppositions remain rooted in philosophy or sociology, but they find in semiotics a useful tool to advance these disciplines. It is, perhaps, the absence of a common approach to the status of legal semiotics that makes the field at one and the same time puzzling yet vibrant.

References

Alphen, E.A. van. 1988. No Constitutive Rule, No Contract? *International Journal for the Semiotics of Law/Revue Internationale de Sémiotique Juridique*, 1, 189–194.

Amselek, Paul, ed. 1986. *La Théorie des Actes de Langage, Ethique et Droit*. Paris: P.U.F.

Arnaud, André-Jean. 1973. *Essai d'Analyse Structurale du Code Civil Français*. Paris: L.G.D.J.

Arnaud, André-Jean. 1981. *Critique de la Raison Juridique I*. Paris: L.G.D.J.

Arnaud, André-Jean. 1985. Fact as Law. In *Semiotics, Law and Social Science*, ed. D. Carzo and B.S. Jackson. Rome and Liverpool: Gangemi and Liverpool Law Review, 129–144.

Atkinson, J. Maxwell and Drew, Paul. 1979. *Order in Court*. London: Macmillan.

Austin, John. 1954. In *The Province of Jurisprudence Determined*, ed. H.L.A. Hart. London: Weidenfeld and Nicolson.

Azzoni, G. 1987. Regula tecnica tra ontico e deontico. *Rivista internazionale di filosofia del diritto*, 64, 297–321.

Balkin, J.M. 1987. Deconstructive Practice and Legal Theory. *Yale Law Journal*, 96(4), 743–786.

Ballweg, Ottmar. 1987. Analytical Rhetoric, Semiotic and Law. In *Law and Semiotics*, Volume 1, ed. R. Kevelson. New York, NY and London: Plenum Press, 25–33.

Ballweg, Ottmar and Seibert, T-M. 1982. Rhetorische Rechtstheorie – im Zusammenhang gesehen. In *Rhetorische Rechtstheorie*, ed. O. Ballweg and T-M. Seibert. Freiburg and München: Alber, 15–24.

Beck, Anthony. 1988. Adjudication and the Sign. *International Journal for the Semiotics of Law /Revue Internationale de Sémiotique Juridique*, 1, 7–22.

Belvedere, Andrea, Jori, Mario, and Lantella, Lelio. 1981. *Definizione Giuridiche e Ideologiche*. Milan: Giuffrè.

Bennett, W.L. and Feldman, M.S. 1981. *Reconstructing Reality in the Courtroom*. New Brunswick, NJ: Rutgers University Press.

Benson, Robert W. 1988. How Judges Fool Themselves: The Semiotics of the Easy Case. In *Law and Semiotics II*, ed. R. Kevelson. New York, NY: Plenum Press, 31–60.

Blanché, R. 1966. *Les structures intellectuelles*. Paris: J. Vrin.

Bobbio, Norberto. 1950. Scienza del diritto e analisi del linguaggio. *Rivista trimestrale di diritto e procedura civile*, 4, 342–367 (reprinted in Scarpelli 1976).

Bogoch, B. 1994. Crossexamining the Client: Lawyering in a Legal Aid Office. In *Legal Semiotics and the Sociology of Law*, ed. B.S. Jackson. Oñati: International Institute for the Sociology of Law, 333–369.

Bourcier, D. and Bruxelles, S. 1984. D'ailleurs: Un Argument Non-Nécéssaire? Ses Fonctions dans Discours du Juge. In *Le Droit en procès*, ed. J. Chevallier et al. Paris: P.U.F, 126–146.

Brion, Denis J. 1987. The Shopping Mall: Signs of Power. In *Law and Semiotics I*, ed. R. Kevelson. New York, NY: Plenum Press, 67–108.

Brion, Denis J. 1988. What Is a Hay Baler? The Semiotic Answer from Contract Law. In *Law and Semiotics I*, ed. R. Kevelson. New York, NY: Plenum Press, 61–85.

Carcaterra, Gaetano. 1974. *Le norme costitutive*. Milan: Giuffrè.

Carnap, Rodolph. 1942–1943. *Studies in Semantics*, 2 vols. Cambridge: Harvard University Press.

Carnap, Rodolph. 1956. *Meaning and Necessity*, 2nd ed. Chicago, IL: University of Chicago Press.

Carrión-Wam, Roque. 1985. Semiotica Juridica. In *Semiotics, Law and Social Science*, ed. D. Carzo and B.S. Jackson. Rome and Liverpool: Gangemi and Liverpool Law Review, 11–67.

Carzo, Domenico. 1981. *I Segni del Potere*. Milan: Giuffrè.

Carzo, Domenico. 1985. A Model of Legal Communication: Succession. In *Semiotics, Law and Social Science*, eds. D. Carzo and B.S. Jackson. Rome and Liverpool: Gangemi and Liverpool Law Review, 179–202.

Carzo, Domenico. 1986. Considérations sur la sémiotique juridique: la point de vue sociologique. *Droit Prospectif*, 2, 357–363.

Carzo, Domenico. 1994. Le droit comme fait social total. In *Legal Semiotics and the Sociology of Law*, ed. B.S. Jackson. Oñati: International Institute for the Sociology of Law.

Carzo, Domenico. 1994. Towards Socio-Pragmatics of Legal Discourses: Discourse and Decision-Making in a Spanish Court. In *Legal Semiotics and the Sociology of Law*, ed. B.S. Jackson. Oñati: International Institute for the Sociology of Law, 151–225.

Casanovas, I Romeu, Pompeu. 1988. Metaphor and Adlinguisticity in the Literacy Language of Michel Foucault. In ed. R. Kevelson, *Law and Semiotics II*. New York, NY: Plenum Press, 105–121.

Conte, Amadeo. 1983. Paradigmi d'analisi della regola in Wittgenstein. In ed. R. Egidi, *Wittgenstein. Momenti di una critica del sapere*. Napoli: Guida Editore, 37–82.

Conte, Amadeo. 1985. Phénoménologie du langage déontique. In *Les fondements logiques de la pensée normative*, eds. G. Kalinowski and F. Selvaggi. Rome: Editrice Pontificia, Università Gregoriana, 179–195.

Conte, Amadeo. 1985. Materiali per una tipologia delle regole. *Materiali per una storia della cultura giuridica*, 15, 345–368.

Conte, Amadeo and Mazzarese, Tecla. 1988. Founding Rules on Rules. In *Reason in Law*, vol. II, ed. C. Faralli and E. Pattaro. Milan: Giuffrè, pp. 283–288.

Cornell, Drusilla. 1987. The Problem of Normative Authority in Legal Interpretation. In *Law and Semiotics I*, ed. R. Kevelson. New York, NY: Plenum Press, 149–157.

Coulon, Raymond. 1988a. Discourse Analysis Versus Text Analysis: The Reading of Ideology in Foreign Language Texts. *International Journal for the Semiotics of Law/Revue Internationale de Sémiotique Juridique*, 1, 195–215.

Coulon, Raymond. 1988b. Indicatif présent et socio-sémiotique du discours constitutionnel. *Archives de Philosophie du Droit*, 33, 347–368.

Culler, Jonathan. 1975. *Structuralist Poetics*. London and Henley: Routledge & Kegan Paul.

Danet, Brenda. 1980. Language in the Legal Process. *Law and Society Review*, 14(3), 445–564.

Danet, Brenda. ed. 1984. Studies of Legal Discourse, Special issue of Text, vol. 4–1/3, including her own "The magic flute: a prosodic analysis of binomial expressions in Hebrew", at 143–172.

Danet, Brenda. 1990. Language and Law: An Overview of 15 Years of Research. In *Handbook of Language and Social Psychology*, ed. H. Giles and W.P. Robinson. London: Wiley, 537–560.

Danet, Brenda and Bogoch, Bryna. 1994. From Oral Law to Literate Law: Orality, Literacy and Formulaicity in Anglo-Saxon Wills. In *Legal Semiotics and the Sociology of Law*, ed. B.S. Jackson. Oñati: International Institute for the Sociology of Law, 227–292.

Deggau, Hans-Georg. 1988. The Communicative Autonomy of the Legal System. In *Autopoietic Law: A New Approach to Law and Society*, ed. G. Teubner. Berlin and New York, NY: Walter de Gruyter (European University Institute, Series A, Law/Droit/Recht/ Diritto, 8), 128–151.

Douzinas, Costas and Warrington, Ronnie. 1987. On the Deconstruction of Jurisprudence: Fin(n)is Philosophiae. In *Critical Legal Studies*, ed. Peter Fitzpatrick and Alan Hunt. Oxford: Blackwell, 33–46.

Douzinas, Costas, Warrington, Ronnie, and McVeigh, Shaun. 1991. *Postmodern Jurisprudence*. London: Routledge & Kegan Paul.

Ducrot, Oswald. 1972. *Dire et ne pas dire*. Paris: Hermann.

Ducrot, O., et al. ed. 1980. *Les mots de discours*. Paris: Editions de Minuit.

Dworkin, R. 1977. No Right Answer? In *Law, Morality and Society*, ed. P.M.S. Hacker and J. Raz. Oxford: The Clarendon Press, 58–84.

Dworkin, Ronald. 1978. *Taking Rights Seriously*. London: Duckworths.

Dworkin, Ronald. 1986. *Law's Empire*. London: Fontana.

Edelman, Bernard. 1979. *Ownership of the Image*. London: Routledge & Kegan Paul.

Ferrajoli, Luigi. 1988. Guarantees and Truth in Criminal Law. In *Reason in Law*, Proceedings of the Conference Held in Bologna, 12–15 December 1984, ed. Carla Faralli and Enrico Pattaro. Milan: Giuffrè, I.301–311.

Ferrajoli, Luigi. 1989. *Diritto e ragione. Teoria del garantismo penale*. Rome-Bari: Laterza.

Fish, Stanley. 1980. *Is There a Text in this Class?* Cambridge, MA: Harvard University Press.

Fish, Stanley. 1989. *Doing what comes naturally. Change, Rhetoric and the Practice of Theory in Literary and Legal Studies*. Oxford: Clarendon Press.

Frank, Jerome. 1949. *Courts on Trial*. Princeton, NJ: Princeton University Press.

Frege, Gottlob. 1879. *Begriffsschrift und andere Aufsatze*, 2nd ed. Hildesheim: G.Olms, 1964.

Garapon, Antoine. 1985. *L'âne portant des reliques*. Paris: Le Centurion.

Garapon, Antoine. 1988. Forme Symbolique et Forme Linguistique du Droit. *International Journal for the Semiotics of Law/Revue Internationale de Sémiotique Juridique*, 1, 161–176.

Giddens, Anthony. 1984. The Consitution of Society: Outline of the Theory of Structuration. Cambridge: Polity Press.

Goffman, Erving. 1974. Frame Analysis. In *An Essay on the Organisation of Experience*. New York, NY: Harper & Row.

Goffman, Erving. 1981. *Forms of Talk*. Oxford: Blackwell.

Gonzalez Ruiz, Samuel. 1989. Semiotic Codes and Deontic Operators: Consequences of Norberto Bobbio's Promotional Function of Law. *International Journal for the Semiotics of Law/Revue Internationale de Sémiotique Juridique*, 5, 183–198.

Goodrich, Peter. 1986. *Reading the Law*. Oxford: Blackwell.

Goodrich, Peter. 1987. *Legal Discourse, Studies in Linguistics, Rhetoric and Legal Analysis*. London: Macmillan.

Goodrich, Peter. 1990. *Languages of Law*. London: Weidenfeld and Nicolson.

Greimas, Algirdas J. 1970. *Du Sens*. Paris: Editions du Seuil.

Greimas, Algirdas J. 1976. Pour une Théorie des Modalités. *Langages*, 43, 90–107.

Greimas, Algirdas J. and Landowski, Eric. 1976. Analyse sémiotique d'un discours juridique. In *Sémiotique et sciences Sociales*, ed. A.J. Greimas. Paris: Seuil, 79–128.

Greimas, Algirdas J. and Rastier, R. 1968. The Interaction of Semiotic Constraints. *Yale French Studies*, 41, 86–105.

Guastini, Ricardo. 1983. Teorie delle regole costitutive. *Rivista internazionale di filosofia del diritto*, 60(4), 548–564.

Harris, J.W. 1981. Olivecrona on Law and Language—The Search for Legal Culture. *Tidsskrift for Rettsvitenskap*, 94, 625–646.

Hart, H.L.A. 1961. *The Concept of Law*. Oxford: The Clarendon Press.

Hermann, Donald J. 1975. A Structuralist Approach to Legal Reasoning. *Southern California Law Review*, 48, 1131–1194.

Hohfeld, Wesley N. 1923. *Fundamental Legal Conceptions as Applied in Judicial Reasoning*. New Haven, CT and London: Yale University Press.

Hoven, Paul J. van den. 1988. Legal Argument as an Illocutionary Act Complex. *International Journal for the Semiotics of Law/Revue Internationale de Sémiotique Juridique*, 1, 29–45.

Hunt, Alan. 1986. The Theory of Critical Legal Studies. *Oxford Journal of Legal Studies*, 6(1), 1–45.

Hymes, Dell H. 1974. *Foundations of Sociolinguistics: An Ethnographical Approach*. Philadelphia, PA: University of Pennsylvania Press.

Jackson, Bernard S. 1975. From Dharma to Law. *American Journal of Comparative Law*, 23, 490–512.
Jackson, Bernard S. 1980. Towards a Structuralist Theory of Law. *Liverpool Law Review*, 2, 5–30.
Jackson, Bernard S. 1982. Structuralisme et 'sources du droit'. *Archives de Philosophie du Droit*, 27, 147–160.
Jackson, Bernard S. 1985a. *Semiotics and Legal Theory*. London: Routledge and Kegan Paul.
Jackson, Bernard S. 1985b. Hart and Dworkin on Discretion: Some Semiotic Perspectives. In *Semiotics, Law and Social Science*, ed. D. Carzo and B.S. Jackson. Reggio and Rome: Casa del libro editrice, 145–167, French version in Archives de Philosophie du Droit, 34, 1990, 243–258.
Jackson, Bernard S. 1986a. Semiotics and Critical Legal Studies. Working Papers di Sociologia, Università degli Studi di Messina, Facoltà di scienze politiche, No.4; French version in Droit et Société 8, 1988, 61–70.
Jackson, Bernard S. 1986b. Emerging Issues in Legal Semiotics. *Droit Prospectif. Revue de la Recherche Juridique*, 2, 17–37.
Jackson, Bernard S. 1987. Rationalité consciente et inconsciente dans la théorie du droit et la science juridique. *Revue Interdisciplinaire d'Etudes Juridiques*, 19, 1–18.
Jackson, Bernard S. 1988a. Can One Speak of the 'Deep Structure of Law'? In *Theory and Systems of Legal Philosophy*, ed. S. Panou et al. Stuttgart: Franz Steiner Verlag, 250–261.
Jackson, Bernard S. 1988b. *Law, Fact and Narrative Coherence*. Merseyside: Deborah Charles Publications.
Jackson, Bernard S. 1988c. Narrative Models in Legal Proof. *International Journal for the Semiotics of Law/Revue Internationale de Sémiotique Juridique*, I(3), 225–246.
Jackson, Bernard S. 1988d. Conscious and Unconscious Rationality in Law and Legal Theory. In *Reason in Law*, Proceedings of the Conference Held in Bologna, 12–15 December 1984, vol. III, ed. Carla Faralli and Enrico Pattaro. Milan: Giuffrè, 281–299.
Jackson, Bernard S. 1988e. Narrative Models in Legal Proof. *International Journal for the Semiotics of Law/Revue Internationale de Sémiotique Juridique*, 1(3), 225–246, reprinted in Narrative and the Legal Discourse, ed. David Ray Papke. A Reader in Storytelling and the Law, Liverpool: Deborah Charles Publications, 1991.
Jackson, Bernard S. 1989. Ideas of Law and Legal Administration: A Semiotic Approach. In *The World of Ancient Israel: Sociological, Anthropological and Political Perspectives*, ed. R.E. Clements. Cambridge: Cambridge University Press, 185–202.
Jackson, Bernard S. 1990. The Normative Syllogism and the Problem of Reference. In *Law, Interpretation and Reality, Essays in Epistemology, Hermeneutics and Jurisprudence*, ed. P. Nerhot. Dordrecht: Kluwer Academic Publishers, 379–401 (Law and Philosophy Library, 11).
Jackson, Bernard S. 1994. Towards an Interdisciplinary Model of Legal Communication. In *Legal Semiotics and the Sociology of Law*, ed. B.S. Jackson. Oñati: International Institute for the Sociology of Law, 97–110.
Jackson, Bernard S. and Paychère, F. 1989. Semiotics and MacCormick's Institutional Theory. In *Legal Semiotics Papers*. Edinburgh: 1989 IASL Pre-Conference Booklet, 6–14.
Jameson, Fredric. 1972. *The Prison-House of Language: A Critical Account of Structuralism and Russian Formalism*. Princeton, NJ: Princeton University Press.
Jori, Mario. 1979. Hart e l'analisi del linguaggio. *Materiali per una storia della cultura giuridica*, IX(1), 161–228.
Jori, Mario. 1985. *Voci: Comunicazione, Referente, Segno, Semiotica, Significato, Sistema e Discorso. In Gli strumenti del sapere contemporaneo*. Torino, UTET.
Jori, Mario. 1987. Semiotica e teoria del diritto. *Rivista internazionale di filosofia del diritto*, LXIV(2), 196–239.
Jori, Mario. 1989. Tendances en sémiotique juridique. *International Journal for the Semiotics of Law*, II(6), 277–300.
Kalinowski, Georges. 1965. *Introduction à la logique juridique*. Paris: P.U.F.

Kalinowski, Georges. 1972. 'L'Axiomatisation et le formalisation de la théorie hexagonale de l'opposition de M.R. Blanché (Système B)", Les Etudes Philosophiques (1967), 201–209. Reprinted in G. Kalinowski, Etudes de logique déontique I (1953–1969). Paris: L.G.D.J., 161–167.

Kalinowski, Georges. 1976. Un aperçu élémentaire des modalités déontiques. *Langages*, 43, 10–18.

Kalinowski, Georges. 1980. Loi juridique et loi logique. Contribution à la sémantique de la loi juridique. *Archives de philosophie du droit*, 25, 123–136.

Kalinowski, Georges. 1985. *Sémiotique et Philosophie*. Paris and Amsterdam: Editions Hadès-Benjamins. Collection Actes Sémiotiques.

Kalinowski, Georges. 1988. Sémiotique Juridique. In *Dictionnaire Encyclopédique de Théorie et de Sociologie du Droit*, ed. A.-J. Arnaud et al. Paris and Bruxelles: L.G.D.J. and E. Story-Scientia, 370–371.

Kalinowski, Georges. 1990. Ontic and Deontic. *International Journal for the Semiotics of Law*, II(8), 133–146.

Kelsen, Hans. 1967. *Pure Theory of Law* (trld. M. Knight) Berkeley, CA and Los Angeles, CA: University of California Press.

Kelsen, Hans. 1981. On the Basis of Legal Validity (trld. S. Paulson). *American Journal of Jurisprudence*, 26, 178–189.

Kennedy, Duncan. 1979. The Structure of Blackstone's Commentaries. *Buffalo Law Review*, 28(2), 205–382.

Kevelson, Roberta, ed. 1987. *Law and Semiotics*, vol. 1. New York, NY and London: Plenum Press.

Kevelson, Roberta, ed. 1988a. *Law and Semiotics*, vol. 2. New York, NY and London: Plenum Press.

Kevelson, Roberta. 1988b. *The Law as a System of Signs*. New York, NY: Plenum Press.

Kevelson, Roberta 1994. Some Reinterpretations of the Meaning of Customary Law in International Law-making. In *Legal Semiotics and the Sociology of Law*, ed. B.S. Jackson. Oñati: International Institute for the Sociology of Law, 119–131.

Kramer, M.H. 1988. The Rule of Misrecognition in the Hart of Jurisprudence. *Oxford Journal of Legal Studies*, 8, 401–433.

Kramer, M.H. 1991. *Legal Theory, Political Theory and Deconstruction, Against Rhadamanthus*. Bloomington, IN and Indianapolis, IN: Indiana University Press.

Kurzon, Dennis. 1986. *It Is Hereby Performed*. Amsterdam: Benjamins.

Kurzon, Dennis. 1988. Prolegomena to a Speech Act Approach to Hearsay Evidence. *International Journal for the Semiotics of Law/Revue Internationale de Sémiotique Juridique*, 1, 263–273.

Kurzon, Dennis. 1994. Silence in the Legal Process. In *Legal Semiotics and the Sociology of Law*, ed. B.S. Jackson. Oñati: International Institute for the Sociology of Law, 297–332

Lachmayer, Friedrich. 1988. The Law of Domesticated Man. In *Reason in Law*, ed. Carla Faralli and Enrico Pattaro. Proceedings of the Conference Held in Bologna, 12–15 December 1984, vol. II Milan: Giuffrè, 333–341.

Lachs, J. 1988. Law and the Importance of Feelings. In *Law and Semiotics II*, ed. R. Kevelson. New York, NY: Plenum Press, 221–227.

Landowski, Eric. 1985. Semiotics in Social Science Research. In *Semiotics, Law and Social Science*, ed. D. Carzo and B.S. Jackson. Rome and Liverpool: Gangemi Editore and Liverpool Law Review, 69–79 (French original in Sémiotique et Bible 31, 1983).

Landowski, Eric. 1988a. "Sémiologie juridique", "Sémiotique juridique". In *Dictionnaire de théorie et de sociologie du droit*, ed. A.J. Arnaud. Paris and Bruxelles: L.G.D.J. and E. Story-Scientia, 368–372.

Landowski, Eric. 1988b. Towards a Semiotic and Narrative Approach to Law. *International Journal for the Semiotics of Law/Revue Internationale de Sémiotique Juridique*, I(1), 79–105.

Landowski, E. 1988c. Sémiotique du droit: interdisciplinarité et pertinence. *Droit et Société*, 21, 85–90.

Landowski, Eric. 1988/1989. Vérité et véridiction en droit. *Droit et Société*, 8, 45–59 (English version in International Journal for the Semiotics of Law/Revue Internationale de Sémiotique Juridique II/4, 1989, 29–47).
Landowski, Eric. 1989. Du référent, perdu et retrouvé. *International Journal for the Semiotics of Law/Revue Internationale de Sémiotique Juridique*, II(6), 301–312.
Landowski, E. 1994. Deux points de vue pour une socio-sémiotique. In *Legal Semiotics and the Sociology of Law*, ed. B.S. Jackson. Oñati: International Institute for the Sociology of Law, 9–21.
Luhmann, Niklas. 1984. Soziale Systeme. In *Grundriß einer allgemeinen Theorie*. Frankfurt: Suhrkamp.
Luhmann, Niklas. 1985. The Self-Production of Law and Its Limits. In *Dilemmas of Law in the Welfare State*, ed. G. Teubner. Berlin and New York, NY: Walter de Gruyter.
Luhmann, Niklas. 1988. Closure and Openness: On Reality in the World of Law. In *Autopoietic Law: A New Approach to Law and Society*, ed. G. Teubner. Berlin and New York, NY: Walter de Gruyter (European University Institute, Series A, Law/Droit/Recht/ Diritto, 8), 335–348.
Luzzati, Claudio. 1990. *La Vaghezza delle norme. Un' analisi del linguaggio giuridico*. Milan: Giuffrè.
MacCormick, D. Neil. 1973. *Law as Institutional Fact*. Edinburgh: Edinburgh University Press. reprinted in The Law Quarterly Review 90, 1974, 102–29.
MacCormick, D. Neil. 1978. *Legal Reasoning and Legal Theory*. Oxford: Clarendon Press.
MacCormick, D. Neil. 1987. Legal Deduction, Legal Predicates and Expert Systems. Paper delivered at a seminar of the Legal Expert Systems Association in Tokyo, August 1987.
MacCormick, D. Neil. 1988. Institutions, Arrangements and Practical Information. *Ratio Juris*, 1(1), 73–82.
MacCormick, D. Neil, and Weinberger, O. 1986. *The Institutional Theory of Law*. Dordrecht: D. Reidel.
Manning, Peter K. 1977. *Police Work*. Cambridge, MA: M.I.T. Press.
Manning, Peter K. 1980. *Narcs' Game*. Cambridge, MA: M.I.T. Press.
Manning, Peter K. 1988. *Signifying Calls: Symbolic Communication and the Police Response Game*. Cambridge, MA: M.I.T. Press.
Martin, R.M. 1959. *Towards a Systematic Pragmatics*. Amsterdam: North Holland Publishing Co.
Martino, Antonio. 1975. *Le Definzioni Legislativi*. Turin: Giappichelli.
Mellinkoff, David. 1963. *The Language of the Law*. Boston, MA: Little, Brown & Co.
Milovanovic, Dragan. 1986. Juridico-Linguistic Communicative Markets: Towards a Semiotic Analysis. *Contemporary Crises*, 10, 281–304.
Milovanovic, Dragan. 1988. *A Primer in the Sociology of Law*. Albany, NY: Harrow and Heston.
Mimin, P. 1978. *Le Style des Jugements*. Paris: Librairies Techniques.
Montague, Richard. 1974. In *Formal Philosophy*, ed. R. Thomason. New Haven, CT: Yale University Press.
Montague, Richard. 1976. *Formal Logic*. New Haven, CT: Yale University Press.
Morris, Charles W. 1938. Foundations of the Theory of Signs. In *International Encyclopedia of Unified Science*, vol. I. Chicago, IL: University of Chicago Press, 1–59.
Morris, Herbert. 1960. Verbal Disputes and the Legal Philosophy of John Austin. *University of California Law Review*, 7(1), 27–56.
Morris, Charles W. 1971. *Writings on the General Theory of Signs*. Paris: The Hague Mouton.
Nelken, David. 1994. Rules and Stories. In *Legal Semiotics and the Sociology of Law*, ed. B.S. Jackson. Oñati: International Institute for the Sociology of Law, 111–118.
Norris, Christopher. 1988. Law, Deconstruction, and the Resistance to Theory. *Journal of Law and Society*, 15(2), 166–187.
O'Barr, W.M. 1982. *Linguistic Evidence*. New York, NY: Academic Press.
Olivecrona, Karl. 1971. *Law as Fact,* 2nd ed. London: Stevens.
Oppenheim, Felix. 1944. Outline of a Logical Analysis of Law. *Philosophy of Science*, 11, 142–160.

Pattaro, Enrico. 1985. *Lineamenti per una teoria del diritto*. Bologna: CLUEB.

Pattaro, Enrico. 1986–1987. *Filosofia del diritto*, 2 vols. Bologna: CLUEB.

Pattaro, Enrico. 1986a. Pour une théorie des impératifs juridiques. La Contribution de Karl Olivecrona. *Droit Prospectif*, 2, 189–208.

Pattaro, Enrico and Gonzalez Ruiz, Samuel. 1988. Linguistic Functions, Usages and Rules. *International Journal for the Semiotics of Law/Revue Internationale de Sémiotique Juridique*, 1, 123–142.

Paychère, François. 1989. La place des foncteurs déontiques dans l'analyse du discours juridique. *International Journal for the Semiotics of Law/Revue Internationale de Sémiotique Juridique*, 5, 199–214.

Paychère, François. 1991. Hohfeld Revisited: A Matter of Viewpoint? *Archir für Rechts-und Sozialphilosophie*, LXXVII/3, 374–384.

Pencak, William. 1987. The United States Constitution: A Semiotic Interpretation. In *Law and Semiotics I*, ed. R. Kevelson. New York, NY: Plenum Press, 311–340.

Perelman, Chaim. 1976. *Logique Juridique – Nouvelle Rhétorique*. Paris: Dalloz.

Perrott, David L. 1980. Has Law a Deep Structure? – The Origin of Fundamental Duties. In *Fundamental Duties*, ed. D. Lasok et al. Oxford and New York, NY: Pergamon Press, 1–15.

Pintore, Anna. 1990. *La teoria analitica dei concetti giuridici*. Napoli: Jovene.

Posner, R. and Krampen, M. 1981. Semiotic Circles in German. *American Journal of Semiotics*, I(1–2), 169–212.

Price, Robert. 1987. The Merely Symbolic. In *Law and Semiotics I*, ed. R. Kevelson. New York, NY: Plenum Press, 341–348.

Robertshaw, Paul. 1975. Unreasonableness and Judicial Control of Administrative Discretion: The Geology of the Chertsey Caravans Case. *Public Law*, 113–136.

Robertshaw, Paul. 1985. Semantic and Linguistic Aspects of Sex Discrimination Decisions. Dichotomised Woman. In *Semiotics, Law and Social Science*, ed. D. Carzo and B.S. Jackson. Rome: Gangemi, 203–227.

Ross, H.L. 1960. *Settled Out of Court*. Chicago, IL: Aldine Publishing Co.

Ross, Alf. 1968. *Directives and Norms*. London: Routledge & Kegan.

Sartorius, Rolf. 1966. The Concept of Law. *Archiv für Rechts- und Sozialphilosophie*, LII(2), 161–190.

Sbisà, Marina and Fabbri, Paolo. 1980. Models (?) for a Pragmatic Analysis. Working Papers and Pre-Publications, Centro Internazionale di Semiotica e di Linguistica, Università di Urbino, Serie A, 91; a later version in Journal of Pragmatics 4, 1981, 301–319.

Scarpelli, Uberto. 1959/1985. *Contributo alla semantica del linguaggio normativo*. Turin: Accademia delle scienze (2nd ed. by A. Pintore, Milan, Giuffrè, 1985, with her Introduzione at 1 31).

Scarpelli, Uberto, ed. 1976. *Diritto e Analise del Linguaggio*. Milan: Edizione de Comunità.

Scarpelli, Uberto. 1988. Una rivendicazione dell' empirismo e del pragmatismo. Considerazioni a partire dalla semiotica di John Locke. Paper delivered to Legal Philosophy Congress on Semiotica e Analisi del Linguaggio at Siena, March l988.

Schreckenberger, W. 1978. *Rhetorische Semiotik*. Munich: Alber.

Searle, John R. 1969. *Speech Acts*. Cambridge: Cambridge University Press.

Seibert, T.-M. 1979. Zur Entwicklung semiotischer Fragestellungen in der rechtswissenschaftlichen Grundlagenforschung. *Zeitschrift für Semiotik*, 1, 277–288.

Seibert, T.-M. 1981. *Aktenanalysen. Zur Schriftform juristischer Deutungen*. Tübingen: Narr.

Seibert, T.-M. 1989. Schriftform und Mündlichkeitsprinzip im rechtsdiskurs. In ed. L. Hoffmann, *Rechtsdiskurse, Untersuchungen zur Kommunikation in Gerichtsverfahren*. Tübingen: Narr.

Sheleff, Leon. 1994. Four Truths: Legal and Political, Judicial and Historical. In *Legal Semiotics and the Sociology of Law*, ed. B.S. Jackson. Oñati: International Institute for the Sociology of Law, 73–96.

Sobota, Katharina. 1990. *Sachlichkeit, Rhetorische Kunst der Juristen*. Frankfurt: Peter Lang.

Sourioux, Jean-Louis et Lerat, Pierre. 1976. *Le Langage du Droit*. Paris: P.U.F.

Stockinger, Peter. 1988. The Conceptual Representation of Action and its Normative Background. *International Journal for the Semiotics of Law/Revue Internationale de Sémiotique Juridique*, I(2), 143–159.

Strawson, P.F. 1950. "On Referring", Mind 59, 320–344, reprinted in The Theory of Meaning, ed. G.H.R. Parkinson, Oxford U.P., 1968, 61–85, and in Strawson's Logico-Linguistic Papers, London and New York: Methuen, 1971, 1–27.

Sudnow, David. 1965. Normal Crimes. *Social Problems* 12, 255–276, reprinted in Deviance. Interactionist Perspectives, ed. E. Pubington and M. Weinberg, 3rd ed., New York: MacMillan, 1978, 211–222.

Tarello, Giovanne. 1950. Orientamenti analitico-linguistici e teoria dell'interpretazione giuridica, In Scarpelli 1976, 375–395.

Teubner, Gunther. 1988. Introduction to Autopoietic Law. In *Autopoietic Law: A New Approach to Law and Society*, ed. G. Teubner. Berlin and New York, NY: Walter de Gruyter (European University Institute, Series A, Law/Droit/Recht/ Diritto, 8), 1–11.

Wróblewski, Jerzy. 1983. *Meaning and Truth in Judicial Decision*. Helsinki: A-Tieto Oy.

Wróblewski, Jerzy. 1989. Legal Language and Legal Institutions. *International Journal for the Semiotics of Law/Revue Internationale de Sémiotique Juridique*, II(4), 3–16.

Wróblewski, Jerzy. 1990a. Semantics and Pragmatics of Normative Qualification Statements. *International Journal for the Semiotics of Law/Revue Internationale de Sémiotique Juridique*, III(7), 35–53.

Wróblewski, Jerzy. 1990b. Semiotics of Law in Poland. *Bulletin of the International Association for the Semiotics of Law*, 6, 6–8 (with further bibliography).

Chapter 2
Firstness and Phenomenology—Peirce and Husserl on Attitude Change

Jan M. Broekman

Possibly . . . Firstness is the embryo of being

Peirce (1903)

2.1 Introduction

Close encounters between Husserl and Pierce never took place in biographic reality, and philosophical closeness was never described in philosophical or semiotic essays. An important exception is the 1957 Spiegelberg essay (Spiegelberg 1957), and an earlier mention in Ogden and Richards' 1929 path breaking book "The Meaning of Meaning" (Ogden and Richards 1923, p. 269 ff.), which gave successively attention to Husserl and Peirce in their Appendix D. Husserl's phenomenology was characterized as "having reference to a manifest multiplicity of conscious subjects communicating with one another. A systematically consistent development of phenomenology leads necessarily to an all-comprehensive logic concerned with the correlates: knowing-act, knowledge-significance, knowledge-objectivity". Peirce was acknowledged for his attention to logic as the doctrine of the formal conditions of the truth of symbols; i.e., of the reference of symbols to their objects. But the idea, not to purely compare the two thinkers but rather to understand their mutual inspiration and their philosophical project in its entirety is an important issue in its own right. Especially the concepts of *First*, *Firstness* and *First Philosophy,* which they have in common and gave a role far beyond the originally Aristotelian notion, plays a central role and could elucidate much of direct semiotic interest. At issue is for both philosophers a breach with the evident and with the naturalness in which we all live our daily life. What meaning and philosophical implications does that breach embrace?

Peirce notices how a sheriff's hand on one's shoulder cannot be gently taken away, treated as an undesirable gesture or as just an incident: it confronts us with

J.M. Broekman (✉)
Dickinson School of Law, Penn State University, Pennsylvania, PA, USA
e-mail: jmb56@dsl.psu.edu

A. Wagner, J.M. Broekman (eds.), *Prospects of Legal Semiotics*,
DOI 10.1007/978-90-481-9343-1_2, © Springer Science+Business Media B.V. 2010

the law! The sheriff's gesture introduces an awareness of *Firstness* because it wakes you up from your naively lived life—the gesture means that you are a bearer of rights and duties. Peirce used biographical experiences (Pencak 1993, p. 17 ff.) where Husserl explored the same questions in the philosophical tradition of Plato and Kant, which he analyzed in view of his concept of a transcendental phenomenology (Husserl 1956, pp. 5, 237; Broekman 1963, pp. 14, 87, 138). He observed how a notion of attitude change (Einstellungsänderung) is necessary to reflect upon what appears in hindsight as evident or natural in life. In both cases, life is enhanced, enriched and deepened by this change, which often implies a fundamental change of meaning caused by a rupture in the situation of evidence or naturalness. Kant called that change a "Copernican turn" (Husserl 1956, p. 240; Kant 1990, p. B22). Husserl used the very same expression to designate the origin and essence of his phenomenology. We highlight *firstness* in Peirce and Husserl in order to understand their respective idea of phenomenology as a background for further semiotic investigations pertaining to future law-society relations. That focus should find its place is the broader context of studies pertaining to the relations between Peirce and Husserl. The most impressive research on that topic is in the recent publication of Stjernfelt (2007), who not only offers an investigation on the borderlines of Phenomenology, Ontology and Semiotics—as his subtitle suggests, but also on hitherto unrevealed components of the Peirce-Husserl relations, especially in the first decades of the twentieth century.[1] His general observation shows the

> . . .strange fact that so little comparison between Husserl and Peirce has been undertaken. Probably the historical reason is that the two philosophers both stand on the initial edge of the analytical/continental split and ended up as founding fathers for each their main currents in philosophy – phenomenology and pragmatism/semiotics, respectively. Seemingly rooted in each their specific tradition, the large bulk of common ideas and interests in their works has been ignored. Distorted parodies of the two – Husserl the transcendental solipsist, Peirce the pan-semiotician – have added to preclude a closer Auseinandersetzung between the two. Correspondingly, it is a little known fact that the two of them did in fact know the other's work – albeit not, unfortunately, to a degree sufficient to reveal the crucial convergences to any of them. Husserl's interest in Peirce lies mainly in the beginning of his career; he refers to Peirce's early semiotic work at several occasions around the *Philosophie der Arithmetik* period, but there is no reference later than the nineties, so Husserl never came to know the mature Peirce's phenomenology and semiotics from around the turn of the century, and so he hardly influenced Husserl's later thinking. Conversely, Peirce several times refers to Logical Investigations which came out in the midst of Peirce's last fertile period of thought – but he only mentions it in a pejorative manner, classing it alongside other German logic studies as

[1]"Peirce and Husserl were mathematicians who had common interests in language, ontology, and phenomenology. Yet the terminology they coined was so different that they misunderstood one another: each accused the other of 'psychologism'", and focuses on that publication: "Stjernfelt shows that they had a closer affinity to one another than either had to Frege or Heidegger. In fact, the writings of each frequently illuminate and extend the insights of the other. . .. Peirce and Husserl were cultivating a broad and fertile common ground, which was largely neglected by both the analytic and the continental philosophers during the twentieth century and which promises to be an exciting area of research in the twenty-first." (John F. Sowa at Amazon.com). The IJSL, vol. 21, No. 3 issue has an extended book review, written by G. Sykes. An in-depth study beyond comparative notions of the Peirce-Husserl relationship seems to be overdue.

despicable examples of psychologism. This characterization evidently rules out that he may in fact have read very much of the book himself (Stjernfelt 2007, p. 141 f.)

2.2 Phenomenology in Semiotic Eyes

2.2.1 Peirce and Phenomenology

Stjernfelt's general description focuses immediately the concept of phenomenology itself, although the two have different approaches and in particular different ideals to realize:

> ...The early Husserl thus may, to some extent, be influenced by Peirce through Schröder. The degree of Peirce's indebtedness to Husserl is equally difficult to ascertain. The mature Peirce decides upon the term 'phenomenology' for a part of his study, which is, in some respects, rather close to the early Husserl's use of the word as referring to the study of essences. It is the study of universal elements of all phenomena; it is a study explicitly anti-psychological (and ante-psychological) of nature; it is the most basic of all positive studies (by 'positive', Peirce does not refer to empirical '*Tatsachenwissenschaften'* only, rather, 'positive' refers to sciences of the given as opposed to sciences of the merely possible), and logic is founded upon it; it is a study that includes all kinds of possible experiences, including dreams and abstract thought; and it is a study – almost an outline of a Peircean phenomenological reduction – bracketing whether the phenomena it studies exists or not. Of course, Peirce does not share the later Husserl's basing phenomenology on a study of conscious acts, but this difference seems more a difference of emphasis within a field than it is a foundational difference (Stjernfelt 2007, p. 142).

Peirce suggests that a pragmatic phenomenology (which he also called "phaneroscopy" the Ancient Greek *phaneron* meaning *the manifest*) should help us to better grasp everyday reality. Stjernfelt researched those differentiations profoundly, including the precise use of the concepts "phenomenology" and "phaneroscopy", which are intertwined in many years of Peirce's developments.

> 'Phenomenology' did not play any important role in the papers published in Peirce's lifetime, but it rose to prominence due to Hartshorne and Weiss' edition of CP where they picked it as a headline term – Hartshorne having studied by Husserl in Freiburg in the 1920s. That was no bad choice; Peirce's use of the term 'phenomenology' is indeed intense, but covers a rather short timespan: (...) what I have called phenomenology, [Peirce writes] that is, just the analysis of what kind of constituents there are in our thoughts and lives, (whether these be valid or invalid being quite aside from the question). It is a branch of philosophy I am most deeply interested in and which I have worked upon almost as much as I have upon logic. It has nothing to do with psychology (...) Phenomenology has no right to appeal to logic, except to deductive logic. On the contrary, logic must be founded on phenomenology (Peirce 1958, vol. 8, p. 297) The word is also used in the passing in a letter to Lady Welby (Peirce 1958, vol. 8, p. 328; Peirce 1997, p. 196–197), as well as in a 1906 commentary to a proposal by a Mr. Peterson to discuss philosophical terminology (Peirce 1931, vol. 5, p. 610). As is evident, the main period for Peirce's use of the term covers the years 1902–06 with the main emphasis on three years only, 1902–04. From around 1905, Peirce substitutes the terms 'phanerology', 'phanerochemy', 'phenoscopy', and especially 'phaneroscopy' for 'phenomenology' (Stjernfelt 2007, p. 143)

A first difficulty is *firstness* itself and the general fact that what is manifest requires an insight, which does not occur when the manifest seems ready to be perceived. So we should first try to methodically understand the universal categories of human experience, which helps us to bring some order in our experiences—an order far beyond psychological components or any type of psychologism. As a consequence, *Firstness* and phenomenology must deliver us appropriate ways of perception and understanding reality. They thus became appreciated as intertwined concepts at the end of the nineteenth into twenty-first century semiotics (Peirce 1998, p. 145)

One should pay attention in this context to Peirce's interpretation of pragmatism as the moment in which he opened up to a general reception of his philosophy (Deely 1994). The general public knew Peirce mainly as a mentor to better known US protagonists such as Willliam James, F.C.S. Schiller and John Dewey. So Peirce introduced 1905/1906 the expression "pragmaticism" for what they (especially William James, after he had introduced the word) had called pragmatism. He wanted to explain his *pragmaticism*, a neologism used in a third *The Monist* paper on phaneroscopy (Peirce 1998, p. 360 ff.). His classical words indicated the same desire, which Husserl circumscribes as "...strenge Wissenschaft":

> ...the word [pragmatism] begins to be met with occasionally in the literary journals, where it gets abused in the merciless way that words have to expect when they fall into literary clutches. ... So then, the writer, finding his bantling "pragmatism" so promoted, feels that it is time to kiss his child good-by and relinquish it to its higher destiny; while to serve the precise purpose of expressing the original definition, he begs to announce the birth of the word "pragmaticism", which is ugly enough to be safe from kidnappers (Peirce 1931, vol. 5, p. 414).

The pragmaticist maxim formulates:

> Consider what effects, that might conceivably have practical bearings, you conceive the objects of your conception to have. Then, your conception of those effects is the whole of your conception of the object (Peirce 1931, vol. 5, p. 438).

In doing so, Peirce revealed his intention to concentrate on a philosophy in the optic of Locke's *doctrina signorum* (Parker 1998, p. 234). But what Locke achieved can in our days not be developed without scientific context. Peirce thus introduces a method of experimental and mental reflection to found conceptions who can be refuted or accepted. The hinge of that phenomenological method is in the attitude change provoked by experiencing *firstness*.

2.2.2 *Phenomenology and* Firstness

Phenomenology is founded on an "attitude change" or "change of approach to reality". Peirce embraces that theoretical goal and describes how

> ...there can be no question that *phaneron* means primarily *brought to light, open to public inspection throughout*. The *manifest* is that which a person who does not willfully shut his eyes to has no choice but believe in (Peirce 1931, vol. 1, pp. 317–321)

The expression "believe in" indicates already an attitude change. Not a *fact* is at stake, but a *basic attitude*. This is a clear contrast to Hegel's phenomenology, which analyzes experience without engaging in whatever is or might be experienced. This attitude is essential for transcendental phenomenology as well as semiotics, and makes Peirce create a link between *firstness* and *feeling*—the latter understood in an epistemological, not in a psychological sense. Feeling indicates a state in which a consciousness can temporarily experience, lighten up or create awareness without referring to a definable or perhaps even objective fact. "A feeling is a state, which is in its entirety in every moment of time as long as it endures" and "a lapse of time..." Peirce notes (Peirce 1931, vol. 1, p. 306 ff.). Only today, in a next century, we perceive clearly how Husserl and Peirce were inspired by a common interest and a shared commitment to establish an "eidetic phenomenology" on the basis of a strict scientific philosophical method. That method creates an a priori science delivering sound foundations for the project called "eidetic phenomenology". Husserl therefore emphasizes changes or transitions of philosophical *optics* when he writes:

> In it, every self-enclosed field of possible experience permits *eo ipso* the all-embracing transition from the factual to the essential form, the *eidos*. If the phenomenological actual fact as such becomes irrelevant; if, rather, it serves only as an example and as the foundation for a free but intuitive variation of the factual mind and communities of minds *into* the a priori possible (thinkable) ones; and if now the theoretical eye directs itself to the necessarily enduring invariant in the variation; then there will arise with its systematic way of proceeding a realm of its own, of the "a priori". There emerges therewith the eidetically necessary typical form, the *eidos*; this *eidos* must manifest itself throughout all the potential forms of mental being in particular cases, must be present in all the synthetic combinations and self-enclosed wholes, if it is to be at all "thinkable", that is, intuitively conceivable ... an "eidetic phenomenology" (Husserl 1927, p. 5)

One can experience through Peirce what it means to read Husserl with semiotic eyes! Semiotics implicates for Husserl a privileged apparatus of possible changes in attitude, which he famously characterized as the "transcendental-phenomenological reduction". This reductive ability, to be practiced by every philosopher, is the central issue that marks a new beginning in twentieth century philosophy, in particular as a new and most radical form of Cartesian doubt. Understanding *First* and *Firstness* is of utmost importance in the heart of this philosophical operation.

2.2.3 *Philosophy and* Firstness

One often remembers how for Plato philosophy emerges from a state of perplexity. Does not Socrates himself claim to be in a state of *aporia* when he becomes confronted with phenomena of self-contradiction? Such a situation of cognitive embarrassment awakens when propositions that are plausible on their own appear to be inconsistent when confronted with others. Can such a perplexity be the beginning of philosophy, of Plato's *thaumazein*? And what to *do* or what to *be,* once confronted with that perplexity?

What distinguishes the philosopher from the non-philosopher is a sensitivity to solve or to overcome perplexity between competing characters of propositions or other fragments of discourse. Aristotle regards *aporia* not only as the *beginning* of philosophical inquiry, but also as the *method* by which any philosophical inquiry proceeds. A philosopher examines the assumptions on which an argument is build, so that his sensitivity for *aporia* becomes crucial for the viability of an unfolding philosophy. From Socrates through Plato to Aristotle, we notice how philosophy is not characterized by some vague notion of *wonder*, *thaumazein*, but rather by the more sophisticated notion of *aporia*. Does this diminish the importance of *firstness*? Plato's *thaumazein* is a matter of rationality, not of a vague perplexity. However, logic as such cannot resolve aporetic inconsistencies, whereas a more rational *thaumazein* initiates philosophy.

Both Husserl and Pierce concentrated on the *aporetic* relations between the idea of a natural world on the one hand and human knowledge as an artifice in that world on the other. The parallel between Peirce's *firstness* and Husserl's *phenomenology* is in their emphasis on the how to focus *aporia*—a problem of general philosophical interest. The two strive for a new philosophical theory, which, in the words of Husserl, is explicitly based on a *revolt* of our everyday life's natural way of thinking.

Husserl highlighted that revolt as a new and scientific view belonging to our sense of the world and constituting what Peirce called "world quality" (Husserl 1956, p. 240). He parallels Husserl in his use of this expression, because "world quality" does not refer to the physical world but to the life world, which Husserl articulates as "Lebenswelt"—a well-known theme of the mainstream in continental European philosophy of the century's twenties and thirties. Remember how problems of *firstness* were always enshrined in Occidental philosophy, and how they resurfaced at a very central place in the semiotics and phenomenology of Peirce and Husserl. *Firstness* comprises indeed much of our semiotically relevant philosophical images, among them those of immediacy, pureness, beginning or naturalness. These were indeed enshrined in sometimes very different philosophical designs in different periods of its history.

2.2.4 Peirce and **Firstness**

In daily life, the idea of *firstness*—always surprisingly close to "the manifest" or "the natural"—is not always and everywhere evident. Peirce begins his manuscript "Phenomenology" with an attempt to understand *firstness* philosophically:

> "The idea of First is predominant in the ideas of freshness, life, freedom..." and more precisely: "The free is that which has not another behind it, determining its actions..." (Peirce 1998, p. 150)

In writing those lines, he forms a classic argument in the definition of *firstness* by means of the phrase "absence of any reference". Freedom and *firstness* are clearly associated for him with his philosophy of a sign and a sign's reference. Maintaining that philosophical climate, however, includes still other problems:

> But so far as the idea of the negation of another enters, the idea of another enters; and such negative idea must be put in the background, or else we cannot say that the *firstness* is predominant.

His descriptions become circumscriptions; the quoted parallels fade away in the history of philosophy itself:

> Freedom can only manifest itself in unlimited and uncontrolled variety and multiplicity; and thus the first becomes predominant in the ideas of measureless variety and multiplicity. It is the leading idea of Kant's "manifold of sense" (Peirce 1998, p. 150)

There is, however, a decisive difference. Kant spoke about the manifold as a totality, because

> In the idea of being, *Firstness* is predominant, not necessarily on account of the abstractness of that idea, but on account of its self-containedness. . . .The first is predominant in feeling, as distinct from objective perception, will, and thought (Peirce 1998, p. 150)

Feeling again: not as a psychological concept but as an epistemological issue. Is that not a weakness? The many jokes people make about Peirce's *firstness*, *secondness* and *thirdness* underline his own reluctance to introduce this sort of concepts. He mentions to Lady Welby in 1904 a strong uneasiness with the formulation of his own ideas, when we consider how their simplicity and vulnerability as well as their intrinsic difficulty should be properly defined. All those go in the first place to the triad of *firstness*, *secondness* and *thirdness*, but *firstness* is the most important, especially if one considers how this triad has a history in its own right within Peirce's philosophy. Here is a remarkable limitation if one wants to interpret *Firstness as a beginning*. A First is not conceivable without its triadic relations with a Second and a Third, so that any concentration on Firstness is at the same time a process of division within what is in essence an infinite totality. Stjernfelt suggests in precisely this context:

> A variety of hundreds of sign definitions are disseminated all over Peirce's work, but a certain agreement among Peirce scholars seem to focus on a few of them, among those the following: 'A Sign, or Representamen, is a First which stands in such a genuine triadic relation to a Second, called its Object, as to be capable of determining a Third, called its Interpretant, to assume the same triadic relation to its Object in which it stands itself to the same Object' (Peirce 1931, vol. 2, p. 274). This sign definition from 1902 involves explicit reference to the three phenomenological categories. The sign relates a quality (1) to an actual object (2) and, by doing so, involves a more or less general regularity (3). This regularity now stands in the same relation to the object as did the initial First, that is, it is to the same degree a sign of the object. Thus, Peirce's sign definition is recursive; the fact that the interpretant is in itself a sign implies that it has its own interpretant and so on ad infinitum. In this recursivity of the sign definition lies Peirce's famous 'unlimited semiosis' (Stjernfelt 2007, p. 23)

Notice, how Peirce writes almost biographically about *Firstness*:

> . . .I was long ago (1867) led, after only three or four years' study, to throw all ideas into the three classes of *Firstness*, of *Secondness*, and of *Thirdness*. This sort of notion is as distasteful to me as to anybody; and for years I endeavored to pooh-pooh and refute it; but it long ago conquered me completely.

> Disagreeable as it is to attribute such meaning to numbers, and to triad above all, it is as true as it is disagreeable. The ideas of *Firstness*, *Secondness*, and *Thirdness* are simple enough. Giving to being the broadest possible sense, to include ideas as well as things, and ideas that we fancy we have just as much as ideas we do have, I should define *Firstness*, *Secondness*, and *Thirdness* thus: *Firstness* is the mode of being of that which is such as it is, positively and without reference to anything else... (Peirce 1958, vol. 8, p. 29)

> The ***first*** and foremost is that rare faculty, the faculty of seeing what stares one in the face, just as it presents itself, unreplaced by any interpretation, unsophisticated by any allowance for this or for that supposed modifying circumstance (Peirce 1931, vol. 5, p. 42)

The philosophical impetus of his remarks seem evident—do we not all remember Immanuel Kant's turgid definition of the "Ding an Sich" [The Thing As Such], and Peirce suggested:

> This ideal first is the particular thing-in-itself. It does not exist as such. That is, there is no thing, which is in-itself in the sense of not being relative to the mind, though things, which are relative to the mind doubtless are, apart from that relation (Peirce 1958, vol. 8, p. 829)

That description has definitely its place in Occidental philosophy, and in particular *firstness* plays a major role here! But how could Kant suggest that we cannot know the "Ding an Sich"? Does it confront us with a riddle of knowing the unknowable? Does *firstness* do alike? Those questions are perhaps not Peirce's because *firstness* is for him clearly related to analyses of a *sign*.

First and second are fundamentally dependent upon one and another, because "independent of" is also a matter of reference, like "relative to"—the only difference being a difference between "nothing else" and "something else". Structurally there is no difference to observe. We should not forget, that *firstness* is the outcome of insight in the *triadic* character of a sign, which is in itself a revolutionary move, but difficult to defend in view of *firstness*. A year before he opened 1903 his third Harvard Lecture with another sentence, which indicates the same struggle to grasp *firstness*—and, as we understand now, was in his mind as a philosophical idea long before he gave it this name:

> Category the First is the idea of that which is such as it is regardless of anything else...

> Category the First, owing to its Extremely Rudimentary character, is not susceptible of any degenerate or weakened modification... (Peirce 1931, vol. 5. p. 66; Peirce 1998, p. 160)

Splinters of bewilderment as with the "Ding an sich" are, however, also perceived in Peirce's strains of thought. There is relativism in the articulation of *firstness*, where he declares during the year of his Harvard Lectures:

> *Firstness* is the mode of being, which consists in its subject's being positively such as it is regardless of aught else. *That can only be a possibility* (my italics). For as long as things do not act upon one another there is no sense of meaning in saying that they have any being, unless it be that they are such in themselves that they may perhaps come into relation with others. ...That I call *Firstness*. We naturally attribute *Firstness* to outward objects, that is, we suppose they have capacities in themselves which may or may not be already actualized, which may or may not ever be actualized, although we can know nothing of such possibilities [except] so far as they are actualized (Peirce 1931, p. 25)

The 1904 letter to Lady Welby shows an interesting approximation:

> The unanalyzed total impression made by any manifold not thought of as an actual fact, but simply as a quality, as simple positive possibility of appearance, is an idea of *Firstness*.

Two years earlier, Peirce wrote:

> We can only guess; for *nothing is more occult than the absolute present.* [my italics]... It would be something which is what it is without reference to anything else within it or without it, regardless of all force and of all reason ... we mostly neglect them; but there are cases ... in which such isolated flashes come to the front (Peirce 1931, vol. 2, p. 85)

All this is, however, is not considered beyond cosmological and metaphysical contexts. Two texts with polemic viewpoints and discussions with Peirce's rhetorically constructed "metaphysical friends", accompanied by occasional "skeptics", show how also the reader is involved for him, most often in expressions like "I hear you say" followed by an "I grant" or "I reply". A first example is in Peirce's fourth Harvard Lecture, delivered 16 April 1903, which contains a paragraph entitled "The Reality of *Firstness*". The paragraph finishes with statements about the Universe and our premises of clearly metaphysical relevance:

> ...to my mind there is a degree of baseness in ... shamefully slinking away from anthropomorphic conceptions of the Universe.
>
> Therefore, if you ask me what part Qualities can play in the economy of the Universe, I shall reply that the Universe is a vast representamen, a great symbol of God's purpose, working out its conclusions in living realities. Now every symbol must have organically attached to it, its Indices of Reactions and its Icons of Qualities.... the premises of nature, however, though they are not the perceptual facts that are premises to us, nevertheless must resemble them in being premises for us. ...As premises they must involve Qualities.
>
> Now as to their function in the economy of the Universe, —the Universe as an argument is necessarily a great work of art, a great poem, —for every fine argument is a poem and a symphony, —just as every true poem is a sound argument.

The second fragment is of an earlier date, 1886, when Peirce concluded

> If the universe is thus progressing from a state of all but pure chance to a state of all but complete determination by lam, we must suppose that there is an original, elemental, tendency of things to acquire determinate properties, to take habits. This is the Third or mediating element between chance, which brings forth First and original events, and law, which produces sequences or Seconds (Peirce 1998, vol. 1, pp. 234, 1886)

So *Firstness* seems to lead us to a Beginning or at least to a *flash* of a Beginning—Walter Benjamin would have said "Blitzartig", a lightening flash. There is, however, a specificity to mention here: if *firstness* recapitulates a Genesis, then it is about man's entrance into a not-yet-articulated *process,* and not about Genesis as a *fact*! But how should we understand this? Should we understand *firstness* as a *process* AND as a *fact*—but both withstanding purely rational articulation because we are confronted with a process? That might be the metaphysical dimension Peirce could have in mind but was reluctant to explore! Peirce quotes Emerson in his definition of "Feeling" who articulated what the Sphynx once proclaimed:

> "Thou art the unanswered question;
> Couldst see thy proper eye,

> Always it asketh, asketh;
> And each answer is a lie." (Peirce 1931, vol. 1, p. 310)

But whatever he may have meant, [Peirce comments the words of the Sphynx] it is plain enough that all that is immediately present to a man is what is in his mind in the present instant. His whole life is in the present. But when he asks what is the content of the present instant, his question always comes too late. The present has gone by, and what remains of it is greatly metamorphosed.

> . . .though a feeling is immediate consciousness, that is, is whatever of consciousness there may be that is immediately present, yet there is no consciousness in it because it is instantaneous. For we have seen already that feeling is nothing but a quality, and a quality is not conscious: it is a mere possibility (Peirce 1931, vol. 6, p. 494)

Constitutive for any initial understanding of *firstness* in the sense of Peirce and his pragmatic-semiotic project are at least four components:

(1) *Beginning: Firstness* is neither unfettered *beginning* nor pure *immediacy*. As was said, reference to *firstness* is not to a recapitulation of any Genesis. *Firstness* is not the same as a Beginning. It is the process of taking a step in a certain direction, not a matter of knowledge and rationality but rather a matter of orientation and awareness. *Firstness* is indefinable, a concept that emerges only when accompanied by retrospection.
(2) *Relations: Firstness* is unique in as far as it is in an absolute sense a matter of *relations*—structural, logical, conceptual, linguistic as well as social. As long as things do not act upon one another, there is no meaning. That has consequences for semiotics in general: signs have to be a relation to other signs, sign systems and eventually language in order to be a bearer of meaning. Meaning is in Peirce's view not the result of the constitutive power of an individual subject but of relationships between elements. The position of an active semiotic subject in Peirce's philosophy is an issue of special consideration (Colapietro 1989, p. 27–49; Kevelson 1996, p. 6)
(3) *Feeling:* Peirce describes *firstness* consistently and repeatedly as a quality of *feeling* and of appearance. *Firstness* as quality is simple, not divided in parts, it is a flavor *sui generis* and the mode of being itself. In feeling, a flash of self-consciousness, of being without reference to anything else, a mysteriously but specific tone of life, of pure change can come up. Once it is there, it is away beyond any grip and substituted by unidentifiable darkness. One should consider *feeling* in its importance for phenomenology and for semiotics.
(4) *Structuralism:* A Peircean approach fits De Saussure's linguistics and anticipates structuralism: texts are *patterns* of predominantly linguistic relationships, which create meaning through sign relations (Broekman 1974, Chap. 4; De Saussure 1915, Engl. 1983). Those who read and meditate Peirce will never be able to accuse semiotics of adhering to an idealistic and logocentric tradition, which exclusively focuses utterances of individuals! Ducrot and Todorov as well as Kristeva have formulated this viewpoint and it dominated large parts of the French debate on semiotics and discourse. The background idea

is that *discourses are signifying ensembles equivalent to speech acts*, whereby that equivalence sometimes grounds a purely metaphorical use of the concept "speech act" in view of the concept "discourse" (Ducrot and Todorov 1972, p. 449; Kristeva 1969, p. 443f.). Firstness does for Peirce not only relate to linguistic phenomena, but plays a far broader semiotic role and reaches all dimensions of reality. To understand *firstness* in proximity to *feeling* implies an attempt to place the creation of significance beyond the capacity of the individual: an ego *awakens* rather than *creates* meaning and significance. In other words: the creation of meaning is in the awakening, the process of making meaning is a secondary process, a matter of appropriating a pre-owned matter. This is an important implication of the distance of Peirce' semiotics takes in view of any logocentric tradition. The adage "why there is something rather than nothing" is fully compatible with the semiotic position: *firstness* has to be thought in order to think! A surprising idea: there is no human history feasible without *firstness*. How does history begin? Dóes history begin?

2.3 *Firstness* and Feeling

The close relation between *firstness* and *feeling* requires indeed a deeper analysis of feeling. (a) One has to consider the epistemological position: feelings do not primarily engender human knowledge or intelligence—they are rather substance, material, tissue for those two. (b) The use of the word "feelings" in connection with *firstness* does not imply any reappearance of psychology, Peirce underlines repeatedly. (c) Feelings have a sign function: they indicate that human experience a breach or rupture is always imminent. (d) Feelings are furthermore not static, they are not a stable property nor any other stable feature, but imply change. (e) One should therefore understand feelings in their interrelationship with signs: a sign stands for something else, and so do feelings. The *firstness—feeling* relationship is, in other words, a sign relationship. (f) We should, however, take care not to completely identify *firstness* and *feeling;* they cannot be duplicated one into another.

2.3.1 Peirce and Feeling

Peirce notices: A feeling, then, is not an event, a happening, a coming to pass, since a coming to pass cannot be such unless there was a time when it had not come to pass; and so it is not in itself all that it is, but is relative to a previous state. A feeling is a ***state***, which is in its entirety in every moment of time as long as it endures. But a feeling is not a single state, which is other than an exact reproduction of itself. For if that reproduction is in the same mind, it must be at a different time, and then the being of the feeling would be relative to the particular time in which it occurred, which would be something different from the feeling itself, violating the definition which makes the feeling to be all that it is regardless of anything else. Or, if the reproduction were simultaneous with the feeling, it must be in another mind, and thus the identity of the feeling would depend upon the mind in which it was, which is other than the feeling; and again the definition would be violated in the same way. Thus, any feeling must be identical with any exact duplicate of it, which is as much as to say that the feeling is simply a quality of immediate consciousness (Peirce 1931, vol. 1, p. 307).

Feelings relate to "*attitude*". *Attitude change is the moving energy of firstness.* Change of attitude is the essence of understanding *firstness. The understanding of firstness is the awareness of attitude change, which expresses itself as feeling.* This is why "feeling" is temporary and why there is no standard definition possible. When we try to understand Peirce's "feeling", we try to understand its semiotic function and how feeling occurs to be the sign for a yet indeterminable change of attitude. The question arises: attitude towards what? The only answer is a vague and vaguely philosophical articulation: attitude towards reality, towards "all there is"! This is expressed in the frequently quoted 1904 letter to Lady Welby:

> The typical ideas of *Firstness* are qualities of feeling, or mere appearances. . . .It is simply a peculiar positive possibility regardless of anything else. . . The unanalyzed total impression made by any manifold not thought of as actual fact, but simply as a quality, as simple positive possibility of appearance, is an idea of *Firstness*. Notice the naiveté of *Firstness*. . . The idea of the present instant, which, whether it exists or not, is naturally thought as a point of time in which no thought can take place or any detail be separated, is an idea of *Firstness*. . . (Peirce 1958, vol. 8, p. 329)

This is a consistent approach; Peirce already wrote at the end of the nineteenth century:

> By a feeling, I mean an instance of that kind of consciousness which involves no analysis, comparison or any process whatsoever, nor consists in whole or in part of any act by which one stretch of consciousness is distinguished from another, which has its own positive quality which consists in nothing else, and which is of itself all that it is, however it may have been brought about; so that if this feeling is present during a lapse of time, it is wholly and equally present at every moment of that time. To reduce this description to a simple definition, I will say that by a feeling I mean an instance of that sort of element of consciousness, which is all that it is positively, in itself, regardless of anything else (Peirce 1931, vol. 1, p. 307)

The *dynamic* character of feeling is identical with the dynamics of a philosophical insight or achievement, which Peirce characterizes as "elliptic"; what does this mean? It means in any case, that we should not recur to a world of stable facts but to transient issues, which are by definition dynamic and thus in transition:

> Elliptic philosophy. Starting-point and stopping-point are not even ideal. Movement of nature recedes from no point, advances towards no point, has no definite tendency, but only flits from position to position (Peirce 1931, vol. 6, p. 582)

A feeling feels its temporary character, *which is of itself all that is*. [italics JMB] Peirce adds that any conscious feeling *is* in itself, regardless of anything else. Feeling, one should conclude, *creates a notion of wholeness, which expects a being broken, or ruptured.* The epistemological essence of *firstness* is in the last part of this phrase, not in the first. The wholeness-to-be-broken is a wholeness, which is only perceivable *after* it has actually been broken—not before. *Firstness* is wholeness only in the light of that breach. This constitutes the sign-function of *firstness*; it is a sign that a rupture is unavoidable! *Firstness* might only be the sign of a future event or plurality of events, and not the description of something that there is, so that for that reason, as Peirce notices, *firstness* is *feeling* rather than *fact*. This Peircean interpretation has several philosophical connotations pertaining to (1) the implicit epistemology, (2) the concept of history and (3) the annotated metaphysical dimensions.

2.3.1.1 Epistemology

The denomination *firstness* is problematic. Peirce was right when he hesitated to introduce *firstness*, *secondness* and *thirdness* as categories that help ordering and articulating human knowledge. His remarks did not only touch the psychological dimension of how his colleagues would receive this categorization, but also the difficulties to properly understand their epistemological components, which is in particular difficult for *firstness*. His commentary has two perspectives. On the one hand he tells us "They are conceptions so very broad and consequently indefinite that they are hard to seize and may be easily overlooked." But on the other hand, Peirce recurs to the indisputable authority of logic to accept its principles, in saying

> Among the many principles of Logic, which find their application in Philosophy, I can here only mention one. Three conceptions are perpetually turning up at every point in every theory of logic, and in the most rounded systems they occur in connection with one another. I call them the conceptions of First, Second, Third. First is the conception of being or existing independent of anything else. Second is the conception of being relative to, the conception of reaction with, something else. Third is the conception of mediation, whereby a first and second are brought into relation (Peirce 1931, vol. 6, p. 32)

Consider the epistemological implications that are suggested in Peirce's observation:

> They are the being of positive qualitative possibility, the being of actual fact, and the being of law that will govern facts in the future (Peirce 1931, vol. 1, p. 27)

If *firstness* is a "positive qualitative possibility" then this possibility has to be realized, and that realization can only occur through a rupture of the equilibrium, which is the positive qualitative possibility called *firstness* (Broekman 1984). *Firstness* is not *secondness* and their relation is not so arithmetically clear as numbers suggest. Nor is the rupture itself the *feeling* expressing *firstness*. In other words: the relation between *firstness* and *secondness* itself is not a rupture. The breach has to be located in *firstness* itself! If there would not be a rupture in *firstness*, there would be no *secondness*. In this light, the triadic character of our relation to reality and modes of being is less uncomplicated then we initially thought. We thought that continuity dominates *firstness*, and conceived discontinuity as the birthplace of *secondness*. But we concede that discontinuity is encapsulated in *firstness* itself, and that the latter is the germ of meaning as well as the energy that unfolds semiotics. The germ of semiotics is, in other words, in *firstness as rupture*.

This insight fits the basic observations of Edmund Husserl in his transcendental phenomenology. Husserl distinguishes between a "naïve-natural" and a "non-naïve-natural" attitude towards knowledge and reality (Broekman 1963, p. 59 f.). The distinction elucidates that what Peirce calls *firstness* is not something simply being there, but the "simply there" is already a matter of epistemological activity to be performed. The "naïve-natural" attitude is like Peirce's *firstness*, the "non-naïve-natural" parallels his *secondness* and *thirdness*. The "non-naïve" characterizes the latter, but their "naturalness" varies amongst them amongst the progressing attitude changes. Notice how the famous epistemological "bracketing"-procedure (epoché) fits only the realm of a "non-naïve-natural" attitude, which is solely possible after leaving the "naïve-natural" attitude behind. Peirce and Husserl are in concordance as far as the epistemological structure of *firstness* is concerned, which necessitates an imminent *rupture*—for Peirce the rupture between firstness and secondness, for Husserl the rupture between the "naïve-natural" and the "non-naïve-natural" attitude, which includes all diverse stages of a phenomenological view. Husserl uses strong words to express the importance of this rupture, saying:

> It will perhaps become clear one day, that the complete phenomenological attitude and its *epoche* brings a fundamental and personal attitude change, solely to be compared with a religious reversal (Husserl 1954, p. 139).

Peirce concludes:

> For principle of progress or growth, something must be taken not in the starting-point, but which from infinitesimal beginning will strengthen itself continually. This can only be a principle of growth of principles... (Peirce 1931, vol. 6, p. 585)

2.3.1.2 Paradigm

The problem with the dynamics of that breach are today more encompassing than in earlier days, because our relation to actually experienced qualities has changed considerably under the influence of cultural changes. The rupture between the "naïve-natural" and the "non-naïve-natural" as well as between *firstness, secondness* and *thirdness* is decidedly a matter of paradigm change. Husserl suggests, that we are "always free to perform the fundamental change from one attitude towards the other", since "such a change is at home in the realm of our perfect freedom" (Husserl 1913, p. 348). He is certainly aware of cultural relativisms, which influence the power to initiate the breach with a naïve-natural worldview and the stimuli to perform that rupture. He also notices how our naïve-natural evidences break down when we perceive how truth of others "which are fixated and generally guaranteed are absolutely not ours..." (Husserl 1913, p. 141). Every human being has the capacity to fundamentally change attitude, but only in as far as a human being is embedded in a pattern of culture and its paradigms, its system of values and norms of perception! These changed considerably during the last period of the preceding century and are in essence always in a state of change. It is debatable whether there is any continuity in human experiences because of the discontinuity in cultural developments of all sorts. That is an issue for any transcendental philosophy, including those who recur to categories and principles of possible experience, as we meet in the thoughts of Peirce and Husserl.

It appears that the dynamics of history will ultimately determine our expressiveness of feelings and with this the possibility of articulating *firstness*. That leads Peirce as well as Husserl to interpret the rupture as an epistemological basis for attitude change as a breach in the continuum of possible qualities. The existence of such a historic and cultural unity of qualities is at stake in a simple question Peirce analyzed in an exemplary manner, a question one finds already in David Hume's *Enquiry*. How can we conceive a shade of blue we never experienced, Hume asks. In other words: how can we express feelings based on materials, which are not available in our paradigms? How to experience what we never experienced in any form or substance before? Peirce answers that any particular feeling means that "an infinitesimal continuum of all feelings differing infinitesimally from that is present" is given. He and Husserl agree upon the idea that the actual is always experienced in the context of a continuum of the possible, so that firstness could be characterized as a continuum of possible qualities in itself, or in other words: a universe partially beyond our horizon (Peirce 1931, vol. 6, p. 132; Parker 1998, p. 119)

This clarifies why semiotics cannot be limited to linguistics and language utterances alone, but must relate to all reality within the boundaries of perception and experience. The philosophical problem pertains to those boundaries and their influence on our paradigms (Broekman 1986, vol. 19, p. 3; Broekman 1996, Chap. 1). Peirce clarified that our conception of qualities is indeed determined by qualities we already experienced plus those we expect to experience because they are part of our horizon of expectations. The dynamic character of *feeling* prevails and expresses itself in any wholeness determined by its expectation of being-broken. This is today difficult to understand because of the cultural situation in which we are entangled. We know that the concept of *firstness* must be imperfect, since we are more than ever aware of what appears to be below thresholds of perception, such as sounds beyond human hearing, wavelengths of light beyond the visible spectrum, tactile stimuli we cannot experience.[2]

---

[2]Applicability of semiotics to law and legal discourse in particular is a problem in legal practice, legal education and semiotic theory formation. Analyses of legal discourse ex post facto are not enough, as legal doctrine, reflections on Court decisions and the contrasting traditions between formal and non-formal law show. Law may be understood as an example for semiotics and a system of signs (Kevelson 1988), semiosis in itself is deeper and more extended so that other forms of semiosis influence the problem of applicability. Where semiotics concentrates on signs (Peirce) or underlines the arbitrary character of signs (Saussure), the complexity and multitude of semiotic systems disturbs clarity about any straightforward applicability. Since there are animal features, mental organizations, neurological processes, structures of perception, systemic hierarchies, genetic and cultural developments, general ideas about applying semiotic fragments, one cannot satisfy the individual lawyer with simple semiotic instruments to improve his reasoning or his logical skills. An issue that fits our notion of accelerations in history is in a semiotic reengineering of law. This would contribute to redesign law semiotically as an organization process. Law is

2.3.1.3 Continuity

A further thought about the link between paradigm as an ordering and conditioning knowledge on one hand and *feeling* on the other is in the philosophical understanding of *continuity* as a requirement for experience and articulation. In continuity, ideas, concepts, articulations and feelings are connected, so that *gaps* have coordinates and thus become determinable. That logical and mental operation has, however, been changed and still changes continuously. Peirce notices in that context:

> Of the continuity of intrinsic qualities of feeling we can now form but a feeble conception. The development of the human mind has practically extinguished all feelings, except a few sporadic kinds, sounds, colors, smells, warmth etc., which now appear to be disconnected and disparate (Peirce 1931, vol. 6, p. 132; Apel 1973, p. 170)

It interests therefore that *firstness, secondness* and *thirdness* are described as specific concepts which harbor continuity. A tendency of any popular exposé on Peircean semiotics is to find more continuity and equilibrium in *firstness* and more rupture and discontinuity in *secondness* with a culmination of discontinuity together with restoration of equilibrium in *thirdness*. But are the three Peircean categories closed circuits so that it would be incorrect to suppose *firstness* to be in need of rupture in itself?

We ventured the viewpoint that *firstness* is always within a zone of rupture in order to be *firstness*, and that *feeling* is the nearest expression for that articulation. Is there a tension between this thesis and the central ideas about continuity as a continuum of the possible? Well, one can observe in Peirce's thoughts that the differences between the three categories also show a certain order among themselves. In that regard exists indeed a difference between the primary notion of possible qualities in *firstness* and the *thirdness* that transcends the boundaries of individuality and reaches out towards greater wholes. The issue of interrelations between categories is therefore important in Peircean semiotics and phenomenology.

One could state that the allocation of rupture is *in categories* and the most important of all categories is *firstness*. What seems to be of essence in the proximity of *feeling* and *firstness* is also in *rupture* and *firstness*—or should one say: in *rupture* and *continuity*? It is difficult to say because we are not used to *enter* categories and look at the semiotic processes that take place *in* them. When we do so, we could conclude that rupture and discontinuity can be instruments for achieving continuity. This might very well be the case in phenomenological attempts to understand

---

in that case regarded as a series of interconnected processes or otherwise as an architectural complexity. Reengineering law in semiotic perspective would be an alternative for applying semiotics to law. It includes (a) a reversal of the usual top-down approach of legal analysis, and (b) introduce communicative criteria, for instance in understanding the levels in legal hierarchy and the numbers of citizens involved, (c) approach the subject in law as a partner, not as subjected to the law, and finally (d) include all levels of reality, the virtual level in the first place.

firstness, the *first* or even a phenomenological and rather non-Aristotelian *first philosophy*. One argument for it is, that none of the categories in a Peircean sense is completely independent from the others. They can be thought apart but they are not apart in the realization of experiences. All function in the constitution of everything and every phenomenon.

But when Peirce writes "A Firstness is exemplified in every quality of a total feeling" (Peirce 1931, vol. 1, p. 531) then one has to consider how *firstness* is envisaged as dissolved from the interrelations between categories and how solely one phenomenon is called *firstness* ("a" *firstness*) to be exemplified in all qualities. One in all—what does this mean, is this implicative relationship the continuity we should find in thoughts and experiences, in particular in semiotics? This should lead us to an important issue in Peircean as well as Husserlian phenomenology: the semiotic unity when we experience and interpret the world, which causes the existence of a particular semiosis. If ever signs represent reality in their pragmatic interpretation and if ever signs are agreed upon, then humans confirm not only separate issues within the boundaries of their cultural pattern, but also all possible judgments as expressed in their concept of justice or—more modern—human rights (Broekman 1984, vol. 5, p. 369). In Peircean words:

> Whatever is wholly incomparable with anything else is wholly inexplicable, because explanation consists in bringing things under general laws or under natural classes (Peirce 1931, vol. 5, p. 289)

The importance of coherence and continuity is overwhelming:

> No present actual thought (which is a mere feeling) has any meaning, any intellectual value; for this lies not in what is actually thought, but in what this thought may be connected with in representation by subsequent thoughts; so that the meaning of a [one single (JMB)] thought is altogether something virtual (Peirce 1931, vol. 5, p. 89, Note 2)

Peirce adds in a Wittgensteinean style:

> ... just as we say that a body is in motion, and not that motion is in a body we ought to say that we are in thought and not that thoughts are in us. ... (Peirce 1931, vol. 5, p. 289, Note 2)

Only one conclusion convinces here: the continuity as a precondition for intelligent *articulation* as well as for *feeling* is a matter of accepted reflection and culturally embedded concept-construction. Both are vital for our understanding of *firstness* and its epistemological signature. That ultimate focus is in Peirce's words:

> We have seen that the content of consciousness, the entire phenomenal manifestation of mind, is a sign resulting from inference. Upon our principle, therefore, that the absolutely incognizable does not exist, so that the phenomenal manifestation of a substance is the substance, we must conclude that the mind is a sign developing according to the laws of inference.
>
> ...the fact that every thought is a sign, taken in conjunction with the fact that life is a train of thought, proves that man is a sign; so, that every thought is an external sign, proves that man is an external sign. That is to say, the man and the external sign are identical, in the same sense in which the words homo and man are identical. Thus my language is the sum total of myself; for the man is the thought (Peirce 1931, vol. 5, p. 313)

And,

> ...the identity of a man consists in the consistency of what he does and thinks, and consistency is the intellectual character of a thing; that is, is its expressing something (Peirce 1931, vol. 5, p. 315)

Those words lead to an interim conclusion with anthropological implications:

> Finally, reality depends on the ultimate decision of the community; so thought is what it is, only by virtue of it's addressing a future thought which is in its value as thought identical with it, though more developed. In this way, the existence of thought now depends on what is to be hereafter; so that it has only a potential existence, dependent on the future thought of the community.
>
> The individual man, since his separate existence is manifested only by ignorance and error, so far as he is anything apart from his fellows, and from what he and they are to be, is only a negation. This is man,
> ... proud man,
>
> Most ignorant of what he's most assured,
>
> His glassy essence (Peirce 1931, vol. 5, p. 316/317).

2.4 Rupture

The notion of rupture, breach or attitude change, which we encounter in Husserl and Peirce is situated at the end of the nineteenth and the beginning of the twentieth century. Our contemporary philosophy became intimately acquainted with transition, translation, difference and comparable terminologies as rooted in existentialism, critical philosophy and structuralism. From there, these notions fulfilled also an epistemological role in semiotics.

2.4.1 Peirce's Rupture

The epistemological necessity of breach and rupture is for Peirce concealed in the relations between the three categories. One can observe how Peirce sometimes stumbles over the need to clarify their connections and entanglements. Breaches are difficult to understand since they relate to social conditions of human life and to patterns of intersubjectivity, which need continuity and withstand breaches. The latter comes to the fore when Peirce discusses the properties of signs and sign-relations.

> When we think, then, we ourselves, as we are at that moment, appear as a sign. Now a sign has, as such, three references: first, it is a sign to some thought which interprets it; second, it is a sign for some object to which in that thought it is equivalent; third, it is a sign, in some respect or quality, which brings it into connection with its object (Peirce 1931, vol. 5, p. 238)

Signs are, generally spoken, a something that represents for someone (an interpretant) something else within the framework of a view or a quality. Peirce's words are more precise:

> A sign, or representamen, is something, which stands to somebody for something in some respect or capacity. It addresses somebody, that is, creates in the mind of that person an equivalent sign, or perhaps a more developed sign. That sign which it creates I call the interpretant of the first sign. The sign stands for something, its object. It stands for that object, not in all respects, but in reference to a sort of idea, which I have sometimes called the ground of the representamen (Peirce 1931, vol. 2, p. 228)

One should not forget, however, that the relations between *firstness, secondness* and *thirdness* are implicative, and where are implications, there are breaches and ruptures necessary to determine precisely one of the chain as separated from the other! Even that distinction, as provoked by ruptures among them, is difficult to articulate. This is not only true for *firstness* and the two other categories, but in particular for *pure firstness, secondness* and *thirdness*:

> Secondness is an essential part of Thirdness though not of Firstness, and Firstness is an essential element of both Secondness and Thirdness. Hence there is such a thing as the Firstness of Secondness and such a thing as the Firstness of Thirdness; and there is such a thing as the Secondness of Thirdness. But there is no Secondness of pure Firstness and no Thirdness of pure Firstness or Secondness. When you strive to get the purest conceptions you can of Firstness, Secondness, and Thirdness, thinking of quality, reaction, and mediation – what you are striving to apprehend is pure Firstness, the Firstness of Secondness – that is what Secondness is, of itself – and the Firstness of Thirdness (Peirce 1931, vol. 1, p. 530)

The triangle is just a thought-experiment, whereas the reality of the three categories is resulting form distinctions. That is far-fetching indeed!

There are at least three expressions and metaphorical narratives in Peirce's prose that relate to rupture or breach: the train's *whistle*, the sheriff's *hand*, and the sense of *shock* or *struggle*. All three bring an everyday experience before one's eye that makes clear how a rupture is needed to understand reality. In an extensive text on this subject (1875), Peirce brings the train's whistle intruding a pastoral landscape together with experience and shock, we would say: "a wake-up call":

> A whistling locomotive passes at high speed close beside me. As it passes the note of the whistle is suddenly lowered from a well-understood cause. I perceive the whistle, if you will. I have, at any rate, a sensation of it. But I cannot be said to have a sensation of the change of note. I have a sensation of the lower note. But the cognition of the change is of a more intellectual kind. That I experience rather than perceive. It is [the] special field of experience to acquaint us with events, with changes of perception (Peirce 1931, vol. 1, p. 336)

In his subtle, detailed and perceptive essay on Peirce's life in his Arisbe estate, Pencak describes how Peirce

> Sometimes used the interruption of his peace and quiet by a railway whistle. This must have occurred frequently at Arisbe, as a train whistle would be audible four and one-half miles away in the stillness of the Pike County wilderness. Since Peirce was an insomniac in his last years who fell asleep writing in his chair he must have been awakened and disturbed and felt it keenly. . . .Peirce described an approaching train whistle as 'disagreeable' and a shock' (Pencak 1993, p. 40 ff.)

The shock has its particular task and value, "The sense of shock is as much a sense of resisting as of being acted upon", Peirce wrote for the Harvard Lecture he delivered on April 2, 1903, and completed: "so it is when anything strikes the senses."

(Peirce 1931, vol. 5, p. 46). The senses, once stroked, are awakened and possess more knowledge than before they are awakened! The landscape becomes less the evident pastoral and idyllic and more a "landscape" as an element of culture after the whistle that announces the influence of human activity as well as the existence of a socialized environment:

> Now that which particularly characterizes sudden changes of perception is a shock. A shock is a volitional phenomenon. The long whistle of the approaching locomotive, however disagreeable it may be, has set up in me a certain inertia, so that the sudden lowering of the note meets with a certain resistance. That must be the fact; because if there were no such resistance there could be no shock when the change of note occurs. Now this shock is quite unmistakable. It is more particularly to changes and contrasts of perception that we apply the word "experience." ...It is the ... absolute constraint upon us to think otherwise than we have been thinking that constitutes experience (Peirce 1931, vol. 1, p. 337)

The train driver's whistle causes sudden changes of perception—apart from the fact that it is a signal indicating eventual danger and implies other sign functions—which transform an unnamed and unarticulated piece of land into a landscape, a domain of culture. *The train driver's whistle makes meaning and he doesn't know it*, he simply drives a whistling train! Peirce did not notice the epistemological impact of his observation. The rupture in the peace and quiet caused by the whistle, appeared to be essential for the existence of new meaning. In the words of Husserl: the naïve-natural changed into a non-naïve-natural, which is an attitude-change that equally changes meaning.

A parallel is the hand of the sheriff. William Pencak refers to Peirce's financial difficulties and how the Sheriff of Pike County has visited him at least four times in 1895 and 1896 to tell him to post a bail of $1,000. Pencak suggests that this could be why Peirce illustrates around 1896 *Firstness* with "bitter, tedious, hard, and heartrending..." and *Secondness* with the same attitude:

> ...we feel facts resist our will. That is why facts are proverbial called brutal ... the senses we are furnished with are adapted to reveal; and it can hardly be doubted that the specializing effect of the evolutionary process which has made us what we are has been to blot the greater part of the senses and sensations which were once dimly felt, and to render bright, clear, and separate the rest (Peirce 1931, vol. 1, pp. 418, 419; Peirce 1931, vol. 6, p. 452 ff.; Pencak 1993, p. 37)

The hand of the sheriff comes back many times in Peirce's notes and letters. One example, explaining the relevance of actuality as a "then and there" relates to his difficult situation:

> Let us begin with considering actuality, and try to make out just what it consists in. ...A court may issue injunctions and judgments against me and I not care a snap of my finger for them. I may think them idle vapor. But when I feel the sheriff's hand on my shoulder, I shall begin to have a sense of actuality. Actuality is something brute (Peirce 1931, vol. 1, p. 24)

A second example is in his letter to Lady Welby of Oct 12, 1904:

> Living in the country on this side of the Atlantic, unless one is multimillionaire is attended with great friction...

The law of gravitation is the judge upon the bench who may pronounce the law till doomsday, but unless the strong-arm of the law, the brutal sheriff, gives effect to the law, it amounts to nothing. True, the judge can create a sheriff if need be; but he must have one.

Like in the case of the train driver and his whistle, the major epistemological crux remains in both examples widely unformulated. One cannot dismiss the gesture of the sheriff as incidental or inadequate but *the sheriff's gesture makes meaning: I am a bearer of (legal) rights and duties!* The rupture in decent human relations, realized in the brute gesture of the sheriff's hand, makes me into an actual and acute legal subject. This meaning is new and this meaning is legal: the sheriff is a meaning maker like our lawyers today. Change is the keyword here, shock and struggle, bruteness, constraint and compulsion:

They cannot exist without resistance, and resistance is effort-opposing change. Therefore there must be an element of effort in experience; and it is this, which gives it its peculiar character. But we are so disposed to yield to it as soon as we can detect it, that it is extremely difficult to convince ourselves that we have exerted any resistance at all. It may be said that we hardly know it except through the axiom that there can be no force where there is no resistance or inertia (Peirce 1931, vol. 1, p. 336; Peirce 1931, vol. 5, pp. 41–56)

2.4.2 Rupture and Epistemology

There is an interesting observation to rely upon when we conclude this paragraph. Peirce's examples and the many causes for reflection on deeply philosophical issues are often biographical; they contain everyday life occurrences and brute reactions on issues of his immediate social context. And his real-life situations show that breaches and ruptures repeat continuously. The whistle has always to blow somewhere, in different surroundings and conditions; its performance must always be repeated in order to make new meanings. There is never an end to the process of meaning making, and never a moment of meaning fixation for good and forever. In Peirce's words "...there is no Secondness of pure Firstness and no Thirdness of pure Firstness or Secondness". We will meet the same structure of epistemological relevance in Husserl's phenomenology. The proximity of the two reinforces the relevance of their philosophical and semiotic project.

Peirce did not fully exploit the epistemological importance of *firstness*. We perceive *firstness* as a receptive attitude, abstaining from any alteration of phenomena and articulated naïvely as "What the world was to Adam on the day he opened his eyes to it, before he had drawn any distinctions, or had become conscious of his own existence...." (Peirce 1958, vols. 8, 1, p. 357). However, *Firstness* is also the result of what Peirce called in 1867 "prescission"—an abstraction without which it should not be possible to distinguish between categories (Peirce 1998, p. 270). Now, how can one cultivate a passive-receptive attitude, and at the same time exercise "prescission", which seems a subtle and highly unusual type of abstraction? Is this epistemological question answered by reference to "attitude change"—or are such changes *beyond* the power of the human mind? Whatever the answer is, it will remain an epistemological issue, which reaches beyond any comparison between Husserl's and Peirce's phenomenology!

That question focuses on the semiotically relevant issue about the *linkage of categories*. What is the purpose of keeping that linkage intact if the idea of rupture seems basic to human knowledge? This observation shows several fascinating aspects, which all relate to the epistemological importance of breach and rupture. Take Umberto Eco's interpretation of semiotics in cultural context. A semiotic approach, he writes, is "more like exploring a forest where cart-trails or footprints do modify the landscape". Modification, change, rupture, breach again; and these make the meaning of forest, footprints appear as knowledge creating ruptures (Eco 1979a, p. 29) Should semioticians provoke ruptures? Legal academicians were critical in view of traditional forms of legal meaning and procedure as well as their forms of legal education in the CLSM (Critical Legal Studies Movement) a decade before legal semiotics was a topic in the US Law Journals. Jeremy Paul, Jack Balkin and Duncan Kennedy inspired the debate whether there is a common progressive political agenda among legal semioticians, which is more than just a shared interest in a theoretical field! There should be a decision whether "The Promise of Legal Semiotics" (title of Balkin's 1990/1991 essay), leads to political action or semiotic reflection (Paul 1991, p. 1782; Balkin 1991, p. 1831) Politics and critical knowledge: is there a parallel between semiotic knowledge stimulated by *ruptures* and semiotic knowledge sustained by *political agendas*?

The *linkage between categories*, subject of Peirce's constant consideration, pertains undoubtedly to the *pragmatic* dimension of sign functions. Do not all signs require a guarantee that consistent knowledge can be realized, so that signs function in a reliable manner? Does semiotics treat such a practical problem philosophically? If that were the case, the central question to discuss would be twofold: (a) whether consistency in knowledge is in reach, and not diffused by varieties in patterns of culture, and (b) in how far that reliability includes reference to a sign-interpreting community. Two remarks are relevant in this context:

(a) Category linkage is one of the most expressive means to underline how knowledge is in the mediation of triadic signs. The triadic cannot be reduced to dual or single properties, because knowledge is based on interpretations of a "something" as a "something mediated through signs" (*thirdness*). If any part or element of the triadic relationship fails, there is no knowledge or any function of a paradigm. There exists no knowledge if knowing is reduced to pure sense data perception or to binary subject-object relations. It means, that concrete knowledge is always based upon semiotic transformations, and the latter cannot function without rupture or breach—an insight that enforces the triadic sign functions.
(b) Consider Peirce's remark about the foundational function of the sign-interpreting community:

> ...all the followers of science are animated by a cheerful hope that the processes of investigation, if only pushed far enough, will give one certain solution to each question to which they apply it (Peirce 1931, vol. 5, p. 407)

> ...The real, then, is that which, sooner or later, information and reasoning would finally result in, and which is therefore independent of the vagaries of 'me' and 'you'. Thus, the very origin of the conception of reality shows that this conception essentially involves the notion of a COMMUNITY, without definite limits, and capable of a definite increase of knowledge (Peirce 1931, vol. 5, p. 311)

This community is essential because it demonstrates semiotic relevance through its unity of interpretation and experience. Peirce speaks about a central issue, expressed in an important word!

Who speaks about Words, speaks about "Together": the word "community" points on the one hand to *semiotics* because of its social practice to engender consistency in interpretation of signs and meanings, and on the other to *logic* because of the structure of its experiences. Apel refers to this community as "a supra-individual unity of interpretation on the basis of experimental experience in the long run" (Apel 1973, p. 173). The sociological implication of quasi-transcendental viewpoints is important in this context. Ruptures have community as their epistemological precondition.

2.5 Husserl's *Einstellungsänderung*

In October 1961, Edmund Husserl's daughter Elisabeth wrote me in a personal letter "... that our [Harvard] President Pusey has forwarded Phenomenology strongly through supporting already from earlier years on Herbert Spiegelberg and his studies about the philosophy of my father (Lawrence College, Wis.). His two volumes appeared recently at Nijhoff." A few years before, in 1957, Spiegelberg published his essay (mentioned in the Introduction) on the wave of that upcoming sympathy for phenomenology in Philosophy Departments of US Universities (Spiegelberg 1957, p. 170; Stjernfelt 2007, p. 141 ff.). Lawrence College was open to comparisons between a German and a US philosopher, who were both fascinated by phenomenological viewpoints. Peirce's and Husserl's phenomenology were founding new interest in semiotics. Apart from exposing the nucleus of Husserl's phenomenology, the article attempts to understand Peirce's *phaneroscopy* in the light of Husserl's *phenomenology*. *Firstness* draws much attention in this context. Spiegelberg notes elaborately how

> it is not surprising that Peirce never gave any systematic development of his phenomenological program, a fact, which is actually the major obstacle to a full-scale comparison between the two phenomenologies. Husserl, much as he realized that in this area precise mathematical description was essentially impossible, he was never that pessimistic as to the chances of phenomenological description. And while he never arrived at a final formulation of his phenomenology, he left at least an impressive array of concrete systematic studies.
>
> Nevertheless, it would seem that even Peirce had become more hopeful as to the chances of a scientific study of *Firstness* by the time he had adopted the term "phenomenology" for his science of categories (see Peirce 1931, vol. 5, p. 42).

I can think of few, if any, passages in Husserl's writings in which the primary requirements of the phenomenological approach are stated with equal impressiveness. ...Husserl indicates no preference for qualities as having a privileged status over other types of properties such as quantity or even of substance. In fact, from Husserl's original viewpoint there seems to be no reason for assigning priority to any particular aspect of phenomena. If at all, such priority pertains to the phenomenon as a structured and interrelated whole, which, for Husserl as well as for the Gestaltists, is characterized primarily by the character of unity in the context of a horizon, or world. . ..

Peirce, when he advanced the program of phenomenology as a science in his Lectures on Pragmatism of 1903, he merely stressed the need for the student of phenomenology . . . to develop the following three qualities:

(1) "Seeing what stares one in the face, just as it presents itself, unreplaced by any interpretation, unsophisticated by any allowance for this or that modifying circumstance;"
(2) delete "discrimination, which fastens itself like a bulldog upon the particular features that we are studying;" and
(3) "the generalizing power of the mathematician who produces the abstract formula that comprehends the very essence of the feature under examination purified from all admixture of extraneous and irrelevant accompaniments." (See Peirce 1931, vol. 5, p. 42 ff.)

There is, to be sure, in Husserl's analysis of phenomena an element, later on designated as the "hyletic datum," which one might feel tempted to relate to Peirce's Firstness. But this raw material for fully constituted phenomena is so closely linked up with Husserl's whole conception of knowledge as an "intentional" process that there would seem to be little sense in correlating it with Peirce's thought, without discussing at the same time this very conception, for which, as will be shown, there is no clear equivalent in Peirce (Spiegelberg 1957, p. 170 f.)

It is remarkable how this analysis with its many insights and conclusions could be conceived long before final editions of the works of Peirce and Husserl were completed.[3]

Already one year before Spiegelberg's publication, one could conclude how *firstness* is not only Peirce's concern, but in the form of what he called "First Philosophy", Husserl came considerably near. We focus on Husserl's concept *attitude change (Einstellungsänderung)* as the hinge of his transcendental phenomenology and of what Peirce called *firstness*.

2.5.1 First Philosophy

Feeling in Peirce's philosophy is *attitude* (*Einstellung*) in Husserl's. Th.W. Adorno, who developed a lifelong allergy against any "bourgeois" philosophical mentality, misunderstood *attitude* in the sense of "bourgeois-private everyday-relativism" and

[3] Of course, the Peirce edition volumes I–VI of Charles Hartshorne and Paul Weiss was published between 1931 and 1935, and the Arthur W. Burks edited volumes VII and VIII followed 1958. There was, and still is, however, no undisputed and entirely complete text edition. The Husserliana were not—and are not yet until today—completed when Spiegelberg presented his opinion on the comparison between Peirce and Husserl. The volume "Erste Philosophie" [First Philosophy] presenting lectures in Freiburg 1923/1924 was published in Husserliana Bd VII, 1956.

suggested that this word was derived from the language of photography (Adorno 1956, p. 205; Edelman 1973, Engl. 1979). Yet Adorno fortifies his thesis with another argument, suggesting that *attitude* is fundamental to Husserl's epistemology. The photographic context is not appropriate: *attitude* played already a role in the second volume of Husserl's Logical Investigations, 1913, linked with his semiotic interest in expressions such as "sense" or "meaning". The epistemological context is, however, correct: the concept of *attitude* is subject of the *first*, being in itself the necessary first phenomenological step! Again, the intertwining of *feeling* and *firstness* is in parallel to *attitude* and *first*.

What is more: every philosophical attempt requires an ego that concentrates on a particular theme. A violinist reads a score written in the G clef and immediately changes into lines in an Alto clef and/or an F clef. The switch becomes a theme of reflection only after the musical performance. The famous reductive procedure, the *epoché*, is in the first place a matter of concentration on a specific issue. No wonder that Husserl spoke about an unlimited number of possible attitudes, which he tried to systematize and to understand as a cornerstone for his phenomenological approach. The expression "first philosophy" is Aristotelian and became only later understood as "metaphysics". The expression suggests the seriousness and importance of a beginning in philosophy as a philosophical problem in its own right. That beginning is laid down in concepts like *feeling* and *attitude change*. *Feeling* is more difficult to precisely circumscribe than *attitude change*.

First philosophy is based upon a most fundamental attitude change, which divides or even splits reality. Reality corresponds to two attitudes, the naïve-objective and the phenomenological. The separation of the two *is* Husserl's first philosophy—the separation, rupture or breach into the two realities is the basis for a new tradition following Aristotle's notion. That foundational rupture results from the difference between a *naïve-natural* and a *non-naïve-natural* vision on reality. The latter, non-naïve-natural attitude is often presented as the transcendental-phenomenological attitude, which includes further differentiations.

2.5.2 Two Worlds

There are many "two-worlds" notions in occidental philosophy. Some of them are descriptive, others are speculative, and again others are influenced by religion, psychology or insights and feelings about the relativity of the world perceived and accessed. The Husserlian two-worlds thesis is unique for two reasons. First, the two worlds idea is *not* directly intended as a philosophical theory but the result of a hands-on discovery of the epistemological relevance of attitude change. Second, the change is not durably fixated in time and reality—an attitude change can and should always take place again and again. Peirce's examples are applicable here: the train whistle ruptures the naïve-natural attitude in which we were experiencing the landscape. It takes a philosophical discussion whether the landscape was a landscape before the whistle became audible. What was the landscape before it became a landscape?

The landscape was *firstness*, Peirce would answer; was *a naïve-natural sense datum*, Husserl would add. The sheriff's hand on my shoulder is a wake-up call for me: I am a bearer of duties and rights and should position myself accordingly, for instance pay my debts. Was I a bearer of duties before the hand of the sheriff touched me? Yes, Husserl would say, but in a naïve-natural manner that remained without consequences or even knowledge about the facts. The hand was a rupture in that situation, and created a different (a non-naïve-natural) attitude. Each attitude change creates worlds of facts and experiences. The change can be forced from outside, as with the train whistle, but also in social relations, as with the sheriff's hand, or even from within one's mind. Look at a person who for instance is suddenly incapable to act or is fed up with a situation and changes in what we call an irrational manner. A *non-reflective* life, Husserl would say, changes by means of such ruptures into a *reflective* life: one knows things otherwise and acts accordingly. It interests how this change has many semiotic consequences: language is challenged, names acquire a new meaning and expressions must be revised. Not only the whistle is a sign, as Pierce suggests, but that sign is itself a sign for the rupture it causes.

There is logic in semiotics, Peirce states. According to him, logic and propositionality are internal processes to the sign process itself! Husserl would completely agree; the rupture causing a transition away from non-reflexivity is precisely the moment where another life begins and this is a sign in its own right. That observation fits Peirce's intention to link signs to external reality and its processes of inquiry and interference, rupture and transition. Husserl's attempt to distinguish the two worlds and then further differentiate the second, the non-naïve, can be understood as an essential part of semiotic logic as foundation for a transcendental phenomenology. It means, that the rupture of attitude-change is a sign in a semiotic sense, which fits to a larger set of sign processes in general, signifying new kinds of generality and of mental (attitude) processes. Sign processes reign mental processes; meanings never remain external to interpreters and signifiers (Husserl 1952, p. 32; Jackson 1988, p. 72). Living in landscapes and texts means living in meanings engendered by a constant flow of attitudes and their dynamic alterations.

Husserl would repeat his warning about the fact that the inclination to fall back into the naive-natural attitude is strong and difficult to abolish, because the non-naïve-natural attitude is not natural and difficult to maintain because it is an attitude *against* our everyday-life habits (Husserl 1954, p. 204). "Don't think too much!" he would say, as if he read Wittgenstein:

> A child has much to learn before it can pretend. (A dog cannot be a hypocrite, but neither can he be sincere) (Wittgenstein 1958, p. 229)

2.5.3 A Rupture and Three Steps

When invited in 1927 to write the lemma "Phenomenology" for the *Encyclopedia Brittannica,* Husserl explains the goals of a transcendental phenomenology (Husserl 1927, p. 129). That philosophy should lead to science with a universal character by means of exposing the different ruptures realized in diverse attitudes. Two positions are at issue:

I. THE FUNDAMENTAL RUPTURE, which causes a transition from a general and unspecified “naïve-natural attitude” towards a “non-naïve-natural attitude”. Phenomenology is based on this attitude change. This is the change effected by rupture, which Husserl denominates (often misunderstandings raise from this) with various expressions, such as (a) epoché [bracketing], (b) phenomenological attitude, (c) total phenomenological attitude, or (d) transcendental phenomenological attitude. In fact, he always means in the first place *Einstellungsänderung* per se, attitude change being the germ of insight and knowledge caused by distancing oneself from the evident.

II. THE RUPTURES IN THE NON-NAÏVE NATURAL ATTITUDE, which are mainly three:

(a) the non-naïve attitude as natural,
(b) the phenomenological attitude,
(c) the transcendental attitude.

Each of those three attitudes should be described explicitly and completely, thus delivering an in-depth description of the logic and the dynamics of phenomenology in the sense of Husserl as well as Peirce. Both are semiotically relevant and have their own difficulties. The appropriate understanding of the concept “natural” is for instance always multiple, since there is a use of the word “natural” in a naïve, and another use of the same expression in a non-naïve manner. Both are at the other side of *the first* and *firstness*. Naturalness of the non-naïve attitude is final and first at the same time: a final result of the change, but not final in the realm of the non-naïve. In the latter are two more levels at stake, the phenomenological and the transcendental. And the epoché, perhaps Husserl’s most famous expression, is a matter of distancing from the naïve-natural as well as from the non-naïve-natural in the form of the second level of the non-naïve-natural. A first orientation pertaining to all those key-notions indicating different steps *after* the fundamental attitude change shows the importance of three steps. These lead a philosopher towards completion of the project that called transcendental phenomenology. They are important for semiotics and throughout comparable to the elements with which for instance Greimas’ famous semiotic square is constructed (Greimas 1968, p. 269; 1970, p. 135; 1983, p. 176)

Within the realm opened by the distinction between the naïve-natural and the non-naïve-natural attitude, three more steps in the latter are to distinguish. (1) The *first* step is the first in the procedure of reduction, epoché, bracketing, and functions as an orientation in the realm of the non-naïve naturalness. One has to liberate from all diversities of everyday world experiences and direct oneself towards what a constitutive consciousness achieves. Perception and reality now form a new region, in a changed and not a reduced perspective. (2) The *second* step is the eidetic reduction in which the stream of consciousness will be understood in accordance with its multitude of ideas. Psychic structures of perception or volition are subject of this eidetic-reductive phase. Pure consciousness, result of this attitude change, is no longer subject of a Cartesian doubt, pureness, or purity is in this regard quite absolute, a unique directedness towards essence and EIDOS (Greek expression for original image). (3) The *third* step is the truly transcendental, the phenomenological in its own right and essence. Envisaged is here an immanence, which forms the fundamental structure for all facts of experience.

The basic dynamics of these three steps is in the movements of an ego that conscientiously and systematically refers back to concrete phenomena of everyday life as concretization of a transcendental ego. The major breach is evident here: the rupture between (1) a naïvely everyday-life living ego, aware of only minor semiotic dimensions of life, and (2) an ego that transforms itself to a transcendental position with a considerably broadened constitutive power. This is the phenomenological manner to articulate the ego in its structural ties with reality—a reality at a large distance from the naïve-natural world.

Notice how this last step is by no means final, although it is a result booked after difficult philosophical exercises and painfully acquired insights. It is rather a basis to undertake new steps and attempts towards attitude change. The semiotic relevance is here a double: on one hand, the ego with acquired transcendental status has to contribute to an enriched capacity of articulation, and on the other, the ego has to prepare for a repeated and renewed attitude change to diversify perceived reality. That dynamics makes clear how semiotic knowledge and analytical skills in the law-semiotics relationship cannot lead to simple procedures of *application*. Semiotics cannot become applied: neither a Husserlian, Peircean, Greimassian nor any other semiotic insight can become just applied in a social discourse or field of science. The rupture creates new worlds; its dynamics cannot bring a standstill. *Firstness* culminates in this insight and establishes important semiotic relevance.

2.5.4 Lawyers Making Meaning

Lawyers make meaning when they speak, write or use language otherwise. Language is their instrument and their spiritual environment—are they aware of their enormous potential when they do so? This question is difficult to answer. The "floor plan" of the engendering firstness by means of a breach between the naïve-natural and the non-naïve-natural is helpful in this regard, as are the three steps to understand and manage the different stages of non-naïve-natural attitudes. They unveil the logic of meaning making and are at least as important as Greimas' semiotic square.

(1) WORD AND NARRATIVE. The non-naïve-naturalness shows that *Husserl's phenomenology leads beyond the boundaries between word and narrative.* It does so with impressive clarity when legal expressiveness is at stake. Its path is not in the first place through structures of speech and meaning in their contrapositions, contradictions and implications as in the case of Greimas' square, but by going all the way through the reductive stages a constitutive ego goes with its meanings.

(2) MANIFEST FIRSTNESS. A concept of everyday language *becomes reduced* into a binary or even monologue legal meaning through various transitions of semiotic importance. Take the word "responsibility" as an example, which in legal

language reads "liability". In this transition, the word *was set free* from its everyday language meaning and with it, *firstness* became manifest. It thus is singled out of a naïve-natural use and starts to play a role in the legal interpretations of everyday occurrences. A multiplicity of meanings of "responsibility" was at home in the naïve-natural language. But the breach with its naïve use with multiple meanings made people aware of questions like "what the phrase in fact wants to say" or "who uses such expressiveness"? With such considerations, the rupture in the naïve-natural attitude is apparent. *Firstness* appears to be the ground floor for phenomenological bracketing and meaning reduction, so that entrance in a specialized discourse is possible on the basis of *firstness recognition*. The semiotic complexity of our words in everyday language seems threatening: in each word or expression multiplicity accompanies us. Law, and indeed any first step in the realm of legal expressiveness should do better, and deliver semiotic stability! "Legal responsibility" is already an acceptable change in view of "responsibility" in general, but we need more, in particular after we understand what we need and how to satisfy that need. We need a new and specific expressiveness—what dictionary delivers this specificity?

(3) LAW'S WORDS AS SIGNS. A transcendental awareness of the constitutive subject maintains legal expressiveness and thus reinforces the language of law. In legal discourse, one disposes of a set of standardized expressions as well as "how-to-use" manuals, which form the basis of law school programs all over the globe. Jurists sustain justice through speech and social order through precisely engineered words. What semiotic dimension is at stake? Standard expressions in legal literature form new signs. These signs should function in all clarity and safety: jurists can decide about issues which can never become decided in a naïve natural language—they decide between a correct and an incorrect use or application in all sorts of social situations. Pattern recognition is required: does one recognize the pattern of an outstanding legal mind?

(4) THE LEGAL MIND. Can a legal mind do with the word "responsibility"? *Quod non*! Words create their "talking heads" (Lee 1997, pp. 97, 321) and these forge new words. The word awakens my awareness of being a bearer of rights and duties. That's what Peirce's sheriff did, naïve but effective in clearly not being just a gesture of friendship or love! A better expression, more precise, reduced, safeguarding social life, more legally acceptable, is the word "liability". The question soon arises: "what *is* 'liability' "? Any response refers to (a) the necessity of introducing this new expression and (b) a reference to the EIDOS of the word in its outstanding binary quality.

We are left with one more question: when precisely occurs "legal liability" and can we completely forget about "responsibility" once we are in legal language? Somewhere between steps 1 and 3, should be the answer. Where precisely? In any case one should say, after 1, after the naïve-natural word is set free and, as is the case in 2 or 3, when the legal mind is able and institutionally entitled to articulate its peculiar expressiveness. Remember "liability" as one of the highlights when reconstructing legal language. The word is derived from the fifteenth century French use going back to the Latin word "ligare", which means: "to bind". That word is a closed dialogue circuit in itself. *Ligare* does express *the power* of a constitutive subject *to bind* (also making meaning obligatory) and *the preparedness* of the subject *to be in a position to incur*—for instance to pay a fine. Legal language goes for the latter, takes this it a clear sign and interprets that sign as if it only pertains to the realm of obligations, which are understood in an individualistic manner without any reference to the existence of an other. In reconstructing this logic, one understands how legal discourse interprets its subject exclusively as being exposed to action and adverse contingency. That is in clear contrast to the dialogic implications of the word "responsibility". In the latter, the presence of the Other makes the word's meaning and sense. That has disappeared in the concept of "liability", which focuses an individual. So the effect of this meaning transposition from responsibility to liability is that a legal subject appears in essence as subjected to a limited openness for strictly determined legal meanings. The semiotic logic of these steps is clear: they represent the logic of reduction and determination. Law students should be taught how to find, to understand and eventually to manage these steps since they truly unveil how lawyers are making meaning.

2.6 *Firstness* and the Legal Mind

"To *be* 'a legal mind' " is an Anglo-Saxon expression. To parallel the expression with a French "Esprit Juridique" would be a misreading of Montesquieu's "Esprit des Lois" or mean something else. The expression "a legal mind" suggests wisdom, peace and equilibrium, often a successful legal position achieved after *firstness*' rupture followed up by professional training, experience and maturity. One can foresee that a law student will once be a "legal mind" but he *is* not, because the years of training alone are not enough. It is important to notice that, the path to obtain a legal mind begins in the light of Peirce's philosophy and legal semiotics by experiencing *firstness* and its implications. What then follows are new beginnings and recapitulations, sometimes accompanied by forms of regression. Do we truly find here a new view or an interesting detail about the dynamics of legal semiotics? Indeed, our semiotic view is a matter of dynamics: it has been noticed that the breach in *firstness* is not *one unique event* but has to be performed time and again. Peirce used the expression "infinite" because not only the train whistle occurs frequently during one round trip. The whistle is audible because *all* trains in *all* landscapes in a certain society during a specific period time use that sign. The sign is not only a sign for the train, but equally well for the breach in *firstness* that indicates a plurality of signs in the specific form of the train whistle. The same is with the hand of the sheriff—that hand does not display one and the same stable structure but series of events, which are a matter of historical developments in culture. They show a great diversity of pace, energy or direction, which is an issue in any philosophy of history and culture. Today's culture differs considerably from the times in which Roman Law or the US Constitution or eventually the EU Treaties inspired the legal mind!

2.6.1 Understanding Hercules

So it seems to be true that a man receiving legal training will never be the same anymore, as Judith Shklar once remarked. Dworkin introduced his well-known *Hercules* to face this multi-facetted challenge. We follow the Peircean and the Husserlian lines of thought to understand Hercules (Dworkin 1985, p. 146). The Peircean path leads to *firstness* and its first rupture, but one has to concede that there are always infinitely more to follow. Hercules is therefore gifted with superhuman skills, education, wisdom, patience and astuteness (Dworkin 1977, p. 105, 1986). He overcame the rupture in *firstness*, which is undoubtedly heroic, but he must still cope with an important aftermath! Growing interdependencies in law and society cause market systems instead of state lawmakers to create more and more specific (legal) rules. Those systems create unforeseen complexities, which obstruct the smooth emergence and application of legal doctrine. Who's interpreting *legal* law anymore? What are "hard cases" in this newly emerging socio-legal context? Is Hercules able to withstand the growing indeterminacies, so that he can demonstrate his extraordinary qualities? Hercules faces many new situations, which are only feasible in terms of semiotics. Modern indeterminism creates an urge for large-scale solidarity. The latter finds new forms of human relations with their own jargon. That expressiveness includes laws, rules and precedent interpretations, which were hitherto the privilege of jurists and lawyers. Is Hercules still strong enough?

Hercules considers conflict solutions and case interpretations as his main task. But a legal mind also excels in *perceiving* reality and interpreting the world in accordance with existing laws and legal culture! Is Hercules able to perform that semiotic task *beyond* pragmatic considerations and interests? Peirce explained in the wake of his analyses (a) that there is a constant need to return to the experience of *firstness* and its inherent breach, and (b) that there is always *firstness* in *secondness*, or in actions of one subject or substance pertaining to another. In his famous Lowell Lectures 1903, he underlines how one should strive to apprehend *firstness* as "*firstness* OF *secondness*" (Peirce 1931, vol. 1, p. 530). Is *firstness* the legal-semiotic dimension, which Hercules can really enter? There is a remark in Jackson's analysis of Dworkin's Hercules that makes us hesitate (Jackson 1985, p. 223; 1988, p. 31). Jackson emphasizes how the relevant statues and precedents are for Hercules not *signs* of rights but *symptoms* of a comprehensive *system of rights*. If that observation is correct, then Hercules remains the most obedient servant of the system and his power remains limited to the pragmatics of law, which is a serious limitation for semioticians. Do legal semioticians have to play the role of *critics* (as in the CSLM) or become *semiotic guerrilleros*, as Eco (1979) once suggested? Hercules' epistemological power seems at stake!

Husserl would agree with Pierce that Hercules represents the legal mind because he awakened *firstness* through rupture and so actualized legal consciousness. However, that awakening is not enough, Husserl would have suggested, because although Hercules changes from a naïve-natural world into a non-naïve-natural world, the two remain in essence a *natural* world! Hercules' inability to complete semiotic dimensions of his legal task is because of his persisting naturalness, which hardly clarifies the importance of distinguishing naïve from non-naïve attitudes. The lack of radicalism towards naivety and positivistic pragmatism limits his attitude to a given legal system as well as his role therein (Posner 2008). Would Hercules be able to accomplish the legal mind through radicalizing his attitude change? Clearly not: Hercules awakened *firstness* but remains within the realm of naturalness. In other words, his *firstness* does not touch any *firstness of secondness* and certainly not of *thirdness*. There is stagnation in the process of reference. Peirce describes *firstness* as the quality of what one is immediately conscious of, and that quality is resulting from reference, which initiates from being simply itself and not referring to anything nor lying behind anything, so that *secondness* emerges through what it is by force of something to which it is second (Peirce 1931, vol. 1, p. 365). This emergence does not occur in the case of the legal mind, which Hercules should represent.

Husserl's sequence of *attitude changes* can deepen this Peircean insight and elucidate a lawyer's stagnation in reference. The non-naïve-naturalness has (also in the case of a lawyer) to serve as a point of departure towards other, more dynamic and more complex levels of attitude. We described already how the non-naïve has to serve for the next non-naïve, for the phenomenological—which requires the famous epoché or bracketing procedure—and from there for a transcendental level. Hercules is hardly able to reach the second level and will certainly tell us that the third, transcendental level, is of no interest for him—it pertains to a pure theory and philosophy, and that is definitely beyond his interest.

2.6.2 Hercules' Legal Attitude

The legal mind, so fascinatingly represented by Dworkin's hero, will be proud to achieve a transition from naïve towards non-naïve naturalness, but this mind does not touch the transcendental attitude. Roughly spoken, Hercules knows the difference between everyday reality and the law, and he is able to socially and politically defend that viewpoint, and he is able to point at the fact that the two worlds use two different languages. He also knows that in *secondness* (Peirce) or in *bracketing* (Husserl) the choice comes up between solving conflicts and following rules through *principles* or otherwise in line with *precedent cases*. He is even proud to master that choice, since a choice between principle or case seem irrelevant in any non-naïve-naturalness as it is entirely unknown in the naïve natural world. He understands how all this plays within various forms of legal pragmatism (Summers 1982). Questions of law who do not contribute to problem solving or conflict resolution are for him "philosophical issues" from which he distances himself. Only the awakening of *firstness* is for him a matter of understanding the specificity of law. His legal mind enters *secondness* and the implicit bracketing phase as a matter of doctrinal nature and of legal theory—not as a transition to further levels of understanding and maintaining signification. A *stagnating reference* is inherent to great jurists, to the legal mind, to Hercules who makes law in one, and is forbidden to make law in another legal culture.

The problem with Hercules is not that lawyers cannot bridge the gaps between law and society; he shares that specific difficulty with lawyers in all occidental legal cultures. The problem is neither the clear dominance of a specifically legal pragmatism, which is the attitude that best is what serves the interest of the client, or solves the case, or purifies the legal rule and keeps the legal system intact. The problem is *whether the legal mind is aware of the necessity to continuously return to firstness.* That return is a *sign* for a fundamental difference between the project of semiosis and legal discourse. Semiosis is infinite and return a sign of its dynamics. On the other hand is legal discourse finite and return a sign of repetition rather than of any dynamics. One could translate this phrase and formulate the question somewhat differently: how and in what regard does the subject of semiosis (the semiotically operating subject) differ from the subject of law (the legal mind)? "Hercules v The Subject of Semiosis"—what is there to say in this case? Eco highlights the idea of an unlimited semiosis (Eco 1979b, p. 69) as inspired by Peirce, who wrote

Anything which determines something else (its interpretant) to refer to an object to which itself refers (its object) in the same way, the interpretant becoming in turn a sign, and so on *ad infinitum*... If the series of successive interpretants comes to an end, the sign is thereby rendered imperfect, at least (Peirce 1931, vol. 2, p. 303)

Emphasis is in this context on the "ad infinitum", which indicates the importance of the return. Hence Colapietro "...the idea of a process of unlimited semiosis is simply that of a series of infinite interpretants" (Colapietro 1989, p. 34), and Eco: by means of this idea "Peirce has reached the highest level of his realism". The return, the innermost dynamics of meaning, implies that a sign gives rise to an interpretant activity of a subject of semiosis, and a first to a second. Eco again:

> ...there begins a process of unlimited semiosis, which, paradoxical as it may be, is the only guarantee for the foundation of a semiotic system capable of checking itself entirely by its own means (Eco 1979b, p. 68)

This comes close to the widely debated idea of Luhmann (1984, pp. 60, 491; Teubner (1989, p. 16ff)) who suggested that a legal discourse is fundamentally autopoietic. The difference between autopoeisis and semiosis is essential, the first being finite and closed, the second infinite and open. Hercules cannot make a choice between these two, without losing his legal mind!

2.6.3 Legal and Semiotic Subject

Colapietro unfolds an important observation about the position of the acting subject in law and in semiosis. The two are by no means identical, although legal-theoretical and even philosophical studies seem to suggest such an identity. There is, however, another, perhaps more important observation beyond Colapietro's analysis: both subjects, the subject of legal operations and the subject of semiotic action, are characterized by their capability to constantly change from one level of attitude to another, and back again! Here is the central issue: theoretical diagnoses from Adorno to contemporary philosophers underlined that an important difference between an everyday subject in phenomenology and in semiosis cannot be abolished. They say, that a transcendental subject is unable to act socially so that the subject of *firstness* must remain without the power of meaning making. Both positions are therefore the result of isolation, which is in itself the product of breach or rupture in *firstness* or of the transition from naïve-naturalness into non-naïve-natural worlds. The two can never meet social requirements once in that pointed position, formulates the standard criticism. Is that correctly stated?

Two remarks relate to a general underestimation and misunderstanding of *attitude change* in relation to the awakening of *firstness*:

(a) The subject entangled in the unlimited process of semiosis can in exactly this framework change along the lines Husserl laid out from a naïve-natural to a non-naïve-natural and ultimately transcendental position, or which Peirce laid out from *firstness* to *thirdness* eventually via *secondness* and back again as many times as necessary. Those two do not lead to any form of becoming encapsulated in isolation. Individuals in everyday life can carry on conversations of a transcendental character among them or elucidate their position of bracketing with their conversation partners! (Broekman 1963, p. 183 ff.). The semiosis project is unlimited just because of the capacity we called "attitude change".
(b) One should consider how De Saussure underlined what Peirce also noticed, namely that a sign is not a fixed semiotic entity but rather the meeting ground for independent entities—an observation confirmed by Eco (1979, pp. 68, 314) and by Colapietro (1989, p. 35). There *are* no signs, nothing *is* a sign, everything *can become* a sign, so that there are ultimately only sign-functions, and these are only temporary exercising such a function. "Finally, . . . reality depends on the ultimate decision of the community" Peirce noticed (1931, vol. 5, p. 317). Eco highlights how

> the semiotic subject is a way of looking at the world and can only be known as a way of segmenting the universe and of coupling semantic units with expression units: by this labor it becomes entitled to continuously destroy and restructure its social and historical systematic concretions (Eco 1979, p. 315).

Legal cases are signs that fulfill a role in this labor. They are names for sign functions and thus limited by their temporary character and by the limited discourse in which its subjects operate. The limits and definitions of law are defined by lawyers and by what society considers as legal, which includes that the defining procedure happens in a changing society and historical context. Those changes are overwhelmingly mirrored in the pace of today's changing e-technology.

Moore's Law is generally accepted as a first radical attempt to understand this. Gordon Moore, with Robert Noyce the founder of Intel and in the mid-seventies its chairman, had accomplished a series of inventions pertaining to integrated electronic circuits. His law—which he never himself called a law—expressed the observation that every twenty-four month twice as many transistors can be loaded onto an integrated circuit as in the period before. His law laid down the foundations of insight pertaining to our culture's character and pace, and is therefore also important for our legal future, its discourses and institutions included. Legal semiotics attempts to coordinate the unlimited and the limited acceleration of history for reasons of better understanding the dimensions of society's major discourse. No wonder that the future of the law seems extremely precarious. Law is deeply intertwined with a multitude of cultural developments, so that legal discourse and Court practices are often perceived to be based on uncertain premises and unwarranted assumptions. It is true that most legal articulations do by no means include essential knowledge about the powers that shape future cases and legal case materials. And, moreover, they do not include clues about the true character and the pace of technology and culture that are developing in the first decades of this century.

Hence the suggestion of a forthcoming *semiotization*—an acceleration of understanding social processes as sign processes—of law and legal discourse. Moore's law has largely held the test of time to date, indicating a limit for the number of transistors on the most complex chips. This issue becomes gradually interpreted as a sign for historical processes within which law has to function. All particles of the cohesion between *firstness* and phenomenology seem to concentrate on their respective subjects and their actions. That seems essential for the theme of this text: those subjects are, no matter in what attitude level involved, at a certain moment of their life time communicating subjects, and their communication processes function thanks to overarching systems of meaning. Peirce explains

> . . .since the meaning of a word is the conception it conveys, the absolutely incognizable has no meaning because no conception attaches to it. It is, therefore, a meaningless word; and, consequently, whatever is meant by any term as "the real" is cognizable in some degree, and so is of the nature of a cognition (Peirce 1931, vol. 5, p. 313)

And he finalizes his thoughts when writing. . .

> Consistency belongs to every sign, so far as it is a sign; and therefore every sign, since it signifies primarily that it is a sign, signifies its own consistency. The man-sign acquires information, and comes to mean more than he did before. But so do words. . . .But since man can think only by means of words or other external symbols, these might turn round and say: "You mean nothing which we have not taught you, and then only so far as you address some word as the interpretant of your thought." In fact, therefore, men and words reciprocally educate each other; each increase of a man's information involves and is involved by, a corresponding increase of a word's information (Peirce 1931, vol. 5, p. 314)

2.7 Law and Attitude Change

> This science of Phenomenology, then,
> must be taken as the basis
> upon which normative science is to be erected,
> and accordingly must claim our first attention (Peirce 1931, vol. 5, p. 39).

The cohesion of *firstness* and the legal mind depends on our understanding of the subject of legal semiosis in progress. If those subjects are truly involved in those discourses, then they are also involved in meaning making. Their involvement makes or breaks the promise of legal semiotics. They have to be involved because, as Peirce notated

> a sign is something, which stands to somebody for something in some respect or capacity. It addresses somebody, that is, creates in the mind of that person an equivalent sign, or perhaps a more developed sign. That sign which it creates I call the interpretant of the first sign. The sign stands for something, its object (Peirce 1931, vol. 2, p. 228)

The "standing for..." is an essential element of culture and a constitutive particle of the process of reference. However, little attention has been given to the fact that *all reference is a historical process* and that therefore the "standing for..." always takes part in historical developments. Being human implies being part of a civilization that seeks to extend its cultural and humane boundaries, a civilization that reaches out to new horizons whilst overcoming its prejudices with regard to other minds as well as longstanding scientific insights. *Firtsness* is a precious domain, and attitude change is implemented there. Law plays an important role in that semiotically bound extension of a human essence, and this is particularly underlined by the fact that there is no law without attitude change and rupture regarding the naïve-natural world. Husserl and Peirce developed different expressions for their ideas, and each of those them gave us different but clear examples. Peirce's hand of the sheriff shows clearly what was said about law. And, what is more, Peirce begun his reflections on *Phenomenology* with the remark, that "This science of Phenomenology, then, must be taken as the basis upon which normative science is to be erected, and accordingly must claim our first attention" (Peirce 1931, vol. 5, p. 39). The language of the law, becoming almost universal and reaching beyond the boundaries of a specific legal system, is in so far normative as the language that guides us with regard to vital questions and profiles of society today seems central. That observation is in effect even before one considers whether Law is a normative science, or is not! A sheriff's task is to awaken awareness in a person about his or her being a bearer of rights and duties. But that narrative changed considerably since Husserl and Peirce. Law and semiotics will soon be about *reengineering a human subject in a process of accelerating progress* instead of matters of appropriate application. Shrinking seizes will enter the (nano) technology range with hitherto unknown frames, patterns and designs for a new technology and new pattern recognitions taking place. Genetics in parallel with modern electronically sustained neurology in the context of our general e-culture do for instance question the traditional delimitations between the natural and the artifice. Categories of space and time altered during one's lifetime in modern society. Attitude changes are never a fixated fact but rather a process in human history. Changes accelerate in line with scientific and social patterns. Neither Husserl nor Peirce has explicitly considered the issue of changing cultural and semiotic backgrounds of attitude changes. The realm of the "naïve-natural" as well as the "non-naïve-natural" is not determined by fixated boundaries. On the contrary: these are the dynamics of culture, techniques and technology, images of man and changing systems of norms and values. How does the semiotic logic of law fit those sometimes deeply disturbing processes?

A semiotic logic of law is a not-yet undertaken research project in its own right. It would show how a phenomenological distinction between the natural and the non-natural is far from evident and an issue in constant change. All this depends on a host of appreciations for which we are not educated, as little as we are prepared for e-technology, not to mention its technological innovations and the many features we don't acknowledge as specifically human characteristics. Reflections are multiple here: does becoming a *cyborg* imply an estrangement from the humane essence, does technological modification of humans (for example *neurological implants*) make them *in*human, or, to move one more step, is a human with a bionic implant (a heart for instance) no longer a human being? Do limitations of technological nature defy the ongoing merger of humans with technology, which manifests itself in the image of the cyborg? Clark suggests:

The cyborg is a potent cultural icon of the late twentieth century. It conjures images of human-machine hybrids and the physical merging of flesh and electronic circuitry. . . .what is special about human brains, and what best explains the distinctive features of human intelligence, is precisely their ability to enter into deep and complex relationships with nonbiological constructs. . . The familiar theme of "man the toolmaker" is thus taken one crucial step farther. Many of our tools are not just external props and aids, but they are deep and integral parts of the problem-solving systems we now identify as human intelligence (Clark 2003, p. 5).

Does law belong to the tools of newly developing humans? This is not easy to answer, the more because one should also read the question as an important indication of a profound and perhaps disruptive transformation in human nature. *Non-biological intelligence enters the history of mankind more rapidly than ever before*, although that development is by no means accepted—neither universally nor in local cultures.

No wonder that the future of the Law seems extremely precarious. Law is deeply intertwined with a multitude of cultural developments. Legal discourse is often perceived as based on uncertain premises and unwarranted assumptions. It is true that most legal articulations do by no means include essential knowledge about the powers that shape future cases and legal case materials. And, moreover, they do not include any clue about the true character and the pace of technology and culture that are developing in the first decades of the century. The following should be highlighted in view of the position of legal discourse in our modern culture.

[1] It has never been clear whether these ideas are restricted to technological developments or are in essence a matter of a new turn in the philosophy of history. The *pace of technology changes* is after all a matter of course of history in one field of culture, which can become extrapolated into others. Kurzweil suggests the latter, and a worldwide reception beyond the realm of electronic technology suggests the same (Kurzweil 2005). This is unique in so far as an analysis of *technology* leads to a new view on the *history* of our Western globalizing culture. Such a view reaches far beyond classical distinctions between reality and the virtual, or between the human body and mind (Massumi 2002, p. 124). Our central interest focuses, however, another aspect and challenges a different

conclusion. *If these developments have to be seen as a twenty-first century philosophy of history—especially regarding linear and exponential development with a new formulation of the position of the transcendental subject—then it's time that legal theoreticians and philosophers of Law take notice!*

[2] Components that define the traditional concept of *history* have changed. Subject of historical changes that form the materials of a philosophy of history are no longer local and national attitudes, government decisions or economic strategies. Technological progress and its social consequences, changes in scientific paradigms, including the rate of change in all regions of daily life, which altogether change in an accelerating mode, have taken a role in a new paradigm. The self-understanding of subjects in history takes place in the context of what nowadays is called *an accelerating change* (Unger 2007, p. 6ff.). Each traditional linear or intuitive understanding of history became an obstacle to understand the structure of the future when paradigms shift at such a hitherto unimagined pace.

A group of scientists that focuses the accelerating rate of change as a predominant force in modern history (together with the interpretation of the pace of time as a non-linear but rather exponential phenomenon) emphasizes the concept named "*Singularity*". Singularity is a period of extremely rapid technological progress. Ray Kurzweil argues that such an event is implied by a long-term pattern of accelerating change in modern history, as explained in his 1989 *The Age of Intelligent Machines*, Hans Moravec's *Robot: Mere Machine to Transcendent Mind* or Damien Broderick's 1997 and 2001 books *The Spike*, as well as the Internet-mediated philosophical texts of John Smart. The concept of *singularity* is philosophical as well as technological, and it does by no means carry univocal meanings. It coordinates the notion of ever-higher rates of paradigm shifts, of exponential growth of information technologies, of the possible hardware and software that is able to emulate human intelligence, of new mental models of reality and human intelligence. With it, the position of the extreme non-naïve-natural, which is in development versus a point of transcendence could become newly understood and defined. It would introduce a truly twenty-first century philosophy. The modern forceful non-invasive brain scan techniques relate to those ideas-to-become a fact in history.

[3] This observation becomes even more complex when one understands that the authors focusing *singularity* do not write and contemplate computers or computer technologies. Computers are not subjects of specific paradigms in the history of science and technology. They simply bring underlying technologies to surface. Different images of man and a new history of mankind are involved. Technology became linked with human features through *new imaging techniques* and understandings of the human *body and brain in terms of wirings and information*. All lay the groundwork for a new language in the human sciences. That jargon is at a large distance to the *philosophical anthropology* in the twenties of the last century. Philosophical and scientific discourses on man are embedded in a jargon that comprises fragments of biology, neurology, psychiatry, genetics, electrophysiology and computer sciences. One has to take into

account that not only ethical, but also technological changes determine human sciences of this century.

As exposed in the above paragraphs, Eco (1979a, b) as well as Colapietro (1989, 2008) have given attention to the question of the subject in semiosis. Its position is indeed a matter of interest to law and legal discourse as well as a cornerstone for understanding the law-semiotics relationship. If law belongs to the context of new human sciences, does legal discourse express this development? Analysis of the relations between Husserl and Peirce have indicated how the two forward the notion of a subject in semiosis developing its attitude and constitutive power from *firstness* to *thirdness*, from a naïve-natural to an ultimately transcendental position without loosing contact with everyday society, its demands and its languages. Those steps can be conceived as important in the process of accelerating history with images beyond the traditional boundaries of biological or technological nature. *Does the law speak and understand this discourse on man, and what are the contributions of semiotics in this regard?*

References

Adorno, Theodor W. 1956. *Zur Metakritik der Erkenntnistheorie*. Stuttgart: W. Kohlhammer.

Apel, Karl-Otto. 1973. *Transformation der Philosophie, Band II: Das Apriori der Kommunikationsgemeinschaft*. Frankfurt am: Suhrkamp.

Balkin, Jack M. 1991. The Promise of Legal Semiotics. *Texas Law Review*, 69, 1831–1852.

Broekman, Jan M. 1963. *Phänomenologie und Egologie. Faktisches und Transzendentales Ego bei Edmund Husserl. Phaenomenologica, Bd 12*. Den Haag: Martinus Nijhoff.

Broekman, Jan M. 1974. *Structuralism. Moscow, Prague, Paris*, Synthese Library, vol. 67. Dordrecht: D. Reidel.

Broekman, Jan M. 1984. Justice as Equilibrium. *Law and Philosophy*, 5, 369.

Broekman, Jan M. 1986. Semiology and the Medical Discourse. *Methodology and Science, International Journal for the Empirical Study of the Foundations of Science and Their Methodology*, XIX(1).

Broekman, Jan M. 1996. *Intertwinements of Law and Medicine*, Leuven Law Series, vol. 7. Leuven: Leuven University Press.

Clark, Andy. 2003. *Natural-Born Cyborgs. Minds, Technologies and the Future of Human Intelligence*. Oxford: Oxford U.P.

Colapietro, Vincent M. 1989. *Peirce's Approach to the Self. A Semiotic Perspective on Human Subjectivity*. New York, NY: SUNY Series in Philosophy.

Colapietro, Vincent M. 2008. Peircean Semeiotic and Legal Practices: Rudimentary and "Rhetorical" Considerations. *International Journal for the Semiotics of Law*, 21, 27–49.

De Saussure, Ferdinand. 1915. In eds. Charles Bally and Albert Sechehaye, *Cours de linguistique générale*. Paris: Payot.

De Saussure, Ferdinand. 1983. *Course in General Linguistics*. London: Duckworth.

Deely, John. 1994. Membra Ficte Disjecta. Editorial Introduction to the Electronic Edition of the Collected Papers (CP) of Charles Sanders Peirce.

Ducrot, Oswald and Todorov, Tzvetan. 1972. *Dictionnaire Encyclopédique des Sciences du Langage*. Paris: Ed. du Seuil.

Dworkin, Ronald. 1977. *Taking Rights Seriously*. London: Duckworth & Co.

Dworkin, Ronald. 1985. *A Matter of Principle*. Oxford: Clarendon Press.

Dworkin, Ronald. 1986. *Law's Empire*. Cambridge, MA: Bellknap Press, Harvard UP.

Eco, Umberto. 1979a. *A Theory of Semiotics*. Bloomington: Indiana U.P.
Eco, Umberto. 1979b. *The Role of the Reader: Explorations in the Semiotics of Texts*. Bloomington: Indiana U.P.
Edelman, Bernard. 1973. *Le Droit Saisi par la Photographie*. Paris: Flammarion.
Edelman, Bernard. 1979. *Ownership of the Image*. London: Routledge & Kegan Paul.
Greimas, Algirdas J. 1968. The Interaction of Semiotic Constraints. *Yale French Studies*, 41, 269.
Greimas, Algirdas J. 1970. *Du Sens. Essais Sémiotiques*. Paris: Du Seuil.
Greimas, Algirdas J. 1983. *Du Sens II. Essais Sémiotiques*. Paris: Du Seuil.
Husserl, Edmund. 1913. *Logische Untersuchungen Band II*, 2 vols. Hall a.d.s: Max Niemeyer.
Husserl, Edmund. 1927. In eds. Palmer and Sheehan, *Phemenology, Encyclopaedia Britannica*. Dordrecht: Kluwer 1997, pp. 129–261, [Revised Ed. Richard Palmer].
Husserl, Edmund. 1952. *Ideen zu einer Reinen Phänomenologie und Phänomenologischen Philosophie Bd. II: Phänomenologische Untersuchungen zur Konstitution. Husserliana*, vol. IV. Den Haag: Martinus Nijhoff.
Husserl, Edmund. 1954. *Die Krisis der Europäischen Wissenschaften und die Transzendentale Phänomenologie. Husserliana*, vol. VI. Den Haag: Martinus Nijhoff.
Husserl, Edmund. 1956. *Erste Philosophie (1923/24). I: Kritische Ideengeschichte. Husserliana*, vol. VII. Den Haag: Martinus Nijhoff.
Jackson, Bernard S. 1985. *Semiotics and Legal Theory*. London: Routledge & Kegan Paul.
Jackson, Bernard S. 1988. *Law, Fact and Narrative Coherence. Legal Semiotics Monographs*. Roby, Merseyside: Deborah Charles Publications.
Jackson, Bernard S. 1996. *Making Sense in Jurisprudence. Legal Semiotics Monographs*. Liverpool: Deborah Charles Publications.
Kant, Immanuel. 1990. *Critique of Pure Reason*, tr. J. M. D. Meiklejohn. New York, NY: Prometheus Books.
Kevelson, Roberta. 1988. *The Law as a System of Signs*. New York, NY: Plenum Press.
Kevelson, Roberta. 1996. *Peirce, Science, Signs*. New York, NY: Peter Lang.
Kristeva, Julia. 1969. *Semiotikè. Recherches pour une sémanalyse*. Paris: Du Seuil.
Kurzweil, Ray. 2005. *The Singularity is Near. When Humans Transcend Biology*. New York, NY: Viking.
Lee, Benjamin. 1997. *Talking Heads. Language, Metalanguage and the Semiotics of Subjectivity*. Durham & London: Duke U.P.
Luhmann, Niklas. 1984. *Soziale Systeme. Grundriss einer Allgemeinen Theorie*. Frankfurt am: Suhrkamp.
Massumi, Brian. 2002. *Parables for the Virtual. Movement, Affect, Sensation*. Durham & London: Duke U.P.
Ogden, Charles K. and Richards, Ivor A. 1923. *The Meaning of Meaning. A Study of the Influence of Language upon Thought and of the Science of Symbolism*. New York, NY: Harcourt, Brace & World Inc.
Parker, Kelly A. 1998. *The Continuity of Peirce's Thought*. Nashville & London: Vanderbilt U.P.
Paul, Jeremy. 1991. The Politics of Legal Semiotics. *Texas Law Review*, 69, 1779–1829.
Peirce, Charles Sanders. 1931–1935 ed. In eds. Charles Hartshorne and Paul Weiss, *The Collected Papers of Charles Sanders Pierce*, vols. I–VI. Cambridge, MA: Harvard University Press.
Peirce, Charles Sanders. 1958 ed. In ed. Arthur W. Burks, *The Collected Papers of Charles Sanders Pierce*, vols. VII–VIII. Cambridge, MA: Harvard University Press.
Peirce, Charles Sanders. 1977. In ed. Charles S. Hardwick, *Semiotic and Significas. The Correspondence Between Charles S. Peirce and Victoria Lady Welby*. Bloomington: Indiana U.P.
Peirce, Charles Sanders. 1998. *The Essential Peirce, Selected Philosophical Writings*, vol. 2, (1893–1913) ed. the Peirce Project. Bloomington: Indiana U.P.
Pencak, William A. 1993 *History, Signing in: Essays in History and Semiotics*. New York, NY: Peter Lang.
Posner, Richard A. 2008. *How Judges Think*. Boston/Cambridge, MA: Harvard U.P.

Spiegelberg, Herbert. 1957. Husserl's and Peirce's Phenomenologies: Coincidence or Interaction. *Philosophy and Phenomenological Research*, 17, 170.
Stjernfelt, Frederik. 2007. *Diagrammatology: An Investigation on the Borderlines of Phenomenology, Ontology, and Semiotics*, vol. 336. Dordrecht: Springer, Synthese Library.
Summers, Robert S. 1982. *Instrumentalism and American Legal Theory*. Ithaca: Cornell U.P.
Teubner, Gunther. 1989. *Recht als Autopoietisches System*. Frankfurt am: Suhrkamp.
Unger, Roberto M. 2007. *The Self Awakened*. Cambridge: Harvard U.P.
Wittgenstein, Ludwig. 1958. *Philosophical Investigations*, tr. G. E. M. Anscombe. Oxford: Basil Blackwell.

Chapter 3
The Gift and the Meaning-Giving Subject: A Reading of *Given Time*

Jacques de Ville

> *How is one to think the fact that everything that is only is insofar as it is given?*
>
> Jean-Luc Marion

3.1 Introduction

Derrida's *Given Time I. Counterfeit Money* (1992a), stemming from a seminar presented for the first time in 1977–1978, with its exploration of inter alia the gift and of time, stands in close relation to his thinking on justice and law. This can clearly be seen in *Force of Law* where Derrida (2002a, p. 254) describes justice in terms of a "gift without exchange, without circulation, without recognition or gratitude, without economic circularity, without calculation and without rules, without reason and without theoretical rationality, in the sense of regulating mastery".[1] The exploration of the notions of time and the gift in *Given Time* takes place with reference inter alia to Heidegger's well-known statement in his 1962 lecture in *On Time and Being* (2002a), "*es gibt Sein, es gibt Zeit*" ("it gives Being, it gives time"; or "there is Being, there is time") as well as Marcel's Mauss's analysis in *The Gift* (1990) of the gift in archaic societies. *Given Time* has not as yet received much attention from legal scholars.[2] This is unfortunate since, as the quotation above shows, justice in Derrida's texts clearly has to be understood with reference to his analysis of the gift. Derrida's analysis of the gift furthermore relates to an issue which is of central

J. de Ville (✉)
University of the Western Cape, Cape Town, South Africa
e-mail: jdeville@uwc.ac.za

[1]See also Derrida (1994, pp. 22–27).

[2]For helpful "non-legal" analyses of *Given Time*, see Bischof (2004, pp. 354–363), Bennington and Derrida (1993, pp. 188–203), Derrida and Caputo (1997, pp. 140–151), Horner (2001), Marrati (2005, pp. 190–197), as well as the analysis of the 'gift section' in Derrida's *Glas* (1986a, pp. 242a–244a) by Gasché (1994, pp. 192–198).

A. Wagner, J.M. Broekman (eds.), *Prospects of Legal Semiotics*,
DOI 10.1007/978-90-481-9343-1_3, © Springer Science+Business Media B.V. 2010

importance for legal thinking, namely the origins of law. This issue is of course also addressed in other texts.[3] *Given Time* nevertheless explores the question of law's origin from a unique angle which in turn makes possible a better understanding of Derrida's other "legal" texts. As will be shown, the importance of Derrida's analysis of the gift furthermore lies in its ability to address the so-called impasse that is often said to characterise constitutional interpretation (Ackerman 2007, p. 1756). *Given Time* in addition points to the necessity of exploring the relation between the thinking of Derrida and Heidegger. Although Heidegger's thinking as well as the relation between Heidegger and Derrida are not completely unexplored in the legal context, much remains to be said in this regard. The current essay, although brief in this respect, will seek to elaborate on the complexity of the inter-relation of their thinking insofar as this ties in with the origins of law.

Given Time is a relatively long and complex text. It would be impossible to explore all the different aspects of this text within the space of a short essay. To nevertheless make an analysis of the main elements of this text possible insofar as it relates to Derrida's thinking on law and justice, the focus in this essay will primarily be on the first two chapters of *Given Time*. Notions that are mentioned in passing in these chapters such as sexual difference, mourning, desire, forgetting and repression, but which are essential for an understanding of the gift will be explored with reference to other texts of Derrida. The essay will start in Section 3.2 with a brief exposition of Heidegger's evaluation of metaphysics. As Derrida notes in *Positions* (2002c, p. 8), his own thinking would not have been possible without the "attention to what Heidegger calls the difference between Being and beings, the ontico-ontological difference such as, in a way, it remains unthought by philosophy".[4] In *Given Time* Derrida then also specifically engages inter alia with Heidegger's thinking on Being as well as the difference between Being and beings, by contemplating that which precedes this difference, through the notions of the gift and of time.[5] An outline of Mauss's *The Gift* will be given in Section 3.3, specifically with reference to the way in which Mauss views the gift in terms of a circular economic exchange. This will be followed by a brief discussion of Derrida's analysis of Mauss's text. Here we will see the first signs of a development in terms of which the concept of the gift will be exceeded towards a certain ecstasy, "a *jouissance* of the concept to the point of overflowing" (Derrida and Roudinesco 2004, p. 5). In Section 3.4, Derrida's own analysis of the gift will be enquired into in more detail. This will take place in four parts. In paragraph 4.1 Derrida's analysis of Heidegger's thinking on the *es gibt* and its relation to the gift and time will be enquired into with reference to *On Time and Being* (Heidegger 2002a). In paragraph

---

[3]This includes texts of Derrida such as "Before the Law" (1992b, pp. 181–220), "Force of Law: The 'Mystical Foundation of Authority'" (2002a, pp. 230–298) and "Declarations of Independence" (2002b, pp. 46–54).

[4]See also Derrida (1973, pp. 153–154).

[5]It is perhaps important to note here that Derrida does not distinguish strictly between Heidegger's thinking before and after the so-called turn (*Kehre*). The same approach will be followed in the current essay in elaborating on Heidegger's thinking.

4.2 an analysis of the "notion" of sexual difference will be undertaken. As we will see, the gift, as well as justice, is closely related to sexual desire. This cannot be completely unexpected as the traditional idea of origin as well as of law and reason are implicitly tied to phallogocentric privilege—the privilege of the one, the unitary origin, the father (Derrida 1991, pp. 313–314). This in turn leads us to the notion of *Mitsein* in Heidegger's texts which is explored in paragraph 4.3 with reference to the notion of mourning. The gift's relation to pleasure beyond pleasure and thus to the "notion" of *différance* is explored in paragraph 4.4. Section 3.5 will briefly consider the implications for law of the analysis of the gift, specifically with reference to *Force of Law*.

3.2 Heidegger and Metaphysics

3.2.1 The Question of Being

For Heidegger, all philosophy since Plato, including its derivatives, constitutes metaphysics. Heidegger points out in this regard that metaphysics concerns itself with the question of being: *ti to on* (what is being?). Heidegger wants us to return to this question and to think it through in a more fundamental way. He wants to in a sense get behind the guiding question metaphysics poses and to pose a more original question, that is: What sustains and directs the guiding question of metaphysics? (Heidegger 1991, vol. II, p. 193) Heidegger's thinking can be said to be motivated by the completion of metaphysics or idealism brought about by Hegel's thinking of the absolute Idea as well as its consummation in Nietzsche's thinking of the will to power. Relying on the metaphor of harvesting we can say that Hegel succeeded in bringing in the first great harvest. Metaphysics now only involves the threshing of empty straw. Heidegger therefore seeks to go back to the source of metaphysics so as to, as he puts it, "come to know the field and what it is capable of yielding" (Heidegger 2005, p. 34). Heidegger is more specifically of the view that Western philosophy has forgotten the question of Being (*das Sein*).[6] Although it has concerned itself with Being throughout its history, metaphysics has not as yet adequately thought Being. The question Heidegger concerns himself with is the more fundamental question (as compared to what happens in metaphysics) of the Being of beings. Being for Heidegger is not "a being" (*ein Seiende*). A being can be any thing such as what we can grasp with our hands, mountains, a river, the moon, a group of people, the Japanese, Bach's fugues, Hölderlin's hymns, day, night, heat, noise, law etc. (Heidegger 2000, p. 81, 1984a, p. 40, 2005, p. 111). Why is the question of Being important? According to Heidegger, the question of Being determines the way in which we relate to the world around us. This can be explained with reference to the word "is" in language. Even though "is" can be said to drift about "as

[6]The use of the capital B is in line with the practice followed in many translations of Heidegger's texts, to distinguish "Being" (a substantive, formed by turning the verb *sein* (to be) into a noun) more clearly from "beings" or "a being".

the most threadbare word in language", it also sustains all our saying, Heidegger contends. We implicitly use the "is" in every verb we employ. It is the same with all substantives and adjectives, all words and articulations of words. Even in our (silent) conduct towards beings, for example by walking in a forest or reading a book, their "is" or Being is at stake. We also are in relation with the "is" when we for example relate in our thinking to a thing that is no longer or not yet, and even a thing that simply is not (Heidegger 1991, vol. IV, pp. 188–193). The question of Being is thus extremely important and it is something we already have a pre-understanding of, even though we tend never to think about it. We could say that because of the brightness of beings, the light of Being is obscured. Being in other words withdraws when it reveals itself in beings (Heidegger 1984a, p. 26). Our relation to Being is according to Heidegger made possible by man's essential nature prior to any philosophical undertaking, for otherwise man would not have been able to relate to himself as a being or to other beings at all (Heidegger 2005, p. 88). Philosophy itself, which as we saw primarily concerns itself with the question of Being (although it has done so in an inadequate way), is thus made possible by this essential nature of man. Philosophy is not simply thought up, but awakened in man through his relation with Being (Heidegger 2005, p. 32). As we will see in more detail below, philosophy has grasped the question of Being in different ways: Plato represented Being as Idea, Aristotle as *energeia*, Kant as position, Hegel as the absolute concept, Nietzsche as the will to power, but consistently as constant presence, which is what Heidegger wishes to place in question (Heidegger 2002a, p. 9, 2005, p. 39).

3.2.2 The Understanding of Being in Metaphysics

Despite the high regard in which Heidegger holds Plato and Aristotle, he regards, as we saw above, Plato as the first metaphysical thinker and views Western philosophy as having been caught up in metaphysics ever since. The early Greeks were not as yet under the sway of metaphysics (Heidegger 1991, vol. IV, p. 165). Plato and Aristotle nonetheless, like all philosophers after them, still contemplated Being, that is, the arche (principle) or ground of beings (Heidegger 2005, p. 71). What then happened with Plato's thinking? Plato thought of Being in a way different from the early Greeks. He did not think Being as such, but thought it from the perspective of and with reference to (the essence of) beings (Heidegger 1991, vol. IV, pp. 207–211). More specifically, for Plato Being is the idea or the universal—that in which the particular thing (a being) has its subsistence and from which it proceeds. Plato's interpretation of Being as idea has according to Heidegger shaped the whole history of Western philosophy. One could say that all philosophy since Plato is "idealism": Being is thought in the idea, the idea-like and the ideal (Heidegger 1991, vol. IV, pp. 162–164). The Christian understanding that all beings have a first cause in God as creator is similarly metaphysical (Heidegger 1991, vol. III, p. 7). It also proceeds by thinking Being with reference to beings. That which "is" in the Christian understanding, is the *ens creatum*, that which is created by the personal Creator-God as the highest cause (Heidegger 1977, p. 130). Christianity in other words states that the

Being of a being is that it has been created by God (Heidegger 1991, vol. IV, p. 88). Beings according to Christianity have been thought out rationally beforehand. As soon as the link between Creator and creation is broken in modernity (Nietzsche's "God is dead"), this idea is adapted and man now takes the place of God, so that the rationality and calculation of man becomes the measure of everything, that is, interpreted as Being (Heidegger 2000, p. 207, 1977, p. 148). This is the enlightenment idea of reason (Heidegger 1991, vol. III, p. 7). Heidegger (1991, vol. III, p. 51) puts this as follows as the profound insight of Nietzsche in his reflections on the will to power:

> Only what represents and secures rational thinking has a claim to the sanction of a being that is *in being*. The sole and highest court of appeal, in whose field of vision and speech is decided what is in being and what is not, is reason. We find in reason the most extreme pre-decision as to what Being means.

What "is" in metaphysics, is therefore necessarily determined by a specific understanding of Being (Heidegger 1977, vol. 117, pp. 127–128). The understanding of Being in modernity, Heidegger ascribes in the first place to Descartes' *Ego cogito, ergo sum*. This statement entails that "[a]ll consciousness of things and of beings as a whole is referred back to the self-consciousness of the human subject as the unshakable ground of all certainty" (Heidegger 1991, vol. IV, p. 86).[7] In modernity, the idea (Being) in Plato has thus become that which man posits for himself (Heidegger 1991, vol. IV, p. 174). Accordingly only that "is" which is correctly thought (Heidegger 2000, p. 207). Reason has become synonymous with the subjectivity of the human subject, entailing "the self-certain representing of beings in their beingness, that is, *objectivity*" (Heidegger 1991, vol. III, p. 96). All beings are furthermore turned into objects (Heidegger 1993, p. 251).

When Being is in the above-described ways turned into idea or "whatness", the latter is promoted to the status of *the* Being of beings, to what really is or to what is most in being about beings, whereas beings are relegated to *me on*—that which really should not be and really is not. A disjoining in this way takes place between *on* and *phainomenon*. The idea furthermore becomes the *paradeigma*, the model and also the ideal (Heidegger 2000, pp. 194–199). Heidegger (2000, p. 197) describes the consequences of the cleft that opens up between the idea and the imitation as follows:

> Because the *idea* is what really is, and the *idea* is the prototype, all opening up of beings must be directed toward equalling the prototype, resembling the archetype, directing itself according to the idea. The truth of *phusis* – *alētheia* as the unconcealment that essentially unfolds in the emerging sway – now becomes *homoiōsis* and *mimēsis*: resemblance, directedness, the correctness of seeing, the correctness of apprehending as representing.

If Being becomes an idea then there is no longer any link between beings and Being or between beings and truth (understood here as unconcealment or the happening of

[7] See also Heidegger (1991, vol. IV, p. 179) and Heidegger (1977, p. 129). This is not to be understood in an individualistic sense as the random opinion of an individual "I" (Heidegger 1991, vol. III, p. 221).

beings)—only between beings and idea. The foundations upon which metaphysical thinking is built, are thus not foundations at all, as they are themselves derived (and falsified) (Heidegger 1991, vol. IV, p. 163).

One can summarise Heidegger's diagnosis of metaphysics by saying that metaphysics does not draw a clear distinction between beings and Being. Metaphysics regards Being as the most abstract and emptiest of concepts and in no need of being determined any further. Being is overshadowed by beings (Heidegger 1991, vol. IV, p. 157). This is not because of a mistake in thinking, but because in the appearance of beings, Being withdraws, conceals itself (Heidegger 1991, vol. IV, pp. 226–227). Being itself and consequently also the difference between Being and beings thus remains unexplored because metaphysics does not take account of the fact that there is a fundamental difference between Being and beings (Heidegger 1991, vol. IV, pp. 195, 196). This difference between Being and beings is referred to by Heidegger as the ontological or ontic-ontological difference. We already saw above that everywhere and continually, man stands in a relationship with Being when comporting himself towards beings. Man could thus also be said to "*stand in the differentiation of beings and Being*" (Heidegger 1991, vol. IV, p. 153). It is this differentiation which makes possible "every naming, experiencing, and conceiving of a being as such" (Heidegger 1991, vol. IV, p. 154). The ontological difference is thus the unknown and ungrounded ground and foundation of (the possibility of) ontology and of all metaphysics. The differentiation between Being and beings, we could also say, forms the basic structure of metaphysics even though it has remained unexamined as such (Heidegger 1991, vol. IV, p. 182).

3.2.3 A Different Understanding of Being, in Relation to Time

Heidegger reflected on the question of Being in a number of ways. In *Being and Time* (1962) he explored the question of Being as a first step with reference to that being for whom its Being or existence is a question: man or in Heidegger's terminology: Dasein (literally: there-being). Being can furthermore be understood only when we understand time (Heidegger 2005, p. 88). According to Heidegger, one of the problems with the usual conception of time is that it is generally referred to in the same context as space. The reason for this approach lies in the metaphysical conception of Being—in terms of beings, which appear in space and in time. This conception fails to recognise that space and time are not the same (Heidegger 2005, p. 84). In terms of the metaphysical concept of time, also to be found in Kant, time furthermore gives expression to permanence (Heidegger 2005, p. 118). This involves viewing time as a calculable sequence of nows (the present as actual now, the past as no longer now and the future as not yet now) (Heidegger 2002a, p. 11) and in terms of things that are present in time. This also informs the understanding of causality (Heidegger 2005, pp. 109, 113). One of the limitations of the conception of time in Kant (time as a mode of comportment of the human subject) is that it does not address the question of Being. It more specifically involves an implicit understanding of Being as constant presence. Heidegger points out that Kant's view of time simply involves that it occurs in man, instead of viewing time more fundamentally as "*the ground of the possibility of the understanding of [B]eing*" (Heidegger 2005, p. 88). Kant in this respect fails to investigate adequately the finitude of man, despite the fact that man stands at the centre of his enquiry in the *Critique of Pure Reason* (Heidegger 2005, p. 119). Instead Kant implicitly views man's way of being as being-present (Heidegger 2005, p. 134). Kant's discussion of time is nonetheless important as it tells us, as Aristotle and Augustine also do, that time is not something that can be found somewhere like a thing. Time can be found only in ourselves (Heidegger 2005, p. 85). To this "vulgar" metaphysical concept of time, Heidegger opposes authentic temporality. He arrives at this notion of temporality through an enquiry into the way in which Dasein actually experiences time. Stated briefly, this notion of temporality according to Heidegger involves a unitary relation of Dasein to the present, the past and the future, stretched along "ecstatically" (Heidegger 1962, p. 462).[8] Ecstatic refers here to Dasein's being carried to or stretching toward a certain "whither" (Kockelmans 1989, p. 283; Taminiaux 1994, p. 52). What Heidegger refers to as Dasein's ecstatico-horizonal temporality, involves awaiting (the future), retaining (having-been) and making things/beings present. These ecstases do not follow in succession upon each other as in the ordinary conception of time. The future is thus not later than the having-been and the having-been is not earlier than the present. As Heidegger (1962, p. 401) explains, "[t]emporality temporalizes itself as a future which makes present in the process of having been". The present or making things present in authentic temporality is dependent on an understanding of one's own having-been thrown forth, which is in turn determined by an anticipation of one's ultimate and ownmost possibility (Kockelmans 1989, pp. 32, 257; Taminiaux 1994, p. 51). The future furthermore has priority in authentic temporality as the future relates Dasein to his own Being-towards-death. Authentic temporality is therefore primordially finite (Heidegger 1962, pp. 378–379). The awareness of its own Being-towards-death places Dasein in a relation to Being and makes resolve and authentic existence possible. Heidegger refers to death in this regard as the ownmost possibility of Dasein, which is at the same time Dasein's utter impossibility (Heidegger 1962, pp. 354, 378). The awareness of Dasein's own death thus structures temporality as it entails an anticipation of the future which determines the way in which Dasein relates to what has been and in making present.

Heidegger (1962, pp. 246–252) moreover contends that Dasein is already thrown into the world and "is" thus Being-in-the-world. This means that there is no world or reality outside of Dasein the existence of which has to proven (as Descartes attempted) or to which one has no access (Kant's "thing in itself"). Both these (metaphysical) approaches assume a subject that is world-less and that seeks to assure itself of a world (Heidegger 1962, p. 250). In this respect Heidegger's thinking is not very far removed from Hegel's critique of Kant regarding the noumenon. Things for Hegel are simply phenomena and there is no reason to go beyond the phenomena

---

[8] Greek ecstasis = standing outside. This word is used by Heidegger "to emphasize a connotation of stretching towards or openness to" (Taminiaux 1994, p. 52).

to the things-in-themselves (Hyppolite 1974, p. 125). Heidegger's thinking in this regard can be better understood when we relate it to what was said above regarding temporality. According to Heidegger (1962, pp. 429, 472), entities other than Dasein are strictly speaking non-temporal; they are nonetheless entities within-the-world that are encountered by Dasein "in time" due to Dasein's temporality. It is because of Dasein's awareness of its own mortality that its existence is an issue for it, although it tends to hide this from itself by finding refuge in beings because of the security they seem to offer. Death is therefore for Heidegger not something that stands apart from life or beyond life, but is connected to the life of Dasein in a fundamental way. Heidegger believes that an authentic life (as compared to the inauthentic life of the "they"—*das Man*) would entail being fully aware of one's mortality:

> Death is a possibility-of-Being which Dasein itself has to take over in every case. With its death, Dasein stands before itself in its ownmost potentiality-for-Being. This is a possibility in which the issue is nothing less than Dasein's Being-in-the-world. Its death is the possibility of no-longer-being-able-to-be-there (Heidegger 1962, p. 294).

In the above quotation we can see that the intricate relation between life and death is what for Heidegger defines Being. This comes out very clearly in another passage a few pages later in *Being in Time* (1962, p. 298): "Dasein is always dying already; that is to say, it is in a Being-towards-its-end." We see a similar kind of relation between life and death in Freud's thinking in relation to the death drive which Freud views as a "desire" of all living beings.[9] Western philosophy, it appears from the reflection of these two thinkers, has "hidden" the relation between life and death from itself, thereby turning itself into a metaphysics of presence. This is borne out by the way in which Being is implicitly viewed by metaphysics through all its epochs:

> Of what do we say and has one said from times of old: This "*is*"? What does one take as in being even when one has fallen away from the *primordial* Platonic way of perceiving? We say something *is* of that which we always and in advance encounter as always ready to hand; what is always present and has constant stability in this presence. What really is, is what already in advance can never be removed, what stands fast and resists any attack, survives any accident. The beingness of beings signifies permanent presence. What is *thus* in being is the true, the "truth" one can always and truly hold on to as what is stable and does not withdraw, on the basis of which one can gain a foothold (Heidegger 1991, vol. III, pp. 59–60).

This notion of constant presence is for example expressed by Kant when he describes appearances in the *Critique of Pure Reason*: "All appearances contain the permanent (substance) as the object itself, and the transitory as its mere determination, that is, as a way in which the object exists" (Heidegger 2005, p. 116). Changes of appearance are in other words viewed simply as alteration and not as "rising up from nothing and disappearance into nothing" (Heidegger 2005, p. 124). The reason for Being taking this form in metaphysics is related to the interest of life

[9] See paragraph 4.4 *infra*.

in constantly maintaining and securing itself. This is why the true world in metaphysics was taken to be the one that is constant and unchanging rather than one that is changing and transforming (Heidegger 1991, vol. II, pp. 61–62). What was at first experienced as "presencing" has due to metaphysics become "something present" (Heidegger 1984a, p. 50). Heidegger's discussion of chaos encountered by knowing (as compared to the commonsensical view that we encounter things or objects in an ordered way), in the context of a discussion of truth in Nietzsche, is revealing in this regard. Heidegger speaks in this respect of every living being, and especially man as "surrounded, oppressed and penetrated by chaos, the unmastered, overpowering element that tears everything away in its stream" (Heidegger 1991, vol. III, p. 84). Heidegger contends, in words that cannot but remind one of Freud's contemplation of the death drive, that Being (in metaphysics) entails an overcoming of this sheer dissolution and annihilation. It is however because of a denial of death as part of his life that man takes his refuge in a particular conception of Being as what is permanent and stable. Instead of viewing this chaos as on the outside whilst praxis or reason provides stability on the inside (as metaphysics does), the chaos must according to Heidegger (1991, vol. III, p. 88) be seen as what is inside:

> Rather, the living being as praxis, that is, as the perspectival-horizonal securing of stability, is first installed in chaos as chaos. Chaos as the onrushing urge of living beings for its part makes the perspectival securing of stability necessary *for* the survival of the living being.

3.2.4 Assessment

Although acknowledging the necessity of Heidegger's questioning of the metaphysical tradition, Derrida's assessment thereof (suspending for a moment the necessarily heterogeneous nature of Heidegger's texts, which will be explored further below), is that it was not followed through to the end. What is called for according to Derrida is an even more rigorous thinking through of Being and of the metaphysical tradition. Heidegger's enquiry into the truth of Being, although it involves a radical questioning of the tradition, ultimately seeks in very metaphysical style a more fundamental truth and origin. Heidegger (2005, p. 71) in this respect for example describes Being as "the primary and ultimate ground of the possibility of every actual and conceivable being". Heidegger furthermore retains in traditional metaphysical style, oppositions such as in his discussion of time and of Dasein between the authentic and the inauthentic (or fallen-ness), and of the proper and the improper, in spite of having suspended all ethical evaluation (Derrida 1982, pp. 63–64). In respect of the ontological difference, Derrida (1973, p. 153; 1982, pp. 66–67) asks whether the thinking of the difference between Being and beings does not still come from the metaphysical order and whether there is not a difference still more unthought than the difference between Being and beings, thereby alluding to *différance*. Heidegger's analysis of temporality raises a similar kind of question, that is, whether an alternative conception of time—here, authentic temporality—does not still remain within a metaphysics of presence, as any conception of time inevitably must (Derrida 1982, p. 63). Lastly, Heidegger's view of death as a possible impossibility of Dasein raises the question whether it does not risk inscribing death within a circular economy (Derrida 1993a, pp. 29–30, 62–64). Viewing death and time in this way, as we will see below, has important implications for our conception of justice. Despite these reservations, Derrida's description of justice in terms of the gift and the invocation of justice in "Force of Law", as well as his distancing of this conception from the Kantian regulative idea, is clearly indebted to Heidegger's destruction of the metaphysical understanding of Being as idea (Derrida 2002a, pp. 254–255). This destruction is a necessary step should one ultimately attempt to think Being in terms of the gift. Marcel Mauss's study of the gift further opens this possibility, as we will see in the discussion that follows.

3.3 Mauss's *The Gift*

Mauss's exploration of the gift in archaic or ancient societies understandably has a prominent place in Derrida's analysis in thinking the gift and time in a way that exceeds metaphysics. Mauss shows that gifts in these societies have a structure of circular exchange and are motivated by economic self-interest. Gifts are in other words coupled with an obligation to give (generously), an obligation to receive, and an obligation to reciprocate with interest, taking due account of prescribed time limits (Mauss 1990, p. 46). A failure to participate in this reciprocal exchange could have fatal consequences as it would amount to an act of war (Mauss 1990, p. 7). In the societies analysed, acts of destruction, giving of alms to the poor, giving of children in marriage, the invitation of others to share meals, drink and tobacco, the exchange of presents, are all forms of obligatory gifts. The exchange of gifts, according to Mauss (1990, pp. 46, 60–61, 90) lies at the origin of law, morality and economy in modern society. Mauss specifically contends in this regard that the principle of justice in modern legal systems has taken the place of the gift—justice derives from the obligation resting upon those in primitive societies who had in abundance; they had to show generosity in giving alms on certain occasions on pain of being punished by the gods in avenging the poor, and in expectation that they would be richly rewarded by the gods should they do so (Mauss 1990, p. 23). This obligation furthermore relates to the belief that the gods and the dead are the true owners of things and possessions of this world (Mauss 1990, p. 20). This at first required destruction in sacrifice to the gods (killing of slaves, burning of precious oil, casting copper objects into the sea, and setting the houses of princes and blankets on fire), which of course also fulfilled the function of displaying power, wealth and lack of self-interest (Mauss 1990, pp. 20, 47–48, 95). The giving of alms to the poor and of gifts to children, instead of to the gods, amounts to an evolution in society, entailing that men act in a way as representatives of the gods and the dead (Mauss 1990, p. 22). It is only relatively recently, Mauss furthermore contends, that a distinction has been drawn in legal systems between obligations and services that are not given freely on the one hand and gifts on the other (Mauss 1990, p. 61). According to Mauss, the exchange of generous gifts in these societies served and still serves the important function of preventing war and establishing peace between families, clans and tribes (Mauss 1990, pp. 104–106). It brings about a certain degree of stability on the basis of which legal and economic systems can develop. This is an interesting conclusion, in light of Mauss's own remarks concerning the destruction of wealth (in times of peace) as a kind of gift which he equates with war (Mauss 1990, vol. 8, pp. 141–142, fn 141, p. 147, fn 166). The preference expressed for the exchange of gifts presumably lies in it being a war or defence of oneself without resort to arms (Mauss 1990, p. 106). Mauss concludes his analysis by arguing for a return to the notion of generous giving, calculated but not excessive, found in ancient civilizations (thus effectively a return to nature) in accordance with the principles of charity, social service and solidarity and a movement away from cold-hearted, utilitarian, calculating laws and actions (Mauss 1990, pp. 83–100; Derrida 1992a, pp. 66, 82).

Although in praise of Mauss's study and of his re-introduction of the word and category of the gift as lying at the origin of legal, economic and moral systems as compared to other authors who seek to do without it, Derrida (1992a, pp. 26, 37, 42) is of the view that Mauss is not sufficiently concerned with his (that is, Mauss's) own observation that all the gifts he analyses are caught within a circular exchange. The same could be said of Mauss's conception of justice. An exchange of gifts, Derrida (1992a, pp. 24, 37) comments, surely amounts to the annulment of the gift. Another important comment of Derrida on Mauss's study deserves mention here. Derrida (1992a, pp. 25–26) questions the unity of meaning, which Mauss ascribes to the many different cultural practices, that is, that they all amount to the exchange of gifts. Derrida does not do this in order to say that these practices cannot be described as gifts, but instead to contend and ultimately to show that the word gift does not have a unitary meaning, that is, that it loses its meaning. This questioning ties in with Derrida's later comments on Mauss's description of a specific kind of gift. As we saw above, certain forms of "gift", those involving the honour of a chief, are described by Mauss as going even beyond this still limited notion of generosity—they involve a "madly" extravagant destruction and consumption, without limits, of all kinds of property. Derrida (1992a, pp. 46–47) notes that Mauss has some difficulty in describing the actions of the destruction carried out here in terms of the gift, where there appear to be no giving and returning and also no desire of expecting a return. This madness of a gift forgetting itself, of dissemination without return, "threatens *a priori* the closed circle of exchangist rationality", Derrida (1992a, p. 47) notes. Mauss in other words wishes to describe the gift in terms of a system of circular exchange, but in the process of describing it, he shows that the concept of the gift exceeds this system.[10] This is of course not to say that these actions which Mauss describes constitute gifts in the perfect sense. As we saw above, they can clearly also be inscribed within the system of circular exchange. Derrida (1992a, pp. 45–48) is concerned here rather with the language Mauss uses in describing these gifts which

[10]See for example (Mauss 1990, p. 47): "In certain kinds of potlatch one must expend all that one has, keeping nothing back." "In a certain number of cases, it is not even a question of giving and returning gifts, but of destroying, so as not to give the slightest hint of desiring your gift to be reciprocated."

seems to exceed his text on the gift as a system of circular exchange. Mauss, in giving us a narrative on the gift of circular exchange, is himself overtaken by the gift without exchange. We will see why this happens, also in the case of a constitution, in the discussion that follows. In his conclusion, Mauss furthermore acknowledges that the terms "present" and "gift" which he had been using throughout the text "are not themselves entirely exact" (Mauss 1990, p. 93; Derrida 1992a, p. 55). Derrida (1992a, p. 55) points out that Mauss here admits that the word "gift" has no centre or identity; that its meaning is marked by dissemination and asymmetry.

3.4 Derrida on the Gift

3.4.1 The Gift and Heidegger's es Gibt

In order to understand Derrida's reading of Mauss, it is necessary to further analyse chapter one of *Given Time* where Derrida sets out the usual conception of the gift. This entails that someone (A) wants, desires, or intends to give something (B) to someone (C). As Derrida (1992a, pp. 10–12) points out, this definition supposes a subject and a verb. It supposes, more specifically, a subject identical to itself and conscious of its identity, seeking through the gesture of the gift, to have its own identity recognised so that identity comes back to it. This definition—the condition of possibility of the gift—points also to the impossibility of the gift, to the destruction, annulment, and annihilation of the gift. The circular economy involved in this exchange in other words destroys the gift. Some "thing" cannot strictly speaking be a gift if it involves a relationship of circular exchange. As Derrida (1992a, p. 12) notes, "[f]or there to be gift, there must be no reciprocity, return, exchange, countergift or debt". In every instance where something is given back, the gift is annulled. There can only be a gift if it does not lead to a debt, to a contract, to a circular exchange, either in consciousness or the unconscious (Derrida 1992a, pp. 15–16). As soon as the gift appears as gift, it annuls or destructs itself, that is, even before it leads to gratitude. A gift can thus only be a gift if it does not appear as gift either to the donor or to the donee (Derrida 1992a, pp. 13–14). As soon as someone gives with the intention to give, a process of self-congratulation and self-approval and thus circular return to self takes place. As soon as the gift gets caught up in the temporalizing synthesis, as soon as it is accepted, and even when it is refused, destruction of the gift takes place.

In metaphysics, as Derrida points out, the gift and the debt, the gift and the cycle of restitution, the gift and the loan, the gift and credit, the gift and the countergift, have been thought together as a system. Derrida seeks to depart from this tradition by pointing to that in the tradition which posits that there can only be gift if this does not involve return, if it interrupts the system and the symbol. This requires a gift-event that would not be caught up within a system of economic exchange. In describing this impossible gift-event, Derrida notes that it would not be sufficient for the gift to be forgotten by the donor and the donee only consciously and still be kept in the memory of the unconscious. The latter would simply entail a displacing—not an annulling or destruction (Derrida 1992a, p. 16). The gift would have to involve an absolute forgetting and an absolute unbinding as distinguished from repression or displacement to the unconscious. This forgetting would involve an instant that no longer belongs to the economy of time (Derrida 1992a, p. 17).[11] It may appear strange to refer to the gift in terms of repression. Why would one want to suppress the giving of a gift? At this point Derrida is however no longer simply concerned with the giving of gifts in the ordinary sense, that is, someone giving something to someone other. He is engaging with the Heideggerian phrases *es gibt Sein, es gibt Zeit*. Through these phrases Heidegger, in *On Time and Being* (2002a), attempts to speak about time and Being, which as we already saw above are not present beings, in a non-propositional manner, that is, without referring to them as present-being/being-present and without speaking of them in terms of a subject-predicate relation (Derrida 1992a, p. 20). Both Heidegger and Derrida can in other words be said to attempt to think Being and time as made possible or "given" by "something" else: *Ereignis* (event).[12]

In his exploration of the *es gibt* in *Given Time*, Derrida (1992a, p. 22) specifically focuses on the notion of "play" which is mentioned by Heidegger in his discussion of time in *On Time and Being*.[13] Heidegger is contemplating here the *es* (it) of *es gibt*. He asks what the source is of Being that is sent to man in presence, or the becoming-presence of Being. According to Heidegger, and this ties in with what was said above concerning temporality in *Being and Time*, not only the present presences, but also what has been insofar as it still concerns us and what comes towards us from the future as it already concerns us. We can in other words say that

---

[11] Law has an essential relation to time, as has been recognised by a number of legal scholars in recent times (see inter alia Rubenfeld 1998, 2001; Douzinas and Warrington 1994, pp. 211–241; Douzinas 2007, pp. 34–50; Cornell 1992, pp. 116–154; Van der Walt 2005, pp. 191–231; Fitzpatrick 2001, pp. 84–90). As the analysis that follows will indirectly seek to show, this law-time couple and the circularity of economic exchange which it necessarily entails, are nevertheless unlikely to be interrupted or exceeded when one seeks to think of time in terms of an Oedipal past, a time of reconciliation, a time of repetition, a diachronic relation between the actual Other and the system, or as an extension over time.

[12] As Derrida (1992a, p. 19) indicates, *Ereignis* is a difficult word to translate. It is usually translated as event. However, as Krell points out in Heidegger (1993, p. 396), in introducing "The Way to Language", *Ereignis* in Heidegger's texts is used in a special sense, related to the Latin *proprius* or own-ness (see also Heidegger 1993, pp. 415–417). Krell therefore translates *Ereignis* as propriation (In *Identity and Difference* (2002b) and *On Time and Being* (2002a) it is translated by Stambaugh as Appropriation). *Ereignis* is furthermore closely related to Heidegger's thinking on death which is in turn viewed as the most proper possibility of Dasein; see Heidegger (1962, p. 294) and Heidegger (1993, p. 417). *Ereignis* could be said to draw Dasein into its own; into its mortal becoming in other words; see Sheehan (1998, p. 315).

[13] In other texts Derrida has indicated how the *es gibt* can be thought of in terms of a promise that makes language possible, and therefore as "preceding" the "is" which Heidegger has shown is a characteristic of all language as well as the "what is" question of philosophy; see Derrida (1989a, pp. 146–148, 1989b, pp. 129–136, fn 5, 1979, p. 111, 1992b, p. 302). Thinking of the *es gibt* in terms of a promise of course ties in closely with Heidegger's thinking on the relation between language, Being and *Ereignis*.

a giving of presencing prevails in the present, the past and the future. This giving, Heidegger contends, reaches us because it is in itself a reaching. Heidegger (2002a, p. 13) sees a reciprocal relation here between the past, present and future which he expresses as follows:

> Approaching, being not yet present, at the same time gives and brings about what is no longer present, the past, and conversely what has been offers future to itself. The reciprocal relation of both at the same time gives and brings about the present. We say "at the same time," and thus ascribe a time character to the mutual giving to one another of future, past and present, that is, to their own unity.

Heidegger then asks about the source of the unity of this three-dimensionality of what he refers to as true time. The unity of time's three dimensions, Heidegger (2002a, p. 15) concludes, "consists in the interplay of each toward each". This interplay of the three dimensions amounts to a fourth dimension of time. A fourth dimension of time thus keeps together the dimensions of the past, present, and future. It is this dimension that Heidegger refers to as the play of the *es gibt* and as *Ereignis*. The latter does not simply belong to time or to Being, but gives Being and time. This fourth dimension of time, Derrida (1992a, p. 22) notes, is not a figure, but is a reference to "the thing itself". "This thing itself of time", he furthermore comments, "implies the play of the four and the play of the gift".

Heidegger's *On Time and Being* thus appears to make possible a thinking of the gift in the strict sense indicated above: a gift which does not involve the giving of some thing by some one (a subject) to an other (subject). At the same time this traditional definition of the gift could be employed if we hear something else in the words "one", "thing" and "other" (Derrida 1992a, pp. 11–12). In the giving of the *es gibt*, as Derrida (1992a, p. 20) points out, the *es* (it) is not a thing; it also entails a giving "without giving anything and without anyone giving anything—nothing but Being and time (which are nothing)". The last phrase in parenthesis is to be understood within the context of Heidegger's analysis in *On Time and Being* which shows that time in itself is nothing temporal; it is also not a thing, and therefore in a certain sense, nothing. Time also does not properly belong to anyone (Derrida 1992a, p. 28). Nothing however appears which does not need time or take time. Time is in other words the condition of possibility of phenomenality (Derrida 1992a, p. 6). We could say that time, as determined by the revolution of the sun, day-time, makes phenomena appear. Similarly Being is not something, a thing or a being-present/present-being. This is why one cannot say "time is" or "Being is", but only *es gibt Sein* and *es gibt Zeit* (Derrida 1992a, p. 20). If the gift, rigorously thought, entails exactly this—the giving of nothing that is and that appears as such, then time is what should be given as gift. In the words of Derrida (1992a, p. 29), "[w]hat there is to give, uniquely, would be called time". This also explains the first part of the title, *Given Time*. We could say regarding time and also regarding the gift that each of them "is what it is *without being (it)*" (Derrida 1992a, p. 28). Neither time nor the gift therefore exists as such. Nevertheless, there is gift and there is time.

Derrida (1992a, pp. 21–22), however, points out that Heidegger's thinking in *On Time and Being* is clearly ordered by a desire for the proper. *On Time and Being* all the same opens the way to a thinking of the gift which, although not completely unrelated to the proper, exceeds the proper and reciprocation. Such a reading is made possible by thinking of the gift as exceeding economy. This furthermore allows for a thinking of *Ereignis* in terms of ex-appropriation or appropriation caught in a double bind, which would exceed the Heideggerian understanding thereof as propriation (Derrida 1995a, pp. 270, 321). Without a re-thinking of the notion of the gift and of *Ereignis*, the *es gibt* in *On Time and Being* risks being understood in terms of *oikonomia* (the home, property, *nomos*) (Derrida 2002c, p. 48). Thinking of the event in terms of a gift beyond exchange would conversely allow for the gift to be thought as opening the "history of Being" (which Heidegger (1991, vol. III, p. 179) defines as the history of the transformation and the devastation of Being's ungrounded truth) without belonging to it.[14]

3.4.2 The Gift and Sexual Difference

As we saw above, Heidegger's contention is that Western philosophical thinking has forgotten the question of Being. This is a question that was first posed by the early Greeks (Heidegger 1962, p. 2, 1993, vol. IV, p. 193; Derrida 1992a, p. 18). We also saw that a certain thinking of forgetting plays an important role in Derrida's analysis of the gift. The forgetting that Derrida refers to is undoubtedly tied to Heidegger's notion of forgetting, but it also goes beyond a forgetting of Being; it is said to involve an absolute forgetting. For Heidegger, the forgetting of Being is not a psychological or psycho-analytical category. Absolute forgetting, as Derrida refers to it and as we will see shortly, is indeed related to psychoanalytic repression, but at the same time exceeds it. Forgetting in this sense is closely related to Derrida's thinking on time. In closely associating forgetting and the gift, Derrida seeks to go not only beyond the Heideggerian notion of a forgetting of Being, but also beyond the psychoanalytical idea of repression or the unconscious (Derrida 1992a, pp. 16–18, 23). The radical forgetting that Derrida is referring to here is first of all required of the donor(s), whether individual or collective. Derrida (1992a, p. 23) stresses the fact that even the intention to give on the part of the donor, already suffices to annul the gift:

> The simple intention to give, insofar as it carries the intentional meaning of the gift, suffices to make a return payment to oneself. The simple consciousness of the gift right away sends itself back the gratifying image of goodness or generosity, of the giving-being who, knowing itself to be such, recognizes itself in a circular, specular fashion, in a sort of auto-recognition, self-approval, and narcissistic gratitude.

The above happens immediately and automatically when a subject or subjects are involved. A gift cannot therefore come about between two subjects exchanging objects, things or symbols (Derrida 1992a, p. 24). Heidegger's thinking in *On Time and Being* is for this reason of great importance in attempting to think the gift. As we saw above it seeks to go back beyond a construction of Being in terms of subjectivity

---

[14] See also Derrida (1986a, p. 242a) and Gasché (1994, pp. 194–198).

and objectivity (Derrida 1992a, p. 24). To understand what is at stake in the notion of absolute forgetting, a number of other texts of Derrida on Heidegger and on the gift need to be briefly referred to. Derrida's invocation in *Given Time* of numerous psychoanalytic notions, such as the unconscious, desire (beyond desire), repression, forgetting, mourning and sexual difference as well as their relation to the gift can be understood only with reference to these texts.

In *Women in the Beehive* Derrida (2005a, p. 150) is asked a question relating to an earlier remark of his concerning the relation between sexual difference and the impossible idea of the gift (Derrida 1988, p. 172). It is important to note that sexual difference, as Derrida uses this concept, does not refer to a separation of the traditional two sexes as in Hegel where "[i]n each sex the organic individuals form a totality" and where sexual difference entails a hierarchical opposition of male activity/female passivity (Derrida 1986a, pp. 110a, 112a–113a). Sexual difference, in Derrida's texts, entails a sexuality which is "completely out of the frame, totally aleatory to what we are familiar with in the term 'sexuality'" (Derrida 2005a, p. 151). Sexual difference, which Derrida associates at this juncture with the gift, in other words goes beyond sexual duality (Derrida 2005a, p. 151; Derrida 1979, p. 121). Derrida relies here on his reading of Heidegger's *Being and Time* (1962) in "*Geschlecht*: Sexual Difference, Ontological Difference" (1991).[15] In this essay Derrida (1991, p. 382) mentions the seeming silence about sex in Heidegger's texts. Dasein in *Being and Time*, and therefore also the meaning of Being, appear to bear no sexual mark. Derrida however refers to a lecture in 1928 at Marburg University where Heidegger explained the need to conceive of Dasein as sexually neuter, that is, as belonging to neither of the two sexes (Derrida 1991, p. 385; Heidegger 1984b, p. 136). It is interesting to note, Derrida (1991, p. 386) comments, that Heidegger, in *Being and Time* (1927), makes no mention of the asexuality (*Geschlechtslosigkeit*) of Dasein, only Dasein's neutrality, yet in the Marburg course, which was meant to clear up the many misunderstandings in the reception of *Being and Time*, this is one of the first traits he mentions. Derrida notes the strangeness of this observation or clarification, seeing that it appears commonsensical that if Dasein is neuter, it does not belong to one of the sexes. How should this observation regarding the neutrality as to sexual difference therefore be understood? Rather than simply understand this as a subtraction or negativity in characterising Dasein, Derrida notes with reference to Heidegger's comments that this characterisation should be understood as a positivity, a richness, or a power of Dasein (Derrida 1991, p. 387; Heidegger 1984b, pp. 136–137). The sexual neutrality of Dasein does not therefore point to the absence of sexuality; not to the absence hence of libido, instinct or desire, but simply to the absence of any mark belonging to one of the two sexes (Derrida 1991, p. 387; Derrida 1988, p. 180). The meaning of the neutrality as to sexual difference that Heidegger refers to could thus be summarised as follows:

> If *Dasein* as such belongs to neither of the two sexes, that does not mean that its being is deprived of sex. On the contrary: here one must think of a predifferential, or rather a predual,

---

[15] See Kamuf (2001) for an excellent analysis.

> sexuality – which does not necessarily mean unitary, homogeneous, or undifferentiated. . .. [I]t would indeed be a matter here of the positive and powerful source of every possible "sexuality" (Derrida 1991, pp. 387–388).

This asexuality is thus also not to be understood as an allusion to some primitive or subsequent bi-sexuality (Derrida 1988, p. 180). Derrida could consequently be said to read Heidegger as saying that "sexuality" is an essential part of the structure of Dasein and therefore influences, or rather, necessarily determines the meaning of Being and the ontological difference (Derrida 1991, pp. 390, 393).[16] This more originary structure of ipseity (*Selbstheid*) understood in terms of Dasein's sexuality furthermore makes possible the emergence of the *ego* and of the you (Derrida 1991, p. 391).[17] As with sexual difference, the word "sexuality" should not be understood here in its usual sense. Derrida notes that Heidegger explicitly relates sexuality to the internal possibility which Dasein harbours within itself of dispersal, dissemination, destruction, shattering, and fragmentation (Derrida 1991, pp. 391–392; Heidegger 1984b, pp. 137–138). This dissemination is thus not an ontic structure, but an originary structure of Dasein that affects it with lack-of-binding. The analysis of Dasein that is at stake here also necessarily affects the meaning of Being as this originary dissemination belongs to the Being of Dasein (Derrida 1991, p. 393). This "theme" of dissemination in Dasein's relation to objects and itself is already to be found in *Being and Time* (Heidegger 1962, pp. 439–444). Although Heidegger sometimes refers to the dispersion of Dasein as a mode of inauthenticity (*Uneigentlichkeit*) or as the falling of Dasein in its everyday-being, this is not always the case. At times, it is used to describe the general structure of Dasein (Derrida 1991, pp. 399, 400). Inauthenticity is furthermore not a moralizing critique, a philosophy of culture, a dogmatic religious account of the fall from an original condition or a corruption of human nature (Derrida 1991, p. 400; Minkkinen 1999, p. 59, n 36). Nevertheless, Heidegger does sometimes make use of the distinction between the authentic/proper and the inauthentic/improper to impose a hierarchical opposition, the very typical metaphysical nature of which cannot be denied (Derrida 1982, pp. 63–64). In exploring further the structure of Dasein in *Being and Time*, Derrida notes that its dispersion makes Dasein occur as *Erstreckung* or *Ausdehnung* (stretching, expansion, elongation, prolongation) which as Derrida (1991, p. 394) points out—

> names a spacing which, "before" the determination of space as *extensio*, comes to extend or stretch out being-there, the *there* of Being, *between* birth and death. As an essential dimension of *Dasein*, the *Erstreckung* opens up the *between* that links it at once to its birth and to its death, the movement of suspense by which it itself *tends* and extends itself *between* birth and death, these two receiving their meaning only from that intervallic movement. *Dasein* affects itself with this movement, and that auto-affection belongs to the ontological structure of its historicity.[18]

---

[16] See also Heidegger (1991, vol. I, p. 194).

[17] See similarly Derrida (1993a, p. 61) on originary mourning.

[18] See also Heidegger (1962, pp. 424–429).

This pre-spatial dispersion of Dasein is manifested inter alia in language (Derrida 1991, p. 395; Heidegger 1984b, p. 138). In writing, which as we know has been "repressed" by metaphysics because of its relation to the trace, this dispersion is for example expressed by the spacing of signs, punctuation, intervals, and differences between signs (Derrida 1976, pp. 68, 167, 2002c, p. 23). All graphemes, Derrida (1976, p. 69) notes, are of a testamentary essence. Dasein's originary dispersion is furthermore closely linked to its thrown-ness (*Geworfenheit*). Thrown-ness, as Derrida (1991, p. 396) points out, has to be understood as preceding any project on the part of Dasein, the categories of passivity and activity which are closely related to the subject, images of the fall, whether Platonic or Christian, as well as of spatiality. The originary spatiality of Dasein thus depends on the throw. The (disseminal) thrown-ness of Dasein, as Heidegger points out, becomes particularly manifest in Dasein's Being-with (*Mitsein*) other Dasein, a notion, as Derrida notes, which also has sexual connotations (Heidegger 1984b, p. 139; Derrida 1991, pp. 396, 401). The *Mitsein* and thrown-ness of Dasein could also be thought in relation to the Levinasian notion of the hostage (Derrida 1995a, pp. 275–276, 283–284; Derrida 1999a, pp. 55–57; Derrida 1993a, pp. 61–62, 65–66).

3.4.3 The Gift and Mourning

The notion of *Mitsein* and its relation to Derrida's thinking can be better understood when taking account of his reflections on mourning.[19] Derrida, following the analyses of Nicolas Abraham and Maria Torok (1994, pp. 125–138), draws a distinction in a number of his texts between the work of mourning on the one hand and mourning which does not take place in the normal way or what could also be referred to as the non-work or the play of the gift on the other hand.[20] The relevance of mourning lies in the role it plays in the structure and formation of the self (Krell 2000, p. 16; Derrida 1989a, pp. 33–34). Briefly stated, the work of mourning or normal mourning according to Freud would entail the total digestion, assimilation, introjection and idealisation of the dead person in order to withdraw the libidinal investment in that person and to re-constitute the self. Although introjection is inevitable, being a desire for presence as counter-reaction to identification with the dead, total assimilation is strictly speaking impossible (Derrida 1999b, p. 235). This is because death makes clear the distinction between self and other, seeing that it requires of a self to bear some one outside of them that absolutely exceeds them within them (Derrida 1989a, pp. 33–34; Derrida 2001a, p. 159). "Abnormal" mourning on the other hand

[19] See also Derrida (1992a, p. 36). Attempts to translate the thinking of Derrida and Freud on mourning into a general approach to law or to apply it to a specific area of law have been undertaken elsewhere (e.g. Cornell 1992, pp. 72–81; Barnard 2006). The present account differs in various respects from these. Derrida's exploration of friendship and of telepathy could also be relied on in exploring the notion of *Mitsein*; see Derrida (1997, 2007, pp. 226–261).

[20] See inter alia Derrida (2001a, 1992a, p. 36, 1988, pp. 57–59, 1989a, pp. 3–43, 1995a, pp. 320–322, 1986b, p. xvi).

would involve the incorporation of the dead person in a crypt in the ego (Derrida 1986b, pp. xvi–xvii). The dead person would thus not be internalised or become a part of us as in the work of mourning, but would nonetheless be taken inside the self, inhabiting the ego as a stranger, a persecutor, having been granted absolute hospitality and left in his/her alterity. The "living-dead" person can in this way haunt our body, look at us and speak through us, become our law, *the* law, stronger and more forceful than us (Derrida 2001a, p. 160).[21] Even before their death, we already carry those we love, our friends, in us outside us in anticipating their death, which constitutes the self and the relation to the self (Derrida 1989a, pp. 28–29):

> Even before the death of the other, the inscription in me of her or his mortality constitutes me. I mourn therefore I am, I am – dead with the death of the other, my relation to myself is first of all plunged into mourning, a mourning that is moreover impossible. This is what I call ex-appropriation, appropriation caught in a double bind: I must and I must not take the other into myself; mourning is an unfaithful fidelity if it succeeds in interiorizing the other ideally in me, that is, in not respecting his or his infinite exteriority (Derrida 1995a, p. 321).

In *Given Time* as well as in other texts, Derrida seeks to extend the structure of mourning, noting that all work is a work of mourning, that is, we are always attempting to reappropriate ourselves as a reaction to our thrown-ness or loss of autonomy (Derrida 1986a, p. 86b, 2001a, p. 161). This motivates his call for a mourning of mourning or an end of mourning work, a beyond of the mourning principle (Derrida 1995a, pp. 48–52; Derrida and Dufourmantelle 2000, pp. 111–119). This is not the same as the successful completion of mourning, but the giving of affirmation "to an other end", which Derrida (1995a, p. 52) brings into relation with Freud's speculation on the death drive in *Beyond the Pleasure Principle*. If we think of mourning in terms of a certain being-with others, it is possible to attain some insight into *Mitsein*. *Mitsein* in Derrida's reading, as the discussion of mourning suggests, does not refer simply to a peaceful togetherness or "reconciliation" between self and other as might be thought. Through a doubling, the boundaries between self and other are breached

[21] Within the notion of mourning a further distinction has to be drawn, following Abraham and Torok, between "the foreigner incorporated in the crypt of the Self" as described in the text above and "the ghost that comes haunting out of the Unconscious of the other" (Derrida 1986b, pp. 118–119, fn 21; Abraham and Torok 1994, pp. 140–141, fn 1, pp. 171–205). This "ghost" or "phantom" also has a place in the unconscious, but "is not an effect of repression 'belonging' to the subject he comes to haunt with all kinds of ventriloquism; he is rather 'proper' to a parental unconscious". The ghost coming back to haunt is therefore not a return of the repressed (Derrida 1986b, pp. 118–119, fn 21, 1988, p. 59). Derrida relies on both of these structures in his extension of the notion of mourning to the field of the political. This can for example be seen in his discussion of the consequences of the encounter in Baudelaire's *Counterfeit Money* of the two friends with a beggar (or at least with the beggar insofar as he represents a purely receptive, expending and consuming agency within this particular culture) (Derrida 1992a, pp. 134–145). The beggar could be said to function here as a "hetero-cryptic ghost" (Derrida 1986b, p. xxxi). As Derrida (1992a, p. 138) notes, the poor, "[a]s marginal people excluded from the process of production and circulation of wealth... come to represent the gods or the dead. They occupy the place of the dead man or the spirit, the return of the ghost, that is, of an always imminent threat."

to the "point" of dissolution of the self.[22] In extending the notions of *Mitsein* and mourning to law, extreme caution is furthermore advised. *Mitsein* which could be another "name" for justice can hardly be viewed simply as a reference to the (reconciliation of the) interests of the two or more parties to a legal dispute. As a number of Derrida's texts make clear, the position analogous to the I, the self or the subject as described above is that of a "we", for example a people, nation or community (a collective subject) who relies on the law in general in an attempt to protect or safeguard themselves in their own interest from their "destruction" or from absolute hospitality (Derrida 1992c, pp. 9–10, 2002a, pp. 230–298, 2005b; Derrida and Dufourmantelle 2000; Derrida 1994, p. 83). The self-destruction that is at stake here would be equivalent to *Mitsein* and also to the gift. A similar possibility of self-destruction is at stake in the case of a sexual bond and the human race (Derrida 1986a, pp. 123a–124a, 2007, pp. 387–409).

3.4.4 The Gift and Différance

The Heideggerian notions of a stretching-along between birth and death, of *Mitsein*, of thrown-ness, and of the gift are invoked by Derrida to contend, as he does elsewhere, that death is a part of life, although in a different way than Heidegger does. This becomes clear from a reading of Derrida's *To Speculate—On Freud* which involves a further engagement, through Freud's *Beyond the Pleasure Principle* (2001b, pp. 3–64),[23] with Heidegger's existential analytic of Dasein, although this time not with reference only to Dasein as providing privileged access to Being, but with reference to all beings (every organism, corpus, movement, organisation), and their "relation" to a certain sexuality and death (Derrida 1987, pp. 328, 347, 356).[24] Derrida shows here in his reading of Freud the link between the death drive and "sexual" desire. The primary process, death drive, absolute pleasure, or what Derrida also refers to as un-binding or final orgasm, entails a "desire" to return to the inorganic state and thus to an absolute past that is no longer a past present (Derrida 1987, p. 397). Every organism could be said to have a "relation" with this desire. This is however more specifically a "relation without relation" or, as we will see below, a *differantial* relation, because this desire or at least the trace thereof becomes effaced in its appearing (Derrida 1973, p. 156). Absolute desire or the secret of enjoyment, Derrida notes within the context of the Hegelian discussion of desire between the two sexes, has to "sacrifice[] itself, immolate[] itself to

[22]This is also suggested by a number of other texts of Derrida (1994, pp. xviii–xix, 154, 162, 1993b, 1998a, pp. 63–65, 1976, pp. 184–192, 1993a, pp. 61–62, 65–66), where he deals more exclusively with being-with, and where mourning is also often referred to.

[23]This is not an isolated engagement with this text of Freud. Derrida comes back to it in a number of other texts, e.g. in Derrida (2001b, pp. 246–291, 1998b, 1995b).

[24]I have explored this in more detail elsewhere and will therefore only give a very brief summary here.

itself, say on the altar of enjoyment, in order not to destroy (itself), itself and the other, one in the other, one for the other" (Derrida 1986a, pp. 123a–124a). Absolute desire would in other words amount to the annihilation of self in the enjoyment of the other and of the self by the other, death coinciding with the act of copulation (Derrida 1986a, p. 123a; Freud 2001a, p. 198, c, p. 47). A similar kind of incorporation and self-destruction appears to be at stake here as in the case of "abnormal" mourning described above; a death drive thus "shared" by all organisms, *the* law of sharing or partition [*partage*], the law of the gift (Derrida 1992a, p. 6, 2005b, pp. 42–62). The "relation" of every organism to self-destruction or what Derrida elsewhere calls autoimmunity, can also, as noted above, be extended beyond auto-eroticism (Derrida 1976, pp. 152–157, 179) and the sexual bond (Derrida 1976, p. 155) to a community (Derrida 1998a, p. 51), a nation (Derrida 2002a, pp. 269–270, 2005b) and the human race (Derrida 2007, pp. 387–409).

The movement of binding or striction described above can be understood with reference to the "notion" of *différance*. *Différance* does not, as is the case with the ontological difference, refer to the distinction between Being and beings, but to the difference between the gift or self-destruction on the one hand and economy, law, politics, reason, meaning, experience, science, knowledge and philosophy which are in time, on the other (Derrida 1992a, p. 30). *Différance*, in other words, structures the relation between the desire for presence (which we also find in Heidegger's analysis of Being) and the desire for absolute pleasure, which remains continuously deferred. *Différance* could thus be said to be "situated" between Being/beings and an other which is not "their" other (Derrida 1995c, p. 104). In the current context, *différance* refers to absolute pleasure, the death drive, the gift beyond exchange, the putting in play or to fire of all, which must nonetheless, in order to make possible an economy of self-relation and a dialectic of meaning, engage in a constriction or binding, resulting in the domestic hearth (Derrida 1987, pp. 338–409, 1986a, p. 242a; Freud 2001d, p. 90, fn 1). As soon as there is, as Derrida (1987, p. 66) points out, there is *différance*. "Prior" to this stricture of the for-(it)self, although one is no longer reckoning with time here but with an absolute past or the trace, one can speak of a pure play of difference, of a difference without subject, of indifference, of a seminal effusion without return (Derrida 1976, p. 66, 1986a, pp. 239a–241a). One can also not speak of the space, locus or region of the gift, but rather, as we saw above, of spacing. Spacing is referred to by Aristotle as "ama", the "together of time and space", which allows for what Derrida refers to as the "becoming-space of time and the becoming-time of space" or what could also be referred to as the difference between time and space, to appear or to be experienced (Derrida 1976, pp. 65–66, 69; Harvey 1986, p. 121; Derrida 1973, p. 143; Heidegger 2002a, pp. 14–15). As Derrida furthermore notes in *On the Name* regarding *khora* in Plato's *Timaeus*, this is a site "where the law of the proper no longer has any meaning" (Derrida 1995c, p. 105). In binding itself, the gift puts a supplement or substitute in the place of that which the structure inhibits or forbids (Derrida 1987, p. 393). It is nonetheless the only way in which the gift can appear or show itself as gift.

3.5 The Gift, Time and Law

The above account is, as noted in the introduction, and as the discussion should have indicated, relevant not only in thinking the origin of law, but also of legal decision-making or interpretation. Derrida's analysis of the gift raises questions concerning the traditional model of decision-making in terms of which a collective subject identical to itself simply re-appropriates its identity through the decision (Derrida 1992a, pp. 10–11). This model of decision-making can most clearly be seen in the recent debates in some jurisdictions concerning the common good as the primary function of law, whether viewed communally, nationally, regionally or internationally.[25] It is nonetheless a characteristic of all legal discourses of self-legitimation, also of (legal) positivism, described by Heidegger (1991, vol. IV, p. 99) as "the real, the factual, which is ordered and arranged by. . .reason". The gift without exchange is also to be clearly distinguished from accounts of justice in liberal political theory, such as that of Rawls (1999). These accounts can be assessed in similar terms as Derrida's evaluation of Mauss's concluding remarks on the need for a return by contemporary society to the generous giving of ancient civilizations:

> An expected, moderate, measured, or measurable gift, a gift proportionate to the benefit or to the effect one expects from it, a reasonable gift (that "good but moderate blend of reality and the ideal" that Mauss favored) would no longer be a gift; at most it would be a repayment of credit, the restricted economy of a differance, a calculable temporization or deferral (Derrida 1992a, p. 147).

The founders of a state as well as legal decision-makers, as should be clear from the above discussion, are always already situated within the movement of *différance* and therefore also within the disseminal or thrown non-space and non-time of the gift. It is from this non-localizable point, beyond space and time, and therefore without meaning, without property, without law, without right, without reason, that responsibility in decision-making, a responsibility necessarily without limit and before memory must be thought (Derrida 1986a, pp. 49a–53a, 2002a, pp. 247–248). Responsibility, thought thus, would necessarily also require a negotiation with the possible and therefore a binding, which, as Derrida points out, "is immediately to supplement, to substitute, and therefore to represent, to replace, to put an *Ersatz* in the place of that which the structure inhibits or forbids" (Derrida 1987, p. 393, 2002a, p. 251). The re-appropriation or ex-appropriation which therefore necessarily follows upon such thrown-ness nevertheless cannot in the case of law be absolutely stabilized in the form of a collective subject. As Derrida (1995a, p. 270) puts it:

> The subject assumes presence, that is to say sub-stance, stasis, stance. Not to be able to stabilize itself absolutely would mean to be able only to be stabilizing itself: relative stabilization of what remains unstable, or rather non-stable. Ex-appropriation no longer closes itself; it never totalizes itself.

---

[25] See Schuppert (2003, pp. 215–260) for a summary.

This is why, in *Force of Law*, Derrida insists that there is the possibility of "general strike", or what we could refer to here as "the gift", in every interpretive reading (Derrida 2002a, p. 271). A written text such as a constitution opens itself to such a reading, as such a text, like the gift, does not return to the author. This is because a constitution ultimately amounts to a gift, in a similar way as does Mauss's *The Gift*, Heidegger's *On Time and Being*, the fragment from Madame de Maintenon (the morganatic wife of Louis XIV) and Baudelaire's *Counterfeit Money*, the gift-giving character of which Derrida explores in *Given Time*. This gift-characteristic of a constitution is of course not the result of the intentions of its authors, but because of the gift "itself" which as we saw sets law in motion through the giving of time and Being (Derrida 1992a, p. 101). The gift, because of the stricture of *différance*, inevitably forms a part of the structure of every text.[26]

The possibility of the impossible gift in every interpretive reading entails also the "right", granted by the gift, to suspend all norms of reading which ultimately also stand in the service of the preservation of law (Derrida 2002a, pp. 271, 272). Constitutional interpretation cannot therefore, thought rigorously, consist simply of calculation or the application of norms of reading in an attempt to find, establish or create meaning. Set in motion by the gift, it should, it *must* affirm the gift. A legal reading affirming the gift has to defy the circularity of economic exchange; it has to involve a certain madness which "allows" itself to be "taken" by the gift.[27] At the same time, because of the inevitable calculation and re-appropriation which is provoked by the unbearable demand of the gift; because of the necessity therefore of time becoming space and space becoming time, constitutional reading also requires the taking account of or negotiation with law and rules (Derrida 1992a, p. 142, 2002a, p. 252). The gift, as we saw, inevitably erases, effaces itself in this negotiation and thus in the giving, so that we can never say, "this is/was a gift or a just decision".[28] A thinking of the gift and its relation to the establishment of meaning nevertheless could allow us to think with Derrida in a different, or perhaps rather *differantial* way and therefore without falling into relativism, about issues of constitutional interpretation such as the death penalty (Derrida and Roudinesco 2004, pp. 139–165), immigration/citizenship (Derrida and Dufourmantelle 2000; Derrida 1997), stem cell research (Derrida 2005b, pp. 141–159), the notion of the family (Derrida and Roudinesco 2004, pp. 33–46), man's relation to "animals" (Derrida 2008), terrorism (Derrida 2003), the punishment of "criminals" (Derrida and Roudinesco 2004, pp. 139–196), dealing with "rogue" states (Derrida 2005b), addressing poverty (Derrida 1995d, pp. 85–86, 1992a, pp. 134–145), the concepts of equality and freedom (Derrida 2005b, pp. 19–62; Derrida and Roudinesco 2004, pp. 47–61), the idea of self-government, and the issue of the sovereignty of the nation-state (Derrida 2005b). Without this thinking of the gift the meaning-giving subject would be forever simply caught in the circle of economic exchange.

---

[26] See also Horner (2001, p. 202).

[27] See also Derrida (2002a, pp. 255, 252, 1995d, p. 95).

[28] See also Derrida (2002a, p. 251).

Acknowledgement The author would like to acknowledge the generous funding provided for the research by the Alexander von Humboldt Foundation and the South African National Research Foundation.

References

Abraham, Nicholas and Torok, Maria. 1994. *The Shell and the Kernell: Renewals of Psychoanalysis*, vol. I, tr. Nicholas Rand. Chicago, IL and London: University of Chicago Press.

Ackerman, Bruce. 2007. The Living Constitution. *Harvard Law Review* 120, 1737–1812.

Barnard, Jaco. 2006. Death, Mourning and Melancholia in Post-Modern Contract – A Call for (Re)establishing Contract's Connection with the Ethical. *Stellenbosch Law Review*, 17, 386–411.

Bennington, Geoffrey and Derrida, Jacques. 1993. *Derridabase/Circumfession*. Chicago, IL and London: University of Chicago Press.

Bischof, Sascha. 2004. *Gerechtigkeit – Verantwortung – Gastfreundschaft: Ethik-Ansätze nach Jacques Derrida*. Freiburg, Schweiz und Freiburg, Wien: Academic Press Fribourg und Verlag Herder.

Cornell, Drucilla. 1992. *The Philosophy of the Limit*. New York, NY: Routledge.

Derrida, Jacques. 1973. *Speech and Phenomena and Other Essays on Husserl's Theory of Signs*, tr. David B. Allison. Evanston: Northwestern University Press.

Derrida, Jacques. 1976. *Of Grammatology*, tr. Gayatri Chakravorty Spivak. Baltimore, MD and London: The John Hopkins University Press.

Derrida, Jacques. 1979. *Spurs: Nietzsche's Styles*, tr. Barbara Harlow. Chicago, IL and London: University of Chicago Press.

Derrida, Jacques. 1982. *Margins of Philosophy*, tr. Alan Bass. Chicago, IL: University of Chicago Press.

Derrida, Jacques. 1986a. *Glas*, trs. John P. Leavey, Jr. and Richard Rand. Lincoln and London: University of Nebraska Press.

Derrida, Jacques. 1986b. Foreword: *Fors*: The Anglish Words of Nicholas Abraham and Maria Torok. In eds. Nicolas Abraham and Maria Torok, *The Wolf Man's Magic Word: A Cryptonomy*, tr. Barbara Johnson. Minneapolis, MN: University of Minnesota Press, xi–xlviii.

Derrida, Jacques. 1987. *The Post Card: From Socrates to Freud and Beyond*, tr. Alan Bass. Chicago, IL and London: The University of Chicago Press.

Derrida, Jacques. 1988. In ed. Christie McDonald, *The Ear of the Other*, trs. Peggy Kamuf and Avital Ronell. Lincoln: University of Nebraska Press.

Derrida, Jacques. 1989a. *Memoires for Paul de Man*, trs. Cecile Lindsay, Jonathan Culler, Eduardo Cadava, and Peggy Kamuf. New York, NY Columbia University Press

Derrida, Jacques. 1989b. *Of Spirit: Heidegger and the Question*, trs. Geoffrey Bennington and Rachel Bowlby. Chicago, IL and London: University of Chicago Press.

Derrida, Jacques. 1991. In ed. Peggy Kamuf, *A Derrida Reader: Between the Blinds*. New York, NY: Columbia University Press.

Derrida, Jacques. 1992a. *Given Time: I. Counterfeit Money*. Chicago, IL and London: University of Chicago Press.

Derrida, Jacques. 1992b. In ed. Derek Attridge, *Acts of Literature*. New York, NY and London: Routledge.

Derrida, Jacques. 1992c. *The Other Heading: Reflections on Today's Europe*, trs. Pascale-Anne Brault and Michael B. Naas. Bloomington and Indianapolis: Indiana University Press.

Derrida, Jacques. 1993a. *Aporias*, tr. Thomas Dutoit. Stanford, CA: Stanford University Press.

Derrida, Jacques. 1993b. Heidegger's Ear: Philopolemology (Geschlecht IV). In ed. Johan Sallis, *Reading Heidegger: Commemorations*, tr. John P. Leavey, Jr. Bloomington and Indianapolis: Indiana University Press, 136–159.

Derrida, Jacques. 1994. *Specters of Marx: The State of Debt, the Work of Mourning, and the New International*, tr. Peggy Kamuf. New York, NY and London: Routledge.

Derrida, Jacques. 1995a. In ed. Elisabeth Weber, *Points...Interviews, 1974–1994*, trs. Peggy Kamuf et al. Stanford, CA: Stanford University Press.

Derrida, Jacques. 1995b. *Archive Fever: A Freudian Impression*, tr. Eric Prenowitz. Chicago, IL and London: The University of Chicago Press.

Derrida, Jacques. 1995c. In ed. Thomas Dutoit, *On the Name*, trs. David Wood, John P. Leavey, Jr., and Ian McLeod. Stanford, CA: Stanford University Press.

Derrida, Jacques. 1995d. *The Gift of Death*, tr. David Wills. Chicago, IL and London: University of Chicago Press.

Derrida, Jacques. 1997. *Politics of Friendship*, tr. George Collins. London and New York, NY: Verso.

Derrida, Jacques and Caputo, John D. 1997. *Deconstruction in a Nutshell: A Conversation with Jacques Derrida*. New York, NY: Fordham University Press.

Derrida, Jacques. 1998a. Faith and Knowledge: The Two Sources of 'Religion' at the Limits of Reason Alone. In eds. Jacques Derrida and Gianni Vattimo, *Religion*, tr. Samuel Weber. Stanford, CA: Stanford University Press, 1–78.

Derrida, Jacques. 1998b. *Resistances of Psychoanalysis*, trs. Peggy Kamuf, Pascale-Anne Brault, and Michael Naas. Stanford, CA: Stanford University Press.

Derrida, Jacques. 1999a. *Adieu: To Emmanuel Levinas*, trs. Pascale-Anne Brault and Michael Naas. Stanford, CA: Stanford University Press.

Derrida, Jacques. 1999b. Marx & Sons. In ed. Michael Sprinker, *Ghostly Demarcations: A Symposium on Jacques Derrida's Specters of Marx*. London and New York, NY: Verso, 213–269.

Derrida, Jacques and Dufourmantelle, Anne. 2000. *Of Hospitality*, tr. Rachel Bowlby. Stanford, CA: Stanford University Press.

Derrida, Jacques. 2001a. *The Work of Mourning*, eds. Pascale-Anne Brault and Michael Naas. Chicago, IL and London: University of Chicago Press.

Derrida, Jacques. 2001b. *Writing and Difference*, tr. Alan Bass. London and New York, NY: Routledge.

Derrida, Jacques. 2002a. *Acts of Religion*, ed. Gil Anidjar. New York, NY and London: Routledge.

Derrida, Jacques. 2002b. In ed. and tr. Elizabeth Rottenberg, *Negotiations: Interventions and Interviews 1971–2001*. Stanford, CA: Stanford University Press.

Derrida, Jacques. 2002c. *Positions*, tr. Alan Bass. London and New York, NY: Continuum.

Derrida, Jacques. 2003. Autoimmunity: Real and Symbolic Suicides: A Dialogue with Jacques Derrida. In Giovanna Borradori, *Philosophy in a Time of Terror: Dialogues with Jürgen Habermas and Jacques Derrida*. Chicago, IL: University of Chicago Press, 85–136.

Derrida, Jacques and Roudinesco, Elisabeth. 2004. *For What Tomorrow . . . A Dialogue*, tr. Jeff Fort. Stanford, CA: Stanford University Press.

Derrida, Jacques. 2005a. Women in the Beehive: A Seminar with Jacques Derrida. *Differences: A Journal of Feminist Cultural Studies* 16, 139–157.

Derrida, Jacques. 2005b. *Rogues: Two Essays on Reason*, trs. Pascale-Anne Brault and Michael Naas. Stanford, CA: Stanford University Press.

Derrida, Jacques. 2007. In eds. Peggy Kamuf and Elizabeth Rottenberg, *Psyche: Inventions of the Other*, vol. 1. Stanford, CA: Stanford University Press.

Derrida, Jacques. 2008. *The Animal that Therefore I Am*, tr. David Wills. New York, NY: Fordham University Press.

Douzinas, Costas and Warrington, Ronnie. 1994. *Justice Miscarried: Ethics and Aesthetics in Law*. New York, NY: Harvester Wheatsheaf.

Douzinas, Costas. 2007. *Human Rights and Empire: The Political Philosophy of Cosmopolitanism*. London and New York, NY: Routledge-Cavendish.

Fitzpatrick, Peter. 2001. *Modernism and the Grounds of Law*. Cambridge: Cambridge University Press.

Freud, Sigmund. 2001a. *The Standard Edition of the Complete Psychological Works of Sigmund Freud. Volume VII (1901–1905)*. London: Vintage.
Freud, Sigmund. 2001b. *The Standard Edition of the Complete Psychological Works of Sigmund Freud. Volume XVIII (1920–1922)*. London: Vintage.
Freud, Sigmund. 2001c. *The Standard Edition of the Complete Psychological Works of Sigmund Freud. Volume XIX (1923–1925)*. London: Vintage.
Freud, Sigmund. 2001d. *The Standard Edition of the Complete Psychological Works of Sigmund Freud. Volume XXI (1927–1931)*. London: Vintage.
Gasché, Rodolphe. 1994. *Inventions of Difference: On Jacques Derrida*. Cambridge, MA and London. Harvard University Press.
Harvey, Irene E. 1986. *Derrida and the Economy of Différance*. Bloomington: Indiana University Press.
Heidegger, Martin. 1962. *Being and Time*, trs. John Macquarrie and Edward Robison. San Francisco, CA: Harper & Row.
Heidegger, Martin. 1977. *The Question Concerning Technology and Other Essays*, tr. William Lovitt. New York, NY: Harper Perennial.
Heidegger, Martin. 1984a. *Early Greek Thinking: The Dawn of Western Philosophy*, trs. David Farrell Krell and Frank A. Capuzzi. New York, NY: Harper & Row Publishers.
Heidegger, Martin. 1984b. *The Metaphysical Foundations of Logic*, tr. Michael Heim. Bloomington and Indianapolis: Indiana University Press.
Heidegger, Martin. 1991. *Nietzsche*, vols. I–IV, tr. David Farrell Krell. San Francisco, CA: Harper & Row.
Heidegger, Martin. 1993. In ed. David Farrell Krell, *Basic Writings*. New York, NY: HarperCollins Publishers.
Heidegger, Martin. 2000. *Introduction to Metaphysics*, trs. Gregory Fried and Richard Polt. New Haven and London: Yale University Press.
Heidegger, Martin. 2002a. *On Time and Being*, tr. Joan Stambaugh. Chicago, IL and London: University of Chicago Press.
Heidegger, Martin. 2002b. *Identity and Difference*, tr. Joan Stambaugh. Chicago, IL and London: University of Chicago Press.
Heidegger, Martin. 2005. *The Essence of Human Freedom: An Introduction to Philosophy*, tr. Ted Sadler. London: Continuum.
Horner, Robyn. 2001. *Rethinking God as Gift: Marion, Derrida, and the Limits of Phenomenology*. New York, NY: Fordham University Press.
Hyppolite, Jean. 1974. *Genesis and Structure of Hegel's Phenomenology of Spirit*, trs. Samuel Cherniak and John Heckman. Evanston: Northwestern University Press.
Kamuf, Peggy. 2001. Derrida and Gender: The Other Sexual Difference. In ed. Tom Cohen, *Jacques Derrida and the Humanities: A Critical Reader*. Cambridge: Cambridge University Press.
Kockelmans, Joseph J. 1989. *Heidegger's 'Being and Time': The Analytic of Dasein as Fundamental Ontology*. Washington, DC: Center for Advanced Research in Phenomenology and University Press of America.
Krell, David Farrell. 2000. *The Purest of Bastards: Works of Mourning, Art, and Affirmation in the Thought of Jacques Derrida*. Pennsylvania, PA: Pennsylvania State University Press.
Marrati, Paola. 2005. *Genesis and Trace: Derrida Reading Husserl and Heidegger*. Stanford, CA: Stanford University Press.
Mauss, Marcel. 1990. *The Gift: The Form and Reason for Exchange in Archaic Societies*, tr. W.D. Halls. London and New York, NY: Routledge.
Minkkinen, Panu. 1999. *Thinking Without Desire: A First Philosophy of Law*. Oxford: Hart Publishing.
Rawls, John. 1999. *A Theory of Justice. Revised Edition*. Cambridge, MA: Harvard University Press.

Rubenfeld, Jed. 1998. Legitimacy and Interpretation. In ed. Larry Alexander, *Constitutionalism: Philosophical Foundations*. Cambridge: Cambridge University Press, 194–234.

Rubenfeld, Jed. 2001. *Freedom and Time: A Theory of Constitutional Self-Government*. New Haven and London: Yale University Press.

Schuppert, Gunnar Folke. 2003. *Staatswissenschaft*. Baden-Baden: Nomos Verlagsgesellschaft.

Taminiaux, Jacques. 1994. Philosophy of Existence I: Heidegger. In ed. Richard Kearney, *Routledge History of Philosophy Volume VIII: Twentieth-Century Continental Philosophy*. London and New York, NY: Routledge, 38–73.

Sheehan, Thomas. 1998. Heidegger, Martin (1889–1976). In ed. Edward Craig, *Routledge Encyclopedia of Philosophy*. London and New York, NY: Routledge, 307–323.

Van der Walt, Johan. 2005. *Law and Sacrifice: Towards a Post-apartheid Theory of Law*. London and Johannesburg: Birkbeck Law Press and Wits University Press.

Chapter 4
Resources for a Dialectical Legal Semiotics?

Michael Salter

4.1 Introduction

This study discusses the possibilities for developing a model of legal semiotics based upon the distinctly dialectical theories of language, culture and society contained in the writings of Hegel and Theodor Adorno. It builds upon, and contributes to, a growing interest in Hegel's theory of language more generally (Schmit 1961; Lowith 1965; Coltman 1966; Simon 1966; McCumber 1993; Schalow 1993; Bodammer 1969; De Boer 2001; Salter 1992; Surber 2006). For both Hegel and Adorno, it is not possible to develop a theory of culture, social integration and cultural and intellectual development occurring over various transitional stages, without attending to the primary role played by the semiotic dimensions of human experience (Burbidge 1982; Collins 2000; Cook 1973, pp. 28–30; Adorno 2005, p. 141). Hegel argues that law, and every other academic discipline, needs to focus explicitly on the semiotic dimensions that underpin it's own interpretative operations. This is required as a necessary—but typically overlooked—enabling contribution: "signs and language are usually foisted in somewhere as an appendix, without any trouble being taken to display their necessity and systematic place in the economy of intelligence" (Hegel 1971, §458). The routine employment of various signs associated with, for example "law", "legality", "legal procedure" etc. and the relations between them, helps generate, sustain and modify an overall, and collectively shared, interpretative framework. This, in turn, makes it possible to study and formulate distinct ideas about law, including semiotic analysis.

Hegel discussed a number of different features of the operation of linguistic sign systems that a broadly neo-Hegelian semiotics of law could usefully discuss and possibly adapt, and which comprise the subheadings of the present study. These include core semiotics distinctions, the mediating role of signs, and, thirdly, the application of a semiotically-informed methodology of "immanent criticism".

M. Salter (✉)
University of Central Lancashire, Preston, UK
e-mail: msalter@uclan.ac.uk; msalter1@aol.com

A. Wagner, J.M. Broekman (eds.), *Prospects of Legal Semiotics*,
DOI 10.1007/978-90-481-9343-1_4, © Springer Science+Business Media B.V. 2010

4.2 Key Semiotic Distinctions

Hegel anticipated many semiotic distinctions and interpretative relations whose identification writers in this field often attribute to later writers, such as Saussure (Saussure 1983). For both Hegel and Adorno, the process of using signs to signify the topics of our lived experience is essentially (re)interpretative in nature. The quality of interpretation is not an accidental attribute of legal and other signs; it is rather essential to their presence for us. Being actually or potentially interpreted (and hence always re-interpretable otherwise) remains integral to what it essentially means to be a sign. Signs operate in and through the medium of our interpretative work, just as much as our acts of interpretation function largely in and through the medium of systems of signs.

Indeed, these are two sides of the same ongoing cultural process. We interpret signs by saying what they mean for us, with this expression "determining", as distinct from merely registering passively, the ongoing significance of the signified. Such determination is a "performance", an actively carried out (but not necessarily self-conscious) "synthesis": one that is broadly analogous to how a musician "interprets" a song by playing it. Hence, for Adorno: "interpretation is essential to ... language ... to interpret language means to understand language" (Adorno 1956, p. 3).

Hegel recognised the nature and implications of the key semiotic distinction between that which is experienced as a given through immediate intuition, i.e., a referent or signified, and signs themselves. He argued that signs possess a degree of independence from the referent, and that this continues to hold good even during the interpretative act of bestowing a layer of meaning upon it. Within the modern world, words typically operate as comparatively independent, even apparently *arbitrary*, signs expressing ideas and concepts. For example, the meaning of the sign "building contract" is autonomous from, and hence irreducible to, the experience of intuiting the tangible qualities of a sheet of paper interpreted as forming the material nature of this contact. A Hegelian approach to legal semiotics would, therefore, need to differentiate the experience of perceiving a sheet of paper covered with writing and signatures as a tangible object, and the sign "building contract" deployed to make sense of this perceived object.

Hegel's explanation is that the meaning of signs is neither tied to, nor dependent upon, any perception of the tangible qualities of external objects: "in the sign, strictly so-called, the natural attributes of the intuition, and the connotation of which it is a sign, have nothing to do with each other" (Hegel 1975, §458). In other words, as socially and historically contingent assignments of meanings to objects through acts of interpretation, no particular sign can claim to possess, in itself, a logically *necessary* relationship to any specific process of signification. Semiotic analysis cannot explain the latter processes wholly in terms of the former. Hence, a key semiotic issue for Hegelian research is how, that is, on what context-specific basis, does our culture associate, connect and differentiate signs and signified objects? (Hoffmeister 1936, pp. 195–217; Cook 1973, p. 25; Adorno 2005, p. 90)

For Hegel, signs, lived-experience and signified topics are internally related. The referent that is signified by the sign may appear as an entirely cultural entity, such the meaning and implications of a semiotic debate, or as something physical with tangible qualities of mass, weight, chemical composition etc. It may also appear to us as a hybrid of both natural and cultural qualities. The meaningfulness of lived-experience takes shape through a continual unification of the sign's representational role, with the specific contents of pre-linguistic intuitions supplied, for example, by our acts of perceiving a written contract.

Our interpretative acts of using legal signs to signify the meaning, value and implications of an experience of law, brings about a *transformation* of that experience. However, such a transformation only becomes visible upon close semiotic reflection. What then becomes clear is that we transform the intuitive contents of our lived-experience by making sense of it through *the mediation* of those specific categories of legal meaning contained in signs, such as "offer", "acceptance", "counter-offer" and "contractual agreement". These simultaneously direct attention beyond themselves towards the significance of their referent, towards whatever is being signified by them.

Adorno notes that the identity of the ideas expressed by signs lies not, as is the case with music, "in their own nature" but rather: "in a signified outside them" (Adorno 1956, p. 2). Having performed their interpretative work of "mediation" (discussed below), legal signs continue to appear within my act of interpretation. However, they persist only as something superseded, as an enabling condition that, in the absence of semiotic reflection, is not "in focus" as the express topic of interpretation.

Provocatively, the Hegelian tradition resists the fashionable idea that an allegedly arbitrary relationship between signs and what they signify ("the signified") is somehow an inherent and fixed feature of semiotic practice as such. The latter supports the poststructuralists' extreme claim that linguistic signs somehow *fully constitute* the meaning of experience to the point where, for this form of reductionism, there is "nothing outside" the free play of semiotic systems. For Adorno, signs are, in principle, capable of accumulating and preserving aspects of how subjects have experienced the distinctive qualities of objects, situations and contexts. However, this possibility is aborted where a fundamental discrepancy arises historically between our qualitative lived-experience of the meaning of legal topic X, and the signs typically used to signify X. Under such circumstances, the sign will appear to be entirely arbitrary and free-floating. Yet the *explanation* of this disconnection does not lie in conventional semiotic analysis. On the contrary, is requires analysis in terms of the sociology of professional specialisation and social disenchantment, and the official disregard for the implications of lay persons' lived experience of their everyday life.

Adorno argues that where this appears to be the case, it represents a symptom of distinctly negative aspects of current social practice. That is, a distortion of how prevailing language is currently relating to our lived experience involving the domination of the communicative and argumentative dimensions of language over the expressive. Where this occurs, our use of signs has already lost its expressive power by becoming uprooted and alienated from its experiential moorings within the subjectively lived world of everyday culture. Hence, for Adorno, the experience of extreme arbitrariness of the sign/signified relationship is not that of an essential semiotic structure. Instead, it is a symptom of a socially and historically contingent fracture, a deeply problematic form of alienation and estrangement that has become all too characteristic of late modernity.

The "healing of this wound" created by the severing of sign from signified would require the relationship between them to both reflect and express an intelligible order of lived-experience, to appear as an "identity-within-difference" (Adorno 1971). That is, as a *strictly relative and contingent* distinction between internally related levels, where the sign and signified both share an affinity and interact through mutual translation and fulfilment. Adorno indicates that this would be a situation that, under current conditions, more closely resembles a utopian dream than an accurate description of current forms of social existence.

Faced with this historical problem, Hegelian semiotics monitors the situation, prospects and possibilities for resistance within the deployment of sign systems. It thus critically addresses the historical tendency of instrumental forms of linguistic communication to break away from the expressive dimensions of language use. Such instrumental usages flatten out metaphorical and rhetorical moments in which the playful engagement of expressive words with others delights in its own activity as a life-affirming end in itself. Hegel's exploitation of the cognitive implications of evocative word play, puns and both the striking inversions and contradictory implications of words remains especially relevant here. As a form of resistance, such academic analysis must address the self-correction of conceptualisations of signs, which are then made to fold back onto themselves. This reflexive act must, at least at some point, be given priority over the more mundane task of articulating their definite communicative content. Yet, we must always remain conscious of the contradictory, even threatening, implications that may stem from this, particularly in terms of legal semiotics' claimed status as a social science.

How, according to the Hegelian tradition, do legal signs relate to subjective and objective dimensions of discursive practices? Hegel addressed the two-sided operation of signs connecting subjective and objective dimensions of our lived-experience. Through their deployment of signs, individuals are able to overcome problems created by an excessively stark opposition between their subjectivity and the objective elements of their surrounding environment. They can do this by subjectively appropriating for themselves the significance and relevance of this selected aspects of environment. Such appropriations entail assigning a particular cultural meaning (or range of meanings) to these selectively addressed objects. In turn, this meaning transcends the tangible physical qualities of such objects. Physical killing, for instance, can be legally reinterpreted as an instance of a judicially authorized act following a trial that found the defendant guilty of the offence of murder. Hence, through the semiotic contrast between the "crime of murder" and "judicially authorized forms of punishment", members of our society can interpret their experience of two deliberate acts of killing as different in kind. Without the mediation of this semiotic distinction, the trial judge could be interpreted as complicit in murder.

Hegelian semiotics also addresses the difficult issues of the relationship between natural and cultural dimensions of sign usage. The categories of "murder" and "capital punishment", and the semiotic contrast between these signs, clearly articulate the legal significance of a material killing and associated physical transformations in the human body. No one can kill the sign "murder". Hegel also noted that signs do not in themselves possess any material qualities. A sign's significance lacks, for example, qualities of weight, physical mass, chemical composition, limited life-span, vulnerability to physical damage etc. Whilst both the original act of 'murder', as well as the judicially authorised killing of the 'murderer' in the name of justice, remain located in a specific time and place, for Hegel the meanings of these signs do not. Instead, they are comparatively transcendent. This is because they refer equally to all previous and future acts of their specified type (Cook 1973, pp. 30–31).

A Hegelian semiotics also draws attention to the manner in which signs give persons, groups and even entire cultures the capacity to raise their level of expression to an enhanced level. Signs enable expression to rise above those infantile signifiers that are excessively determined by external natural or quasi-natural factors. One example would be where relatively undeveloped verbal signs merely "imitate" the distinctive noises of different animals, such that sheep are signified as "baa baas", or pigs as "oinkers". Such signs lack any significant reference to human purposes and intelligence. Where they predominate, the sign still remains excessively tied to the most obvious materials qualities of the signified. The result is an obvious restriction on the scope for conscious and deliberate adaptation and refinement of signs systems to better meet the changing social and cultural interests and specific needs of citizens (Hegel 1975, p. 459).

By contrast, the incremental enhancement of cultural expression requires the cultivation of signs that are no longer externally determined in this way. These expressions must be transformed so that their significance can be made to articulate whatever it is that the particular society, or sub-culture, in question needs or wants them to express, with the result that members of such collectives can recognise them as a distinctive creation of their way of life. Signs functioning at this enhanced level of "anthropological articulation", which generally requires a written, alphabetical designation, have largely lost accidental qualities of mere imitations, sometime humorous and trivial, of material qualities of external objects. For instance, legal signs, such as "contract", "offer", "agreement", "invitation to treat" and "contractual acceptance", can be devised and have their meanings and practical implications judicially refined and supplemented virtually at will. This is *only because* they are free of any possible moorings to the material qualities of external nature (Hegel 1975, p. 459).

The *meaning* of the sign must thus be recognised as having an ideal, cultural existence. This exists "above and beyond" the spatio-temporal features of the following three strata: that to which it refers, the sign itself and, thirdly, the subjective awareness of the persons who deploy it to make sense of their experiences of legal topics.

For Hegel, the meanings of signs and their ideal subsistence stem from the *signifying activity* of human subjectivity operating in specific cultural and institutional contexts (Cook 1973, p. 31). The results of semiotic analysis make it clear that both material objects employed as signs, and human subjectivity, are essentially two-sided. This means that such objects are experienced as existing both autonomously "in themselves", and as "signs for" particular human subjects. Hence, treating natural physical objects, including court insignia, *as* signs, entails them being interpreted as *other than what they are in themselves*. Signs—as distinct from pre-linguistic symbols—remain wholly dependent for their significance upon cultural proceses of signification taking place during ongoing social interactions.

Hegel further clarifies his interpretation of the nature of signs in terms of the nature/culture distinction by distinguishing them from the role physical symbols play. Here, we can point to those images of physical objects symbolising the authority of the judge, and the state more generally, which often adorn courtrooms. He claims that only *linguistic* signs, in the strict sense of this term, possess a measure of independence from the visible attributes of whatever they signify. Hegel insists that a "sign object" of this kind does not have its full meaning in itself. It lacks a meaning that is relative to purely conventional *linguistic* signs in the strict sense of this term. Although linguistic signs are relatively independent with respect to the signified, in the case of physical symbols, for Hegel: "the original characters (in essence and conception) of the visible object are more or less identical with the import which it bears as symbol" (Hegel 1975, §458).

Hegel's distinction between symbols and linguistic signs possesses important cognitive implications (Magnus 2001). Symbols typically exhibit less cognitive potential and are, in this respect, less developed (Cook 1973, p. 32). By contrast, the intelligence of both speakers and writers is afforded far wider choice and ampler authority in the use of pre-linguistic intuitions whenever signs are treated them as: "designatory (significative) rather than as symbolical" (Hegel 1975, §458). In addition, our acts of communication through the exchange of linguistic signs are less restrained in comparison with what is possible through resort to mere symbols, including pictorial imagery and bodily gestures (Peters 1997). This is because we can deploy a range of different possible linguistic signs to express and nuance the same legal point for example. We are able to select the one that appears most appropriate to both the specific context of this communication, and our underlying cognitive and rhetorical goals for taking part in it (Hegel 1975, §458; Peters 1997). If, for instance, a lawyer wishes to doubt the good faith of a party to a dispute, she can certainly convey this by producing a physical caricature of this party that portrays him as a snake, or as having snake-like attributes such as the proverbial "forked tongue". However, compared with the interpretative range of choices that *linguistic* signs provide to make the same point, and to develop its implications for the dispute in question, such reliance upon symbols tied to the claimed qualities of objects and natural entities, is highly limited and restraining, a mere gesture.

Our routine use of signs both opens up sustains the realm of culture. A Hegelian approach to legal semiotics addresses other aspects of the relationship between natural and cultural aspects of our use of legal signs. It recognises that the exchange of signs during legal negotiations, for example, generates a sense of what may be possible for both parties. In turn, this sense remains independent of the relationship to time and space of any relevant intuitions of physical objects operating as the source and bearer of these ideas.

For instance, where legal negotiations relate to compensation for defective building work that has violated the terms of a prior contract, the spatial and temporal relations of the situation conjured up by this conversation *are not themselves tied to those of physical nature*. Indeed, a distinct cultural significance of time and space becomes superimposed through our reiteration of patterns of sign usage. This holds good even where some of the signs themselves carry with them specific material and physical associations, such as "causation" and "recoverable damage". In this running illustration, the allegedly defective building work has resulted in material damages that are scientifically explicable in terms of the laws of physics. However, our lawyers' resulting exchange of verbal and written statements takes place within a *qualitatively different, and culturally-specific*, realm of ideas, categories and institutional practices. In this realm, human motivations and interests typically predominate over material cause and effects.

Hegel further notes that, in comparison with physical nature, the cultural realm inhabited by legal signs possesses its own distinct temporal and spatial qualities and dimensions. Our experience of signs' original state of being rooted within a specific time and space, their spatio-temporal belonging, becomes transformed through our use of language. In other words, the immediate phase of the sign's presence to us as something simply given as a spoken sound or perception of writing, becomes instantly "superseded" and "sublimated". Hegel notes that this occurs at the very moment that signs perform their interpretative and mediating role: "the peculiar characteristic of existing only as superseded and sublimated" (Hegel 1975, §459). What signs express, that which is said in the act of saying, independently persists even as the experience of the act of expression itself instantaneously disappears (Adorno 2005, p. 90; Hahn 1994). Unlike the situation with musical expression, that which is expressed in language is detachable and takes its place within: "a semiotic system" (Adorno 1956, p. 1). The existence of such verbal articulations, and deliberate acts of keeping silent, remains fleetingly temporal. They appear as fast disappearing events within an ongoing stream of lived-experience: one whose: "existence vanishes in the moment of being" (Hegel 1975, §459).

Hegel gives a certain priority to the spoken word; whilst—for his part—Adorno compares the idiom and intonation of speech to that of musical notes (Adorno 1956, p. 1). Hegel seeks to explain why it is that although the sound of the spoken word disappears almost as soon as it appears, the significance of whatever is being said need not (McCumber 2003). His explanation is that as cultural outcomes, the meaning of signs possess an ideal, cultural quality, which allows them to persist almost indefinitely whenever specific conditions are met.

For Hegel, exchanges of statements between participants within legal culture displace any interpretation of the events referred to that are causally explicable (scientifically or otherwise) in terms of their natural properties alone. Instead, this exchange of linguistic signs effectively *overlays* a level of cultural meaning onto both social actions and natural events. It:

> [N]ow gives its own original ideas a definite existence from itself, treating the intuition (or time and space as filled full) as its own property, deleting the connotation which properly and naturally belongs to it, and conferring on it an other connotation as its soul and import. This sign-creating activity may be distinctively named 'productive' memory ... (Hegel 1975, §458)

In other words, Hegel interprets our use of linguistic signs as an interpretative activity that opens up, perpetuates and revises the significance of the cultural objects to which it refers and their immediate contextual relations of time and space. Even where communications between lawyers uses signs that have a literal physical referent, such as "opening the floodgates", the cultural layer of significance retains its interpretative priority: the meaning of this judicial metaphor is explicable only by those who have already learned that this phrase forms part of the rhetorical vocabulary of common law judges. Both Hegel and Adorno recognise the vital and irreducibly character of such metaphors and other rhetorical device, and the limitations of attempts to prioritise literal interpretations of words (Adorno 1956, p. 1).

A Hegelian semiotics of law confronts the difficult question of the relationship between distinctly cultural dimensions on the one hand, and biological and bodily aspects of linguistic expression, on the other. That is, the ability of our bodies to make sounds and write signs and symbols. Clearly, this capacity remains at least partially grounded in our biological nature. Yet, a Hegelian theory of signs is radically distinct from any biological reductionism or one-sided materialism. Irrespective of their type of their reference, whether this is a natural or cultural object, or even a complex hybrid of the two dimensions, Hegel regarded systems of signs and symbols as rooted in a partial transcendence and sublimation of our purely biological qualities. Such qualities remain preserved as the bodily ability to make sounds expressive of ideas, as: "an institution growing out of its (anthropological) own naturalness. This institution of the natural is the vocal note, where the inward idea manifests itself in adequate utterance" (Hegel 1975, §459).

For Hegel, legal and other signs exist as historical constructs emerging out of, and transforming, natural, or at least quasi-natural, properties of human beings. During acts of signification, the latter are simultaneously overcome (as determinative) and preserved (albeit in a culturally mediated form). This complex relationship between bodily and cultural dimensions is "dialectical": the use of signs remains governed by the prior human need to give an adequate external expression to oneself and to others of what would otherwise remain a purely internal experience. That is to say, it expresses a basic social need for subjective *externalisation* through acts of communication (Peters 1997). In turn, these acts necessitate the overcoming (or "negation") of the form at least of its previously inward state.

According to Adorno, our use of signs to "communicate meanings" draws heavily upon the "language of intentionality", a subset of language more generally. In turn, this indicates: "what it [the signified] means and determines this" (Adorno 1956, p. 3). The language of intentionality is a subset because clearly we can also deal with legal and other signs irrespective of questions of intentionality (Adorno 1956, p. 3). One example would be where law students write down lecture notes without addressing the meaning of what is they are writing, or copy another's lecture notes in the same mechanical way.

Outside of such mechanical deployments, however, linguistic signs can be used expressively as: "a product of intelligence for manifesting its ideas in an external medium" (Hegel 1975, §459). To some extent, such negation of inward form appears as a willed and consciously controlled act of purposeful intelligence, which brings the pre-linguistic phase of our ideas, intuitions and feelings to a more adequate and complete state. Hence, the activities of both keeping silent and speaking can both exhibit and clarify aspects of persons' obscure tactics and strategy for manipulating aspects of their immediate situation. This instrumental aspect is particularly evident during various kinds of legal discourse, such as police interrogations, courtroom statements, cross-examination etc.

For Hegel, the complex relationship of mutual determination that signs exhibit with respect to both nature and culture, also affects the material elements of the spoken word. At one level only, the original sound of the spoken word possesses a common form with that of rain, wind and other naturally occurring noises. However, unlike these, we experience the sounds of spoken words as always already mediated (and hence infiltrated) by aspects of culture. For Hegel, this means that mediating social categories animate these sounds with relations of sense. Adorno agrees, noting that speech appears as: "a temporal sequence of articulated sound which are more than just sounds. They say something, often something human" (Adorno 1956, p. 1). Without assimilating the two, Adorno draws an analogy with "musical gestures" taking shape within our experience of a musician playing a succession of notes. In both situations, the phrasing of sounds, the deployment of exclamation, the rise and fall in volume, tone, punctuation and the use of subordinate phrases, all contribute to the expressive qualities of musical notes and spoken words. In terms of such expressions of meaning, the sounding of an individual name is broadly akin to that role played by a single musical note: "a pure vehicle of expression." Furthermore, the lexical terms of a language are broadly analogous to the tonality of musical expression (Adorno 1956, p. 1).

For human listeners at least (and perhaps also for certain domesticated animals?), the sound of our spoken words does not ever appear as *merely sound* (McCumber 2003). Hegel suggests such animation of sound with sense immediately elevates the experience of the spoken word to a "higher" (in the sense of extra-natural) second level: an "ideational" or "cultural realm", which effectively sublimates the first. Once transposed through acts of interpretation, the spoken words take their "rightful place" as one of a multitude of different cultural constructs, each of which is expressive of humanly invented values, meanings, interests and purposes (Hegel 1975, §459). Hence, sign making involves a potentially intelligent reworking and articulation of the lived-experience of external objects, such that this takes its place within the realm of ideas and beliefs. Relations of human purposefulness and intelligence can thus mediate our deployment of signs in different ways. This is because the original creation and ongoing modification of such signs gives expression to specific human purposes and concerns; whilst their deployment will often also exhibit strategic qualities.

Hegel also identifies a social psychological aspect of our use of signs, which is related to our faculties of cognition. He claims that "sign-creating activity" is rooted in "productive memory", a capacity which: "has always to do with signs only" (Hegel 1975, §458). Our experience of signs, such as the judicial metaphor of "opening the floodgates", triggers and reactivates specific and culturally learned associations with how an earlier understanding of this judicial metaphor has been used. Once we grasp this metaphorical phrase in the way or ways legal culture deems to be appropriate, the later experience of hearing or reading it again can endlessly reactivate the meaning of our initial interpretation of its implications. This potential for reactivation persists even where later judges have altered the connotation of this rhetorical expression by, for example, doubting its appropriateness in certain cases as a resource for legal argumentation. Here, "productive memory" reactivates simultaneously both the "original" and the "modified" connotation together, affording the latter great weight.

The surplus of a legal sign's potentially expressible meanings over those currently articulated is important. It highlights the importance of the distinction between that which deployed signs, treated as clues, can be made to reveal, and that which they currently articulate in an express manner. Because of the expressive force of concepts, semiotic analysis must, according to Adorno, include a repeated interpretative effort and struggle to give voice to things, to bring things to language. This can even involve efforts to "say the unsayable"; that is, to render explicit legal meanings that are currently implicit and unarticulated, or at least only partially expressed within our available discourses (Foster 2006, pp. 16–17).

Adorno's published studies on Hegel distinguish three distinct, and sometimes incompatible, dimensions to the usage of linguistic signs: expressive, argumentative and communicative (Adorno 1973, pp. 105, 137). It is mainly the expressive aspect, the moment of articulating through signs the contextual meaningfulness of our experiences, which makes it possible for us to aim to say what has proved "unsayable" to date.

This expressive dimension also enables semiotic researchers to identify something more in the social use of signs than is typically communicated by their specific content to a third party listener or reader. A "surplus" of this kind nevertheless remains open to semiotic interpretation and analysis. Indeed, it can become possible to identify something "extra" that a particular person is saying but which someone else making the identical statement in the same or similar context, would *not* be expressing. Of course, the ability to identify this surplus aspect will typically presuppose some familiarity with the subjectivity of the speaker or writer in question.

More generally, the additional yet-to-be-grasped aspect is not "bolted on" to the meaning of such use of signs. Instead, it forms part of the fulsome contextual significance of what it is we are putting into words about our lived-experience. It us part of the *content* of the act of signification shaped by, and reacting to, its immediate context(s) (Adorno 1971). For example, the conception articulated by the linguistic expression "right to equal treatment" has multiple connotations. The implications of some of these may well exceed that which the judiciary have, to date, articulated expressly during their interpretation of actual cases of discriminatory treatment. From a Hegelian perspective, the "logos" of a "semio-*logy*" of law stems from its interpretive elucidation and explication in words of what legal concepts mean, a "spelling out" of what language can itself be made to disclose about these ideas (cf. Hegel 1969, p. 27).

In turn, if we are able to successfully recover language's expressive element, this may result in the broadening out of both the horizons and scope of our discourse as legal scholars. It may be possible for semiotics to make a modest constructive contribution to the re-activation of the expressive potential of contemporary patterns of speaking and writing. This contribution is certainly needed given the increasingly deadened, hollowed out and levelled down condition of the meanings of legal and other signs, considered both individually and in their internal connections with one another. However, the more such recuperation is needed, the less likely it is to happen to a sufficient degree to reverse the process of decline. This is because the narrowing down and impoverishment of signs applicable to, and expressive of, the distinctive features of law typically brings with it a corresponding degeneration in the qualities of our cognitive experience of this social practice. Such qualities are precisely what is needed to better articulate the endangered expressive dimensions. One vital task for a Hegelian semiotics is to engage critically with this vicious circle of decline, with the aiming of breaking its power.

4.3 The Mediating Role of Linguistic Signs

It is not possible to outline the fundamental distinctions made by a broadly Hegelian semiotics of law without recognising the mediating role of signs at both individual and collective levels of lived-experience (Cook 1973, pp. 28, 30, 78). Hegel's analysis of *collective* forms of such mediation suggests that its analysis forms a vital task for any viable theory of culture, social integration and cultural and intellectual development. In other words, he challenges such social sciences to attend to the primary mediating role played by semiotic dimensions of human experience, and to grasp the systematic qualities of this (Cook 1973, pp. 28, 30–35). According to Hegel's Jena writings, the specifically cultural dimensions of sign systems are grounded in collective social institutions, customary patterns of life, and belief systems. In turn, these are essentially subject to ongoing historical development shaped by a range of specific human needs, interests and purposes located at different levels. Nor can signs makes sense if considered in isolation from an overarching and collective system of signs and associated cultural and institutional processes (Cook 1973, pp. 30–38).

Hegel's early statements in his Jena lectures addressed the "organic" nature of linguistic categories. He suggested that these function as a pervasive cultural force mediating between the subjectivity of human subjects and their surrounding natural and social worlds. These comments emphasise the essentially historical and constitutive character of such mediation. For Hegel, linguistic mediation of individual experience by forms that are essentially collective in nature means that the categories which "are always on our lips ... are the heart and centre of things" (Hegel 1969, §24, n. 2). Language thus operates as a shared medium that mediates our experience of, for example, all legally significant objects, events and actions, thereby affording them a measure of generality even universality.

Adorno extends Hegel's contributions regarding the collective aspects of semiotic mediation when he notes that no linguistic sign "stands alone" as an unmediated atom. Individuals' usage of signs presupposes, and is enabled by, the structures of a prior linguistic system rooted ultimately in a contingent set of social relations: "Everything becomes what it is in memory and in expectation through its physical contiguity with its neighbour and in mental connection with what is distant from it" (Adorno 1956, p. 5). Relative to the contribution of each act of expression, this "semiotic system" appears as a collective set of connections comprising an ongoing—but pre-established—meaningful totality. This is akin to how members of a cultural tradition possess a primordial relation of "belonging" to an overarching network of relations constituting their own distinctive life-medium.

To a greater or lesser extent, such a "structured totality" consistently imposes its own distinctive principles of organisation upon every component part (Adorno 1956, pp. 1, 5). Each linguistic sign remains essentially mediated by this moving totality of organised and interconnected relations of similarity and contrasts between them, a: "system of mutually dependent meanings" (Adorno 1956, p. 4). To say what, for example, a contract "really is" requires us to distinguish it, and its various elements, from other related but not identical parts. A legally valid contract imposes an essential civil and private law (as distinct from criminal and public law) form of liability; but not all forms of civil liability are contractual. Hence, to provide a fulsome elucidation of the meaning of a single legal sign reveals how it is mediated by other signs and relations of contrast, differentiation and affinity, which are themselves equally mediated (Adorno 1956, p. 4). The familiar processes of comparing, differentiating and contrasting one legal category from another, of comparing the meaning of "murder" to that of "manslaughter" for example, which forms a key aspect of doctrinal analysis, is made possible precisely by such reciprocal mediation(s).

For the Hegelian tradition, semiotic mediation functions as something essentially immanent. Signs do not mediate the objects of legal experience as an independent third party moving back and forth between these objects and our subjective experience of them. Instead, such mediation takes place within the experience of the objects themselves as something always already integral to both these elements. Mediation *is* an integral part of which it is to experience these objects. Furthermore, the condition of being mediated by signs remains an essential part of what it is for the objects of legal experience to attain their cultural intelligibility for us. In this respect, semiotic mediation is both immanent and reciprocal (Adorno 1974, p. 562).

Mediation of legal experience by signs means that the particular qualities of the object form legible surfaces from which general linguistic categories that are materially and uniquely tied to such qualities, take shape contextually. As a result of such mediation, these qualities take shape not as abstract generalities (such as "contracts in general") but as "concrete universals" ("this specific contract for building work"). In turn, this allows the meanings of such concrete universals to be reflected in our experience of the particular qualities of the object of legal experience as part of a unique configuration, with "this specific building contract", for example, arising out of a complex of contextual relations of difference and identify (Foster 2006, pp. 3, 13). Without the semiotic mediation of concrete experiences by general categories, there could be no concrete universals, only meaningless stream of fleeting intuitions. On the other hand, in the absence of the semiotic mediation of general categories by the contents of lived-experience, we would be left with merely abstract general categories (the idea of contracts in general), not concrete universals. The reciprocity of semiotic mediation is thus the precondition for the interpretation production of concrete universals (this specific instance of that particular "type" of legal case such as breach of contract, personal injury claim, etc.), which form the bulk of mundane legal experience.

Indeed, it is important to recognise that our interpretation of cases of such mediation by non-individual signs remain inevitably tied to social and historical contexts that are specific. These are contexts of both the original emergence and subsequent reception of semiotic mediations. Recognition of such contingencies and contextual dependencies by a Hegelian form of semiotic analysis can be useful in helping to "redeem" aspects of the *sheer particularity* of individual instances. In turn, such redemption combats a variety of unwelcome tendencies, particularly those of subsumption, abstraction and reductionism, which will be discussed more fully in the final section of this study (Adorno 1956, p. 2). Such contextual factors are not exterior to the functioning of a system of legal signs. Instead, as mediating dimensions, they are articulated from within this system as part of the very meaning of legal signs. Every judicial articulation of the significance of a specific dispute, its doctrinal meaning contains a claimed validity-for-here-and-now, which may not go beyond the unique facts of the dispute itself. In turn, this context specificity implies that such semiotic meaning can be transferred to other, later disputes if, but only if, some relevant commonality or affinity to a different context can be identified which allegedly justifies this extension.

Such conceptualisation shows how the meaning of legal concepts remains dependent on the functioning of a "living language" within ongoing social practices. It also suggests that our experience of "negative" aspects of such practices, such as unwarranted forms of social exclusion and alienation, can impact upon the use and meaning of signs rendering them impoverished, even brutal.

To date our analysis of the mediation of legal experience by semiotic systems has focused on the collective level. It is now appropriate to counter-balance this by an analysis of how such mediation functions at the level of *individual experience*. A Hegelian semiotics of law highlights the mediating process of contextualisation, or "universalisation", which occurs whenever individual speakers or writers express a particular object of their lived-experience in words (Cook 1973, p. 35). A particular contractual agreement concerning, for example, proposed litigation can appear unique, specific and individual with respect to both the parties, and the agreed terms and conditions. Before actually speaking or writing, I may subjectively believe that I can say precisely what I mean about my own experiences and ideas. Yet, this changes whenever I articulate the immediate experience, or "conception", of these specific features through the mediation of the legal sign "contractual agreement". The latter represents a more general and universal category of common law legal culture (Cook 1973, p. 34).

Here, according to Hegel's approach, our use of language raises and transforms such unique particulars into an instance of a certain "general type". In turn, such usage relocates these particulars to the more general level of a "contractual relationship" embodying the qualities typically ascribed to *all* legally recognised contracts:

> Now language is the work of [rational] thought: and hence all that is expressed in language must be universal. What I only mean or suppose is mine: it belongs to me—this particular individual. But language expresses nothing but universality; and so I cannot say what I [alone] merely *mean* (Hegel 1969, §20).

Consider, for example, a context in which I have to articulate aspects of my contractual dispute with a builder during an interview with a lawyer, during which she asks a series of incisive questions and then records "relevant" part of my answers. During this exchange, she cannot avoid transforming the expression of unique and ineffably subjective aspects of my experience into examples of a generally intelligible "type" of situation. Only then does it become possible for her to connect, and then reduce, the particular qualities of my situation to a range of standard legal opportunities and responses available for "cases of this type". The unique features of this specific and unique contract become available *precisely because* our experience of it remains mediated by the non-specific sign "contracts-in-general", which in turn thereby becomes conceptualized.

Hegel's illustration of this general point concerning mediation is radical and far-reaching in its implications. He deploys the distinction between the immediate experience of being a particular self, and the relation of generality, even comparative universality, which arises whenever anyone uses the word "I" to characterise themselves during their communications (Cook 1973, p. 46). The very expressions that I select and deploy to both identify and communicate "my" internal subjective beliefs and concerns are themselves contextual (i.e., comparatively "universal") in nature. They are "mine" only the qualified sense of not being exclusively mine alone but—insofar as they are intelligible at all—already "ours", those of a specific linguistic community.

Hegel's account refuses to treat the transformation of our pre-linguistic experiences through the mediation of signs, as a corrupting distortion of a supposedly "authentic" level of subjective lived-experience. Instead, he insists that acts of communication bring the meaning of such experience, including the experience of signs, "into its own", with its cognitive value and possibilities raised up and significantly enhanced (Cook 1973, p. 42; Peters 1997). In other words, when expressed through the mediating level of signs, even the most subjective and inward of legally relevant experiences, becomes raised up to a higher cognitive level of generality and relative abstraction. It takes on significance for all those who can understand the concepts of the particular language in which I have expressed these words.

By implication, Hegel qualifies, perhaps even reverses, commonly held individualistic assumptions. These relegate language to a mere tool for a ready-made subjects to expressing their own, and already complete and unmediated, "ideas" and "thoughts". By contrast, a Hegelian semiotics suggests that our very sense of being an individual stems, in part at least, from the mediation of signs we use to define who we are. Such mediating signs are, as already discussed, themselves vital elements of collective institutions and cultural processes (Cook 1973, pp. 34, 77).

For instance, whenever our self-understanding becomes mediated by the word "I", the legal subject appears to itself and others under a double aspect. On the one hand, it appears as pre-linguistic, unique and subjective; whilst on the other, for speakers of the English language at least, this subject exhibits objectively universal qualities. Following Hegel's lead, Adorno also identifies language as a collective mediating factor that counterbalances any writers' extravagant claims to have personally achieved total originality, for example, concerning their thoughts about law and other topics: "As language, culture migrates into the earliest impulses of its consciousness; a mortgage on all talk of originality" (Adorno 2001, p. 116). Adorno goes on to analyse such semiotic mediation in terms of the pervasive operation of concealed ideologies. These initially call for a strictly "internal" form of criticism of a type discussed below in the final section of this study. He thus recognises that comparatively general and abstract linguistic categories mediate the core of individual experience.

On the other hand, Adorno also claims that such mediation can take place in a manner that allows space for the specificity of individual topics to attain expression (Adorno 1956, p. 2). Mediation of our lived-experience by generic signs is not, therefore, necessarily a reductionist form of subsumption, a collapse of difference into sameness, that he criticizes as an instance of "identity-thinking" (discussed below). Indeed, the fact that our interpretation of cases of such mediation by non-individual signs remain inevitably tied to socially and historical specific contexts of both their original emergence and subsequent reading or listening, is important. It can "redeem" their particularity and thereby combat unwelcome reductionism (Adorno 1956, p. 2).

The semiotic dimension of legal experience typically remains implicit, and in need of deliberate and reflective acts of elucidation in order to render it explicit, and thus available for further scholarly analysis. Because of the mediation of everyday consciousness of law by linguistic signs, statements that purport to identify the existence of a "miscarriage of justice", already presupposes the meaning of each of these foundational signs. For Hegel, this remains the case even concerning those signs that are most fundamental for law as an academic subject, such as the precise sense in which we can say that "rights", "justice" and "law" exist. Such categories are "apparently at least, perfectly familiar objects. But things thus familiar are usually the greatest strangers." Within ordinary as well as specialised types of language use, such fundamental categories are rarely made "an object of investigation", even though the signs expressive of their meaning permeate everyday life. Hence, an initial finding of a Hegelian semiotics concerns the reasons justifying its own existence, and the task of uncovering and elucidating the typically implicit and taken for granted relations between the experience of signs, meanings, objects and acts of interpretation. The semiotic mediation of legal experience typically provides an enabling lens through which the objects of such experience take shape, but without the mediating process itself coming into view as a topic in its own right. Hence, although typically taken for granted, Hegel maintains that any number of foundational categories remain: "directly before us, so present that so long as we think, we must, though without express consciousness of it, always carry it with us and always use it. Language is the main depository of these types of thought" (Hegel 1969, §24, n. 2).

Within unreflective forms of legal awareness, acts of interpretation using such signs take place in a manner that typically camouflages this act of presupposing a particular signification. A Hegelian semiotics, by contrast, aims to elucidate and clarify that level of "genuine experience" which everyday language usage renders implicit. For Adorno, it strives to respond to: "the philosophic spur to express the inexpressible". And yet, a Hegelian semiotics must do this without renouncing the effort of sustained conceptualization within a language aware of its own contingency, fallibility and unwelcome mediation by ideologies (Adorno 2001, p. 116).

Within the Hegelian tradition, the covert nature of mediation by cultural signs can exhibit a specifically ideological dimension, whose results must be subjected to critical analysis. Familiar signs make an invisible contribution to the interpretation of legal experience, or at least one that draws attention away from them, towards whatever it is they are referring to (Cook 1973, p. 37). Such camouflaging, in turn, encourages speakers and writers to adopt a "taken for granted"—and potentially ideological—way of dealing with these familiar words and expressions, which the elucidating trajectory of semiotic analysis needs to both address and ideally optimally reverse (Cook 1973, pp. 69–70). Adorno builds upon Hegel here by noting that signs can operate as ideologically powerful and entrenched stereotypes. In turn, the camouflaging operations sustaining such stereotypes actively promote an unreflective and dogmatic acceptance of questionable ideas about law, rights and justice, even—or perhaps particularly—those incapable of withstanding critical scrutiny.

A Hegelian semiotics is thus committed to the idea that the sheer persistence across successive generations of cultural stereotypes embedded in signs, and operating as predictable and congealed formulas, does not confirm their proven validity. Instead, it merely provides evidence of their deepening resistance to change, which prompts an attitude closer to suspicion than uncritical acceptance. For Adorno, in the absence of critiques of ideology, which successful expose their interpretative relativities and assumptions, such mediating stereotypes are "sedimented like a second nature". This occurs whenever they become increasingly hardened, "ossified" and even "fossilised" (Adorno 1956, p. 2).

Recognition of the fact and implications of such mediation of experience by signs requires more than communications that take note and retrace its existence in a descriptive way. For Hegel, such recognition should also prompt semiotic researchers to engage in reflection upon, and thoughtful analysis of, both the contextual operation and significance of such signs (Hegel 1969, §20). The unfolding by semiotic analysis of the mediation of experience by signs involves elucidating the connection and reciprocal illumination of internal elements that interact with each other.

Recognition of the mediation of legal concepts by signs embedded in a network of specific cultural and material relations, and which are reflected in these concepts, ought to immunise legal scholarship from succumbing to the dangers of formalistic analysis. The latter of course detaches concepts, such as "rights", from contextual relations by treating them as isolated and abstract cognitive puzzles. Such puzzles, which may be found in many of the exercises set for law students within black letter forms of legal education, purport to connect "general principles of law" to specific rules and cases, themselves treated as mere repeatable exemplars. By contrast, if we recognise the contextual mediation of legal experience by signs, this allows us to better appreciate how these concepts operate within language as the expression of a complex of specific cultural and social relations. Such concepts thereby attain an expressive force, the capacity when suitably coaxed to disclose more historically accumulated meanings than they currently articulate in conventional patterns of language use. In turn, an appreciation of these forms of expression can help offset the tendency of mainstream legal analysis and scholarship to rest content with formalistic types of doctrinal analysis lacking sensitivity to the explanatory force of historical and social contexts.

4.4 Telling the Truth About Deception? Legal Semiotics as Cognitively Advanced Critical Analysis of Both Naturally Occurring and More Specialist Discourses

Hegel suggested that our ordinary, or "vernacular", language can contain, or at least imply, insights that we ordinarily pass over in silence during everyday discourse. However, such language also often fails to make what are, for his semiotic analysis, vital distinctions. Hence, during mundane and unreflective types of writing and speech, we often use certain signs in a manner that unhelpfully confuses, or conflates, distinct themes and levels in a manner that impedes semiotic analysis. For example, one or more of the follow strata of legal experience are typically conflated in cognitively unhelpful ways: the target of interpretation, subjective acts of interpretation directed towards this target, a system of semiotic signs enabling the meaning(s) of such targets to appear and stand out as such, the subjective orientation of speakers and writers towards these targets containing specific concerns and interests (Adorno 2005, p. 65; Hegel 1975, p. 402).

Hegel argues that despite such conflations, valuable lessons can still be derived from scholars reflecting upon semiotic issues raised by both everyday and more specialist discourses. These issues can then be treated as resources for both cognitive inspiration and substantial "internal" or "immanent" critique (whose nature is discussed below). We have already seen how a dialectical analysis of signs addresses the mediating role of language in the transition from one state of awareness to another. From a Hegelian stance, developing a viable semiotics of law represents a "higher", and more intellectually advanced and reflective, form of legal analysis than mainstream formalistic analysis of legal doctrine unaware of its semiotic preconditions. This is a potential that must, however, be constantly demonstrated anew by the comparative success of concrete semiotic analyses.

According to Adorno, dialectical semiotics positively uncovers and elucidates both primitive and more advanced concepts mediating our sign systems. However, only the more primitive types are analogous to the recurring ciphers' of musical expression (Adorno 1956, p. 1). Semiotic elucidations of the type promoted by a Hegelian semiotics of law depend upon reflective acts of conceptualization. In turn, the results of such acts ought to enhance our linguistic self-consciousness, and thereby raise levels of both individual and cultural self-awareness more generally. This is certainly the case when semiotic analysis is compared to those other approaches to legal research and scholarship, which blithely ignore the linguistic elements and preconditions for both their topics, and their own analytical activity directed towards these. The justification for making this apparently self-promoting claim is that linguistic self-reflection clearly plays a key role in the ongoing refinement of ideas about not only legal semiotics, but also legal thought in general. Linguistic expression remains immanent to the idea of such thought. Furthermore, this dynamic tendency unleashed by semiotic (self)-reflection also fuels the engine for a strictly internal, or "immanent", form of criticism of ideological distortions of our experience of law, which—if successfully applied—also enhances the level of scholarly debates about legal topics. The nature of such critical analysis will be discussed more fully in the final section of this study.

A Hegelian approach to legal semiotics locates itself firmly within the specifically cultural and social sciences. This is because the meaning of our deployment of cultural categories studied by semiotics does not properly belong to the sphere of the objects of natural science research amenable to the materialism of causal-explanatory analysis. Instead, they form part of the realm of human interpretation and social interaction studied by the qualitative social sciences—and given the emphasis Hegelian semiotics places upon historical contextualisation and transformation—possibly also the humanities as well. Studying the meaning of legal signs does not require a methodology of controlled observation of external events. Instead, it depends upon empathetic, reflective participation in, and later critical engagement with, the particular cultural "sub-worlds" of those who use such signs as part of their own interpretative practices. In short, a Hegelian semiotics of law takes its place amongst those interpretative social sciences that deploy qualitative methodologies, albeit in ways that also take account of the findings of empirical forms of historical and cultural analysis more commonly associated with the humanities.

In addition, our approach distances itself from formalistic forms of doctrinal analysis in various ways, some of which have already been mentioned in passing. In particular, the prime methodological question for a Hegelian semiotics is not what is the "essence" of a legally recognized doctrinal distinction between "murder" and "capital punishment". Instead, it asks: "how and under what contextual conditions do specific state authorized interpreters deploy these signs during their ongoing social interactions, to reiterate and modify various semiotic distinctions?"

For Hegel, in this context, meaning is an interpretative outcome of ongoing historically contingent patterns of our use of linguistic signs, a claim that predates and anticipates those of the later Wittgenstein (Lamb 1980). Hence, its study can require ethnographic fieldwork deploying the social scientific (or more specifically "phenomenological"), methods of participant observation. Such methods are diametrically opposed to the type of research which prides itself on never leaving the four corners of law reports and statutes regarded falsely as "primary sources" of legal research and analysis.

4.5 Towards a Semiotically-Informed "Immanent Criticism" of Law

In addition to the largely descriptive approach of phenomenological qualitative social science, a Hegelian semiotics recognizes a need to apply a distinctly critical methodology of "immanent criticism" or—in Hegelian terminology—"determinate negation" (Salter and Shaw 1992; Pearson and Salter 1999). This is founded upon Hegel's contrast of two models for the generation of truthful statements.

In contrast to poststructuralist semiotics, both Hegel and Adorno insist that statements about signs, or any other phenomena, can be true or false in a perfectly workable sense of these terms. For Adorno, "true language" embraces expressions in which: "the content is apparent in it" (Adorno 1956, pp. 2–3). Here, the resulting cognitive—as well as ethical—obligation is to cut through ideological euphemisms by calling things by *their* right names even—or rather especially—where this contradicts pressure from specifically ideological tendencies to name them otherwise by resort to standard rose-tinted euphemisms.

Hegel contrasts a credible dialectical model for making truthful social scientific statements, with the manner in which we typically interpret the sign "truth" during everyday discourse. During the latter, the sign "truth" is typically interpreted as a direct and accurate "correspondence" between our *statements about* things and situations, such as the outcome of litigation, and the "things themselves", e.g., what was actually decided in the case (Reid 2006; Adorno 2005, p. 51). Hegel states that: "In common life truth means the agreement of an object with our conception of it. We thus presuppose an object to which our conception must conform" (Hegel 1969, pp. 51–52). Unfortunately, this "common sense" approach to the sign "truth" presupposes that is both possible and—in the name of objectivity—desirable, to purge language of supposedly purely "subjective" value-judgements. Such a claim presupposes the existence and operation of an essentially "undialectical", that is, non-reciprocal, relationship between the subject and object of knowledge—as if there is no possibility of interactions or mutual dependences between these two dimensions (Harvey 1982; Adorno 2005, p. 51).

However, Hegel recognises that even those who operate with this "correspondence" model of truth continue to use expressions, such as "true friend", "genuine law", "legitimate law-making" etc. These expressions contain a quite different, and often incompatible, interpretation of a sign's meaning that refers to the degree of relative internal consistency between implied ideals stemming from such concepts, and relevant instances of lived-experience of real-life situations. Such norms operate to include and exclude certain actions and outcomes on the basis of specific moral or other normative criteria. In other words, it invites comparison between the meaning of "true friendship" as generally understood as containing a range of normative expectations, and our experience of the actions of someone we take to be our friend. One result of such a comparison could be the conclusion that thus person's actions exhibit genuine friendship in some but not all respects. Hegel thus claims:

> [T]ruth may be described, in general abstract terms, as the agreement of a thought-content with itself. This meaning is quite different ... the deeper and philosophical meaning of truth can be partially traced even in the ordinary usage of language. Thus we speak of a true friend; by which we mean a friend whose manner of conduct accords with the notion of friendship (Hegel 1969, §24n).

According to Hegel, these two models of truth, correspondence and internal consistency, can however, come into conflict. This occurs in contexts where we make statements that, at the descriptive level, are accurate, but which nevertheless fail to articulate the nature of a wholly, or partially, *false state of affairs*. One example could be where the actions of a legal system typically fail to "meet the requirements of the notions" of justice, fairness and respect for equal rights on which depend its claims to democratic legitimacy. Here we can could identify a conflict between the descriptive statements of legal positivism recognising properly enacted state degree as "laws", with the discourse of a more critical natural law approach. The latter could refuse to identify such acts or degrees as laws because of their claimed failure to meet either a contextually appropriate internal or external moral or ethical standard. The model of truthful discourse carried forward by Hegelian immanent critique more closely resembles the natural law position. It too is capable of contrasting legality with legitimacy by deploying a notion of truth that recognises the possibility of making descriptively accurate, yet nevertheless false, statements about law.

For present purposes, semiotic reflection upon ordinary, or "natural", language reveals traces of the typically unreflective acceptance of both these models of truthful statement. This is important because only the second model recognises the problems with any simple polarity between true and false statements by highlighting the pervasiveness of, for example, institutional "falsehood" in the sense of legitimation deficits (Hegel 1969, §24, n. 2). By contrast, the first correspondence model of truthful statements operates in a cognitively deficient and ideologically conservative manner (Adorno 2005, p. 5). It renders such institutional falsehood invisible by reinterpreting purely descriptive statements, which accurately register the factual details of an institutional legitimacy deficit as objectively truthful, precisely because they refuse to identify the deficit itself. An analogy here is with a medical researcher's statement that accurately corresponds to the detailed findings of a medical experiment; but without recognising these as the symptoms of an underlying, and extra-discursive, disease process.

4.6 The Methodological Stages of a Semiotically-Informed Immanent Critique

Hegel's alternative semiotic model of truthful statements and truth more generally, provides the basis for his "methodology" of "immanent criticism". This, in turn, articulates the truth-content of the second model of truth over six "methodological" stages, which themselves may need to be modified when applied to different semiotic fields (Pearson and Salter 1999). Such critique rejects the idea that any extrinsic criteria, even that of clarity of semiotic exposition, should be prescribed in advance of the initial results of concrete semiotic research. The character of the topic itself must instead lead the latter, even where this appears "abstruse" (Adorno 1972, pp. 336–337).

The application of immanent criticism involves two movements. It combines an initial phase of empathy, which is necessary to immerse oneself within, yield to and appropriate the meaning and implications of norms immanent to legal discourse, with later partial estrangement from what is being carried out in the name of these normative signs. This back and forth movement from empathy to estrangement is closer to "tough love" than to sado-masochism.

The latter, specifically critical impulse, stems from a concern that the prevailing condition of a topic of semiotic analysis is confronted by, and brought ever closer to, whatever is required by a rationally compelling articulation of its meaning. However, there still remains an enduring "tenderness" and receptivity towards the immanent norms and the possibility of a potential experience of their more fulsome realisation. The latter is linked to the expressive potential of language to articulate undistorted subjective experience of the significance and implications of legal norms for example. Semiotically-informed immanent critique attempts to optimise the expressive potential. However, this aspect is combined with a negative reaction to experiencing the institutional betrayal of these normative implications in practice, whose articulation in concepts will need to draw upon the communicative and argumentative potentials of language as well.

The remainder of this section will discuss each of the six stages of immanent criticism. The first stage requires the identification and rejection of potential criterion for analysing a legal topic that are not indigenous to this topic itself; but are rather overlaid and superimposed upon it from the outside as it were. For example, immanent criticism needs to reject the neo-Kantian theory of "communicative action" promoted in Habermasian legal theory. The latter seeks to generate generally applicable norms by reflecting upon the supposedly essential preconditions for any form of discursive debate. However, Habermas' universalising procedure remains extrinsic to the specific indigenous norms already in play within the research field. Prior to the results of concrete analysis, such an approach both presupposes and superimposes the very values it is supposed to validate, including those of autonomy and responsibility. It also relies upon questionable conceptual oppositions between, for example, procedural and substantive norms, and the articulation of contextually specific worldviews. In addition, this approach to criticism rests upon the possibility of formulating a supposedly universally applicable, world-governing and purely formal moral standards for critical analysis (Foster 2006, p. 197). From the perspective of immanent criticism, both the standards and the prejudices underpinning these procedural devices, and which are supposed to convince us of their validity, are unacceptably formalistic and abstract. As such, they fundamentally disrespect already existing standards of contextual appropriateness unless—by some chance—these are capable of "passing" its own testing procedures for universal applicability. Such disrespect provides grounds for rejecting the Habermasian approach to developing norms for the critique of semiotic practices.

The fact that Hegelian immanent criticism "lacks" an overarching and preconceived moral theory, functioning allegedly as a "moral foundation" from which one can logically deduce the validity of criteria for critical semiotic analysis, is more of a blessing than a curse. Freeing oneself from the weight of such intellectual baggage and universalising procedures, allows immanent critics to discover criteria that are more adaptable to, and appropriate for, different contexts of application.

The second phase of immanent criticism requires semiotic researchers to take a step back from immersion in a key aspect of ideological closure within language use. Namely, the discursive misrepresentation of reality as if it *already* fully embodied those ideals expressed in its rhetoric of legitimation. In other words, the supply of "descriptions" of existing institutional practices within our constitutional and legal systems as if these already fully embodied and realised their own legitimating ideals of, for example, "equal rights" and the "rule of law". Such would-be "descriptions", which gloss over contradictions between actual practices and relevant legitimating ideals, contain claims to articulate the immediate truth of these institutional practices. However, from Adorno's perspective, they are little more than make believe advertisements for the *status quo*.

Indeed, he argues that such "closure" of the discrepancy between the implications of words and the experiences of things, falsely conflates sign and signified through the assertion of "predicative identity". However this is achieved at the expense of the future potential of both signs and signified. Adorno maintains that reductionism of this kind succeeds only in reversing one of the central achievements of semiotic reflection; namely, the critical potential unleashed by the results of contrasting rhetoric with experiences of real life practices of, for example, law in action:

> What it criticizes in words, its claim to immediate truth, is almost always the ideology of the positive, existing identity of the word and the thing. Even the insistence on the specific word and concept, as the iron gate to be unlocked, is solely a moment of such, though an indispensable one (Adorno 2001, pp. 62–63).

To further develop semiotic forms of immanent critique, it is necessary to progress to a third phase. This reflects upon, and then grasps from the "inside" of everyday exchanges and interactions, how persons (including judges and other lawyers) routinely use words such as "rights", "justice" and "equal treatment", in the vernacular. It is necessary at this stage to identify those pre-existing legal-constitutional norms that have potential for further progressive development. For example, the discourse of our "liberal democratic" legal-constitutional traditions contains signs whose normative expectations relate to universal entitlements to "freedom", "justice" and "equal treatment". The availability and accessibility of such internal ideals, means that there is an alternative to merely superimposing alien criteria drawn, from example, from the critic's own pre-existing beliefs and commitments (Adorno 2005, p. 134).

Well-directed semiotic reflection and analysis needs to uncover from the inside various cognitive and ethical advances, as well as social prejudices and dubious assumptions, that successive generations of lawyers of various kinds have deposited within law's linguistic categories. Both Hegel and Adorno suggest that contemporary linguistic signs are, to some extent, the work of thought about concrete historical experiences, which is itself shaped by an underlying "telos" (potentialities) seeking fulfilment (Adorno 1956, p. 4). The semiotic assumption here, which many will view as questionable, is that words and signs have been adapted pragmatically in the light of historical experience. The process of adaptation has evolved to the point where they now contain the results of an overarching learning process, a tried and tested wisdom awaiting further development.

There is an internal connection between the last two phases of semiotic critique proposed by the Hegelian model. Uncovering the presence of immanent standards that are indigenous provides semiotic critics with evidence that there is an acceptable alternative to reliance upon extrinsic criteria, and the various contradictions that stem from such dependency. The reasons offered for rejecting the superimposition of extrinsic criterion also positively supports the deployment of *strictly immanent* standards of critical assessment.

For example, defenders of flawed institutional practices within our legal and constitutional systems can dismiss as contextually inappropriate all criticisms stemming only from the critics' deployment of pre-conceived extrinsic criteria. The fact that our constitutional practices diverge from expectations projected upon them by anarchists, Marxists and fascists need give defenders of these practices no cause for concern, or any obligation to issue a reasoned defence of this "failure". However, no such blasé response is possible when faced with the results of immanent criticisms based on the application of the very standards that, as rhetoric at least, our constitutional and legal systems rely upon to justify their existence. In short, according to the Hegelian approach to criticism, semiotic researchers must reject as inappropriate criteria that are extrinsic to the rationale and legitimacy of the *status quo*. Such benchmarks must be replaced by indigenous standards, which—precisely because they are immanent—cannot be renounced by defenders of the *status quo*, at least not without undermining the legitimacy of the criticized practice itself, the normative rhetoric or perhaps even both (Pearson and Salter 1999).

In terms of methodology, this phase of immanent criticism requires semiotic critics to adopt a modified version of the research method of participant observation. This requires researchers to acquire the orientation of a relative "insider" who becomes optimally immersed in the discursive and interpretative framework of prevailing patterns of sign usage; and who then acquires fluency in an insider frame of reference within the relevant context. Immanent critics need to both grasp adequately, and then take seriously, the legitimating words and phrases of the *status quo*, including its public law discourses on the "rights of individuals". This remains the case even where such statements appear to be largely rhetorical, and honoured more in their breach than with respect to their observance.

Both Hegel and Adorno recognized the centrality of internal ideas articulated by language as criteria with which to assess those institutional practices that, in order to promote and sustain their perceived legitimacy, purport to embody them (Adorno 2005, p. 134). For example, many generations of lawyers, legal scholars and political activists have reworked and refined the discourses of law through their cognitive work and purposeful activities of various kinds. Such discourse, therefore, can both embody and preserve many of these contributions and insights, including a series of normative expectations with critical implications for the *status quo*. A collective intelligence continues to be invested not only in specific texts and speech, but also in the form and structure of legal and constitutional language, its categories and distinctions.

Even though later stages of immanent criticism recognize that such "naturally occurring" usage of signs cannot be accepted uncritically, during this early phase critics recognize that it may contain buried normative resources that merit exploitation by semiotic analysis. The aim is to obtain and refine viable internal criteria for critical semiotic analysis by reflecting upon this currently underdeveloped resource of accumulated human learning and received intelligence (Adorno 2005, p. 65).

This goal cannot, however, be secured if critics either rely upon scientifically reworked versions of discourse or themselves translate naturally occurring patterns of sign usage into logical-scientific terminology. Such terminology reflects a commitment to a model of objectivity that typically blunts, or even neutralises, the critical implications of signs, even those associated with human rights. Instead, Adorno notes the requirement is to ascertain: "how language uses the word outside of logic" (Adorno 2001, p. 153, cf. 1956, p. 4).

Following Hegel's lead, Adorno insists that, in such naturally occurring contexts, aptly selected names both contain, and then resonate with, a surplus of unrealised but potentially realisable possibilities over and against whatever topic they currently signify (Adorno 2005, p. 134). Such informal usages contain "negative signs", that overshoot the current ideology and achievements of the status quo (Adorno 2005, p. 51). Potentially, these signs provide vital criteria for a strictly internal form of institutional and social criticism. These normative implications: "live in the hollows between what the things claim to be, and what they are" (Adorno 2001, p. 153). One aim of this phase of immanent criticism is to identify those signs and patterns of semiotic usage that articulate a normative surplus of currently unfulfilled possibilities, and which are therefore capable of providing strictly internal criteria: "No concept could be thought, indeed none would even be possible without the 'more,' which makes language into language. ... that everything would be more than it is ..." (Adorno 2001, pp. 111–112)

Once researchers have identified signs suggestive of potentially applicable norms, they need to subject both their meaning and implications to a process of close descriptive elucidation that spells out their content. Such careful analysis and stringent linguistic exposition of normative implications, transcends the unreflective manner in which these signs are typically used during everyday life (Adorno 2005, p. 51). Critics need to engage in such subsequent interpretative (or "hermeneutical") analysis because the normative achievements embodied in traditional legal and constitutional signs can remain buried, ideologically neutralised and suppressed.

Indeed, Hegel insisted throughout his writings that the customary connotations and all-too familiar usages of our ordinary native language exhibit various negative features. Such usages all too often work to enmesh, implicitly channel and restrict the incisiveness and depth of our thinking; and do so in ways that are essentially contingent and relatively arbitrary (Hoffmeister 1936, pp. 50, 127). For instance, words such as "law", "equal rights" and "justice" have become so familiar that their everyday usage has turned generally indeterminate, vague and imprecise. This process needs to be reversed before such signs could ever be made serviceable for the task of a semiotically informed immanent criticism. Counteracting this tendency requires the elevation of these signs from their currently underdeveloped condition to an optimally precise, stringent and clearly articulated state. A suitably stringent reinterpretation of these signs could, in principle, reawaken previously suppressed normative expectations.

The practical application of this third phase of immanent critique can be both time-consuming and cognitively demanding. The very process of seeking to rationally articulate from the inside our experience of the meaning and implications of such normatively significant signs may, over time, allow us to grasp new shades and nuances of meaning. In turn, this can bring about a transformation in the critic's conception of both these implications and the norms themselves.

The explanation for this is that the very practice of empathetic appreciation of the normative potential of, for instance, legal and constitutional signs remains a skill that is difficult to acquire. It is an interpretative ability that matures and becomes increasingly subtle only through repeated practice and refinement. It is likely, therefore, that later recollection of the results of one's first attempt at immanent criticism will appear embarrassingly crude and inept. With the benefit of hindsight, these earlier attempts were able to articulate and rely upon only the most readily apparent and obvious of a sign's normative implications, and overlooked more subtle shades of meaning, implications and connections that only slowly became evident during subsequent elucidations. It follows that as an extended project, this pivotal phase of immanent criticism will prove self-correcting over time, with important "knock on" consequences for later stages and the concrete results.

The *fourth* stage of immanent criticism requires semiotic researchers to construct a "counter-factual" and ideal-type model of how legal and constitutional institutions ought to operate "in principle". This analytical model sets out a positive vision of how such institutions would need to function before we could conclude with good reasons that the results of their policies and actions have brought their own internal justifying ideals to complete fruition. This counter-factual and hypothetical stage seeks to overcome the temptation towards cynicism that renounces any expectation that institutional practices will, in practice, ever seek to realize their legitimating norms. It further elucidates the implications of immanent norms identified, and the measure of sheer hope for a reformed social practice these express (Adorno 2005,

p. 51). Here, we could focus on the normative implications of legal expressions relevant, in principle, to the rights to poor persons to "equal treatment"—including their right not to experience "discrimination" on grounds of their economic disadvantage. This could be achieved by critics spelling ought how they should be treated by relevant institutions aiming to fully comply with the latter's own justificatory rhetoric.

This phase clearly draws upon the *imagination* of semiotic researchers to project a hypothetical context of complete compliance. However, the actual construction of this counter-factual model still remains guided by the objective trajectory of possibilities projecting beyond the prevailing *status quo*, which work completed during the previous phase of immanent criticism has already identified and faithfully elucidated (Adorno 2005, p. 65). The normative ideas embodied in these vernacular words still manage to radiate from within a degree of "utopian" hope, which immunizes immanent criticism from complete negativity and cheap cynicism. In creating an analytical model and vision, semiotic researchers need to follow the lines of this projected trajectory beyond the *status quo*. What is projected by liberal norms of "individual freedom", "justice" and "equal rights" may, for example, be a vision of a freer and more diverse form of social life. The latter may be unaffected by compulsive or other forms of coerced and manipulated actions that diminish liberal values of autonomy and self-determination.

The process of formulating the most apt and stringent possible expressions to characterize the nature and implications of discourses of "equal rights", for example, can itself highlight problems within our existing interpretations and analysis, their relative failures to attain sufficient *affinity* with the signified (Adorno 2005, pp. 51, 90). For Adorno, uncritical and lax articulations of the implications of legal norms betray cognitive, as well as expressive, weaknesses: "Through expression, stringency is compelled from what is expressed" (Adorno 2001, pp. 29–30). Hence, the very process of elucidating the normative implications of conventional legal and constitutional signs in an optimally stringent manner can, in itself, exert a developmental impact upon these norms, something whose implications are discussed below.

The fifth stage of immanent criticism represents a major change of focus. It reverts from hypothetical projections reliant upon controlled acts of imagination, to a strictly empirical type of socio-legal analysis. Semiotic forms of immanent criticism now come more fully into their own element by contrasting the results of the fourth stage, with detailed social scientific evidence of the results of actual institutional practices. The aim here, sometimes aptly expressed in the rhetorical form of irony, is to identify evidence of *discrepancies* between the practical implications of internal standards contained in already elucidated linguistic signs, and citizens' pertinent lived experiences of events and actions (Adorno 2005, p. 134). Here, the vital question becomes: "to what extent has there been a failure, in whole or part, to fully honour these norms in practice?" In other words, Hegel's dialectical method of immanent criticism identifies and emphasises evidence of contradictions between the implications of normative language deployed to legitimate specific legal and constitutional practices, and the words those with firsthand experiences of their practical effects are using to aptly describe these practices. Here, we can focus, for example, on the normative implications of the institutional denial in practice of normative implications of legal expressions relevant to the supposedly "universal" rights of all citizens to "equal treatment" and "freedom from discrimination". Such critical analysis could investigate the extent to which the very institutions and "free market" mechanisms of liberal society have resulted in the abridgement and selective enforcement of distinctly liberal rights in general, and rights to "equal treatment" in particular. In addition, it may even be possible to identify discrepancies between the promise of "freedom of expression" and the hidden restraints on the use of signs even within conversations imposed ideologically by conformist formulae (Adorno 2005, p. 90).

From a Hegelian perspective, any substantial evidence of the complete or partial betrayal of legal and constitutional norms by our existing institutional and social arrangements tends, in practice, to render them abstract, even imaginary and counter-productive. At this stage criticism fans outs in two directions: firstly, towards both misrepresentations of institutional realities as if they had already fully realised normative promises contained in their legitimating rhetoric; and, secondly towards the results of inadequate institutional practices themselves.

Adorno provides some examples of the first direction of criticism. He argues that to misrepresent an institutional arrangement and context *as if* it has already achieved immanent ideals, when—as a matter of empirically ascertainable reality—it clearly has not, is especially problematic. It leads to a particularly damaging and even counterproductive form of ideological distortion and inversion of the real state of affairs:

> Freedom is solely to be grasped in determinate negation, in accordance with the concrete form of unfreedom. Positively it becomes an "as if." ... If freedom is posited as positive, as something given or unavoidable in the midst of what is given, then it immediately turns into unfreedom (Adorno 2001, p. 230).

He illustrates this point by reference to how the discourse of the criminal justice system operates with a hangman's metaphysics: one that consistently and dogmatically ascribes a purely abstract form of freedom to criminal defendants: "regardless of empirical conditions". This one-sided ascription of freedom is carried out to legitimate unlimited accountability, which in turn is needed to provide a questionable justification for: "the necessity of harsh punishment ... The social emphasis on freedom as something existent coalesces with undiminished oppression" (Adorno 2001, p. 231). For Adorno, affirmations of individual freedom (and related liberal ideas of autonomy, fulsome legal accountability etc.) found within the discourses of law, liberal constitutional doctrines and culture more generally, merely *simulate* something that the core material aspects and processes of society betray in practice (Adorno 2001, p. 281). The illusion of legitimacy degenerates into ideologically concealed mockery.

The *sixth* and, in one heavily qualified sense, "final" stage of a semiotically-informed immanent criticism, involves the open-ended task of both proposing and revising trajectories for institutional reform and incremental social transformation.

These proposals represent the logical culmination of the overall transitions traversed during the previous five methodological stages, and give a sense of coherence, purpose and rationale to each of them. We cannot, of course, prescribe in advance the precise content of proposals for change. Nevertheless, it still remains possible to outline their general form. They will set out in a detailed manner how current institutional practices will need to change to resolve the previously identified discrepancies and contradictions between normative promise and empirical delivery. These proposals will identify which aspects of institutional practice need to change, perhaps over a series of stages and subject to various extrinsic imperatives, so that the vision of total compliance, articulated during stage four, will no longer be dishonoured in whole or part. In other words, immanent criticism identifies those features of the *status quo* that must change because, in practice, they operate in ways that violate and betray the practical implications of their own normative standards. It may become clear that such discrepancies both stem from, and can be explained by reference to, underlying material contradictions located at the level of "social structures". If so, then immanent criticism is bound to advocate structural, as well as purely institutional and legal, reforms.

The practice of immanent criticism at this stage strives to remain optimally objective, albeit in a qualified and distinctive sense of this term. Critics should advocate only those suggestions for change that they have shown to be strictly required to meet the imperatives of the normative vision already faithfully set out. For example, if the discursive norms themselves have been shown to possess "liberalising" implications, then even a critic who is personally opposed to liberalism must still respect these as objectively demonstrated, if subjectively unwelcome. Obviously, the same point regarding qualified objectivity applies if these implications are subjective unwelcome by the researcher because of their authoritarian or socialist qualities.

Adorno maintains that the immanent vision projected by our own comparatively liberal constitutional and legal norms, and developed through immanent criticism as the basis for institutional reform proposals, will probably appear as utopian. That is, for an ideal state of affairs that has finally overcome not only all manner of unreflective conformities, but also the consequences of the contradictions between the promise of legal and constitutional ideals on the one hand, and the reality of contemporary institutional practices on the other. The specifically semiotic dimension of this vision includes the utopian hope for the fulsome practical institutionalization of an alternative, more humanistic and expressive use of signs: one which both articulates and respects the affinities between human beings and things: "a togetherness of what is divergent" (Adorno 2001, p. 153). This includes an aspiration that the relevant institutional activity will finally realize what, for ideological reasons, its deceptive rhetoric holds itself out as already embodying.

One semiotic dimension of such ideological rhetoric remains deeply embedded in the subject-predicate relationship of language; it falsely posits an identity between these two elements. For example, it projects the idea that legal phenomena are nothing other than how they currently appear because the existing predicates fully exhaust the possibilities of the subject. Here, the subject is portrayed as that which its cluster of given predicates suggest; and researchers must simply recognise that this positive state of affairs expresses the final truth of its existence. Such rhetoric is unacceptably ideological because, like all varieties of positivism, it disregards evidence of existing tensions within the subject between realised potentialities and as yet unrealized possibilities for future change. Indeed, for Adorno, such hope: "is contradictorily tied to that which breaks through the predicative identity" (Adorno 2001, p. 153).

In other words, the ultimate goal of proposals for change supported by a semiotically informed type of immanent criticism is that the target of critique will, in practice, be transformed to fully meet the standards that, via the mediation of signs, are already applicable in principle. Sustaining this utopian aspiration based on a vision of transcendence from within, entails a rejection of ideological aspects of current semiotic practices, particularly those which are founded on subject-predicate identity.

In short, the proposals for institutional reform and social change that make up the culminating phase of immanent criticism build upon earlier methodological stages by following up upon the practical implications of possibilities already projected by unrealized "negative signs". They spell out in detail what is now required to realize the positive implications of such signs in terms of a hope for a reformed life-context.

The proposals must be clearly seen to be not only objective but also politically relevant. If, but only if, it becomes clear that basic discrepancies exist that are currently being ideologically glossed over and suppressed, then the final stages of immanent criticism must now—for the first time—take on a decidedly *partisan quality*. Insofar as our cognition of, for example, legal signs has not already become entirely colonized and instrumentalised by dominant ideologies, it: "wishes that which one has been already drilled to renounce, and what the names which are too close ... obscure" (Adorno 2005, p. 51) In other words, a critical form of legal semiotics has no option but to participate in acts of the resistance to linguistic practices of ideological closure and related stereotypical and clichéd usages of signs. Yet, such participation also involves an element of intended subversion of purely instrumental deployments of signs. This is particularly the case for those deployments that force-fit preconceived qualities upon our experiences of legal topics so as to dominate them. A stance of immanent criticism, by contrast, includes a willingness to revise our use of signs so as to better articulate the emerging qualities of such topics, which might otherwise remain buried.

Immanent critique is carried out not in the name of any political counter-ideology but that of a highly qualified form of scientific enlightenment: one that is especially aware of its own inevitable ideological complicities and cognitive fallibilities. And yet such critique must also resist the temptation to posit a fixed goal and terminus for legal and related institutional reforms and social transformations. On the contrary, Adorno recognizes that the very act of engaging in successful immanent criticism, which includes the linguistic articulation of its results, can motivate a reinterpretation, and possibly even an extension, of the underlying normative criteria previous elucidated: one that could, in turn, widen the depth and scope of the critique itself. It is thereby possible, at least in principle and in broad outline, to identify additional phases of immanent criticism where the original normative implications of "negative signs" undergo a process of renewal and transformation driven by semiotic factors.

It may well, for instance, prove to be the case that the stringent expression and repeated redrafting of the implications of identified norms can contribute to their further creative development. The moment of objectifying those features that require a transformation of given legal categories, such as traditional definitions of "legal rights", obviously takes place by means of linguistic expressions, which can also be reformulated to become more stringent and adequate to the qualities of the topic itself. By seeking to express, for example, a viable interpretation of the meaning, scope and purpose of legal rights, which as far as possible generates a sustainable affinity between the relevant signs and signifiers, we can also discover the partial *inadequacy* of traditional expressions of such rights. Any such reconsideration of the meaning and scope of legitimating norms expressed by signs will, of course, add a further twist to the spiraling movement of immanent criticism, which may then have to reactivate the movement through stages three to six.

For example, insofar as a society makes substantive progress towards the realization of liberal constitutional and legal goals of "freedom", "justice" and "equal treatment" under the "rule of law", then the implications of expressions of these internal ideals could become reinterpreted more broadly within this revised context of application. It is possible to speculate that the supplementation of classical liberal notions of constitutional rights, so-called "first generation" human rights, with "second generation" social and economic rights illustrates of this process. Once civil and political rights were articulated linguistically not as exhaustive specifications of rights *per se* but as one "generation" of rights, the expression "generation" opened up the prospect of successive models of a different type. In turn, this pointed to the potential existence of rights yet to be realised and located beyond those conceivable within liberalism's restrictive framework of purely "negative rights" against the state, that is, socio-economic rights positively requiring welfare state interventions.

Hence, the partial realization of the normative implications of existing signs can operate as merely one initial and underdeveloped phase of a wider ongoing and open-ended process. Within the resulting reformed context, the implications of these norms may well inspire a new generation of critics to prompt their reinterpretation and further extension. This, in turn, could project additional proposals for reform and change to better fulfill these revised normative implications. Here, Adorno recognises: "an odyssey of unending mediation to bring the impossible back home" (Adorno 1956, p. 4).

The disclosure through immanent criticism that current social and institutional practices betray their own stated ideals, at least in part, is distinct from claims that the ideals themselves have failed us. And yet there remains a demand that arises within our experience of law's normative expressions, which moves critics to compare what they are currently able to express to that surplus of the signified's unfulfilled sense, which is still striving to be articulated.

According to Adorno's model of semiotics, there exists an impulse supported by an underlying "kinetic force", to open up society's legitimating signs to the meanings of those lived-experiences to which they have yet to fully adapt or articulate sufficiently; and about which they are currently at least partly mute. Part of this impulse is to try to coax these normative signs into remedying such comparative deficiencies by upgrading their expressive power (Adorno 1973, pp. 25–26). In that sense alone, is it fair to say that later stages of immanent criticism turn back upon the legitimating ideals this approach previously accepted as fully valid criteria for an immanently critical form of semiotic analysis. It then proves necessary to subject these ideas to a critical re-assessment in terms of how they figure within the lived-experience of the sign/signified relationship, in terms of how much progress they still have to make towards finally closing the gap between what they currently say, and that which they signify.

Hence, later stages of such criticism, which only painfully graduate to reflective self-criticism, must shake free of the attitude of deference to immanent norms and ideals. Here, critics must seek out and critically analyse experiential evidence of the latter's limitations and internal contradictions, which are also those of immanent critics themselves. Yet whilst grappling with these, we can still experience instructive failures, especially when trying to use signs to fully grasp a legal topic. One lesson from such failures is explicable by the insight that our signs remain at least indirectly tied to social experience and its current restrictions under contemporary historical conditions, limitations which themselves strive to become articulated in signs. Indeed, it becomes possible for new illuminations to arise concerning the relationship of mediation between our lived-experience, the role played by cultural signs, and how each of these point beyond themselves towards the signified object of experience.

Semioticians can even self-critically reconsider the assumptions underpinning how they have habitually used language to express concepts; and develop new ways of articulating the mediation of these concepts by signs that would otherwise be obscured. Such a reappraisal would help break through the illusion that the subjectivity of semiotic researchers merely passively registers from the outside the empirical facts of sign usage before their scientific gaze. As an embodied instance of what it studies, the consciousness of the semiotician remains "this side", and is both internal to, and dependent upon, ongoing historical processes of cultural signification. The contrary assumption of the free-floating objectivity and neutrality of a type of semiotic analysis that superimposes classificatory schemes from the outside, now appears merely a symptomatic reflection of ideological abstraction, which itself merits immanent critique.

At first sight, there may appear to a logical problem with claiming against prevailing ideological closures, that we have experienced the failure of language to adequately capture and express our lived-experience of law. However, in practice, this does not prevent the completion of immanent criticism. It is no more impossible than any other situation where we find that, despite possessing a reasonable broadly vocabulary, we currently lack adequate words to articulate the nature of something we want to communicate, and that others can, through their words, show that they too have had a similar experience. Later stages of immanent criticism seek to give voice to this experience, to disclose the existence of an excess, or surplus, of meaning over what our existing discursive frameworks are able to communicate, even when—of course—the content of that surplus can only be alluded to, not itself immediately "spelled out" expressly. This indicates the distance still to be travelled before it would be possible to claim that signs and signified have finally achieved a coherent relationship, before the articulation of our experience of legitimating legal norms could no longer reasonably be that of a concealed mockery.

The Hegelian tradition thus implies at least that there is something purposeful about our concepts and categories: something that resists simply accepting a deficient expression of lived-experience and, in fact, is positively striving for its adequate articulation and specification in practice. Immanent criticism of both specialist and ordinary language use contains, within itself, the goal of rescuing the particular and distinctive features of our lived-experience of, for example, legal signs, which ideological practices of classification and "identity thinking" either ignore or marginalize.

One goal of immanent criticism of coercive identification is "thinking in constellations". This requires researchers to allow qualitative concepts relevant, for example, to the denial of particular rights to poor person, such as "equal treatment", "justice" and "equal rights", to enter: "into a constellation. These illuminate the specifics of the object. . . . The model for this is the conduct of language" (Adorno 2001, p. 164). In this context, Adorno distinguishes "language" from a "mere sign-system for cognitive functions".

4.7 Conclusion

The goal of critical analysis is to fully articulate the sense in which existing social mechanisms are still betraying promises internal to their own concepts. This takes place by spelling out relevant aspects of these at least partially broken promises as something that is central to the interpretation of the topic itself (Adorno 2001, p. 164). Following Hegel's lead, Adorno has further developed a specifically semiotic model of immanent criticism relevant to legal analysis. This involves a series of stages starting with the rejection of criteria for critical assessment that are not indigenous to the topic in question. Next, critics need to distance themselves, as far as possible, from the grip and closure devices of prevailing ideologies which misrepresent legal topics as if they already full embodied legitimating norms. The third stage involves identifying relevant internal norms expressed in discourses that our society officially endorses. The next phase requires critical semiotic research to develop from within an analysis of the practical implications of these norms, a vision of how the status quo would need to operate before we could reasonably conclude that their key legitimating norms have been fully realised in practice.

The fifth methodological stage investigates evidence of *discrepancies* between these normative implications and the record of accomplishment of institutions responsible for the realisation of these legally relevant norms in practice. The next stage of semiotically-informed immanent criticism entails critics identifying those aspects of the *status quo* that need to be changed to remove, or at least minimise, discrepancies between ideological rhetoric of justification, and the practical outcomes of their institutional practices. However, this phase cannot be regarded as necessarily final because the very process of subjecting internal legal ideals to a process of elucidation and semiotic analysis can itself further develop their implications in a photographic sense of this term, which, in turn, adds a fresh twist and dynamic to this spiralling process, in effect a secondary re-running of at least stages 3–6 of immanent critique.

The present study has only the scratched the surface of the potential richness of a Hegelian semiotics of law. For reasons only of space, I have omitted many other equally vital themes of this approach. These include: the process of individuals acquiring and, with others, refining sign systems as a form of socialisation, and semiotic issues of, for example, "stringency" and the "speculative sentence", relevant to the very language appropriate for the articulations of dialectical semiotics itself (Smith 1974; Surber 1975; Nancy 2001; Lau 2006; Nuzzo 2006). Additional questions that this study could have addressed include the relationships between literal and non-literal, and between rhetorical and metaphorical, usages of legal signs (Smith 1994), and the complex relationship of relative priorities of spoken, as opposed to written signs. The latter is a theme crassly misinterpreted and distorted by Derrida's and related poststructuralist critiques of Hegelian semiology (Derrida 1976; 1982; Smith 1987; Burns 1989; Brockmeier 1990; Burns 2000; McCumber 2003; Stähler 2003).

References

Adorno, T. W. 1956. *Quasi una Fantasia, Essays on Modern Music*, tr. Rodney Livingstone. London: Verso.

Adorno, T. W. 1971. Die Actualitat der Philosophie. In *Die Frühschrifen*. Frankfurt am Main: Suhrkamp.

Adorno, T. W. 1973. Thesen über die Sprache des Philosophen. In *Die Frühschrifen*. Frankfurt am Main: Suhrkamp.

Adorno, T. W. 1974. Henkel, Krug und frühe Erfhrung. In *Noten zue Literatur*. Frankfurt am Main: Suhrkamp.

Adorno, T. W. Negative Dialectics, 2001 revised English translation by Dennis Redmond at: http://www.efn.org/~dredmond/MM3.html

Adorno, T. W. *Minima Moralia*, 2005 revised English translation by Dennis Redmond at: http://www.efn.org/~dredmond/MM3.html

Adorno, Theodor W. and Horkheimer, Max. 1972. *Dialectic of Enlightenment*. London: Verso.

Bodammer, T. 1969. *Hegels Deutung der Sprache*. Hamburg: Felix Meiner.

Brockmeier, J. 1990. Language, Thought and Writing: Hegel After Deconstruction and the Linguistic Turn. *Bulletin of the Hegel Society of Great Britain*, 21–22, 30–54.

Burbidge, J. 1982. Language and Recognition. In ed. M. Westphal, *Method and Speculation in Hegel's Phenomenology* Atlantic Highlands, NJ: Humanities, 85–94.

Burns, T. 1989. Hegel, Derrida, and the Sign. In ed. H. Silverman *Derrida and Deconstruction*. New York, NY: Routledge, 77–91.
Burns, T. 2000. The Purloined Hegel: Semiology in the Thought of Saussure and Derrida. *History of the Human Sciences*, 13(4), 1–24.
Collins, A. B. 2000. Hegel on Language, Citizenship, and the Educational Function of the Workplace: The Marxist Challenge. *Owl of Minerva*, 32(1), 21–43.
Coltman, K. 1966. Gadamer, Hegel and The Middle of Language. *Philosophy Today*, 40, 151–159.
Cook, D.J.1973. *Language in the Philosophy of Hegel*, NY:Den Haag.
De Boer, K. 2001. The Infinite Movement of Self-Conception and Its Inconceivable Finitude: Hegel on Logos and Language. *Dialogue*, 40, 75–97.
Derrida, J. 1976. *Of Grammatology*, tr. G. Spivak. Baltimore, MD: Johns Hopkins.
Derrida, J. 1982. The Pit and Pyramid: Introduction to Hegel's Semiology. In *Margins of Philosophy*, tr. Alan Bass. Chicago, IL: University of Chicago Press, 69–108.
Foster, S. 2006. *Adorno: The Recovery of Experience*. New York, NY: SUNY Press.
Hahn, S. 1994. Hegel on Saying and Showing. *Journal of Value Inquiry*, 28(2), 151–168.
Harvey, I. 1982. The Linguistic Basis of Truth for Hegel. *Man and World* 15, 285–297.
Hegel, G. W. F. 1969. In ed. Werke. *Science of Logic*, tr. A. V. Miller. New York, NY: Humanity Press.
Hegel, G. W. F. 1975. In ed. Werke. *Hegel's Philosophy of Mind*, tr. W. Wallace. New York, NY and Oxford: Clarendon Press.
Hoffmeister, J., ed. 1936. *Dokumente zu Hegels Entwicklung*. Stuttgart: From-mann, reissued, 1974.
Lamb, D. 1980. *Language and Perception in Hegel and Wittgenstein*. New York, NY: St. Martin's.
Lau, C. F. 2006. Language and Metaphysics: The Dialectics of Hegel's Speculative Proposition. In ed. J. O. Surber, *Hegel and language*. Albany, NY: SUNY, 55–74.
Löwith, K. 1965. Hegel und die Sprache. *Die neue Rundschau*, 76, 278–297.
Magnus, K. D. 2001. *Hegel and the Symbolic Mediation of Spirit*. New York, NY: SUNY.
McCumber, J. 1993. *The Company of Words: Hegel, Language, and Systematic Philosophy*. Evanston, IL: Northwestern.
McCumber, J. 2003. A Question of Origin: Hegel's Privileging of Spoken over Written Language. *Bulletin of Hegel of Great Britain*, 47/48, 50–60.
Nancy, J. L. 2001. *The Speculative Remark*, tr. C. Suprenant. Stanford, IL: Stanford University.
Nuzzo, A. 2006. The Language of Hegel's Speculative Philosophy. In ed. J. O. Surber, *Hegel and Language*. Albany, NY: SUNY, 75–91.
Pearson, G., and Salter, M. 1999. Getting Public Law Back into a Critical Condition: The Rule of Law as a Source for Immanent Critique. *Journal of Social and Legal Studies*, 8(4), 483–508.
Peters, J. D. 1997. The Root of Humanity: Hegel on Communication and Language. In eds. D. Klemm and G. Zöller, *Figuring the Self: Subject, Absolute and Others in Classical German Philosophy*. Albany, NY: SUNY, 227–244.
Reid, J. 2006. Objective Language and Scientific Truth in Hegel. In ed. J. O. Surber, *Hegel and Language*. Albany, NY: SUNY, 95–110.
Salter, Michael. 1992. Laws of Language in Hegel's Semiology. *International Journal of Law and Semiotics*, 5(14), 165–180.
Salter, M., and Shaw, J. 1992. Towards a Critical Theory of Constitutional Law: Hegel's Contribution. In ed. Michael Salter, *Hegel and Law*. Aldershot: Ashgate, 90–120.
Salter, M., Shaw, J.J.A. 1994.Towards a Critical Theory of Constitutional Law: Hegel's Contribution, *Journal of Law and Society*, 21(4), 464–486
Saussure, F. 1983. *Course in General Linguistics*, tr. R. Harris. London: Duckworth.
Schalow, F. 1993. The Question of Being and the Recovery of Language within Hegelian Thought. *Owl of Minerva*, 24(2), 163–180.
Schmidt, F. 1961. Hegel's Philosophie der Sprache. *Deutsche Zeitschrift für Philosophie*, 9, 1479–1486.
Simon, J. 1966. *Das Problem der Sprache Bei Hegel*. Stuttgart: Kohlhanner.

Smith, J. 1974. Sentences Against Sentences: An Aspect of the Hegelian Dialectic. *Dialectis and Humanism*, 1, 67–73.
Smith, J. 1987. U-Topian Hegel: Dialectic and Its Other in Post-structuralism. *The German Quarterly*, 60, 237–261.
Smith, J. 1994. The Language of Mastery and the Mastery of Language: The Recognition of Rhetoric in Hegel. *Clio*, 23(4), 377–394.
Stähler, T. 2003. Does Hegel Privilege Speech over Writing?: A Critique of Jacques Derrida. *International Journal of Philosophical Studies,* 11(2), 191–204.
Surber, J. O. 1975. Hegel's Speculative Sentence. *Hegel-Studien*, 10, 210–230.
Surber, J. O., ed. 2006. *Hegel and Language*. Albany, NY: SUNY.

Part II
Legal Semiotics as Communication

Chapter 5
The Problem of the Subject(s)

Louis E. Wolcher

> *The same person has perceptions that, for all their differences, have the same object, which leads one to infer that there are different subjects contained within one and the same person.*
>
> Franz Kafka (2006, p. 71).

5.1 Introduction

It has been said that ours is "the epoch of the subject," in the precise sense that for us the idea of the Individual Human Being has replaced both the Nature of the ancients and the God of medieval Christianity as the "new ground of being and meaning" (Douzinas 2000, p. 84, 93). Nowhere is this shifting of the ground more visible than in the notion of a legal entitlement, including especially "human rights," where the classical declarations—the American Declaration of Independence (1776), the French *Déclaration des Droits de l'Homme et du Citoyen* (1789), and the United Nations Universal Declaration of Human Rights (1948)—all say that the rights they specify belong to an entity called "Man." Conceived of secularly as a "pivot of self-consciousness" (Kojève 1980, p. 86), this human subject is supposed to employ what the Greeks called *logos*, or discourse endowed with a meaning, to give and take grounds for itself in the form of THE LAW. Of course, the linkage between subjectivity and the concept of ground is a well known feature of Western intellectual history. Less visible, however, is the connection between the idea of subject-as-ground and the phenomenon of ethical evasion during the crucial moment in which some individuals threaten or apply "legitimate" legal force against other individuals.

The relationship between grounding and ethical evasion is difficult to see because ever since Kant's day we have been taught to believe that "being principled"—i.e. acting on the basis of textual grounds as opposed to yielding to merely causal influences—constitutes the very essence of being ethical. A good will is supposed

L.E. Wolcher (✉)
Charles I. Stone Professor of Law, University of Washington School of Law, Seattle, WA, USA
e-mail: wolcher@u.washington.edu

A. Wagner, J.M. Broekman (eds.), *Prospects of Legal Semiotics*,
DOI 10.1007/978-90-481-9343-1_5,

to be a law-governed will, and virtue has come to be defined as a struggle against any natural inclinations and passions that might lead individuals away from doing what the moral law requires. On this view, if the law of the land happens to be just, then willing disobedience to the law is the same as willing disobedience to the moral law, and those in charge of the legal system are duty-bound to inflict pain on the transgressor regardless of any "irrational" feelings of pity or compassion they may experience on his account (see Kant 1996, p. 474). Indeed, according to certain redemption-oriented (or quasi-masochistic) accounts of law and justice, the transgressor himself is duty-bound to accept his just deserts, on the theory that he implicitly "chose" them by virtue of having willed his unlawful (= immoral) act (see Hegel 1967, p. 70).

Nevertheless, Walter Benjamin rightly observed that "something rotten in law" (*etwas Morsches im Recht*) (1978, p. 286) is revealed whenever human beings believe that they can legitimately and even justly exercise the power over life and death in the law's name, as they may do, for example, when they administer the death penalty, sentence convicted criminals to understaffed and underfunded prisons, enforce military conscription in wartime, or even evict defaulting tenants onto the mean streets of the city. It will be the task of this essay to enlarge and refocus Benjamin's point. I will try to uncover something analogous to rottenness (a deep sadness, perhaps) in the relationship between the belief that well-grounded action is possible and the phenomenon of legal violence. In addition to whatever else the law may accomplish, I will claim that at the end of the day it also represents the will to deny what Max Weber (1958, p. 117) has called the "tragedy with which all action, but especially political action, is truly interwoven."

5.2 Temporality and the Idea of Ground

What this essay calls "the problem of the subject(s)" cannot be understood apart from a prior understanding of time and temporality. It is a profound truism that this moment, right now, is not the same as any other moment ever was or will be. Whether or not we are aware of it (and most of the time we are not) time continuously restarts itself, wiping the chalkboard of our possibilities clean with each new upsurge of a fresh present. Repetition or iteration is governed by the concept of similarity, which entails a temporal human judgment, and not by the concept of identity, which expresses a timeless (and therefore purely formal) rule of logic. The difference between similarity and identity suggests that time's most precious gift to being—the absolute heterogeneity of each new moment as it arises—is also its greatest affront to the concept of the rule of law. The essence of law is to crave grounds; the essence of time is to dissolve and disperse them. The general notion of "ground" thus represses an awareness of the ineradicable difference that is proper to every beginning, including even those everyday beginnings which appear most boring and routine to the human beings who are involved in them. If a sincerely avowed ground of action is taken to have a continuous history, then the one who says he acts "on its basis" can claim that it is the ground as such, and not the actor, which bears ultimate responsibility for what happens when words and images give way to deeds and their consequences.

When it comes to faith in the possibility of feeling well-grounded by a stable ground, the institutions of law resemble those forms of religion that revere or worship "holy books." Indeed, it is possible to read the original Greek text of the first clause of John 1:1, *En archē en ho logos*, as expressing something like a common ecumenical creed uniting theology and jurisprudence. The customary English translation of this verse is, "In the beginning was the Word," and in this form it expresses a bibliophilic thesis with which most contemporary lawyers and judges would undoubtedly agree. Law construes the concept of ground in terms of the category of "meaning," and it equates meaning with what an authoritative linguistic sign (e.g. a legal norm) correctly signifies to a rational reader of the law, defined as a human subject that is capable of grounding its actions in textual truths. If, as Aquinas says, God signifies his meanings "not by words only (as man can also do), but also by things themselves" (*Summa Theologica* I q. 1 a. 10), then it would appear that at the very least human beings can (and perhaps should) use words to signify the meanings of their earthly laws to one another. Both in legal theory and in legal practice, the supposed *constancy* of grounding statements is identified with their meanings, or as Wittgenstein (1978, p. 54) would say, with their "meaning-bodies" (*Bedeutungskörper*). The supposition that these meanings enjoy a unified existence through time allows legal actors to imagine that something called THE LAW itself spans the temporal gap separating words and deeds, commands and sanctions, proscriptions and punishments, and, more generally, ground and grounded.

Since legal deeds, sanctions and punishments take place "on a field of pain and death," as the late Robert Cover reminds us (Cover 1986, p. 1601), *how* the gap between words and deeds is spanned presents a distinctly ethical problem. The hand that signs a death warrant or default judgment is not in fact attached to a law book—it can be found only at the end of some particular human being's real arm. A hypertrophied awareness of this fundamental truth can produce anxiety (if not anguish) in the mind of anyone whose job it is to set in motion the coercive mechanisms of the law. Let this anxiety be exposed to the seductive influence of Wittgenstein's aphorism, "What the eye doesn't see the heart doesn't grieve over" (Wittgenstein 1983, p. 205), and there begins to emerge a surprising, even scandalous, aspect of the relationship between the phenomenon of gap-spanning and the ethical sensibility of those particular human beings who perform legal deeds. Faith in the metaphysical unity of legal grounds for acting is like the curtain that separated Dorothy and her companions from Professor Marvel, the little man who pretended to be the mighty Wizard of Oz in the motion picture of the same name. Such a faith, like most other instances of blind faith, functions to screen the distinctly ethical dimension of interpersonal legal violence from the view of those who believe they are duty-bound to lay on the lash in the name of the law.

5.3 The History of the Ground in Western Thought

The relentless positivism which characterizes mainstream legal thinking in most modern Western democracies can be traced ideologically to the idea of popular sovereignty, and to the mythical social contract amongst free and equal citizens on which it is theoretically based. Of course, it is a fact that finite human beings have never all been free and equal, and probably never will be, and that treating them "as if" they were all the same (i.e. "free and equal citizens") can reinforce and reproduce very real social and material inequalities. Perhaps no one has expressed this contrast better (or more famously) than Jacques Anatole François Thibault (1844–1924), who wrote under the name of Anatole France (2005, p. 331): "The law, in its majestic equality, forbids the rich as well as the poor to sleep under bridges, to beg in the streets, and to steal bread." The frequently glaring contrast between the abstract idea of formally equal citizens, or legal subjects, and the concrete inequalities experienced every day by real individuals has been a well-known theme in leftwing critiques of liberalism ever since Marx's day. But whatever empirical, conceptual, or ethical difficulties may attend the social contract theories of foundational thinkers such as Hobbes (1914, pp. 87–90), Locke (1939, p. 441) and Rousseau (1993, pp. 181–305), this much, at least, is historically certain: sometime between the sixteenth and eighteenth centuries the concept of ground shifted its location from the infinitely broad shoulders of God onto the much narrower shoulders of "Man."

The story of how the idea of ground passed from nature to God, and thence to the modern human subject, usually begins with Aristotle. Having removed Plato's free-floating "ideas" from their supra-heavenly place and ensconced them in actual things, the Philosopher (as Aquinas called Aristotle) employed the Greek term *to hypokeimenon* (literally, "that-which-lies-under") to denote a given thing's essence or substance. This he placed in opposition to the thing's merely accidental "qualities" (*ta sumbebekota*), such as its particular color or size. The *hypokeimenon* of any given being, X, is what provides X its unity through time, and therefore what founds and supports its ultimate purpose (*telos*), defined as that which each being inherently strives to become (i.e. its *entelecheia*) (192^a25–34). *Hypokeimenon* is what makes each and every X (including human beings) what they are "in virtue of being themselves" (1028^b33–1030^b14).

To paraphrase Heidegger's well-known interpretation (2008, p. 223), for Aristotle, as for the Greeks in general, *constancy* was the unshakeable ground for the possibility of something "accidental." The merely accidental qualities of X transpire in the sphere of what holds as constant or as a rule for X: namely, in the sphere of nature. Nature (*physis*) in the Greek sense was not conceived of as something that had to be created by anything outside of itself. In contemplating nature (including human nature), the Greeks discovered what they took to be an eternal "world-order" which served as their principle of comprehension and evaluation of all things (see Jaeger 1945, i, pp. 150–84). Aristotle (1071^b3–1072^a19), following both Parmenides (1984, p. 65) and Heraclitus (1987, p. 25), believed that the universe was always in existence and will always continue to be in existence. In a nutshell, the Greeks, and later the Romans, were inclined to look "outward"—to what they took to be nature itself—as the measure and *hypokeimenon* (i.e. stable ground) of all of nature's beings, including, for example, mountain ranges, streams, rocks, trees, flowers, animals, human beings, and even the gods themselves.

The proper home for the concept of ground in Western European thought shifted place with the advent of Christianity. Plato, in the *Timaeus* (28*b*1–29*d*3), had argued that the chaotic substance of the universe was first given shape by a demiurge, or creator. But this ur-being did not make the world *ex nihilo*, for as Timaeus says in the dialogue, nothing can come from nothing. Instead, the demiurge bestowed order upon the substance of the universe by imitating that which is eternal and unchanging, namely, the self-showing appearance (*eidos*) of the everlasting world of forms (Plato's *idéas*). Attempting to wed the authority of Holy Scripture to the prestigious philosophical authority of Plato, early and medieval Christian thinkers radically upgraded the role of the creator and downgraded the *idéas* to the status of mere creations. These thinkers interpreted nature as an *utterly* created thing (*ens creatum*), from top to bottom, and made God-the-creator into the omnipotent and ultimate ground of everything that is, including nature-as-a-whole and all of the beings, both real and ideal, that inhabit it.

In particular, the medieval schoolmen, following Aquinas (*Summa Theologica*, I q. 1 a. 7), translated the word *hypokeimenon* as *subjectum* (literally, "that-which-is-thrown-under"), which they placed in opposition to the term *objectum* (literally, "that-which-is-thrown-in-the-way-of"). For them, a *subjectum* was something that is capable of being thought about or acted upon independently of our knowledge or even our existence; whereas an *objectum* was that which is concretely experienced of something by a human agent through this or that power or faculty of perception. Aquinas, for instance, confidently asserts that a colored thing is "the proper [*objectum*] of sight," and he places this example in opposition to the case of the Deity as such, whom he asserts "is in very truth the [*subjectum*] of the science [of sacred doctrine]." The medieval sense of the difference between the subjective and the objective was thus the exact opposite of modern usage. For Aquinas and the schoolmen, the objective was merely that which is thrown-in-the-way-of a human perception, whereas the subjective was what we would today call the "subject matter" itself: namely, reality, and most especially reality's God, to whom all things refer, as Aquinas said, "as their beginning and end."

Instead of imagining that nature was modeled on the basis of eternally preexisting ideas, it would appear that the medieval mind believed that nature and all possible ideas of it were brought into being by the Word of God uttered at the inception of creation—a divine *logos* that, according to the Gospel of St John, not only was *spoken* by God, but also *was* God (John 1:1). By thus identifying the *logos* with the ultimate *subjectum* of the universe, Christianity prepared the way for two monumental changes in Western thought. First, it reversed the ancient Greco-Roman relationship between language and reality: if the world is brought into being by God uttering the divine *logos*, this means that words determine nature and man, and not the other way around. Plato's eternal ideas were replaced by the "sense" or "meaning" of divine words, for as Aquinas said, "nothing false can ever underlie the literal sense of Holy Scripture" (*Summa Theologica*, I q. 1 a. 10 ad 3). Second, Christianity's emphasis on "the Word" unwittingly prepared the way for the rise of another kind of "subject." Aristotle (1253^a10) had defined the latter as *zoon logon echon* ("the animal that has language"), translated into Latin as *animal rationale* ("rational animal"), and this being too could utter words, if not *the* Word.

Now a truly comprehensive explanation of the rise of the modern subject would have to take account of much of the rich intellectual, cultural and political history that transpired between the thirteenth and seventeenth centuries. For example, the emergence of nominalism in the work of the Franciscans Duns Scotus and William of Ockham was critically important to the slow process by which the phenomenon of language in general became fully historicized and humanized (Douzinas 2000, pp. 62–63). In the interest of space, however, I will simply observe that René Descartes is usually credited with having definitively initiated the so-called "subjective turn" in Western philosophy. His skeptical methodological principle of doubting everything about which he was not absolutely certain led him to affirm the one thing he believed he could not doubt: the sheer fact that it was he who doubted, or rather, that it was he who was *thinking* in the mode of doubting. Descartes' *cogito ergo sum* thus redirected thought's gaze, so to speak, from "outward" (to nature and nature's God) to "inward," namely, to the thinking thing that is certain of itself (*res cogitans qua certum*). The I that thinks (*ego cogito*) became for Descartes and his intellectual descendents "the first principle of philosophy" (Descartes 1985, i, p. 127), the one being that is more in being than any other being.

Kant's so-called "Copernican revolution" (Kant 1998, p. 110) in philosophy finally brought to a head the revolutionary tendencies that the advent of Cartesian subjectivism had merely initiated. Kant gave the human subject a systematic form that did not need to be derived from any authority beyond its own capacity for rigorous self-awareness. Descartes' thinking thing grew into the new *subjectum* and ground of everything that is, or rather, of everything that can be thought about or experienced by human beings. In the guise of pure reason, Kant's transcendental subject became a fixed and abiding self hardwired with "forms of intuition," "faculties" and "categories" that allowed it to organize and make sense of its experiences. As Derrida notes, Kant raised this "I" (*das Ich*) infinitely (*unendlich*) above all other beings on earth, thereby achieving an "infinite elevation [that] identifies a subject in the strict sense, for... Kant emphasizes the fact that 'I' signifies a consciousness that remains the same throughout all of its modifications" (Derrida 2008, p. 92).

Its unity secured, the self-certain human subject displaced God and nature as the ultimate foundation of all possible knowledge and truth, and in this sense it became the creator of its own reality. Enlightenment, defined by Kant (1993, p. 145) as "man's leaving his self-caused immaturity, [that is,] the incapacity to use one's intelligence without the guidance of another," became an individual moral imperative. Indeed, the very concept of enlightenment implicitly denounced the medieval notion that individuals should submit without question or hesitation (i.e. without reason) to traditional sources of authority within a hierarchical social order that pretended to be God-given and eternal. With the appearance of Kant's finite human *subjectum*, the entity "Man" no longer needed a pastor or holy book to supply him with a conscience, as Kant (1993, p. 145) himself would declare. The human subject was therefore poised to step into the shoes that hitherto had been occupied by the infinite and divine Thomistic *subjectum*. Transcendental apperception—the self's awareness of its own operations in the mode of the *cogito me cogitare*—gave this new subject the ability to peer within itself and find the conditions of the possibility of all scientific and moral "objectivity" (in the modern sense of the word). The external world as such (i.e. the world independent of human cognition) became an inaccessible cipher (*noumenon*), while "objects" became mere objects of the subject's consciousness (*phenomena*).

In the guise of practical reason, Kant's newly minted transcendental subject was identified with freedom, defined as the will's capacity to lay down the law for itself in accordance with the moral law. This moral law was the categorical imperative: "Act as if the maxim of your action were to become by your will a general law of nature" (Kant 1993, p. 187). In one of the boldest finesse plays (or category mistakes) in the history of philosophy, Kant accepted the categorical imperative as a "fact" of reason, the absolute truth of which is accessible to the internal gaze of all rational subjects. After Kant, the entity "Man" morphed into a self-enclosed rational monad: a being that could, at long last, "free himself from obligation to Christian revelational truth and Church doctrine to a legislating for himself that takes its stand upon itself" (Heidegger 1977, p. 148).

It's not that after Kant people stopped believing in God—far from it. God ceased being a plausible *subjectum*—or as Nietzsche (1968, p. 45) so famously put it, "God is dead"—because belief in Him became *optional*. It was not long before having religious faith was lowered from an unquestioned and unquestionable duty to the level of just one possible human value amongst many others. This loss of prestige was reinforced by the rise of the secular state, which tolerated religion in general, but did not endorse any religion in particular. Once God became a mere preference or choice that individuals considered themselves free to accept or reject (i.e. once people were no longer imprisoned or burned at the stake for not believing in Him), His reign as the universally acknowledged ultimate *subjectum* of the universe was finished. If God had to go a-begging, so to speak, amongst human beings—if believing in Him was truly optional—then it is obvious that the one who actually is free to believe or not believe in the first place ("Man") is really the ultimate (i.e. final) ground. In a word, the Kantian subject became the sovereign subject, and the concept of subjectivity was elevated to a cosmic principle, the very ground of rational grounding itself.

In legal positivism, which remains to this day thoroughly Kantian in spirit despite all that has happened in and to humanity during the past 200 years, the one who posits the law can no longer be confused with nature or God. Whether in the form of a monarch, a legislator, a dictator, a ruling junta, or even the fictional "We the people" of the United States Constitution, the one who posits the law—and the one who can un-posit it—has finally come out from behind the curtain. The one who is at once "free" to posit the law and "bound" to follow it can no longer hide or deny the fact that he or she is a "human, all too human" being (cf. Nietzsche 1996).

5.4 The Fracturing of the Ground

Hannah Arendt reported that the Nazi war criminal Adolf Eichmann, during his 1961 trial in Jerusalem, "declared with great emphasis that he had lived his whole life according to Kant's moral precepts, and especially according to a Kantian definition of duty" (Arendt 1965, pp. 135–136). Although Eichmann's interpretation of Kant is hardly authoritative, his remark does highlight an important tension or paradox within the concept of the sovereign subject. The Kantian subject is both a law-giver and a law-taker, and thus must somehow manage to straddle the ancient Roman legal categories of *sublimus* (he who is chosen to command) and *subditus* (he who turns towards the chosen one to hear and obey the law) (see Douzinas 2000, p. 218). As a temporal being, the Kantian subject must *first* lay down or acknowledge the law (an abstraction), at t_1, and *then* concretely follow it, at t_2. The one who grounds must also be the same as the one who is grounded. The subject *of* the law must also be subjected *to* the law. Despite the temporal gap that separates them from one another, two subjects—or rather two states of affairs—must somehow manage to become one.

Kant's categorical imperative stipulates that moral content ("maxims of action") should be generated, but it is itself devoid of any particular moral content. The alleged universality of the imperative is therefore utterly procedural, and the only constraint on its concrete application is the formal requirement of non-contradiction. Because of its purely abstract universality, Hegel would soon claim that Kant's "universal moral law" can just as easily become a principle of immorality as a principle of morality. Long before postmodern thought and its so-called "indeterminacy thesis," it was Hegel who first drew attention to the radical insecurity of the temporal passage between grounds and grounded in the Kantian system. "'It is only a blunder, an incompetence of reason,'" observed Hegel, "if one can show it incapable of justifying by this principle any determination and therefore any action at all" (Hyppolite 1996, p. 47). Hegel was to Kant what Aristotle was to Plato: a transcendence skeptic. In identifying the rational with the real, and the true with the whole of reality, Hegel (1977, p. 11) dragged Kant's abstract, transcendental subject into time and history in the form of Spirit (*Geist*), and he equated world history with the continuous Sisyphean labors of human beings to negate the given through concrete work aimed at actualizing their ideas. In the assertion that "the power of Spirit is only as great as its expression, its depth only as deep as it dares to spread out and lose itself in its expression" (Hegel 1977, p. 6), the creative *logos* of John 1:1 finally lost its supernatural deistic provenance and assumed a completely human, historicized form.

The Hegelian philosophical system remained mere speculative metaphysics, of interest primarily to philosophers and dreamers, until Marx managed to radically transform Hegel's critique of Kant's abstract moral casuistry into a comprehensive political critique of concrete social life. According to Marx, all moral law-giving of the type that Kant and his intellectual heirs advocated was not only hopelessly abstract, as Hegel had said, but also historically epiphenomenonal, that is, causally linked to the promotion of particular social (i.e. class) interests (Marx 1959, pp. 243–245). In the thesis that the religious, moral and legal ideas of an era are but ideological reflections of the oppressive social relations prevailing during that era, the concept of the human *subjectum* reached its apogee. If, as Marx (1964, p. 44, 52) claimed, "man is the supreme being for man," then the hypostatized norms and ideas peddled by bourgeois institutions such as religion, morality and law could be interpreted as false suns, "about which man revolves so long as he does not revolve about himself." In Marx's thought a new categorical imperative arose that impliedly reproached both Kant and Hegel for their refusals to confront politically the empirical reality of massive human inequality and suffering. Just as the point of philosophy became to change, and not merely interpret, the world (Marx 1959, p. 245), so too Marx would announce the need for a "*categorical imperative to overthrow all those conditions* in which man is an abased, enslaved, abandoned, contemptible being" (Marx 1964, p. 52).

Apart from the intellectual and political radicalism fostered by nineteenth and twentieth century Marxism, "sociological" neo-Kantianism during the same period also subverted Kant's claim that the categorical imperative and the categories of the understanding are universal features of humanity, even amongst those thinkers who were most sympathetic to Kantianism in general (see Beck 1967, v, p. 473). In neo-Kantianism, "categories" and "moral laws" became culturally determined patterns of thinking that happen to prevail at this or that particular moment in history amongst this or that group of people. As a result of this displacement of the universal by the particular, the *causes* of patterns of thinking (historical, economic, psychological, etc.) not only jutted into prominence, but also rendered implausible the claim that any *particular* cultural pattern could constitute an objective, supra-historical ground of truth and knowledge. The transcendental subject became the historical subject, and philosophical epistemology became the sociology of knowledge (see Mannheim 1985). Philosophy had lost its "nimbus," as Wittgenstein (2003, p. 342) put it, and painstaking idiographic inquiry into the particular became more respectable (and more fashionable) than starry-eyed nomothetic inquiry into the universal.

As a result of these trends, "the" human subject (which human subject?) could no longer bear the massive weight of the world in the same way that nature and God, the two previous *subjecti*, had borne it. Rather than serving as an absolute and indubitable foundation, the human being became a specimen to be studied for its various habits and tastes. Science and technology discovered sociology and psychology, but lost speculative philosophy. Economic theory discovered instrumental rationality based on the probabilistic calculation of causes and effects, but gave up all pretence of being a science of *political* economy that is explicitly and unashamedly concerned with the ultimate aims of humanity (see Habermas 1984, i. p. 4). In the form of such disciplines as cost-benefit analysis and law-and-economics, social science abandoned any effort to ground the rationality of human choices in anything beyond the sheer existence of un-analyzable individual preferences.

If we look beyond the narrow confines within which most mainstream social science is conducted, it has become almost commonplace these days for members of the academic intelligentsia to assert that, in a post-Kantian, post-Freudian and postmodern world, "people have no essential identities outside of those constructed in symbolic discourses and practices" (Douzinas 2000, p. 259). Kantian legalism—which also happens to be the legalism of mainstream jurisprudence—gives us "the notion of the human subject as a sovereign agent of choice, a creature whose ends are chosen rather than given, who comes by his aims and purposes by acts of will, as opposed, say, to acts of cognition" (Gaete 1993, p. 125). But to put it mildly, the vociferous counterclaim that the ego is not *in fact* a master of its own house can be found everywhere in postmodern thought. It appears, for example, in the work of well-known thinkers such as Althusser, Foucault, Derrida and Lacan, all of whom in one way or another demote the self from the status of a sovereign subject and author of its own destiny to that of an embodied entity that is constantly being *subjected* to historical, symbolic and psychological forces (i.e. causes). These forces seem to imprison the individual in heteronomy, and they cut the will loose from any ground that it could reliably "choose" on its own by acting autonomously in the capacity of an ultimate *subjectum*.

The point is not that the world is "constituted by consciousness," as a naïve hyper-idealist might claim. The argument is more subtle: whatever the word "consciousness" is attempting to name always finds itself already thrown into its world, and fully at work in it, the very instant it becomes conscious of anything whatsoever. The archetype or ur-text of this way of thinking about the human condition is, of course, Heidegger's *Being and Time* (1962). In one way or another, the thinking enacted in this book has profoundly influenced almost all strands of postmodern thought, and has provided it with such neologisms as *Dasein* (the human being interpreted as always already thrown into its world), *Geworfenheit* (thrownness), *In-der-Welt-sein* (being-in-the-world), and *Miteinandersein* (being-with-others). According to what might be called an almost universal postmodernist thesis, the most that the actual, phenomenal facts of the case give anyone the right to say is just this: any time you choose to look, *something is always already happening* that only *later* will call itself a "self." The self or subject does not magically spring into existence, at t_1, and only then begin to think and feel for the first time, at t_2. Instead, there is always the primordial unity of *thinking-and-feeling-going-on-in-a-world*, and only because of this prior unity—which is supposed to transcend the subject/object dichotomy—can anything like a distinct self or subject then be imagined or constructed. Seen from a postmodem point of view, it would seem that the Enlightenment's beloved human *subjectum* has left the stage of history, and what has reentered it is an over-determined action or interpretation which merely "takes place," so to speak, without any real ground but with plenty of causal influences that an observer could line up to explain it, should he or she be so inclined.

Nietzsche, as usual, was very precise in exposing the unwarranted inference that allowed Kant to hypostatize the existence of an entity called "the subject" on the basis of the undeniable fact that living human beings actually do think and have experiences:

> "The subject" is the fiction that many similar states in us are the effect of one substratum: but it is we who first created the "similarity" of these states; our adjusting them and making them similar is the fact, and not their similarity (—which ought rather to be denied—) (Nietzsche 1968, p. 269).

Although Nietzsche's argument is unimpeachable from a logical point of view, a merely logical critique of the concept of the human subject, however valid and necessary, does not yet reach what the title of this essay has called "the problem of the subject(s)." Merely to deny the subject the right to claim its own ipseity, or simple self-sameness, does not go far enough. The human subject is but the last in a series of grounds that once included nature and God. Questioning the subject-as-ground does not question the notion of ground as such. For what Nietzsche calls a "fact"—a judgment of similarity between different states of affairs—continues to assume that at least the event of judgment itself possesses a kind of metaphysical unity.

Nietzsche's ultimate *subjectum* is a unified being, too, even though its unity is not as resplendent as that of God or nature, or as abstract as the Kantian transcendental subject. In his theory of will-to-power (*Der Wille zur Macht*), Nietzsche's thought "completed" Western metaphysics, as Heidegger (2003, p. 95) put it, because it demonstrated the fact that philosophy had now "gone through the sphere of prefigured possibilities" of beings that could occupy the position of ultimate ground. After the series Nature→God→Man→Will-to-Power had been finally written down, there was no one left to try out for the role of Supreme Being. In his above-quoted critique of the human subject, for example, Nietzsche still assumes that the human act of judgment is "grounded," so to speak, in a judging entity or being ("we"). Identifying the precise name of this being (soul, subject, mind, will-to-power, or whatever) is much less important than noticing the supposition that it is *one* being. The real problem of the subject(s) will only begin to show itself if this last assumption is questioned.

5.5 The Subject as Ground

When Dōgen, a thirteenth century Japanese Zen master, was asked, "Who says 'I'?", he replied: "It is 'I' that says 'who'" (Cleary 2001, iv. p. 174). From a semiotic point of view, this answer is equivalent to the assertion that the linguistic signs "who" and "I" are locked within a sterile circle of mutual self-reference. From a philosophical point of view, the answer can be read more broadly to imply that no actual soul, ego or human subject corresponds to the first-person personal pronoun, "I", and that what ordinary people take to be *the self* is really just an illusion produced by the grammar of our language encountering the fierce urgency of our desires. As we have seen, the Western philosophical tradition as it has developed since Descartes both disagrees and agrees with Dōgen's cryptic text. The previous discussion of the rise and decline of the human *subjectum* shows that tradition has bequeathed us two separate grammars for discussing essentially two different types of subjects. I will call these the *causal subject* and the *grounding subject*.

5.5.1 The Causal Subject

The causal subject () stands *in* a relation to the world, conceived of as a manifold of things () that it keeps on encountering and that it must deal with and manage in some way or other. The concept of the causal subject thus depicts two distinct entities and their relationship (R) to one another:

This subject is a mover and a shaker. It causes effects in the world, and therefore participates fully as a co-citizen, so to speak, in a realm that Hegel (1975, p. 70) calls "the causal nexus." What the causal subject's everyday discourse might call "rationality" or its antithesis (e.g. "spirituality") is always merely epiphenomenal: a product of prior experiences and historical influences of which this subject is not presently conscious. When Freud, for example, reduced the adult mystic's alleged "oceanic feeling" to the status of being an unconscious effect of an antecedent "feeling of infantile helplessness" experienced at the breast of the mother, he was referring to a type of causal subject (Freud 1962, pp. 17–19). Moreover, if the causal subject does act in a way that it would call "rational," its comportment is at best "instrumentally rational" (*zweckrational*) in Max Weber's sense of the term. That is, the causal subject calculates and uses the object world and other human beings as "conditions" or "means" for the attainment of certain ends, *whatever* they may be (Weber 1978, i. p. 24).

For example, in pursuing their various goals, Ghandi and Martin Luther King, Jr. acted as causal subjects, but so too did Stalin and Hitler. What is more, the goals that any of these men pursued, as motives belonging to a causal subject, were no different in kind than any other entity or condition involved in the causal nexus. The various manifestations of causal subjectivity throughout history have been well-nigh infinite in number, as befits the infinite causal web in which every human being is caught. However, what makes all causal subjects into variations on the same basic theme is their utter *groundlessness*: although their behaviors have causes and produce effects, this is the most one can say about them. The causal nexus is relentlessly unsentimental and unflattering to human pride: it stipulates that today's cause is always also yesterday's effect.

One could say that the causal subject stands in what Heidegger called a "non-regarding" (*hinsichtlos*) relationship to beings: it is perpetually losing itself to its immediate perceptions, including its immediate perceptions of language and mental images (Heidegger 2002, p. 148). In the case of the causal subject, this relationship of losing oneself goes far beyond merely occasional bouts of absentmindedness. Heidegger's imagined protestations to the contrary notwithstanding, the relationship of losing oneself also characterizes the causal subject's recognition of the "as"-structure (*die "als"-Struktur*) of beings, which in Heideggerian thought is supposed to distinguish the human being from the animal (see Derrida 2008, p. 142). The frog sits on a lily pad, for sure, but it would seem that the frog cannot experience what it sits upon *as* a being, *as* a "lily pad," in the way that humans can. Therefore Heidegger (1994, p. 176) famously asserted that while beings like the frog are not completely "worldless" (*weltlos*) in the manner of a stone, they are nonetheless "poor-in-world" (*weltarm*) in comparison to human beings, who are "world-forming" (*weltbildend*).

But the Heideggerian concept of the "as"-structure of beings, in this context at least, is a hindrance rather than a help in trying to understand the essential nature of the causal subject. It may very well be that humans are the only living beings capable of noticing a given entity, X, *as* X; it may even be the case that encountering X as X does not depend on language but rather primordially founds it. However, in contrast to the grounding subject, whom we will encounter shortly, the causal subject is a heteronymous being from top to bottom (i.e. *fully* an effect of history). Seen from the standpoint of the causal subject, X in any form (e.g. X *or* "X") is simply a mute *sign*—and there is no "magic" behind a sign that determines how it is to be applied when the *recognition* of X "as" X gives way to *action* in respect of X. When Heidegger stated that "every fact is already understood *as* this and this, i.e. it stands under the knowledge of essence" (2002, p. 203), he unwarrantedly hypostatized what the word "knowledge" seems to be saying. Knowledge is not a thing but a capability for the causal subject. As the following remark by Wittgenstein suggests, the causal subject does not mysteriously "know" (or pre-know) X so much as simply *act* with an image or impression of X in its mind:

> How is it possible even to come up with a thought! Here "How could I have come up with a thought" means: "What does the thought *mean*, to what extent is it a thought anyway, since *nothing* corresponds to it, after all?" As if a thought were magic. What do we mean by the existence of things, i.e. what use does this concept have? After all, a thought is just an expression, and there can be no magic hidden behind an expression. What this expression *accomplishes* can only be seen by looking at its use (Wittgenstein 2005, p. 52e).

Phenomenally speaking, "goals" take the form of representations (words and images), and words and images can be interpreted as causes that are just as effective as sticks and stones are at breaking bones. The so-called "symbolic order" to which the bodies and minds of individuals are subjected does not primordially consist of signs-endowed-with-meanings, for the causal subject does not register "meanings" as *grounds* of action. Rather, the symbolic order shows itself first and foremost as a manifold of words and images capable of producing *effects*. As Schopenhauer (1999, p. 37) put it, at best the causal subject's own mental representations cause its will to turn "like a weathervane on a well-oiled pivot in a changeable wind." This implies that the linguistic expressions of what the *grounding* subject would call "grounds for acting" do not in fact provide the *causal* subject with anything more substantial than, say, a momentary burst of adrenaline. After all is said that must be said in any given situation, and the time has come to act, the causal subject *reacts* but does not *respond* to language: the causal subject it bounces off language, so to speak, without answering it back.

The foregoing phenomenon is easiest to observe in cases in which we react to language automatically or habitually. Consider William James's description of "action grown habitual":

> In action grown habitual, what instigates each new muscular contraction [e.g. a judge announcing a result or signing a judgment] to take place in its appointed order is not a thought or a perception, but the *sensation occasioned by the muscular contraction just finished*. . .. In an habitual action, mere sensation is a sufficient guide, and the upper regions of brain and mind are set comparatively free (James 1904, i. pp. 115–116).

Listen, too, to Derrida's description of this phenomenon in the context of rule-following:

> When there is a determinable rule, I know what must be done, and as soon as such knowledge dictates the law, action follows knowledge as a calculable consequence: one *knows* what path to take, one no longer hesitates; the decision no longer decides anything but simply gets deployed with the automatism attributed to machines. There is no longer any place for justice or responsibility (whether juridical, political, or ethical) (Borradori 2003, pp. 134–135).

For example, in reacting to an order to perform some simple task we may notice *that* the order applies to us, to be sure, but we need not also *take notice* of anything explicit about it, such as what the order "means." In such a case there need not appear any internal event of meaning-recognition before action, even (or especially) action that is judged "correct." The causal subject simply reacts to the linguistic sign that comprises such an order without any question or hesitation. As Wittgenstein (2005, p. 135e) says, this sort of use of language "is better compared to what occurs when, upon pressing a button with the word 'blue' on it, a blue color chip automatically pops up, or doesn't pop up if the mechanism fails."

But the causal subject does not just react to what lawyers call "easy cases" in this fashion. Eventually it reacts to *every* case that way. When the list of justifications for how authoritative language (e.g. a legal norm) "should" be followed comes to an end—when it reaches the bedrock of action, as it always must—our philosophical spade is turned, as Wittgenstein (2005, p. 85e) puts it, for there is then no further event of justifying or grounding to consider. A results-oriented parent or bureaucrat might justify a particular use of linguistic signs by saying that they are supposed to causally induce someone to perform certain actions. Thought from such a point of view, norm-following is a present disposition or ability created by social custom as it continually co-constructs the identities and typical reactions of individual actors through various processes of socialization (see Berger and Luckmann 1967, p. 129–183). But custom in this sense is not a *ground* that is consulted by the actor. Once the causal subject has fully internalized custom through learning or imitation, it does not then fall back on (i.e. explicitly "follow") the memory-image of some past event of learning or imitation to know how to behave according to custom. As Wittgenstein (2005, p. 162e) puts it, the causal subject's behavior is "instinctive later on, whatever its origin." That is, the concept of "custom" is but a shorthand way of expressing the idea that the actor and others like him have been *caused* by social conditioning to behave in certain stereotypical ways.

Speaking more generally, one could say that the causal subject not only causes things to happen, but also is itself caused. Its desires and reactions are effects of history in the largest sense of the term. At any given moment, the motives competing in the mind of the causal subject show themselves concretely as representations. Whether we think of causation in terms of necessity or in terms of invariable sequence, only one of these motive-images is destined to become a cause (but not a ground!) in the strictest sense of the word. That is, the causal subject lets these motive-images "try their strength on his will, whereupon the more powerful motive then decides him and his action ensues with precisely the same necessity with which the rolling of a ball results from its being struck" (Schopenhauer 1974, p. 72).

It almost goes without saying that a creature such as this is also fated to become an object and a means in its own right: an object of scientific inquiry and knowledge, for example, and, more generally, a means to the ends of other causal subjects. The causal subject makes its appearance in the psychiatric and sociological concept of "latent objective rationality," according to which the actions of individuals, however unconscious or automatic, somehow wind up producing effects that "make sense" given some functionally important end of which the actor himself is unaware (see Brubaker 1991, p. 55). Biology, neuroscience, psychology, anthropology and behavioral economics poke and prod the causal subject, trying to find out what really makes it tick beneath all of its own flimsy self-interpretations and self-justifications. Various technologies of disciplinary power (family, law, religion, medicine, advertising, etc.) also act on the causal subject to make it what it is, as Foucault's well-known statement suggests: "In fact, it is already one of the prime effects of power that certain bodies, certain gestures, certain discourses, certain desires, come to be identified and constituted as individuals" (Foucault 1980, p. 98). In sum, though the causal subject may believe that it autonomously uses things and people in its world, whether rationally or otherwise, in fact it is also constantly *being used* by forces beyond its control.

5.5.2 The Grounding Subject

In contrast to the causal subject, the concept of the grounding subject is that of an origin rather than a cause. In Greek terms, this subject is an *archē* as opposed to a mere *aitia*. As we have already seen, the grounding subject also corresponds to the original Latin meaning of the word "sub-ject": it is thrown (*jacere*) under (*sub*). The grounding subject is thrown under its world *as* (not in) an unmediated relation to the projects of its doppelganger, the causal subject. The former attempts to authorize or legitimate the latter's instrumentally rational deeds by freely positing a grounding expression ("X"):

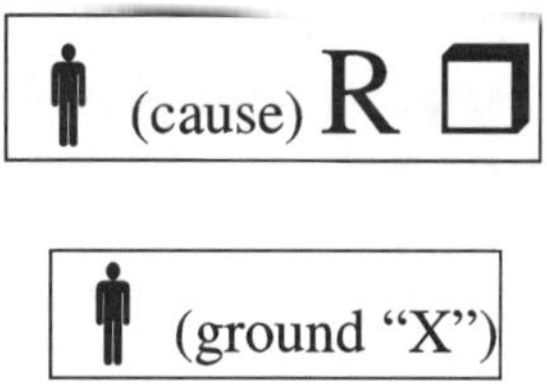

It is said that Hegel used to shout excitedly to his students that modern philosophy arrived only when man was conceived of as a subject (Douzinas 2000, p. 190). In one respect, at least, the way of thinking called Hegelianism has the considerable virtue of highlighting the grounding subject's own attitude towards its grounding expressions. The grounding subject believes that the problem of its identity is inextricably linked to the coherence and vigor of its ideas:

> Now in the Hegelian conception, work can truly be Work, a specifically human Action, only on the condition that it be carried out in relation to an idea (a "project")—that is, in relation to something other than the given, and, in particular, other than the given that the worker himself is. . .. [T]hat man is Wise who is capable of answering in a *comprehensible* or satisfactory manner *all* questions that can be asked him concerning his acts, and capable of answering in such a fashion that the *entirety* of his answers forms a *coherent* discourse (Kojève 1969, 64, 75).

The idea, or project, was discovered (or invented) by Hegel to avoid falling into what he took to be the mind-numbing, soulless abyss of immediacy, where lesser beings such as animals, trees and boulders dwell. The human being, whose subjectivity Hegel determined precisely by its innate capacity to negate the given, is supposed to be uniquely able to lift itself out of the abyss of nature by means of the sky-hook of an idea. According to Hegel's concept of determinate negation (*bestimmte Negation*), the consciousness of the human being keeps on freely expressing ideas to itself in order to become subordinate to them—that is, in order to let the historical progression of its ideas become the dialectical grounds (not the causes!) of Spirit's own self-realization through work and knowledge (see Hegel 1977, p. 51).

Hegel's affinity for the project of grounding on the basis of ideas is hardly unique. It was Parmenides (1984, p. 57) who got the West's grounding ball rolling, so to speak, when he identified being with thinking. According to the Kantian tradition, for example, a grounding expression is the product of a rational evaluation of the rightness of the ends that the causal subject would like to pursue (see Kant 1993, p. 187). Other, less tidy thinkers (e.g. Heidegger 1999, p. 334) have conceived of grounding expressions in terms of an abyssal (*abgründig*) event of appropriation (*Ereignis*), in which a finite human freedom continually undergoes a kind of rupture by simultaneously giving *and* taking grounds as it hurtles through time towards its eventual death. Still other philosophers speak of the grounding subject in terms of its ability to act on its grounds *contra fatum* in a world that is still open and not yet determined all the way to the end (Bloch 1988, p. 162).

As these examples suggest, the grounding subject has shown itself to be a truly protean being during the long history of Western thought. It has taken numerous historical forms and gone by many different names, including "the soul," "practical freedom," "Spirit," "*Dasein*," and "existential freedom." Although it is obvious that there are many philosophically important differences among these concepts, they all have one thing in common. In one way or another, the idea of the grounding subject in any of its various forms performs its primary task within the discursive spheres of politics, law and ethics. The grounding subject is supposed to provide a foundation, beyond all merely causal relations, that can explain how it is possible for the causal subject at once to accomplish something useful in the world *and* to refute Plautus's notoriously corrosive assertion that "man is wolf to man" (*Homo homini lupus est*) (Plautus 1874, p. 226). When Emmanuel Levinas (1999, p. 172) referred to "a certain violence that is implied in all justice," the wolfish causal subject reared its head; but when he praised a "justice always to be perfected against its own harshness" (Levinas 1999, p. 229), a wistful hope for the appearance of a different (and cuddlier) kind of wolf shone forth. To switch metaphors, the grounding subject, like

Dr. Jekyll, yearns to make the causal subject, Mr. Hyde, at least *potentially* more worthy and just than a fully determined (or over-determined) natural force, such as a pouncing animal or a falling boulder.

5.5.3 Conflating the Subject(s)

Time and again, however, the grammatical separateness of these two subjects is forgotten, and the concepts of the grounding subject and the causal subject get conflated. Thus, on the one hand, we are told that the more the human being (*which human being?*) calculates and uses the object world and other people as means—the more strategically ontic and technological it is—the less authentic it is (Heidegger 1962, p. 311), the less it inhabits the cradle of real life (Buber 2000, p. 24), and the more it acts in bad faith (Sartre 1956, pp. 48–49). But on the other hand, we are also told by other responsible and respectable thinkers that the more rationally and strategically this allegedly unitary subject acts, the more effective it is likely to be in achieving its ends and in discharging its ethical duty to take responsibility for the foreseeable consequences of its actions (e.g. Weber 1958, p. 121). Everyday experience confirms this strategic lesson: those who control (or aspire to control) politics, law, and the economic order routinely harness what Marcuse called "the frightful science of human relations" (1964, p. 70) to produce massive results by successfully modelling human beings as biological response mechanisms (i.e. causal subjects). The philosopher Georgio Agamben (2000, p. 138) has identified the potentially devastating meaning of this strategic lesson; in today's world, he remarks, "our private biological body has become indistinguishable from our body politic."

Given the foregoing antinomies, the most pressing juridical and moral question facing twenty-first century humanity seems to be: How can law and politics become at once effective *and* just, coercive *and* compassionate, responsive *and* responsible? How, in short, is it possible (to borrow Kant's somewhat quaint terminology) "to treat man, in your own person as well as in that of anyone else, always as an end, never merely as a means" (Kant 1993, p. 195)?

5.6 Grounds Versus Causes

How indeed. Authoritative legal words (e.g. the linguistic signs contained in statutes and precedents) seem to remain the same from moment to moment, even if every concrete legal deed in which they are involved is always just as unique and unrepeatable as a falling snowflake. The law is therefore compelled to reject, as a matter of principle, the interpretation of John 1:1 that Goethe gave in his poem *Faust Translates the Gospel* (1964, p. 185): "In the beginning was the *Deed!*" (*Im anfang war die* Tat!). Explaining deeds by appealing to the authoritative words of the law appears to ground them in reasons, and hence in the faculty of reason itself. In contrast, explaining deeds by linking them to other deeds (i.e. to history in the largest sense of the word) seems to de-rationalize and diminish the law by demoting its operations to the status of events governed by merely causal forces, such as ideology, tradition and habit. In short, Western thought has privileged the grounding subject over the causal subject ever since Plato put the charioteer of the soul in charge of the chariot steeds of the passions (*Phaedrus* 246*b*).

According to Kant (2000, p. 10), causes occupy a mere "dwelling place" (*domicillium*) in nature, whereas rational grounds possess a sovereign "realm" (*ditio*). The correct meaning of a grounding statement seems to put right and just action on a secure foundation; and the activity of grounding seems to be a laudable exercise in human reason. A historically conditioned intuitive reaction to the signs which express legal norms, on the other hand, is merely causal in nature, and causation is something that also happens to lesser beings such as rocks, icebergs and alligators. "Nothing, Adorno says, is more abhorrent, more hateful, more odious to Kantian man than the memory of a resemblance or affinity between human and animality ... The Kantian has nothing but hate for the animality of the human" (Derrida 2008, p. 103). To compare language to a mechanism of signs that serves to set off certain reactions in us by virtue of previous conditioning and association (see Wittgenstein and Waismann 2003, p. 341) seems to slander reason. It appears to degrade autonomous human beings to the same level as rocks, icebergs and alligators (not to mention Pavlov's salivating dogs), all of which are heteronymous beings incapable of transcending their present circumstances on their own. Reason fancies that in the natural world a cold, pitiless necessity holds sway: an "irksome" necessity, as Aristotle (1015^a31–33) puts it, which "cannot be persuaded [*ametapeìstos angkē*]... for it is contrary to the movement which accords with choice and with reasoning."

Unwilling to be placed on the same level as nature's other beings, conventional legal and political theory believes that its central problem is how to attribute right outcomes to grounds rather than causes, reason rather than history. John Rawls's concept of "stability for the right reasons"—which he claims to be a necessary condition for any realistic liberal conception of justice—furnishes a good illustration of this point of view. For Rawls (1999, pp. 16, 13, n. 2), it is not enough that social stability is "merely a *modus vivendi*" produced by contingent historical forces: "Stability for the right reasons means stability brought about by citizens acting correctly according to the appropriate principles of their sense of justice, which they have acquired by growing up under and participating in just institutions." In other words, although the specific contents of particular grounds and reasons may indeed ultimately owe their existence to history and its panoply of causal influences, the category of right action as such does not. Reason acts *on* (as opposed to *in*) history. And the category of right action is defined a priori as action that is based on a correct reading, by a grounding subject, of historically produced principles that satisfy certain minimal criteria of justice.

The proposition that law requires the support of rational grounds rather than mere historical causes lies at the heart of analytic philosophy's preference for "internal" over "external" explanations of the law (see Dworkin 1986, p. 13; Hart 1961, p. 10). The internal perspective describes the process of legal reasoning from the standpoint of the decider (usually a judge), whereas "external" thinkers are inclined to attribute justice in general, and judicial behaviors in particular, to factors other than the objectively correct subjective decisions of legal decision makers to accept this or that legal reason (ground) for their behaviors. The premise of the external perspective is that historical causes trump rational grounds, or rather, unmask and explain them for what they really are. A good example is Marx's thesis that all past history is really "pre-history": a benighted era in which human beings did in fact control their affairs, but without the sort of autonomous self-determination that can come only to those who realize, at long last, that their historically produced "reasons" are but ideological reflexes and echoes (i.e. effects) of their concrete life-processes (see Marcuse 2007, p. 242).

Causal analysis can unmask the irrational, or at least the pre-theoretical, historical factors (revolutions, invasions, wars, imperialisms, genocides, class interests, racisms, patriarchies, etc.) that "illegally" found the various forms of domination that exist in every society, and that the operations of positive law function to "legally" preserve. The fundamental contrast between law-founding and law-preserving violence helps explain why Foucault, for example, proposed inverting Clausewitz's notorious proposition that war is the continuation of policy by other means to read, quite simply, "politics is the continuation of war by other means" (Foucault 2003, p. 15). Seen from the "external" perspective of a thinker such as Foucault, there are at least three different senses in which the various political relations that prevail in most of today's democratic-capitalistic nation-states constitute the continuation of war by other means. First, existing power relations, including most especially those encoded in legal rights and duties, are in fact causally linked to certain relationships of force that were literally established through warfare, conquest, brigandage, or revolution at some earlier historical moment. Second, political power and its primary instrument, law, only seem to put an end to war in civil society, for they do not actually suspend the present *effects* of previous wars. On the contrary, an extremely important result of the exercise of political and legal power "is perpetually to use a sort of silent war to re-inscribe [previous relations of force] in institutions, economic inequalities, language, and even the bodies of individuals" (Foucault 2003, pp. 15–16). And third, the hypothesis that politics is the continuation of war by other means implies that any imaginable "last battle" in this war would have to put an end not just to war, but also to politics itself. Foucault's deflationary theory of politics suggests that it would be a mistake to view politics as heaven in comparison to the hell of war; rather, politics is best interpreted as a never-ending purgatory in which the sins of the last war are continually being punished and re-punished without ever being fully cleansed or redeemed.

Positive law equates justice with the business of preserving existing legal relations whatever they may be and regardless of any (lawful) asymmetries of power, privilege and prestige they may presuppose and perpetuate. One might say that the law judges people by *what they essentially are* according to their presumptively chosen roles ("shareholder," "director," "worker," "recidivist," "prisoner," "welfare recipient," "father," etc.) rather than by *who they might still become*. The legal order indulges in what Nietzsche (1968, pp. 401–402) called a "great falsification," namely, that the body of a human being belongs to a unitary, diachronic self. Substantively speaking, the internal perspective on the law embodies an ethic that Costas Douzinas has called "legal humanism," according to which human possibilities are defined in advance, "through the axiomatic determination of what it is to be human and the dogmatic exclusion of other possibilities" (Douzinas 2000, pp. 211–212). Methodologically speaking, those who occupy an internal point of view are trained to see words that are not calculated means to officially-certified (well-grounded) legal ends as meaningless distractions. Such individuals are always impatient to get down to what they take to be the real business of the law: *correct administration by grounding subjects*.

The following passage, in which the liberal legal philosopher Ronald Dworkin (1991, p. 360) expresses his honest antipathy towards the external perspective and his strong normative preference for rationally grounded "internal" explanations, typifies this administrative mindset:

> We should now set aside, as a waste of important energy and resource, grand debates about whether law is all power or illusion or constraint, or whether texts interpret only other texts, or whether there are right or best or true or soundest answers or only useful or powerful or popular ones. We could then take up instead how the decisions that in any case will be made should be made, and which of the answers that will in any case be thought right or best or true or soundest really are.

The imperative of correct administration is subverted by the external point of view, which insists on talking about what *might have been* in addition to *what was*, and *what might be* in addition to *what is*. Historians, sociologists and psychologists (not to mention Marxists, critical race theorists and feminist legal theorists) explain legal norms, arguments and outcomes by tracing them to their proximate or ultimate causes rather than to their legal grounds, which they suspect of being ideological. Seen from the external point of view, the question of a juridical result's rationality cannot be separated from an assessment of the rationality (or irrationality) of its concrete historical origins and consequences. In contrast, Dworkin's above-quoted condemnation of the external perspective seems to be saying that no rational person could deny that the law we have now is at least reasonably just on its face, so let's stop whining about its allegedly unjust causes, conditions, and effects and get on with the business of administering it fairly and wisely.

In its impatience for results, traditional jurisprudence consciously or unconsciously subordinates the ubiquitous brutality and sadness of the underlying facts of social life to the necessity of giving them legal form. The real, flesh-and-blood individual who is about to be pushed through the meat grinder of the legal system might be tempted to join Foucault in crying out, "Do not ask who I am and do not ask me to remain the same: leave it to our bureaucrats and our police to see that our papers are in order" (Foucault 1972, p. 17). But as a distinctly *legal* subject, such an individual will quickly discover that once she is subjected to the law—that is, once she is functionally transformed into a causal subject and therefore an object of law's operations—those in charge of the legal order will conclude either that her papers are in order, or that they are not. The law is designed to repress awareness of any raw, un-theorized, "surplus" human suffering so that proper legal grounds can be given to manage, explain, and/or justify that suffering's existence. Moreover, what the internal perspective reveals—the officially certified "reason" for this or that bit of legalized pain—has the effect of concealing that pain from any further scrutiny or notice.

5.6.1 The Sleep of Reason

It is as if the law greatly feared the monsters that might come if it were to fall asleep and risk letting passion and instinct hold sway, as in Goya's famous etching entitled, "The Sleep of Reason Produces Monsters" (*El sueño de la razón produce monstruous*).

But what if there was a sense in which reason is always asleep, even when it is most awake? To be more precise, what if the subject-that-reasons were not one, but two subjects, one of which must always fall sleep before the other can awaken? In that event monsters might come no matter what actions the well-grounded subject takes, and the particular human beings who enforce the law would be like Oedipus the King as he stood on the verge of discovering and punishing the murderer of Laius: damned if they do, and damned if they don't.

Nietzsche once said that the great danger of all direct questioning of the subject *about* the subject lies in the fact "that it could be useful and important for one's activity to interpret oneself falsely" (1968, p. 272). This essay has attempted to heed his warning. The strong distinction it has drawn between the causal subject and the grounding subject is meant to suggest that the most pressing philosophical problem pertaining to subjectivity is definitely *not* how it is possible for a metaphysical entity called the subject, or even for individual human beings embedded in a dynamic post-metaphysical process or temporal milieu, to break free of the given world by using new ideas to overcome old habits. This way of thinking begs the question of *how* new ideas become more compelling than the immediacy they would overcome. No, the real question concerns what I will call the idea-hood of the idea in relation to those who work to implement it. Thinking in terms of passage, the problem is not how a symbol-creating entity or milieu—whether we call it soul, subject, mind, Spirit, will-to-power, *Dasein*, Unconscious, or anything else—can pass from a historically over-determined present (i.e. the given world) to a different, possibly better, future by creating or recognizing new ideas. Rather, the problem is how that-which-appears in the symbolic sphere makes the passage to its subsequent realization. To put the matter even more plainly, the most pressing question is: how it is possible even for the idea of something new to found something new?

The discourse of grounds and grounding conceals a deep contradiction or incommensurability between the causal subject and the grounding subject, and, in concealing it, testifies to the ethically evasive tendencies displayed by all official institutions of law and morality. The grounding subject cannot get anything done in the world without the assistance of the causal subject. Moreover, it cannot communicate with the causal subject except in signs. Considered from the grounding subject's point of view, these signs seem to *speak* in the language of signified meanings (i.e. rational grounds). But the causal subject can only *hear* these very same signs in a lesser language comprised of mere phonemes that trigger historically determined reactions. The very moment the grounding subject whispers grounds into the ear of its more muscular twin, the causal subject, the former falls asleep, like a narcoleptic, so that the latter can react, like Pavlov's dogs, to the stimulus of the ordinary, the run-of-the-mill, the "obvious." The grounding subject may lay down the law as X, but the causal subject always picks up the *sign* "X" in a way that only history can explain.

In response to the query, "Who am I?" Derrida (2008, pp. 53–54) once asked, "what would ever distinguish the response, in its total purity, the so-called free responsible response, from a reaction to a complex system of stimuli?" The point of Derrida's question—and it is a question rather than an answer—was ethical rather than metaphysical. For him, "Casting doubt on responsibility, on decision, on one's own being-ethical, seems to me to be—and is perhaps what should forever remain—the unrescindable essence of ethics, decision, and responsibility" (Derrida 2008, p. 126). From this point of view, it verges on an unpardonable ethical evasion to claim, as Heidegger (1998, p. 127) did, that "freedom is freedom for ground, [and i]n grounding, freedom gives and takes ground." This way of talking about grounding fails to preserve the *problem* of the subject(s) as a ceaseless ethical burden and sorrow. That problem, in a nutshell, is that no decision can be made, and no enduring hierarchy established, between the grounding subject and the causal subject without engaging in bad faith.

The idea of the grounding subject represents a desperate and ultimately futile attempt to repress awareness of (and evade personal responsibility for) the essential sadness and tragedy of the world. But the idea of the causal subject is also a copout: it reduces ethical responsibility to a mere reaction, and thus apologizes for the sadness and tragedy of the real world that lies just beneath the abstraction expressions of law and morals. The grounding subject hides from tragedy behind its grounding expressions; the causal subject rides away from tragedy on the back of necessity. The most that thought and reason (the grounding subject) could ever do is provide the human body (the causal subject) with a thin tissue of grounding statements made up of symbols and images. But these symbols and images will never span the vast existential distance separating the grounding subject from the causal subject, our ends from our means, our words from our deeds, and, more generally, human suffering and all of the seemingly endless casuistries we offer to justify it. Since living in constant awareness of this fact can be unpleasant, there is always the option of finding refuge in sheer stupidity, which, as Vladimir Jankélévitch (2005, p. 75) once said, is the only way that some people have of retaining their innocence. But then again, what if that most acerbic of all statements in the Bible—"In much wisdom is much grief; and he that increaseth knowledge increaseth sorrow" (Ecclesiastes 1:18)—were also the most ethically obligatory?

References

Agamben, Giorgio. 2000. *Means Without End: Notes on Politics*, tr. Vincenzo Binetti and Cesare Cesarino. Minneapolis, MN: University of Minnesota Press.

Alexandre, Kojéve. 1980. *Introduction to the Reading of Hegel*, tr. James Nichols. Ithaca, NY: Cornell University Press.

Arendt, Hannah. 1965. *Eichmann in Jerusalem: A Report on the Banality of Evil*, Revised edn. New York, NY: Viking Press.

Beck, Lewis White. 1967. 'Neo-Kantianism'. In Paul Edwards (ed.), *The Encyclopedia of Philosophy*, 8 vols. New York, NY: Macmillan, v. 468–473.

Benjamin, Walter. 1978. *Reflections: Essays, Aphorisms, Autobiographical Writings*, tr. Edmund Jephcott. New York, NY: Schocken Books.

Berger, Peter and Luckmann, Thomas. 1967. *The Social Construction of Reality*. New York, NY: Doubleday.

Bloch, Ernst. 1988. *Natural Law and Human Dignity*, tr. Dennis Schmidt. Cambridge, MA: MIT Press.

Borradori, Giovanna. 2003. *Philosophy in a Time of Terror: Dialogues with Jürgen Habermas and Jacques Derrida*. Chicago, IL: University of Chicago Press.

Brubaker, Rogers. 1991. *The Limits of Rationality: An Essay on the Social and Moral Thought of Max Weber*. London: Routledge.

Buber, Martin. 2000. *I and Thou*, tr. Ronald Smith. New York, NY: Scribner.

Cleary, Thomas. 2001. *Classics of Buddhism and Zen: The Collected Translations of Thomas Cleary*, 4 vols. Boston, MA: Shambhala.

Cover, Robert. 1986. "Violence and the Word". *Yale Law Journal*, 95, 1601–1629.

Derrida, Jacques. 2008. In ed. Marie-Louise Mallet, *The Animal that Therefore I Am*, tr. David Wills, New York, NY: Fordham University Press.

Descartes, René. 1985. *The Philosophical Writings of Descartes*, 2 vols, trs John Cottingham et al. Cambridge: Cambridge University Press.

Douzinas, Costas. 2000. *The End of Human Rights: Critical Legal Thought at the Turn of the Century*. Oxford: Hart.

Dworkin, Ronald. 1986. *Law's Empire*. Cambridge: Harvard University Press.

Dworkin, Ronald. 1991. 'Pragmatism, Right Answers, and True Banality'. In Michael Brint and William Weaver (eds), *Pragmatism in Law and Society*. Boulder, CO: Westview Press, 359–388.
Foucault, Michel. 1972. *The Archaeology of Knowledge and the Discourse on Language*, tr. A.M. Sheridan Smith. New York, NY: Pantheon.
Foucault, Michel. 1980. In ed. Colin Gordon, *Power/Knowledge: Selected Interviews and Other Writings 1972–1977*, trs Colin Gordon et al., New York, NY: Pantheon.
Foucault, Michel. 2003. In eds Mauro Bertani and Alessandro Fontana, *'Society Must be Defended': Lectures at the Collège de France 1975–1976*, tr. David Macey, New York, NY: Picador.
France, Anatole. 2005. *The Novels of Anatole France: The Gods Are Athirst; Thais; The Red Lilly*, trs A.W. Evans et al. Garden City, NY: Country Life Press.
Freud, Sigmund. 1962. *Civilization and Its Discontents*, tr. James Strachey. New York, NY: W.W. Norton.
Gaete, Rolando. 1993. *Human Rights and the Limits of Critical Reason*. Dartmouth: Aldershot.
Goethe, Johann Wolfgang. 1964. *Goethe: Selected Verse*, ed. and tr. David Luke. London: Penguin Books.
Habermas, Jürgen. 1984. *The Theory of Communicative Action*, 2 vols, tr. Thomas McCarthy. Boston, MA: Beacon Press.
Herbert, Lionel Adolphus. 1961. *The Concept of Law*. Oxford: Oxford University Press.
Hegel, Georg Wilhelm Friedrich. 1967. *Hegel's Philosophy of Right*, tr. T.M. Knox. Oxford: Oxford University Press.
Hegel, Georg Wilhelm Friedrich. 1975. *Hegel's Logic*, tr. William Wallace. Oxford: Oxford University Press.
Hegel, Georg Wilhelm Friedrich. 1977. *Phenomenology of Spirit*, tr. A.V. Miller. Oxford: Oxford University Press.
Heidegger, Martin. 1962. *Being and Time*, trs John Macquarrie and Edward Robinson. New York, NY: HarperCollins.
Heidegger, Martin. 1977. *The Question Concerning Technology and Other Essays*, tr. William Lovitt. New York, NY: Harper & Row.
Heidegger, Martin. 1994. *The Fundamental Concepts of Metaphysics: World—Finitude—Solitude*, trs William McNeill and Nicholas Walker. Bloomington, IN: Indiana University Press.
Heidegger, Martin. 1998. In ed. William McNeill, *Pathmarks*. Cambridge: Cambridge University Press.
Heidegger, Martin. 1999. *Contributions to Philosophy (From Enowning)*, trs Parvis Emad and Kenneth Maly. Bloomington, IN: Indiana University Press.
Heidegger, Martin. 2002. *The Essence of Truth: On Plato's Cave Allegory and* Theaetetus, tr. Ted Sadler. New York, NY: Continuum.
Heidegger, Martin. 2003. *The End of Philosophy*, tr. Joan Stambaugh. Chicago, IL: University of Chicago Press.
Heidegger, Martin. 2008. *Basic Concepts of Ancient Philosophy*, tr. Richard Rojcewicz. Bloomington, IN: Indiana University Press.
Heraclitus. 1987. *Fragments*, tr. T.M. Robinson. Toronto, ON: University of Toronto Press.
Hobbes, Thomas. 1914. *Leviathan*. London: J.M. Dent.
Hyppolite, Jean. 1996. *Introduction to Hegel's Philosophy of History*, trs Bond Harris and Jacqueline Spurlock. Gainesville, FL: University of Florida Press.
Jaeger, Werner. 1945. *Paideia: The Ideals of Greek Culture*, 3 vols, 2nd edn, tr. Gilbert Highet. New York, NY: Oxford University Press.
James, William. 1904. *The Principles of Psychology*, 2 vols. New York, NY: Henry Holt.
Jankélévitch, Vladimir. 2005. *Forgiveness*, tr. Andrew Kelley. Chicago, IL: University of Chicago Press.
Kafka, Franz. 2006. *The Zürau Aphorisms*, tr. Michael Hofmann. New York, NY: Schocken Books.
Kant, Immanuel. 1993. In ed. Carl Friedrich, *The Philosophy of Kant: Immanuel Kant's Moral and Political Writings*, trs Carl Friedrich et al., New York, NY: Modern Library.

Kant, Immanuel. 1996. *Practical Philosophy*, ed. and tr. Mary Gregor. Cambridge: Cambridge University Press.

Kant, Immanuel. 1998. *The Critique of Pure Reason*, eds and trs Paul Guyer and Allen Wood. Cambridge: Cambridge University Press.

Kant, Immanuel. 2000. *The Critique of Judgment*, tr. J.H. Bernard. Amherst, NY: Prometheus Books.

Kojève, Alexandre, 1969. *Introduction to the Reading of* Hegel, tr. James Nichols, Ithaca, NY: Cornell University Press.

Levinas, Emmanuel. 1999. *Alterity and Transcendence*, tr. Michael Smith. New York, NY: Columbia University Press.

Locke, John. 1939. 'An Essay Concerning the True and Original Extent and End of Civil Government'. In Edwin Burtt (ed.), *The English Philosophers from Bacon to Mill*. New York, NY: Modern Library, 403–503.

Mannheim, Karl. 1985. *Ideology and Utopia*, trs Louis Wirth and Edward Shils. San Diego, CA: Harcourt Brace Jovanovich.

Marcuse, Herbert. 1964. *One-Dimensional Man*. Boston, MA: Beacon Press.

Marcuse, Herbert. 2007. In ed. Douglas Kellner, *Art and Liberation*. London: Routledge.

Marx, Karl. 1959. *Basic Writings on Politics and Philosophy*. Garden City, NY: Anchor Books.

Marx, Karl. 1964. *Early Writings*, ed. and tr. T.B. Bottomore. New York, NY: McGraw-Hill.

Nietzsche, Friedrich. 1968. In ed. Walter Kaufmann, *The Will to Power*, trs Walter Kaufmann and R.J. Hollingdale, New York, NY: Vintage Books.

Nietzsche, Friedrich. 1996. *Human, All Too Human: A Book for Free Spirits*, 2nd edn, tr. R.J. Hollingdale. Cambridge: Cambridge University Press.

Parmenides of Elea , 1984. *Fragments*, tr. David Gallop. Toronto, ON: University of Toronto Press.

Plautus, Titus Maccius. 1874. *Comedies of Plautus*, tr. Bonnell Thornton. London: Becket and de Hondt.

Rawls, John. 1999. *The Law of Peoples*. Cambridge: Harvard University Press.

Rousseau, Jean-Jacques. 1993. *The Social Contract and the Discourses*, tr. G.D.H. Cole. New York, NY: Knopf.

Sartre, Jean-Paul. 1956. *Being and Nothingness: An Essay on Phenomenological Ontology*, tr. Hazel Barnes. New York, NY: Philosophical Library.

Schopenhauer, Arthur. 1974. *On the Fourfold Root of the Principle of Sufficient Reason*, tr. E.F.J. Payne. La Salle, IL: Open Court.

Schopenhauer, Arthur. 1999. In ed. Günter Zöller, *Prize Essay on the Freedom of the Will*, tr. E.F.J. Payne. Cambridge: Cambridge University Press.

Weber, Max. 1958. *From Max Weber: Essays in Sociology*, eds and trs H.H. Gerth and C. Wright Mills, New York, NY: Oxford University Press.

Weber, Max. 1978. In eds Guenther Roth and Claus Wittich, *Economy and Society*, 2 vols, trs Ephraim Fischoff et al. Berkeley, CA: University of California Press.

Wittgenstein, Ludwig. 1978. In ed. Rush Rhees, *Philosophical Grammar*, tr. Anthony Kenny, Berkeley, CA: University of California Press.

Wittgenstein, Ludwig. 1983. In eds. G.H. von Wright et al., *Remarks on the Foundations of Mathematics*, tr. G.E.M. Anscombe, Cambridge: MIT Press.

Wittgenstein, Ludwig. 2003. In eds James Klagge and Alfred Nordmann, *Public and Private Occasions*. Lanham, MD: Rowman & Littlefield.

Wittgenstein, Ludwig. 2005. *The Big Typescript TS 213*, eds and trs G. Grant Luckhardt and Maximilian Aue. Oxford: Blackwell.

Wittgenstein, Ludwig and Waismann, Friedrich. 2003. In ed. Gordon Baker, *The Voices of the Vienna Circle*, trs Gordon Baker et al., London: Routledge.

Chapter 6
Law, Code and Late Modern Governance in Prophetic Painting: Notes on Jackson Pollock, Mark Rothko and Gilles Deleuze

Ronnie Lippens

6.1 Late Modern Governance

In a short passage in his book on *Postmodern Ethics*, Zygmunt Bauman remarked that late modern consumer societies, or, in Bauman's view, *postmodern* governance was characterized by two fundamental strategies, i.e. *seduction* and *repression* (1993, p. 139). Allow me to rephrase and expand on Bauman's remark here. Let us have a look at *seduction* first. Populations are now governed by allowing them to freely, and indeed, nomadically roam among a dizzying variety of what might perhaps be called commodity-image, in order to choose elements or fragments from it for consumption and self-constitution. The wandering, nomadic consumer, eager to choose, is allowed to circulate freely amidst freely circulating commodity-image. Late modern consumer nomadism is unlike the nomadism of the desert dweller who, forced by circumstance, must follow beaten tracks, regular as clockwork, like a machine. Late modern nomadism is more akin to the nomadism of the forest dweller who roams freely in search of uncertain opportunity. Drawing upon Foucault's later work, Michael Dillon and Luis Lobo-Guerrero describe this age as one marked by a "permanent state of *emergency*", that is, one that results from "the infinite empiricities of finite life understood as a continuous process of complex adaptive *emergence*" (2009, p. 10; italics RL). Such adaptive nomadics not only thrive on emergence (emergency), they are themselves emergence (emergency). They are emergent circulation. They are emergency circulation. However, all this nomadic circulation is permitted only on the condition that the processes of choice and self-constitution that result from it do not hinder, or worse, block off the very possibility of nomadic circulation itself. Seduction works, or is supposed to work only to the extent that consumers circulate, choose, and self-constitute responsibly, that is, with a certain measure of self-constraint. If there is a lack of self-constraint, or better, as we will see, if such a blockage of circulation threatens to occur, governance falls back on a second strategy, i.e. *repression*. Repression takes place when consumer choice and consumer self-constitution lack self-constraint and consequently

R. Lippens (✉)
Keele University, Newcastle-under-Lyme, UK
e-mail: r.lippens@keele.ac.uk

A. Wagner, J.M. Broekman (eds.), *Prospects of Legal Semiotics*,
DOI 10.1007/978-90-481-9343-1_6,

threaten to undermine the very conditions of free, nomadic circulation itself. That which is (assumed to be) unable to circulate responsibly, or better: *responsively*, should be repressed. That which is assumed to operate according to a non-responsive code should be repressed, for it is bound to obstruct free, nomadic circulation and free and nomadic, responsive choice. That which is assumed to function uncontrolled and uncontrollably, or unconstrained and unconstrainably, according to a blind, mechanistically rigid "logic", or according to an equally rigid, mere biological schema (e.g. a virus, a biological weapon system, fundamentalist ideology, a fanatic's mind, a criminal's depraved biology, an "anti-social" resident, and so on) should be repressed, for it is bound to spread, and infect and destroy the very conditions of free, nomadic circulation and choice. That which is assumed to threaten free, nomadic circulation and choice, should be repressed.

Late modern repression may however take a number of shapes and forms. In one, perceived threats to the possibility of free circulation, or, to be more precise, to the possibility of choice *in* circulation (or the choice *of* circulation), are considered as mere physical mass that needs to be shifted around, managed, or destroyed. The real target of the intervention here is the physical, or mechanical rigidity which this mass is alleged to carry within it. In criminal justice, for example, there has been talk for some time now about the move to what Malcolm Feeley and Jonathan Simon (1994) once termed *actuarial justice*. By that they meant the growing inclination, in criminal justice practice and procedure, to ignore the import of the singularity of individual defendants' capacities and make-up, and to rely, instead, on the stochastic processing of populations, of masses, or indeed, of *mass*. Feeley and Simon stressed the point that the "logic" here is an actuarial one. But that may be only part of the story. The actuary makes his calculations in order to insure against what is deemed to be unavoidable "risk". But the trend in criminal justice practice and, more broadly, governance, may already have moved *beyond* mere managerial "insurance" against "risk". In many cases the dominant logic in criminal justice and in governance is now provided by the *precautionary principle* (e.g. Pieterman and Hanekamp 2002, Pieterman 2008). According to this principle governance should not just aim to insure against risk, but should simply *prevent* all risk, by any means possible if deemed necessary. Instruments such as Anti-Social Behaviour Orders (deployed against the perceived rigidity of disturbing bio-mass), or a block on GM-foods (against the perceived rigidity of "unnatural" genetic codes), are only a few manifestations of the precautionary principle.

Repression can also take the form of punitive interventions whereby those who threaten conditions of free circulation and choice (e.g. the robber, or the bank manager who refuses to extend easy credit, and the manager who *does* extend easy credit easily, and so on) are made to *feel*, physically, how their rigidity is obstructive and therefore unwanted. Here the offender is reduced to his biological substrate. He is a mere biological organism. As with mere physical mass, there is no point in engaging in communication with mere organisms. Mass one shoves around, neutralizes, or destroys. Biological organisms, one makes them *feel*. Authors such as Nicola Lacey (2007) have, recently, noticed how in criminal justice procedure the emphasis is no longer on defendants' capacities (e.g. their capacity for change or self-transformation), but, rather, on their *character.* Character, almost by definition, is fixed, unchangeable, indeed, almost biological. One does not communicate with character. One makes it feel.

Both forms of governance (i.e. the management of rigid, inflexible, and unconstrained mass, and the taming of rigid, inflexible, and unconstrained flesh) share some common ground. Both target unresponsiveness. Neither presupposes or requires an interest in the inner self. Using existentialist words one could say that late modern governance has lost at least some of the typically modern interest in the singularity of surveying, pondering, deliberating, deciding and choosing selves. We will get back to this issue later. But a few words can be said here. Where modern governance, on the whole, *was* interested in finding out about how selves survey their being-in-the-world, how they ponder and deliberate upon this, how, in short, they choose, this interest is now gradually crumbling away. There is now less a need to find out about the singularly particular workings of inner selves, since the typically modern zeal to tap into their potential, to harness their energy, to exploit them, to knead and mould them, to discipline them, to normalize them, to guide and steer them towards predetermined goals and into projects, has nearly completely dissipated. The age of construction, *modern* construction is over.

Much in this picture might be underpinned, one could argue, by a *form of life*—a Nietzschean concept—that emerged in what we now call the late modern era. This is the form of life of a post-material generation whose main preoccupation it is to safeguard nomadic freedom of choice and circulation, or better still: choice *of* circulation, much less the construction of new, institutionalized futures. This is a form of life whereby, beaconless, one *must* constantly deal with, or attempt control over "the emergency of [continuous, unrelenting, RL] emergence" (Dillon and Lobo-Guerrero 2009, p. 17). It's the very same form of life whereby eagerly circulating nomads *must* deal with, or assert control over anything that carries a rigid, inflexible code. The word "generation" is used loosely here; it refers to an attitude and to practices which by no means are spread evenly across populations, although elements in the culturally dominant demographic or segments in late modern consumer societies may harbour or manifest more of such an attitude and practices than others. In this form of life there is no need for communication, and even less for the transformation of self. One does not communicate with mere mass or with mere biological organisms. There is nothing in them that could be transformed. After the end of the age of construction, there is nothing to communicate about, there is nothing to transform *to*. Even the joint consumption of commodity-image in what Michel Maffesoli (1996) has called "neo-tribes" does not require communication; only experience. As we will argue later the embryonic phase of this form of life emerged, faintly, during the immediate post-war years, say somewhere between 1945 and 1955. Fully-fledged, however, it only crystallized about two decades later.

We will return to this embryonic phase later. Let us explore this post-material, post-constructive form of life a little more. Much of the literature on current developments in criminal justice and governance focus on the management of "risk" (and therefore also of opportunity) in "risk societies", or on the prevention and near-total blocking off of potential "risk" (and opportunity), in precautionary societies.

But "risk" may not be the core target of a post-material, non-constructive consumer generation. Indeed, it is this very same generation that has produced what sociologists call *edgework*, i.e. the wilful seeking of, engagement in, and experimentation with all kinds of risk-taking and risk-exploring behaviour. This includes e.g. base-jumping, sky-diving, hiking in the great outdoors, and so on, as well as -why not?- hedge-fund investments, speculation on financial markets, sub-prime crediting, and so on. In all these activities, "risk" is not so much a problem, as a resource. A few years ago Stephen Lyng (2004) showed how edgeworkers take themselves in a zone beyond all code. Beyond the reach of rigid, unresponsive and external constraints embodied in legal and institutional codes, in social codes, in *any* code actually, edgeworkers move into a free zone where in some cases only the mere law of nature—the physical law of mass and the biological one of organism—is left to deal with. The control of nature, the control of mass and organism, is what edgeworkers hope to achieve. It is this control, or at least sense of control, argues Lyng, that allows the edgeworker to regain a sense of self. If Lyng's analysis of edgework is anything to go by, then the post-material, non-constructive consumer generation, roaming and swerving, as they tend to do, do not necessarily have a problem with risk per se. But they do seem to have a serious problem with a lack of control over all kinds of codes. Codes are by definition unresponsive, rigid, and threaten to curtail or constrain the self's potential for choice and circulation, or again: its potential to choose the form of circulation, or the modalities of the form of circulation it might wish to engage in. That is why edgeworkers tend to escape to an imaginary free zone of circulation, outside the reach of codes. In the face of the only code that cannot be escaped—the law of nature, or sheer nature—the edgeworker becomes one with it, and in that moment, or in this zone, he, and he alone (or at least that's how he imagines it), *chooses* freely (that is: un-coded, or coded only by nature's law itself) how to *respond* to, indeed *control* mere mass and organism. This should provide him with a *naturally* skilful self that, once returned to the human world, will know how to deal with all the rigid and unresponsive codes, indeed with the mass and organisms *there*. If this applies to the extreme world of edgework, it may also colour the attitudes and practices within the broader post-material generation more generally. There too nature, or the environment, often tends to be imagined as a free zone, as a zone of free circulation, that needs to be protected from the codes of human intervention. Human intervention, in this imaginary, particularly if it takes the shape of development and construction, cannot be anything but rigid and destructive of choice and circulation. Nature has no need for development and construction. Nature is complete. Out of free circulation, nature magically produces harmony (or so it is then believed). The name of this "magic" is responsiveness. The only thing that needs to be done is to keep at bay, or if necessary to destroy everything that threatens to disrupt or block this magic of nature. Nothing needs to be constructed, and so there is nothing to communicate about. Like nature itself, the post-material self's imaginary world is a, nay *the* natural one. In this imaginary world, harmony emerges spontaneously out of freely choosing and freely circulating natural selves. These selves choose and circulate, and choose their form of circulation, responsively. That means they choose and circulate flexibly, with a certain measure of self-constraint that comes *naturally*. These selves do not carry within them and do not operate according to a rigid, inflexible code (responsive self-constraint could not exist if there *were* such rigidity within the self). This post-material imaginary world is one that needs no further construction or reconstruction either. Anything that carries or operates according to a rigid code (a virus, a radical extremist, an "anti-social" element, and so on) should be kept at bay, managed, neutralized or destroyed. That's all. There's no need to reason with such rigidity. There's no point in communicating with them. It makes no sense to try and transform their operative code, their "inner self". Rigid mass and organism, their "code" is unchangeable anyway.

This post-material, post-constructive imaginary of free circulation and choice, and the need to protect these, sometimes at all cost (e.g. in precautionary societies and cultures), tends to continually spawn measures and interventions that will, paradoxically, undermine their very conditions. The often draconian measures taken against anything that allegedly poses a threat to the capacity and to the ability to choose one's form and modality of circulation quite often result in a severe restriction of this very capacity and this ability. In the longer term such measures may simply drain potentials of resilience and responsiveness, and, consequently, the very ability to even imagine free and chosen circulation. This is the case particularly when protective measures are sanctioned by law, and when they legally allow the officially appointed "protectors" to freely invent, explore and apply definitions, standards and assessments of threat. There is then a significantly paradoxical tension to be noted in the post-material and post-constructive imaginary. This tension is all the more significant in the light of a feature of the late modern, de-traditionalized, and de-institutionalized self, i.e. its decentred condition. Decentred, the late modern self roams and swerves nomadically, either in reality, virtuality, or in the imagination, unbounded. During such roaming and swerving the self (and that includes the protector's self) will be very likely to encounter and explore all manner of opportunity, but will be equally likely to stumble upon all kinds of what it believes to be unresponsive, rigid and therefore threatening code. Quite often the self will experience the very same code encountered as both an opportunity and a threat, sometimes simultaneously so. It is not at all uncommon for local councillors to find that when, at the pressing demand of constituents, they rearrange, with a lot of *precaution,* the road layout in the vicinity of schools, those very same constituents will then also attack them for having blocked off their free circulation to the nearby shopping mall.

Let us now recapitulate the broad contours of what, arguably, could be called the late modern, post-material and post-constructive *form of life* and the mode of governance that flows from it. This form of life is one where the free choice of the form of circulation—whether real or imaginary—is of paramount importance. Free choice of the form of circulation can only be entrusted to nomadic selves that, freely choosing and freely circulating, do so *responsively*, in control. This form of life is assumed to be natural, indeed it is deemed to be nature itself, that is, beyond history, past the need for constructive improvement. This however often leads to drastic, precautionary measures that, aiming to protect this form of life, seek to merely manage, neutralize, or even destroy all sources of rigid and therefore threatening codes. That in turn tends to undermine, in a paradoxical twist, the very post-material and post-constructive form of life itself. As mentioned above this form of life and governance emerged fully-fledged in what some have called late modernity. In the remainder of this essay however we will try to show how traces of this form of life already emerged *visibly* during the immediate post-war years. The use of the word "visibly" here is not at all coincidental. One of the theses which it is hoped this paper will, if not demonstrate then at least illustrate, holds that forms of life and their forms of governance first emerge in the *visual* realm, before they do so, conceptually, in strings of words. The visual traces of an emerging form of life that expresses or imagines life as perfectly natural free choice and circulation that shall be explored here, in the essay at hand, will be those that crystallized, sometime between 1945 and 1955, on the canvases of abstract expressionists Jackson Pollock (1912–1956) and Mark Rothko (1903–1970). But before we analyse these works in more detail, we will have to discuss the issue and problem of emergence first.

6.2 Virtuality and Prophetic Painting

Art historians have on occasion wondered about whether there might be something like prophetic art. The late Francis Haskell was one of them. In his essay "Art as Prophecy" (1993, pp. 389–430) Haskell analysed woodcuts and paintings spanning four centuries, asking himself whether works such as Jacques-Louis David's pre-revolutionary painting *Oath of the Horatii* [1785] somehow prophesied events to come. Haskell himself remained undecided on the issue, and ultimately felt compelled to conclude that the prophetic force of the image, or the "gift of divination" of the artist has "been distributed in a somewhat arbitrary manner". Some artists (Haskell was focussing on painters) seem to possess such a gift, at least to some extent, while others don't. However, if there is reason to suspect any "prophetic power" in artists, then, claims Haskell, it "is related to their exceptional sensitivities rather than to their abilities at making clever guesses or to their faculties of reasoning" (1993, p. 430). Indeed, it is "sensitivity" (the more or less direct route between earth and flesh) and not "cleverness", much less "reason" (faculties firmly embedded in the symbolic order of language and institution) that allows the artist to bring visual traces to the surface first. Conceptual "cleverness" and wordy "reason" should then follow later, that is, after journeys through the symbolic and the institutional.

Haskell's use of terminology such as "gift of divination" betrayed a particular understanding of the possibility of *prophetic painting*. Here the artist, or the painter, appears as someone who makes a deliberate effort to divine what is to happen in the future. The painter, or the artist, pictures himself or sees a scene, in other words, a vision, which he then proceeds to compose and arrange on his canvas, or panel. The thus painted image then holds the representation of a number of scenes or events in a divined, prophesied future. *Prophetic painting* here is painting that paints on canvas, or on panel, events or scenes that were *deliberately* divined, imagined, and prophesied. There is, however, another way of looking at prophecy in painting. That one holds that *all* painting, to an extent, is prophetic. This is because all painting somehow expresses something of *emerging* forms of life. By "emerging" is meant here the transition, of forms of life, from the realm of the virtual, from the not-yet-actualized, to the actual. This transition takes place, so it will be argued below, first and foremost through the senses. The process of transition, or of actualization, is continuous, and non-deliberate. Painting is the location *par excellence* to detect the actualization, in matter, of emerging forms of life. Or at least, painting might potentially be that location, much more so than e.g. sculpture, or installation art, or film. These already require a certain amount of deliberate *reasoning* and reflection, and should therefore be implicated—much more so than painting—in the realm of the symbolic, and the conceptual. Haskell himself hinted at this when he fleetingly remarked that, if there is anything like "prophetic power" in art, it should reside in "sensitivity", that is, in a certain non-reflective, non-deliberate, and non-conceptual emergence, through the bones and the flesh of the artist, and into actual matter, of that which is emergent. To be sure, much in painting *is* the result of reflection, of reason and deliberation. But some of it isn't. Something in painting—in *all* painting, potentially—is the sensory expression of the new, of that which is, continuously, becoming. In that sense one could indeed say that *all* painting is prophetic, at least potentially. All painting will to some extent express something of the newly emerging, before reason, before the concept, before reflective deliberation. It is in this sense that we will consider *prophetic painting*. Emergent forms of life, or elements of it, in other words, are likely to leave traces first on panels and on canvases, before they do so in books and tracts, or on film.

Our guide here will be Gilles Deleuze, particularly the Deleuze who discussed painting in the book on *Francis Bacon: The Logic of Sensation* (2003, originally 1981). There is simply no space here in this essay to situate this book within the massive, massively important though hugely complex oeuvre of Deleuze and his co-author Felix Guattari. It would simply be impossible to even begin to situate Deleuze and Guattari's very extensive conceptual apparatus. But we need to say a few words at least about Deleuze's ideas on emergence (see e.g. Murray 2006 and 2007 on this), and more specifically about emergence in painting (see also Slaughter's work on Deleuze and art, 2004, 2007). One of the crucial concepts in this book is the *diagram*. The concept is not new, and Deleuze relies on earlier work by Peirce and Foucault. A diagram is the result, in virtuality, of the articulation, in and through the flow of desire, and the clash of forces, of a number of what Deleuze calls *intensities*. A diagram then is that which, in virtuality, is produced by *desiring machines*, i.e. articulations (i.e. machines) of intensive (i.e. not yet materialized, or actualized) forces and flows of desire that, in turn, cut into and further machine desire. Diagrams then are *abstract machines*, machined products of desiring machines. Out of the chaotic potential of flowing desire, *desiring production* ultimately produces abstract diagrams, or virtual forms or modes of life. This process of incessant, continuous virtual desiring production takes place on and from the *social unconscious* (mind: not the *individual* unconscious), i.e. from what Deleuze calls the *plane of immanence*. Diagrams emerge from there to move through matter (e.g. a painter's flesh and bones; a local ruler's; a revolutionary's, and so on) in a process of actualization whereby concrete—that is, *extensive*—and coded assemblages are formed (e.g. lines on a canvas, strings of words, subjects, institutions, a policy, and so on). Together these assemblages form a form of life. In his book on *Foucault* (1988, originally 1984), Deleuze would later analyse Foucault's work as essentially preoccupied with emerging diagrams. Diagrams here combine virtual, emerging *visibilities*, on the one hand, and *articulables*, on the other. Visibilities are those productive conditions that make particular *ways of seeing* possible. Articulables are those productive conditions that make particular *ways of saying* possible. Foucault himself, in Deleuze's analysis, considered visibilities and articulables as belonging to two separate, distinct registers, but, nevertheless, emerging virtually and actualizing extensively simultaneously.

In *Bacon* the diagram is, first and foremost, an abstract "possibility of fact" (2003, p. 71). Situated between the sheer chaos of the intensive production on the plane of immanence, on the one hand, and the extensive coded assemblages in the sphere of the actual, on the other, the diagram is, writes Deleuze, "a chaos, a catastrophe, but it is also a germ of order or rhythm" (2003, p. 72). It is the virtual abstract form of a becoming, emerging form of life. Francis Bacon's paintings, according to Deleuze, capture precisely the moment of actualization. In the deformed, stretched, and contorted figures that take centre stage in Bacon's work, Deleuze sees the impact of an emerging diagram on the flesh of matter as it traverses bodies. As it impacts on, or affects extensive bodies and assemblages, it stretches and contorts them, it transforms them, into new bodies and into new assemblages, decoding them and recoding them. Bacon, then, paints emergence, or transformation (both words can be used interchangeably). Traces of the diagram can be seen on the canvas. The diagram, writes Deleuze, "is the operative set of traits and color-patches, of lines and zones" (2003, p. 72). As such these patches, traits, lines and zones are the visual trace of the "possibility of fact" as it crystallized, through matter, on the canvas.

Bacon still painted figures. Abstract expressionists had abandoned the figural years before Bacon. In the work of the former, and especially in Pollock's, according to Deleuze, the diagram of an emerging form of life formed fully on the canvas. Indeed, Deleuze writes, in the work of abstract expressionists "the diagram merges with the totality of the painting; the entire painting is diagrammatic" (2003, p. 74). That however may be a bridge too far. It may be impossible to detect the outline, that is, the full *virtual* "possibility of fact", machined, as it was, out of the full potentiality on the plane of immanence, in the patches, lines, colours, and zones of a painting, including abstract expressionist ones. On its travels through matter, that is, through extensive bodies and assemblages, it will, whilst affecting and stretching and contorting matter, itself get to be stretched, contorted, de-formed, and transformed. The diagram can only leave traces on canvases. It could never be "the entire painting". Moreover, works of art (whether they be painting or scholarship or political tract) are what John Hillis Miller once called "inaugural performatives" (e.g. 1992, pp. 55–60). Expressions of virtually emerging and actualizing diagrams works of art may be, they are also, and simultaneously so, *creative* performances that always and inescapably so, add to, escape from, and exceed their diagrammatic conditions. They are singular configurations of traces that betray only *becoming*. Internally diverse, or hybrid, or multiple, and fleeing its context and conditions on its *performing* move, the work of art is an unstable, moving target. This is a point that Deleuze himself agrees with when he introduces the notion of the figure (2003, p. 109), i.e. that which emerges, in matter, after the diagram has "scrambled" coded figurative forms. That goes for abstract expressionist work too. The visual abstraction on the canvas is only a trace—a trace of the Figure—left by the virtual abstraction of the diagram *after* it has travelled through the singularly *specific* assemblage of bodies and assemblages that form the painter, and his horizon. But these traces are all we've got. The attempt to re-trace the contours of a diagram underneath the patches, lines, zones and colours on a canvas, therefore, can only be that: an attempt.

However, at the exact moment when elements of the virtual diagram appear as traces in and on matter, they form part of an emerging form of life, and, methodologically speaking, they can be considered together with other manifestations of this form of life. As assemblages that were machined out of the diagrammatic virtual, to then traverse matter, and in so far as they are closer to the immanence of the productive earth (the *plane of immanence*) than symbols and concepts, or political tracts and film scripts, these traces are among the first assemblages of an emerging form of life to crystallize. We hope to be able to illustrate below how some of the traces that appeared, in the immediate post-war era, on the paintings of Jackson Pollock, and of Mark Rothko, could be viewed as such early assemblages. They appeared, it will be argued, as harbingers of a late modern form of life, and of a late modern form of governance, well before there was talk of it in works such as those by, e.g. Guy Debord (1967). Indeed they appeared well before the advent of the welfare state, this final attempt at and continuation of the modern project of normalization and discipline which would, on the one hand, slow down the full emergence of late modern, post-material, and post-constructive life, but, on the other, also help shape its final assemblage.

6.3 Two Painters (1945–1955)

The post-war work of Pollock and Rothko is often classified as *abstract expressionist*. Unlike other abstract work, and indeed unlike other abstract expressionist work—e.g., Barnett Newman's static and rather strictly divided colour fields—their painting expresses remarkably tangible tension (on Newman, see also Slaughter 2004, at pp. 253–256). Pollock's paintings on the one hand, and Rothko's on the other, seem to occupy two opposite poles of a visual spectrum. Pollock's so-called action-painting and "drip" technique produced canvases with what on first sight look like randomly splattered and dripped, criss-crossing lines and curves and blots of paint. Rothko's huge squares, or oblong shapes, that seem to hover, pulsating, facing one another, wavering perhaps, or negotiating the thin and hazy zones in-between them, are, visually, quite distinct from Pollock's and one might perhaps be forgiven for situating them at the extreme opposites of the spectrum. And yet there is quite some common ground between both painters. Both Pollock and Rothko tended to paint on large canvases that, in the words of Rothko, one must "be within" (Rothko 2006, p. 99), as one would be—like the edgeworker, perhaps—within the *matter* of a natural environment. Pollock, when painting, placed most of his canvases on the floor of his studio and, bending over them, dripping curves and lines of paint on them. He too inclined towards the sheer matter of a natural earth. The paintings of both Pollock and Rothko, as said, also express a gripping tension. We will get back to this tension below, but here we can already mention the fact that both artists did stress that they wanted to express the irresolvable tension that dwells at the heart of the human condition. Rothko, who, unlike Pollock, left us quite extensive written reflections on his work, on many occasions claimed that his massive squares, floating or hovering in the midst of tangible tension, express entities that are involved in and "perform" the fullness of human "drama" (2006, p. 58). "I'm only interested", he later wrote, "in expressing basic human emotions—tragedy, ecstasy, doom and so on" (2006, p. 119). Both painters had tried to express the fundamental tension of human "tragedy" before, in their earlier work (right up to the end of World War II), mostly in more or less figural paintings of mythological scenes. After the war they abandoned the figural altogether. In their post-war work the subject, and the self, dissolve into the matter of the earth, that is, into the natural environment of universal, irresolvable, and ineradicable human "drama" and "tragedy". Let us now have a closer look at the work of these artists separately.

6.3.1 Jackson Pollock

Jackson Pollock's giant-size canvas *Autumn Rhythm* [1950], for example, envelopes the viewer completely. The viewer notices and experiences traces in the earthy autumn all around him. Those could be his, or perhaps they are traces left by others. On first sight the traces look as if they are the result of random wanderings. Away from the *striated space* (to use Deleuze's terminology) of institutionalized codes and the orders they crystallize, the seemingly random traces betray something of the freedom-searching (and possibly: freedom-experiencing) roaming of nomads who are on their restless way to *becoming*-nature. In Deleuze's terminology: fleeing from the codes embodied in actual assemblages (e.g. institutions, subjectivity, and so on) the nomad explores virtual "possibilities of fact" and, beyond those, reaches for the immanent potentiality of the earth. In some of his earlier and smaller post-war paintings (e.g. *Gray and Red*, and *Black, White and Gray*, both 1948) Pollock seems to have mimicked the wriggling movement of sperm, i.e. the as yet un-coded, *seminal* "possibility of fact".

Autumn Rhythm: Number 30 [1950] (266.7 × 525.8 cm) Courtesy of The Metropolitan Museum of Art, New York. © The Pollock-Krasner Foundation ARS, NY and DACS, London 2009

The Earth—autumn earth at least—is a place full of potential to explore; it is a place where "possibility of fact" emerges, for the nomadic explorer to explore and, possibly, produce. Indeed, nomadic exploration is not just mere exploration. Something emerges from it, i.e. "possibility of fact", as well as, subsequently, the forms and shapes which it forms during its travels through earthy matter. The attentive viewer will notice a number of located shapes and forms on the canvas. There is (let's recall Deleuze's words) "a germ of order or rhythm" to be noted here.

But this freedom-loving nomadism is not just about nomadic freedom of exploration. And it certainly is not about returning to chaos. Pollock once (i.e. in 1950) sent a telegram to the editors of a piece that characterized his work as pre-occupied with chaos: "SIR: NO CHAOS DAMN IT. DAMNED BUSY PAINTING AS YOU CAN SEE..." (cited in Emmerling 2007, pp. 68–69). There is a very tangible tension in Pollock's works. In one of the very few statements made by Pollock on the topic of his work he wrote "Technic is the result of a need... new needs demand new technics... total control... denial of the accident... States of order. organic intensity... energy and motion... made visible... memories arrested in space... human needs and motives... acceptance" (published posthumously, cited in Emmerling, on page 69 and in Varnedoe and Karmel 1998, p. 56). His work is as much about control, that is, about acquiring control, about exercising and about controlling self and environment, as it is about nomadic, un-coded exploration. In fact, both dimensions are inextricably intertwined in Pollock's painting. One may hope to acquire control ("total control" even) by moving away and by placing oneself outside the reach of the "total control" of "States of order", away from the rigid codes of the State and its institutions. This zone can and should not be one of "accidents", or mere chaos. It is, rather, a zone of nature, one of "organic intensity" and, in Deleuze's words, one of potential emergence, which is to be explored with lots of "energy and motion". It is precisely this energetic motion and this exploration that will provide sources of control. But control also is to be exercised *during* these very nomadic, earthy explorations. One must never allow chaos to take over. Now, the nomadic and wandering exploration in itself already constitutes a measure of control. The productive emergence of diagrammatic "possibilities of fact", and indeed the crystallization, in matter, of the new, constitute another form of control. The nomadic traces of the "energetic" and "busy" productive wandering that went before and that led to this emergence are then only the past, "made visible", indeed mere "memories arrested in space" which, in the very moment of painting and contemplation, are already on the move again, exploring and becoming-other yet again.

The issue and importance of control is also noticeable in the very act of painting itself. In his meticulously elaborated essay "Pollock at Work" (in Varnedoe and Karmel 1998, pp. 87–137), Pepe Karmel notes how Pollock usually started his paintings by drawing a number of clearly delineated figures on the canvas. He then dripped or splashed the paint in his typically nomadic curves, and lines and patches, working outward, i.e. from the figures toward and into their environment, ultimately allowing the lines and patches to cover the whole canvas and to erase all outlines of the original figures and therefore all distinction between the subject, or the self, and its natural surroundings. The subject—the coded effect of institutionalized order—and the self thus dissolve in the sheer nature of organism and the law of physical mass ("organic intensity"... "energy and motion") in what Varnedoe calls "gestures of cancellation or eradication" (in Varnedoe and Karmel 1998, p. 50). This, according to Varnedoe, is "an act of opening-up, not suppression" (1998, p. 54). In this sense one could understand why Omri Moses, in a Nietzschean reading of Pollock's work recently (2004) described it as an "address to the nonhuman". Pollock's nomad roams "endlessly" in a world that is devoid of human projects and their rigid codes. That however means there can then be no "accident" ("denial of the accident", says Pollock) in that world either, only nomadic necessity ("technic is the result of a need", etc).

But that, i.e. necessity, claims Moses, "turns quite imperceptibly into the endless of production, that is, production's inability to possess itself in its end" (2004, p. 21). Here though one would be inclined to differ. There is much control, much "possessing itself", involved in Pollock's work. The painter drips and splashes the paint not in a completely random fashion, but, says Karmel, in a "controlled, deliberate fashion" which ultimately leads to the "breakup of the composition into a series of self-contained configurations" (1998, pp. 129–131). There is, to some extent, a "free flow of unconscious imagery" in the "dancelike movements" made by Pollock during his action painting. And this imagery, claims Emmerling, may transfer to the canvas in a process of "immediate communication" (2007, p. 65), but Pollock himself, as we have seen, was at pains to stress the dimension of *responsive* control in the very process of emergence itself ("new needs demand new technics"). In his *Bacon*, Gilles Deleuze captured this moment of tension and ambivalence in the very act of painting when he referred to Bacon's remark "that there is no chance except 'manipulated' chance, no accident except a 'utilized' accident" (2003, p. 67). Deleuze however believed that the abstract expressionists (he mentions Pollock) "abandoned [...] any visual control" in all their "blindness". In "[suppressing] the task of controlling the hand that the eye still had in classical representation", action painting, Deleuze goes on, "subordinates the eye to the hand" and "replaces the horizon with a ground" (2003, p. 75). Pollock would have begged to differ. In Pollock's work, both the eye *and* the hand dissolve in the ground of nature where the boundaries between free experimentation (the hand) and control (the eye) have collapsed, and where the horizon ever-becomes anew in endless transformation. Or, in Omri Moses' words, Pollock's painting is an "adulterated site in which volition shares company with contingency, rather than seeing itself as triumphing over it" (2004, p. 12). But, it should be stressed, control never leaves Pollock's picture. The dissolution of self and subject in the sheer potentiality of earth, both in the act of painting, as in the resulting paintings themselves, takes place not just *with* a measure of control, but *as* control—responsive control. In the act of painting this control manifests itself as choice, i.e. the choice made, by the painter, to drip here, and not there; to splash such, but not so. In the paintings, choice is "made visible" as a series of trajectories—"arrested in space"—of past choices, of past controlled explorations and, possibly, experiments.

Now let us have a look at a painting from 1952, i.e. *Blue Poles*. Again this is a painting of quite substantial dimensions. Clear straight lines now seem to organize the earthy ground. Whether these lines are the original lines of the coded and *striated*

Blue Poles: Number II [1952] (210 × 486.8 cm) Courtesy of National Gallery of Australia, Canberra. © The Pollock-Krasner Foundation ARS, NY and DACS, London 2009

space of State institutions—or any other institution or project for that matter—which the nomad explorers, on their *lines of flight* (again a Deleuzian term), are fleeing in a bid for control, or whether, on the contrary, these straight lines are the manifestations of emerging forms of control through which these very nomads seem to attempt to code and thus control their environment and, consequently, their meandering explorations, remains unclear. But one could argue that in *Blue Poles* something of the inevitably "tragic" dimension of the "human drama" which many, in the immediate post-war years had come to realise (but more on this later), expressed itself. This "something" refers to the sense, more than the insight, or the idea, that the "possibility of fact" of free exploration rests on, and depends on the "possibility of fact" of control (the control of self, as well as the control of nature). And vice versa: "the possibility of fact" of control depends on, and cannot emerge or take shape without the "possibility of fact" of un-coded nomadism (flexible, responsive nomadism *within* the self, as well as within nature). This is probably why Varnedoe is able to conclude that Pollock's work expresses not just a "quasi-religious rejection of modern life in favour of a return to unreasoned awe before, and identification with the elemental forces of nature". It is not just a "Romantic" "atavistic howl". It was equally "nurtured", and bears traces of, an Enlightened legacy of "individual freedom", "civic reason" and "cosmopolitan pluralism" (in Varnedoe and Karmel 1998, p. 75).

Emerging "possibilities of fact", however much they result from flight from coded, or striated space, will produce their own code. Without a virtually emerging diagram and without crystallizing, coded assemblages machined from them, emergence *itself* could never be a "possibility of fact". To use words that are well-known in post-structuralist circles: the one provides the *conditions of possibility* for the other. And vice versa. The other provides the *conditions of impossibility* for the one. And again, vice versa. Mark Rothko too tried to express this "drama" in his post-war work. He used forms and shapes that were very different from Pollock's though.

6.3.2 Mark Rothko

After he left mythology during the early 1940s Rothko gradually developed his signature style. At first he painted his so-called *multiforms* (i.e. patchworks of lots of smaller, fuzzy patches, mostly square shaped) but by the end of the decade he had already moved on to painting the massive squares and oblong shapes that are so characteristic of this mature work. The painting *No. 24* of 1951 is one of these paintings.

The shapes are indeed massive, and seem to be hovering, or floating, against a backdrop which, as a hazy shimmer, is visible in some of the spaces in-between the shapes, as well as in the borders. Some (e.g. Stoker 2008, Svedlow 2008) tend to read Rothko's work as the depiction (as well as the experience) of the religious sublime. Another reading is possible. The shapes, in Rothko's words, are entities, "unique elements in a unique situation", "organisms with volitions and a passion for self-assertion", "actors" that "perform" the "tragedy" of the "human drama". They are "actors who are able to move dramatically without embarrassment and execute gestures without shame". They do so "with internal freedom, and without need to conform with or to violate what is probable in the familiar world" (Rothko 2006, pp. 58–59). In other words: codeless, these entities circulate, responsively, embarking upon "unknown adventures in an unknown space" (cited in Baal-Teshuva 2003, p. 42). Seeing a similarity between Pollock's work and Rothko's shapes (i.e. in their capture of "a moment of flux") Bonnie Clearwater notes how the latter "seem able to move and breathe on their own" (2006, p. 72). The borders are completely open, and suggest a limitless expanse, or world, of ever-continuing tragic drama *beyond*. The entities seem to have some room to manoeuvre, and to negotiate their position in the obvious and undeniable presence of the other shapes, "constantly shifting their position" (Clearwater 2006, p. 77). They may negotiate a path into the beyond and explore the possibilities there. Or they may have returned from there, full with the wisdom of the ineradicable drama of human life, and filled with the tragedy that comes with the acknowledgement that there is no ultimate redemption out there. But for now they are just floating, hovering, and negotiating space, their space.

No. 24 (Untitled) [1951] 236.9 × 120.7 cm Courtesy of Tel Aviv Museum of Art, Gift of the Mark Rothko foundation, Inc., New York, 1986. © 1998 Kate Rothko Prizel and Christopher Rothko ARS, NY and DACS, London 2009

The boundaries of the entities are porous and fuzzy. This is what allows them to negotiate their space, and the other entities in it. This is what allows them to sense their way through the tragedy of life. In places the fuzzy boundaries overlap, and something akin to communication and thus transformation takes place. But that is mostly by way of experimentation. The entity remains, on the whole, its massive self. Within this self there is tremor, tension, and what might be described as indeterminacy. Within the self, things are not all that even, or clear. There too fuzziness abounds. Perhaps there are too many memories of earlier explorations in there, and the choices they once made, all burdened now with the inevitable tragedy of life? Perhaps these selves harbour a wildly diverse and visibly boiling collection of newly prepared plans, intentions, aspiration, all chosen with an eye on yet another hopeful bout of explorations into the world of human drama? The drama within the shapes includes "pre-occupation with death", "sensuality", "tension [. . .] either conflict or curbed desire", "irony", "wit and play", "the ephemeral and chance", and "hope" (Rothko 2006, pp. 125–126).

Although Rothko has, on one occasion, used the phrase "complex inner self" (Rothko 2006, p. 46) to describe that which is depicted within the porous and unclear boundaries of the entities, the particular dynamics that take place in them seem to be, at best, of secondary importance only. The specificity of memories, plans, intentions, deliberations, ponderings, and so on, is not the main issue here. Indeed, in the painter's own words, it goes: "the familiar identity of things has to be pulverized in order to destroy the finite associations with which our society increasingly enshrouds every aspect of our environment" (2006, p. 59). Here again, as with Pollock, there is a sense of nomadic desire to flee all code ("finite associations" that "enshroud"). The particular singularity of each of the entities' inner self is not of paramount importance here. But the deep sense of human drama, regardless of the singularities involved, is. Indeed, by his own account Rothko (2006, p. 39) chose to do away with all figuration in order to "intensify" the expression of the universality of the human drama.

It should by now come as no big surprise that Rothko spent a lot of time reading and thinking about Nietzsche's work (as well as Kierkegaard's). What we see on Rothko's canvases, one may safely assume, could therefore hardly be interpreted as nihilism. Like Nietzsche, Rothko is a *tragic* philosopher. "Tragic" here refers to the ability to fully see the abysmal tragedy of life and not to run from it, but

No. 61 (Rust and Blue)
[1953] 294 × 232.4 cm
Courtesy of The Museum of Contemporary Art, Los Angeles. © 1998 Kate Rothko Prizel and Christopher Rothko ARS, NY and DACS, London 2009

look it *squarely* in the face. A tragic philosopher is someone who understands that life as such is ultimately unstoppable and unfixable. It is impossible to pin it down completely. Life will always find a way to burst forth, to become ever anew, with all its splendour and with all its horrors. Life is "eternal recurrence". The force of life is unquenchable. Nothing human will hold or last forever. Becoming is unstoppable. A tragic philosopher is someone who understands this, and who sees this as an opportunity or as an invitation to stop moaning and to start creating, exploring, venturing, and changing instead.

With Nietzsche, Rothko seems to be saying: since the world is unfixable, nothing will ultimately hold; there is then all the more reason not to despair but to start creating the new instead. This is where the open space in-between the entities and in the expanding borders keeps open the promise of the new, and of exploration. Through this open space the earthy colour of an immanent earth is clearly visible. On this earthy *plane of immanence*, virtual "possibilities of fact" may already be forming, to then start impacting on entities and moving them into further negotiations and explorations which, in turn, will lead to new assemblages, and, possibly, the de-coding and re-coding of old ones.

But this is only part of the story. Rothko's work, like Pollock's, seems to express something of the tangible and paradoxical tension within the human tragedy. Others, such as Phillips and Crow, have noted "irreconcilability" as the main theme in his work (e.g. in Phillips and Crow 2005, pp. 1–9). Let us have a look at painting *No. 61 (Rust and Blue)*, finished in 1953. The borders are still open and, possibly, inviting. The spaces in-between entities are still somewhat fuzzy, and porous, as are the boundaries of the entities themselves, albeit to a lesser extent. Within the shapes of the entities there still is a *tremendous* amount of boiling tension. But there is now also a certain neatness, a certain order. Entities seem to be much more aware now of their position and their place. There is much more constraint (of mass and organism, or in short: entities), and self-constraint ("curbed desire"). The entities seem to be much more aware of their own, and others' possibilities. And perhaps also of the dangers, out there. A certain degree of closure, and indeed perhaps even seclusion, and exclusion, or segregation has crystallized (as it would more forcefully in Rothko's *Seagram Murals*, painted in 1958). Caution, and perhaps also precaution, form part now of the coded assemblages that organize space. As in Pollock's work, this tension could be paradoxical. The code, or *principle,* of precaution, for example, however much it blocks off potential, can be seen as both the condition of possibility and the condition of impossibility of negotiation and exploration (e.g. the degree of boiling within the entities of *No. 61* is much more noticeable than the one in those of *No. 24*). And vice versa: it might very well be the case that constraint, order, and closure as evidenced on canvas No. 61 are the result of their own condition of possibility and impossibility, i.e. the negotiations and explorations, either already undertaken or yet to be undertaken, in the *out there* of human tragedy. The flight *from* code presupposes, requires, depends on, and produces code. What is needed, in Rothko's own words, is "the right number of inhibitions or suppressions to provide the leaven, just right disturbance of equilibrium, to imbue that excitement [...] which demonstrates the difference between dynamic organism and static machination" (2006, p. 11). This paradoxical tension *is* the tragedy of the human drama.

6.4 Back to (Late Modern) Governance

One might perhaps be able, arguably, to detect, in Modern governance, a certain preoccupation with the complexities of inner selves. That which is to be governed, in Modernity, is the inner self. That which lurks secretly underneath the surface of mass and mere organism—a complex of boiling potential, deliberations, aspirations, intentions, imaginary tactical manoeuvres, and so on—is what governance is to divine, access, reflect upon, work with, and put to productive use. One could argue that the first traces of this mode of governance, as well as the form of life it is part of, appeared on panels such as Gerard David's early modern *The Justice of Cambyses* [1498], about two decades before Machiavelli, Erasmus and More would start work on their political tracts (for more on this, see Lippens 2009). In high modernity one could for example note the paintings by Joseph Wright of Derby (see in e.g. Daniels 2000). Wright's meticulously painted scenes characterized by a centrally placed light source that throws a glow on figures whose faces remain half-hidden in shady surroundings somehow seem to be the harbinger of a high modern form of life and governance. Whereas his earlier paintings (e.g. *A Philosopher Giving That Lecture on the Orrery* [1766] and *An Experiment on a Bird in the Air Pump* [1768]) locate the source of light—and thereby the source of self—in scientific instruments that mimic the inevitable mechanics of the law of physics, this later changes. The source of light and self in these earlier paintings is the mechanics of physics. As such the self, including the "inner self", cannot be anything more than a mere *mechanical* logic, not unlike the one in Cesare Beccaria's *Dei Delitti e delle Pene* of 1764. But in subsequent paintings (e.g. *A Blacksmith's Shop* [1771] or *An Iron Forge* [1772]) the light source is provided by a white hot iron that is worked and shaped into a standard, "normalized" form. The source of self, and the self itself, here appear as something that is in need of formation. It has to be formed. The contents of the inner self here is nothing like a mechanistic logic of physics at all. The self appears to be a cauldron of boiling tensions that need to be shaped into form, *productively*. The light here, on these paintings, is a *productive* light. The light on these canvases, one could argue, is the harbinger of the light that Jeremy Bentham—according to Foucault at least—would conceive in his *Panopticon*, some 15 years later. It is a kneading, disciplining, normalizing light that works to productively knead the chaos of boiling inner selves into 'normal' shape.

If what we have explored in the first section of this contribution is anything to go by, this interest in the complex particulars of inner selves—albeit that in high modernity this interest always had an *eye* on normalization—is now on the wane. In a post-material, post-constructive age there is precious little to knead or shape *towards*. The self itself has largely dissolved around its crumbling core and what remains of it finds itself in nomadic wanderings amidst commodity-image. Fleeing from coded territories and from constraint, it explores opportunities and risk, but, doing so, depends on and produces other coded territories and constraint. Pollock"s story and his work, Kirk Varnedoe claims, are about the uneasy "mix of insecurity and ambition, the internal conflicts and the ambivalence of outside observers" (in Varnedoe and Karmel 1998, p. 72). This could very well apply to Rothko as well. Another word for this uneasy mix, says Varnedoe, is "America". The travels of the post-material and post-constructive, "American" self turn around choice (consumer choice, mostly). The self must choose, unrelentingly. There are only very few guidelines or very little guidance available, if at all. What the self strives for is control. Control over the choices it must make. Control, or a sense of control at least, can be found in what the self assumes to be the completely un-coded realm of nature. And control can be exercised in the often even *precautionary* management, neutralization, or even destruction of mere physical mass and biological organism, especially mass and organism that is deemed to be unresponsive, rigid, and a threat to nomadic circulation and the sources of control therein. There is no point in engaging with complex inner selves in a post-materialistic and post-constructive age. The age of construction is over. And so, Guy Debord reminds us, is the age of constructive, that is: *transformative* communication. There is no need for face, nor for figure.

Some of this diagram, or *abstract machine* (in Deleuze's words) of this late modern form of life and governance seems to have crystallized on Pollock's and on Rothko's post-war paintings. The aforementioned paradoxical tension between code and de-code, or between nomadic freedom and control, or between constraint and self-constraint, and so on, seems to have appeared not just in each of both painters' works separately, but also across them. One should of course admit that in both painters' view this tension refers to something universal, to human nature as such. And their paintings appeared at a time when existentialism was at the height of its powers. A few words are needed here. Existentialism (Sartre's [1943] in particular) located *nothingness*, i.e. radical indeterminacy, at the heart not just of the human self, but also of the *matter* of human action (Sartre [1960]). It is through nothingness, through indeterminacy that the human self, or that, indeed, humanity as such, *becomes*. The self is nothing but a collection, or trajectory, of choices made—"memories arrested in space", Pollock would say—within the porous and precarious bounds of a *life project* (i.e. the self's *original choice*, in Sartre's words). *As* choice, or *as* a collection of choices, the human self, and whatever is chooses, can only be that: choices. There can be no universal humanity; there can only be choice. The nothingness at the heart of the human self, indeed at the heart of humanity, can not be eradicated. All choice emerges from it; all choice perpetuates it. This ineradicable indeterminacy, this impossibility of redemption, this *eternal recurrence* (to use Nietzsche's words) is how existentialism views the "tragedy" of the "human drama". All constructions and projects are only choice, and will, *as* choice, carry within themselves their own condition of (im)possibility, i.e. nothingness.

It would be a bridge too far to deny any connection between Pollock's and Rothko's works and their existentialist and, more generally, post-war surroundings. There is, for instance, a way in which one might be able to see Rothko's floating shapes, and Pollock's poles, as reflecting the Cold War stand-off (although neither of them referred to this). More importantly, however, their work appeared at a time which authors such as Nichola Chiaromante and Jeffrey Isaac have called "zero hour humanity" (Isaac 1992, pp. 21, 266), that is, a time when all beacons and idols and codes have crumbled away in utter disillusionment or in horror, and when things have to be built up from scratch, if at all. Existentialism's sense of the absurd, its discovery of nothingness and radical indeterminacy as the source of emergence, as well as Pollock's and Rothko's flight from rigid code into responsive control, may well have shared some common ground. "I lost all faith in the idea of progress and reform", Rothko would later say (in 1959), and "I am still an anarchist, what else" (Rothko 2006, p. 132), fully aware that there can be "no yearning for Paradise, or divination" (2006, p. 143). Their work though moves beyond existentialism. Whereas existentialism remained deeply interested in the inner self, that is, in the intricate and singular surveys, deliberations, imaginings and projects of choosing selves (see e.g. Sartre's Saint Genet [1952]), this is much less the case in the figureless canvases of both painters. Existentialists remained interested in the inner self, and in communicative collective projects (think of Sartre's work on dialectical reason, [1960]), albeit that they did so with a lack of naivety and a sense of the absurd so characteristic of Nietzschean tragic philosophers. Pollock and Rothko seem to have been much more preoccupied with the tension in the human drama itself. And they seem to have been much more interested in the physics of mass, in the biology of organism, in nomadic trajectories, in hovering or floating containers of energy, in the tangible tension between coded enclosure and de-coding escape. Their work hovers and floats around the paradoxical nature of *control*. It even betrays something of a *will to control*. Seen this way their work, as a visual crystallization of traces, somehow announces something newly emerging, a new form of life and governance. Their work, if you wish, had something prophetic about it. Asked whether he was a mystic, Rothko replied, again in 1959, "not a mystic. A prophet perhaps—but I don't prophecy woes to come. I just paint the woes already here" (2006, p. 135). In painting the paradoxical tensions of a form of life that was emerging, Rothko, and Pollock too, expressed what was yet to come fully-fledged. As we now know the modern project of discipline and normalization would maintain itself for a few decades longer, or, depending on your point of view, it would re-emerge as the construction we know as the welfare state. For the late modern, post-material and post-constructive form of life and governance to fully emerge, it would have to wait for *that* beacon, for *that* code to finally fade, and to give way to what Gilles Deleuze, in his essay on control societies (1995, pp. 177–182), called the "essentially dispersive" nature of late modern capitalism. That form of capitalism is no longer focused on production, but, rather, on the control, via "password" codes, of circulation (1995, pp. 180–181). The welfare state however would contribute to and impact on this late modern emergence. It would help replace the post-war dearth of beacons and idols with an overabundance of circulating commodity-image, and it would help transform post-war "zero hour" nomadism into late modern consumer nomadism. The latter in turn spawned the twin strategies of *seduction* and *repression*, mentioned by Zygmunt Bauman, and referred to at the start of this essay.

6.5 Coda

In one of his essays (it was originally published in 1956) Ernst Gombrich once wrote, with slight contempt, about "the vogue of abstract art" (he didn't target abstract expressionism in particular): "It is a commonplace of psychology that nothing is harder to bear than complete freedom from any restraint". Imagine the artist's "state of mind in front of his canvas, really facing that existentialist nightmare, the responsibility for every decision, every move, without any convention to guide him, without any expectation to live up to except the one of creating something recognizably his own and yet significantly different" (1963, p. 144). After a series of drip paintings, and having exhausted his signature style to the point of turning it into a code, Pollock died in an alcohol-fuelled car crash in 1956. Rothko took his own life in 1970, after an equally exhaustive—and exhausting—series.

References

Baal-Teshuva, Jacob. 2003. *Rothko*. London: Taschen.
Bauman, Zygmunt. 1993. *Postmodern Ethics*. Oxford: Blackwell.
Clearwater, Bonnie. 2006. *The Rothko Book*. London: Tate Publishing.
Daniels, Stephen. 2000. *Joseph Wright*. London: Tate Gallery Publishing.
Debord, Guy. 1967. La Société du Spectacle. Paris: Buchet-Chastel.
Deleuze, Gilles. 1988. *Foucault*. London: Athlone.
Deleuze, Gilles. 1995 [1990]. *Negotiations*. New York, NY: Columbia University Press.
Deleuze, Gilles. 2003 [1981]. *Francis Bacon: The Logic of Sensation*. London: Continuum.
Dillon, Michael and Lobo-Guerrero, Luis. 2009. The Biopolitical Imaginary of Species-Being. *Theory, Culture & Society*, 10, 1–23.
Emmerling, Leonhard. 2007. *Pollock*. Köln: Taschen.
Feeley, Malcolm and Simon, Jonathan. 1994. Actuarial Justice: The Emerging New Criminal Law. In ed. David Nelken, *The Futures of Criminology*. London: Sage, 173–201.
Gombrich, Ernst. 1963. The Vogue of Abstract Art. In Ernst Gombrich, *Meditations on a Hobby Horse*. London: Phaidon, 143–150.
Haskell, Francis. 1993. *History and Its Images. Art and the Interpretation of the Past*. New Haven, CT: Yale University Press.
Isaac, Jacob. 1992. *Arendt, Camus, and Modern Rebellion*. New Haven, CT: Yale University Press.
Lacey, Nicola. 2007. Space, Time and Function: Intersecting Principles of Responsibility Across the Terrain of Criminal Justice. *Criminal Law and Philosophy*, 3, 233–250.
Lippens, Ronnie 2009. Gerard David's *Cambyses* [1498] and Early Modern Governance. The Butchery of Law and the Tactile Geology of Skin. *Law and Humanities* 1, 1–24.
Lyng, Stephen. 2004. Crime, *Edgework*, and Corporeal Transaction. *Theoretical Criminology*, 3, 359–375.
Maffesoli, Michel. 1996. *The Time of the Tribes*. London: Sage.
Miller, J. Hillis. 1992. *Illustration*. London: Reaktion Books.
Moses, Omri. 2004. Jackson Pollock's Address to the Nonhuman. *Oxford Art Journal*, 1, 1–22.
Murray, Jamie. 2006. Nome Law: Deleuze & Guattari on the Emergence of Law. *International Journal for the Semiotics of Law*, 2, 127–151.
Murray, Jamie. 2007. Deleuze & Guattari's Intensive & Pragmatic Semiotic of Emergent Law. *International Journal for the Semiotics of Law*, 1, 7–32.
Phillips, Glenn and Crow, Thomas (eds.), 2005. *Seeing Rothko*. Los Angeles, CA: Getty Publications.

Pieterman, Roel. 2008. *De Voorzorgcultuur*. Den Haag: Boom Juridische Uitgevers.
Pieterman, Roel and Hanekamp, Jaap. 2002. *The Cautious Society? An Essay on the Rise of the Precautionary Culture*. Zoetermeer: Heidelberg Appeal Nederland.
Rothko, Mark. 2006. *Writings on Art*. New Haven, CT: Yale University Press.
Sartre, Jean-Paul. 1963 [1952]. *Saint Genet, Actor and Martyr*. New York, NY: George Braziller.
Sartre, Jean-Paul. 1967 [1960]. *Questions de Méthode*. Paris: Gallimard.
Sartre, Jean-Paul. 2002 [1943]. *Being and Nothingness*. London: Routledge.
Slaughter, Marty. 2004. The Arc and the Zip: Deleuze and Lyotard on Art. *Law & Critique*, 15, 231–257.
Slaughter, Marty. 2007. Black and White or Technicolor. *Law & Critique*, 18, 143–169.
Stoker, Wessel. 2008. The Rothko Chapel Paintings and the 'Urgency of the Transcendent Experience'. *International Journal for Philosophy of Religion*, 64, 89–102.
Svedlov, Andrew J. 2008. Hermeneutic Phenomenology of Mark Rothko's Painting. In ed. Anna-Teresa Tymienicka, *Analecta Husserliana XXIII*. Dordrecht: Springer Publications, 287–293.
Varnedoe, Kirk and Karmel, Pepe. 1998. *Jackson Pollock*. New York, NY: The Museum of Modern Art.

Chapter 7
Visual Law: The Changing Signifiers of Law in Popular Visual Culture

Jason Bainbridge

> *Either the world's right-side up or upside down. Depends on how you look at it. I mean, close the book of rules and there's just people caught in situations.*
>
> *Rita Pompano (Ellen DeGeneres),* Goodbye Lover, *(1999, Warner Brothers) dir. Roland Joffe*
>
> *Andrea: 'Unhappy the land that has no heroes!'*
>
> *Galileo: 'No, unhappy the land that* needs *heroes.'*
>
> *Bertoldt Brecht (*The Life of Galileo *qtd* Life On Mars, Episode Six, *emphasis added)*

7.1 Introduction

Law is.

As legal and cultural theorist Steve Redhead notes, conventionally "in jurisprudential and political theory" law is taken as a given—"we assume that we know what it is and where to find it, and also what it does" (Redhead 1995, p. 10).[1] But of course, "law" can be defined in many ways, not just by theorists and practitioners (where law can refer to a range of concepts including case law, statutes, positivist law, natural law, indigenous law or police powers) but also in the wider culture. Law then seems to be a malleable concept, its definition often depending upon the

J. Bainbridge (✉)
Swinburne University, Boston, MA, USA; Swinburne University of Technology, Melbourne, VIC, Australia
e-mail: jbainbridge@swin.edu.au

[1] Interestingly this does not seem to be the case in practice. The adversarial system is, in part, based on the idea that law can be interpreted differently by different people. Similarly the composition of courts acknowledge that judges interpret laws differently; by way of example, some judges believe the American constitution to be a living document while others turn to what the original drafters of the law intended.

A. Wagner, J.M. Broekman (eds.), *Prospects of Legal Semiotics*,
DOI 10.1007/978-90-481-9343-1_7, © Springer Science+Business Media B.V. 2010

context in which it is found, leading Redhead to suggest that the idea of law as a given may in fact be "a powerful (legal) fiction... crucial to the exercise of political power and legal authority across many different fields, especially the 'cultural'" (Redhead, p. 10).

I have previously argued that Swiss linguist Ferdinand de Saussure's (1983 [1916]) notion of *semiotics* provides a set of tools suitable to unpack how law is culturally defined (Bainbridge 2006). Saussure adopts a structuralist approach to communication, breaking down communication practices into a series of units that produce meaning called *signs*. Each sign is comprised of a physical component (*the signifier*) and a mental concept associated with that physical component (*the signified*) with the relationship between the signifier and the signified being defined as *signification,* the process by which meaning is made (see de Saussure 1983, Hawkes 1977). We can therefore understand a statue of justice, an image of a courtroom, or the figure of a lawyer or a policeman as all being physical *signifiers* of a common mental *signified*—law.

This chapter uses Saussurean semiotics to explore how law is culturally defined through popular visual media and how these media representations contribute to wider understandings of both law's functioning and its limitations. It profiles four signifiers of law in popular visual media: the father, the lawyer, the policeman and the vigilante and explores the relationship between them, analysing the impact each of these signifiers has on the corresponding signified of law and their connections to justice and the rule of law. The primary texts I will be looking at are the US series *Law & Order* (NBC), *Dexter* (Showtime) and the UK series *Life on Mars* (BBC). Following Bennett and Woollacott's study (1987, pp. 55–69), these examples are supported by a deliberately wide-ranging series of secondary media texts, with some slippage between filmic and televisual texts, as any other approach runs the risk of being too limiting, abstracting texts from the wider culture and "the shifting orders of inter-textuality" (Bennett and Woollacott, p. 59) which both elucidate their meaning and demonstrate how widespread these ideas of law truly are.

A semiotic approach permits an analysis of culture without the imposition of value judgments (based on artistic or moral merit) and unlike empirical sociology can focus on individual texts rather than large-scale patterns (Fiske 1982, O'Sullivan et al. 1994). Furthermore, despite criticisms that semiotics is too abstract and formalist in its approach, it is committed to the *social* production of meaning. For Saussure, meaning is not contained in a single sign but rather exists in the various sorts of relationships into which a sign enters (Culler 1976)—as in the relationship between law and justice. Saussure therefore seems to be acknowledging that meaning is *contextual*, something which is fundamentally important in any analysis of law because, as noted above, the very meaning of law seems to depend on the context in which it is found; as the physical signifier of law changes, so too does the mental concept of law that is signified.

Furthermore, popular visual media representations of law are important objects of study because, as Joshua Meyrowitz (1985) notes, film and television remain the most prevalent popular cultural forms and therefore the most accessible to mass audiences.

This accessibility makes popular visual media "the main source of *common* knowledge about the law... (exerting) a powerful influence on ordinary people's attitudes to, and expectations of, law and the legal system" (Laster 2000, pp. 10–11)[2] simply because they *are* so much more accessible to the general public than law reports or even visiting courtrooms for themselves. Roland Barthes for example argues that "iconic images [like Perry Mason cross-examining someone on the stand] distil complex details [like legal process] into blissful clarity" (Barthes 1972, p. 143) while John Frow and Meaghan Morris contend that "every aspect of social life", (including law), is shaped by "a network of representations—texts, images, talk, codes of behaviour, and the narrative structures organizing these" (Frow and Morris 1993, p. 345).

7.2 Fathers as Signifiers of Law

While it is risky to generalize in relation to representation across a number of popular cultural forms, overwhelmingly the most common recurring signifier of law in popular visual media is the father, whether they are literal fathers, as in the case of *To Kill A Mockingbird's* Atticus Finch, or symbolic figures as in the male senior partners in law firms, or senior clerks, or the captains of police/law enforcement stations on television series like *LA Law, North Square, Hill Street Blues, CSI* and *Boston Legal*. This idea has its roots in the Roman idea of the "*pater imporiosius* who himself bears both the character of the father and the capacity of the magistrate... the magistrate's *imperium* is nothing but the father's *vitae necisque potestas* extended to all citizens" (Agamben 1998 [1995], p. 89). As Austin Sarat notes, law has long been conceptualised as "patriarchal in its norms and methods" (qtd Goodrich 1997, p. 1047), citing precedents from Abraham and Isaac, to *DeShaney v. Winnebago*,[3] to Freud, to Jerome Frank's famous pronouncement that "the Law... inevitably becomes a partial substitute for the Father-as-Infalliable-Judge" (Frank 1949, p. 18). Though this is not unproblematic, or without its critics (including Sarat himself), Sarat admits that legal scholars continue to display a "longing for... paternal power and the overwhelming power that fathers exercise as basic to legal authority" (Sarat 1999).[4] Legal scholar Peter Fitzpatrick, for example, locates the origins of law in the origin myth Freud outlines in *Totem and Taboo*. Fitzpatrick uses Freud for two reasons—first, because Freud is regarded as "the parent of a self conscious modernism [modernity]" (Fitzpatrick 2001, p. 1) and secondly because Freud saw law as central to "modern, self-sufficient" society. Indeed, Freud grounded law "within

---

[2]It is important to note that while I agree with Laster's proposition that texts form "the main source of *common* knowledge about the law" I downplay the idea of "influence" with its implications of power over the viewer.

[3]408 US 189 (1989).

[4]See also Goodrich (1997) and Fitzpatrick (1997). It should be noted that in relation to this patriarchal model of law, feminist critics like Kaja Silverman (1992) have argued that there is still a lack or absence, in this father figure.

a social existence bereft of the transcendent variety" while at the same time viewing law as bringing together those elements of society which themselves ground it. As such Fitzpatrick seeks an origin for law that accounts for its connections with modernity and in Freud's origin myth, drawing upon Freud's own work in psychoanalysis, Darwin's *Descent of Man* and Atkinson's *Primal Law*, he finds such a nexus point.[5]

This origin myth concerns two sons who slay and eat their father. In the wake of his death the sons realize that neither is strong enough to assume their father's role so rather than struggle between themselves the sons make a social contract. That they choose to recognise mutual obligations and social institutions, over instinctual gratification, leads Freud to locate the "beginnings of morality and law" (Freud 1950, pp. 103–104)—and the beginnings of *society as a whole*—in this contract. In this formulation, law is located in the taboos and transgressions society wishes to control, signified by this totem of the father. Law and society therefore become inextricably linked to the father-as-signifier of both law and the process of modernity more broadly.

It is perhaps unsurprising then that popular cultural signifiers of law are so often paternal, in either a literal or figurative sense. For while popular cultural representations of the father are constantly in flux[6] and always subject to changing "cultural, economic, political, technological, and geographical contexts" (Coltrane and Parke 1998) rather then following any through-narrative of either improvement or decline (LaRossa et al. 2004), the one common element of almost all of these representations of father is the father's continuing signification of law and authority. In her overview of the father on celluloid, from 1946 until 2006, Stella Bruzzi (2005) finds that the father is treated with either desire or fear, loved or loathed because of the authority and stability he signifies. Similarly throughout this time, television sitcoms consistently present the father as the signifier of authority, deriving humour from their success (as in *The Cosby Show*) or failure (as in *The Simpsons*) (Miller 1986).

7.3 The Lawyer as Signifier of Law

More particularly, popular cultural representations of law capitalize on this idea of father-as-signifier with the paternal figure who often runs the legal practice, paternal in the sense that they are invariably older, wiser and male. On television this was perhaps first, and most memorably, embodied in Lawrence Preston (E.G. Marshall) of Preston and Preston in *The Defenders*. Preston is quite literally a father here as

[5]Other origin myths for law include *Antigone*. The Freudian origin myth is selected here because of the connections it makes to modernity and its clear use of a patriarchial/paternal figure as the totem of law, a totemic figure taken up by most popular cultural representations of law.

[6]For more detail see Coontz (1992), Mintz (1996), Atkinson and Blackwelder (1993) and LaRossa (1997).

his partner in the firm is his son, Kenneth Preston (Robert Reed). Lawrence is also a father figure for his knowledge and experience has been refined over two decades at the bar, whereas Kenneth is a recent law school graduate. The lessons Kenneth learns from his father, both as father and paternal mentor, form an integral part of the storylines.

More broadly, in her overview of legal television series, Menkel-Meadow identifies the presence of "professional communities" in series ranging from *The Defenders* to *L.A. Law* (and including non-legal series like *Dr Kildare* and *Ben Casey*) wherein "lawyers help and succour each other while performing [a] difficult, but important, public service" (Menkel-Meadow 2001, p. 1320). She notes that narratives of the 1950s and 1960s commonly involved "character development in the training and mentoring of a younger professional by an older and wiser professional" (Menkel-Meadow, p. 1320). The male paternal figures cited include the afore-mentioned Lawrence Preston and Leland McKenzie (Richard Dysart) of McKenzie Brackman in *L.A. Law*, but could also include John Houseman in *The Paper Chase*, Adam Schiff and later Sam Waterston in *Law and Order*, (who are both always advising younger male and female ADAs) and Denny Crane (William Shatner) in *Boston Legal* (though his relationship with the younger Alan Shaw changed so much over the course of the series, that he eventually married Alan by the series end!)

On film, *Class Action* (1991) is perhaps the quintessential example of the father-as-signifier-of-law. A father Jebediah Ward (Gene Hackman) goes up against his corporate lawyer daughter Maggie Ward (Mary Elizabeth Mastrantonio) and convinces her to seek social justice. While the gender roles are inverted here (male is justice, female is law, see below), the outcome is the same: the paternal signifier of law (even if that law is one based in social justice) successfully wins the other potential signifier of law (his daughter) over to his side. The plot of *Devil's Advocate* similarly hinges on the fact that senior partner Al Pacino (in actuality the devil) is also the protagonist, Keanu Reeve's, father; he spends much of the film trying to win Reeves over and though Reeves rejects his attempts there is enough ambiguity by the film's end to suggest that he has been partially successful. Indeed, senior partners in popular visual culture are invariably older, male and hold themselves out as paternal figures, be they the senior partners of Bendini, Lambert and Locke in *The Firm* or Lucien Wilbanks in *A Time to Kill.*

As officers of the court, and therefore physical embodiments of the legal system, lawyers are one of the most common signifiers of law in popular visual culture. They appear in three main ways: as the heroic protagonists of legal dramas, as the heroic protagonists of legal thrillers, or as supporting cast members (often signifying law as an impediment to justice) in dramas more generally. In legal dramas, drama arises from two sources: the relationship between the lawyer and the criminal and the ability of the lawyer to be able to discharge their duty while working within the constraints of the legal system as in television series like *LA Law, the practice* and *Law & Order* and films like *Compulsion*, *The Verdict* and *In the Name of the Father*. In legal thrillers, drama arises from the tension between the lawyer and the legal system of which they're a part as in films like *To Kill a Mockingbird, The Firm* and

The Rainmaker and television series like *Damages*. Where lawyers appear as supporting cast members in other dramas—like police series (*NYPD Blue, Homicide: Life on the Street*) or action series (*24, Spooks*)—they often act as impediments to ideas of justice, which I will return to below

Regardless of whether they appear in legal dramas, legal thrillers or other types of drama, lawyers consistently signify a *modern* idea of law. By a *modern* idea of law I'm referring to "black letter law", based around the idea of the Rule of Law. I've termed this concept "modern law" because the Rule of Law is itself at the very heart of modernity, both as an important part of the public sphere and as a way of ensuring the continuing maintenance of "order" and "certainty", two of the central concerns of modernity (Sarup 1996, p. 50 citing Zygmunt Bauman). Modernity's belief in progress through rationalism resulted in a corresponding rise in the presence of the courtroom and the idea of empirical argumentation as a locus of justice, leading Max Weber (1991) to conclude that law itself legitimated the modern state.[7]

The Rule of Law is defined by contrast with the "rules of man", arbitrary, ad hoc decisions. Its most basic requirements are consistency, through rules fixed in advance, and public knowledge and fairness, through neutral application (Fallon 1997). The modern idea of law is therefore based around *rationality*. It aims to provide *due process,* ensuring fairness and equality and to a certain extent it also seeks to provide *reassurance* that the legal system is the best forum for dealing with criminal and civil issues as it ensures objectivity and impartiality.

Lawyers serve as signifiers of this modern law signified because they ensure *due process* occurs; when DAs Richard Bey (Jason Kravits) and Helen Gamble (Lara Flynn Boyle) go to lunch after losing a case on the television series *The Practice*, Bey reassures Gamble that they are the heroes because they are trying to uphold justice and put away the criminals (an argument often replicated by the DAs and ADAs in *Law & Order*). *The Practice*'s defence lawyer Eugene Young (Steve Harris) reminds the lawyers at his firm that their courage to represent unpopular clients makes them heroic—an argument that echoes the sentiments of defence lawyers in films from *Compulsion* to *In the Name of the Father*. Similarly, *The Verdict*'s Frank Galvin (Paul Newman) is presented as heroic because he learns how to overcome his alcoholism and depression, work hard and win a case. Here, Galvin's move toward professionalism is presented as heroic. The lawyers in each of these popular culture examples clearly signify the modern ideal of law as their professionalism maintains faith in the legal system; the fact they are heroic simply by discharging their duty, or attempting to discharge their duty, reinforces the need for due process; and the fact that resolution occurs in the courtroom underscores the importance of rational argumentation.

---

[7] American legal historian Jerold Auerback (1983) concurs, stating that: "no longer is it possible to reflect seriously about American culture without accounting for the centrality of law in American history and society" (p. 115) and it is certainly arguable that Auerback's argument regarding the centrality of law in modern society also applies, at the very least, to England and Australia as well.

Lawyers in legal dramas also function as signifiers of the modern ideal of law because, following Thomas (2001, p. 1499) they provide reassurance in the legal system. The modern approach to law is signified in two main ways. First, legal series like *L.A. Law, Picket Fences* and *The Defenders* provide a forum for dealing with complex social issues in the guise of criminal and civil cases (Gillers 1989, p. 1608), the balanced presentation of these issues confirming that equality before the law is maintained. At the same time, the presentation of these social issues in the courtroom helps to legitimise the courtroom as the right forum for the hearing of such issues, an important part of the "public sphere" and the maintenance of "order" and "certainty", two more ideas associated with modernity (Sarup 1996, p. 50 citing Zygmunt Bauman), as in the *L.A. Law* episode "Wattsamatter" where the judge comments "the American courtroom is a reflection of American society and society is a reflection of it", confirming law's prominence in the public sphere.

But legal dramas do not form a homogenised discursive whole and lawyers can signify quite different forms of law as in the *legal thriller* subset of legal dramas. A number of *Perry Mason* episodes bear this out, where Mason has to work *against* the legal system to prove his client's innocence. Similarly, in *To Kill A Mockingbird,* Atticus Finch's struggle to exonerate Tom Robinson is framed as a struggle by a moral lawyer *against* a flawed and bigoted justice system while the protagonists of John Grisham's many novels and their adaptations are often presented as lone, young idealists succeeding in spite of corrupt and moribund legal systems. In modern law, justice remains *procedural* in that it is just another aspect of law, to be considered and balanced against these other requirements, but often implicit in the legal thriller is the idea that a lawyer discharging their duty is simply not enough to be heroic. Rather, to be heroic necessarily requires a combination of legal and extra-legal action. While all of these men remain officers of the court, frequently they must act outside the scope of their role as a lawyer—and sometimes in direct contravention of it— o achieve justice. This is clearly signifying a quite different signified of law, where substantive justice becomes the primary motivator and other legal rights and duties must be suspended to achieve it. As such, these lawyers in the Finch-Mason-Grisham protagonist mould represent the first step in the popular cultural signification of law away from the modern rule of law towards a different signified.

7.4 Justice as Part of Law

As always, it is the relationship between law and justice that remains a central consideration in any analysis of the ways in which law is culturally constructed (Fiebleman 1985). But as Barry (2000, p. 135) notes:

> Despite more than 2000 years of political theorizing the notion of justice still has no settled meaning: it is the paradigm case of an essentially contested concept. It is not simply that there are fundamental disputes at the normative level... it is the fact that there is so little agreement as to what the *concept* stands for that causes serious problems.

Jacques Derrida (1992) claimed in his keynote speech at a Cardozo Law School symposium on deconstruction and law that since justice transcends the legal system it can never be wholly imminent. Following Plato (Balkin 1994) Derrida views justice as something "beyond" the legal system, something quite apart from legal rights and remedies (Derrida 1992, p. 10)—allowing for the possibility that justice can exceed or even exist in contradiction to the law (Derrida 1992, p. 16) Indeed, Derrida quotes Montaigne when he states: "Laws keep up their good standing not because they are *just* but because they are laws" (Derrida 1992, p. 12).

Justice can therefore be categorized in two ways—*procedural justice* (relating to fairness and ensuring that the proper procedures have been followed) and *substantive justice* (relating to getting the "right" or "correct" result, even at the expense of some procedural fairness). This classification reveals justice's relationship with the law. Procedural justice is *subordinate* to the law. Here justice remains just another aspect of the law, with fairness and closure remaining the true aims of the legal system. In contrast, substantive justice *is* the aim of the law. Other aspects of the law (like fairness or closure) may necessarily be suspended or ignored to achieve it.[8]

Clearly then the pursuit of justice has a significant impact on the form that law may take or the idea of law that may be signified. Indeed, Derrida famously pronounced that "deconstruction *is* justice" (Derrida 1992, p. 15). Legal scholar Douglas Litowitz sees Derrida, both here and in his later *Specters of Marx* (1994) as "laying the groundwork for an approach to jurisprudence which insists upon an almost dialectical struggle between law and justice" (Litowitz 1997, p. 97) or more precisely that "the call to do justice to the other is what spurs the deconstructive process into action, and hence the very process of deconstruction is a process of seeking justice" (Litowitz 1997, p. 102) where "justice and law differ *in kind*; justice is transcendent or (quasi-transcendent) and is not deconstructible, while law is imminent and deconstructible" (Litowitz 1997, p. 97). Here then the act of seeking justice itself shapes the law, creating instability in the law and resulting in different signifieds of law, what I have termed *modern* law and *pre-modern* law.[9]

In contrast to the modern signified of law, a pre-modern signified of law privileges justice over equality and emotion over rationality, with emotion often viewed as a conduit to the "truth". This signified is "pre-modern" in the sense that it has a connection to the "sacred", the (pre-modern) forms of church law or divine law

[8]This chapter is therefore adopting a pragmatic view of justice as the "correct" or "fair" result, predicated on the notion that something is "just" when individuals get what is due to them—a definition which fits both these ideas of justice. In part the chapter plays into the debates around moral relativism in accepting that justice does have a different meaning depending on where it is found—though in this case this is produced more by its relationship with law than its social or cultural context.

[9]This is based in part on Lyotard's (1985) notion of a "multiplicity of *justices*, each one of them defined in relation to the rules specific to each [language] game" (Lyotard 1985, p. 100, emphasis added). Here I'm suggesting that the intersection of justice and law actually results in a "multiplicity of laws" each based on "the rules specific to each game" i.e. the place of justice in law. We could include postmodern law here as well, but for reasons of space this chapter focuses on pre-modern and modern law.

in ancient societies. Here, kings or clergy were said to have a direct conduit to the will of the divine and therefore came to personify the law themselves (see Feldman 2000). In pre-modern law justice is clearly substantive in that it is the aim of law, overriding concerns of due process or equality.

Chase (2002) prefers to map popular visual media according to the dilaectical tension between *crime control*—where individual rights are subordinated in favour of the greater societal good (as embodied in films like *Dirty Harry* (by the police), *The Star Chamber* (by judges) and *Jagged Edge* (by defence lawyers))—and *due process*, where individual rights are maintained (as in *Shakedown* and *True Believer*) (Chase 2002, pp. 67–103). For me, crime control and due process are symptomatic of the broader signifieds of pre-modern and modern law. The danger in focussing on terms like crime control and due process is in glossing over both the social forces behind such ideas and the central principles of each: transcendant justice (pre-modern law/crime control) on one hand and equality (modern/due process) on the other. Furthermore, the crime control/due process antinomy does not acknowledge the link between these two conceptions of law, the belief in a "real" truth, be it transcendant (through justice) or discoverable (through due process and the authority of the state). Finally, the use of a binary like crime control/due process does not allow for the possibility of other conceptions of law, skeptical of truth, anti-authoritarian or otherwise interested in non-rational forms of thinking, that I explore in more detail further below.

7.5 The Policeman as Signifier of Law

Ironically, despite the police force being a profoundly modern institution, in popular cultural representations of law it is the police that function as signifier of a *pre-modern* signified of law. This is because in police procedurals, films and series that focus on the workings of the police, the legal system is dispensed with altogether so that the signifer of law becomes either "the police force" (as in England's *Z Cars*, or *The Bill*, Australia's *Blue Heelers* or America's *Hill Street Blues*) or "the individual policeman" (be it *Kojak*, *Columbo* or *Inspector Morse*). DI "Jack" Frost (David Jason) titular character of the English series *A Touch of Frost* and characteristic of the "individual policeman" type sets out the policeman's "pre-modern" approach to the law while trying to cheer up a colleague during *A Touch of Frost: Hidden Truth*:

> Look, this is not the sort of thing that I say out loud too often, but the reason why some of us do this job is because we care. Now I know it sounds a bit naff and all of that... I can't help what the courts do, or what some of these fancy lawyers get away with. All I know is if I can nick a few of those low-life out there then this is what I'll do.

These signifiers represent another step away from the modern ideal of law where rational enquiry is frequently abandoned in favour of instinct or emotion, where individual rights are suspended for the good of the community and crime's "causes and definitions [become] self-evident, that criminals are easily recognisable and the punishments that we should give them, obvious" (Grant 1992, p. 58). Lawyers are therefore sidelined, the renewed focus on police drama meaning that:

> the complexities of social order, law and criminality are reduced to crime, identification, pursuit and capture… detection and apprehension become synonymous with guilt; the police become agents not only of law, but of justice too. (Moran 1985, p. 162)

With a different idea of law at its heart, this genre is clearly advancing a pre-modern ideal of law, one that places a transcendant "justice" over equality (in the figure of the policeman) and physicality and emotion over rationality (as a conduit to "truth"), while still maintaining a sense of progress "nicking a few low-lifes" "cleaning up the streets" i.e. making society better, safer and therefore more efficient. This pre-modern ideal of law is notable in that it prizes emotion over rationality and has crime control (where individual rights are suspended for the greater social good) rather than due process (ensuring fairness and equality) as its objective, thus being protective of community rather than individual rights.

Of course, much like legal dramas, police procedurals do not form a homogenised discursive whole. Police procedurals are not always uncritical of police as exemplars of the law and often foreground "the ideological and coercive work of the police" (Clarke 1986, p. 1992) as most evident in series featuring maverick, ruthless or just plain corrupt cops like *The Sweeney*, *The Shield* and recent seasons of *The Bill*. Similarly police procedurals can take on many hybrid forms creating a shifting signifier of "the law" applicable to series as diverse as *Cagney and Lacey*, *Cracker* (Creeber 2001, pp. 19–23) and the *CSI* franchise.

However, common to all of these series is a narrative Toby Miller identifies as belonging to the detective genre but is just as applicable to the police series:

> The villain and the detective depend on each other through an overarching third term: the law and its embodiment in the state, which one must elude and the other convince that justice be meted out. (Creeber 2001, p. 18).

It is this conception of "the state" that is important here, a "state" that for the most part is seen to exist without the presence of lawyers. When lawyer characters are present they are often treated with, at best, a healthy distrust and skepticism, at worst, outright hostility. But even more commonly, there is a disenchantment with the legal system best demonstrated by what is *not* shown; most police series end with the capture of the criminal, the implication being that it is here that justice occurs, sparing us the intricacies of the legal system, its failures and delays. As Friedman (2000) notes popular culture, particularly through the police procedural, often displays an "impatience with technicality and procedure" through their depiction of technicalities as "obstructions to justice" (Friedman 2000, p. 556).

This distinction between modern and pre-modern ideas of law is well made in the BBC television series *Life on Mars*, a modern police procedural "[v]ery much influenced by TV of the seventies… probably all television and films actually… things like *The Sweeney* and *Starsky and Hutch*… *Get Carter* and *All the President's Men*" (Jane Featherstone, Executive Producer, *Look at that Lawman*). Here DCI Sam Tyler (John Simm), a policeman from 2006 and very much a signifier of a black letter, modern signified of law, is struck by a car and wakes up in 1973, as a DI in Manchester, working under the charismatic and maverick cop, DCI Gene Hunt (Philip Glenister), signifier of a pre-modern signified of law. Unsure whether he is in a coma or whether he has indeed, somehow, traveled back in time, Tyler sets out to "work out the reason" why he is here and therefore find a way to "get home" (from the voiceover, title sequence *Life on Mars* Series 1 Eps 2–8). Over the course of the series Sam frequently clashes with Gene over his policing methods; two signifiers of law that reveal how contestable notions of law and justice really can be. In this way *Life on Mars* "both draws on and challenges the idea of nostalgia... [it] asks the question were things better in the past" and in the process "all of those [modern law] attitudes and beliefs [of Sam's] are challenged" (Claire Parker, Producer, *Look at that Lawman*).

Gene clearly signifies the pre-modern idea of law, describing his style of policing as: "Grab 'em by the balls and their hearts and minds will surely follow, *that* is policing" (*Life on Mars*, Series 2, Ep 8). He describes himself as "the sheriff but I'm deputy to the law" and his precinct as "my kingdom" (Series 1, Ep 1).[10] His idea of law is "putting bad people away" (Series 1, Ep 1), something instinctive ("Snap decision. Guilty. You ever been somewhere and you just know it's about to kick off. That's primeval. You clocked something was wrong. That's why you're a copper not a train driver. Sometimes the job is this [clicks fingers] and all your fancy science and tape machines are useless without it", Series 1, Ep 3), physical ("Nothing puts things right quite like a punch does it?" says Sam to Gene, Series 1, Ep 2) and if it means a little corruption to achieve justice, then Gene will do it; "I try not to think about it [taking bribes]. I do the best that I can. I try to look after *my* men and the people in *my* city" (Hunt, Series 1, Ep 4). Ultimately his goal is crime control; "Got to charge him today Sam, got to keep that bloke off the streets" (Gene, Series 1, Ep 2). All other aspects of law are subordinated to that. "The public don't give a damn what we do", says Gene, "As long as we get results" (Series 1, Ep 7).[11]

As *Life on Mars* makes clear, the courtroom becomes something largely unseen and invisible in the police procedural, replaced by the interrogation room as the locus of "truth" and "justice", as it does in texts like *Dirty Harry*, *NYPD Blue*, *Homicide: Life on the Street* and *Law & Order: Criminal Intent*. *NYPD Blue's* Andy Sipowicz (Dennis Franz) regularly abuses and slaps suspects. Greg Medavoy (Gordon Clapp) strikes a suspect with a telephone book. *Homicide's* Frank Pembleton (Andre Braugher) engages suspects in complex mind games, whittling

[10]In Series 1, Ep 8, Sam provides a different description of Gene as "an overweight, over the hill, nicotine-stained, borderline alcoholic homophobe with a superiority complex and an unhealthy obsession with male bonding", to which Gene responds:

> You make that sound like a bad thing.

[11]The true dangers of this approach are illustrated in *Life on Mars*, Series 1, Ep 7, when DS Ray Carling (Dean Andrews) and DC Chris Skelton (Marshall Lancaster) force a suspect, Billy Kemble (Kevin Knapman), to ingest cocaine to get him "talky". Fifty minutes later Kemble dies. Skelton defends his actions as being: "We were just trying to get a result. That's all. Please the Guv". Ray similarly defends his actions to Gene as "doing what you taught me. I was trying to get a result for you." Gene privately admits the problem to Sam: "These lads... they think they're made in my image. They've never learnt where to draw the line. And it scares the shit out of me."

away at them until they crack. *Criminal Intent's* Robert Goran (Vincent D'Onofrio) does the same. As Sterne (2000) notes, all do this without reference to a code of conduct (like the Amnesty International 1996 Report) and always without the presence of a lawyer. Most often, suspects are tricked into not calling their lawyers in the belief it will "be easier" for them if they don't. Here the policeman becomes the transcendental justice figure. Or as Gene Hunt puts it at the end of *Life on Mars* "I *am* the law" (Series 2, Ep 8).

The production of a confession replaces the verdict as the moment of catharsis in these dramas, providing both resolution and a sense of justice, detectives often rewarding themselves afterwards for getting "results". In police procedurals then it is the arrest (or sometimes execution, as in *Dirty Harry*) of the suspect that provides narrative closure, bypassing the court system with a "Book 'em Dano" (as Jack Lord provides in *Hawaii Five-O*) and a cut to the end credits. Rational enquiry is abandoned in favour of pure emotion and crimes's "causes and definitions [become] self-evident, that criminals are easily recognisable and the punishments that we should give them, obvious" (Grant 1992, 58). In this sense the pre-modern idea of law is similar to the modern in that justice (pre-modern) and equality (modern) both reflect a belief in an objective truth (this person is guilty/not guilty) that will become self-evident when justice/equality is brought into play.

Sam on the other hand signifies the modern idea of law, by-the-book and very much about due process. Gene tells Sam he fancies himself as "The moral compass in a dodgy department" (Series 1, Ep 7). This is set up early in the series when, in 2006, his girlfriend and colleague Maya Roy (Archie Panjabi) tells him to "Screw [Reimes'] psyche evaluation, you used to believe in gut feeling... what happened?" to which Sam replies "Look around you. What use are feelings in this room?" (Series 1, Ep 1). This is a clear endorsement of the modern idea of law, echoed in his advice to DC Skelton, "Nothing beats the satisfaction of a thorough investigative process" (Series 1, Ep 3). He tells Gene "I only know one way to police" (Series 1, Ep 2) and clashes with him over a variety of issues including interrogations under duress (Series 1, Ep 1, Series 2, Ep 6), false imprisonment and destroying evidence (Series 1, Ep 1), planting evidence (Series 1, Ep 2) and covering up a death in custody (Series 1, Ep 7), their different views clearly expressed in this exchange from Series 1, Ep 4:

> There's no way you can police a modern city without a bit of give and take (Gene).
>
> Checks and balances? It can't work like that. Every copper has to be whiter than white or the whole thing falls apart (Sam).
>
> No, you're living in cloud-cuckoo-land Sam (Gene).
>
> Otherwise it spreads like a cancer. A free cut of meat from the butcher at Christmas. You wave the paperwork through for a fella with a funny handshake. And then one morning you wake up and your whole body's riddled with it. And you hadn't even noticed (Sam).
>
> You're a cheerful bastard to have a drink with aren't you? Come on, we're meant to be celebrating. You did ell Sam. Every officer will be walking a little bit taller tomorrow because of you (Gene).

According to Director, Bharat Nalluri, Sam has "forgotten how to live in the jungle" and instead consistently puts his "head over heart" (Bharat Nalluri, *Look at that Lawman*). For Executive Producer, Jane Featherstone "[Sam and Gene] are two halves of the same coin... they're head and heart and when they're working together they're most effective... Sam's wonderful anal meticulous 2006 technology driven brain is pitted with Gene's sort of lumbering instinctive methods and together they solve crimes, and it's only by coming together that they can really get to the heart of the matter" (Jane Featherstone, *Look at that Lawman*). Part of the interest in this series then is how these different conceptions of law can be reconciled with each other.

The father as signifier of law similarly figures into *Life on Mars* as well, when Sam encounters his father in 1973, Vic Tyler (Lee Ingleby) (Series 1, Ep 8). But rather than being the travelling cleaning products salesman Sam remembers, Vic turns out to be a petty criminal trying to make a name for himself in the Manchester underworld. Desperate to believe that his father is innocent, Sam describes himself as his father's "second chance" and sets out to prove his father's innocence:

> My dad walked out on us at a family wedding. Round about this time. I never found him. Not a trace. 30 years... Maybe that's why I'm here. To stop him from leaving. History's repeating itself. But I can change it... Save him. And that will save me (Series 1, Ep 8).

This leads Sam to pull a gun on Gene so his father can escape: "You're not going to set him up Gene" says Sam. "I don't need to Sam. Forget logic, what does that (clicks his fingers) tell you", says Gene. While Vic plays on Sam's tensions with Gene ("Sam. You understand. You know what the police are like. They need to solve cases. They'll do anything..." (Series 1, Ep 8)) when confronted with Vic's violence to WPC Annie Cartwright (Liz White) and his willingness to shoot him in cold blood, Sam realizes Vic cannot be saved. He doesn't arrest him, but lets him get away, to spare his mum (and himself) the truth of his father's criminality in 1973. His father's authority has been found wanting and Sam sides with Gene. Sam has chosen the surrogate father (Gene) over his own father, returning to the paternal signifier of law (even if this is a pre-modern idea law) over the lawlessness signified by his real father.

Ultimately, it is revealed in Series 2, Ep 8, that Sam is indeed in a coma, with a tumour, with Gene and his entire world of 1973 seemingly derived from Sam's own ethical questions over policing and informed by his experiences of growing up, and exposed to media depictions of law, in the 1970s. As early as Series 1, Ep 7, Gene suggested to Sam that "You could have gone home any time you fancied. The truth is, you like it here. You just can't bear to admit it." This is confirmed when, awakening from his coma and bored with his sterile, over-administered and clinical life in 2006, Sam ends the series by jumping off the edge of a building, "returning" to his fantasy world of 1973 in the process where he felt more alive than he had before. Here then is confirmation of Meyrowitz's belief in the power of popular visual representation; a series of representations of law that become preferable to the real world for Sam Tyler, *fictional* signifiers that seem more "alive" than the reality of policing in 2006. This is highlighted in Series 2, Ep 8 through the repetition of

Nelson (Tony Marshall), the bartender's comments that "when you can feel, then you're alive. When you don't feel, you're not" (Series 2, Ep 8).

Throughout *Life on Mars* the importance of popular visual media is consistently underscored through a number of visual motifs: the title sequence is composed of dozens of little television screens that together "make up" Sam's "life" in the seventies; Sam hears messages from the future through media like radio and television (meaning that communication between 2006 and 1973 is, quite literally, mediated); and the one person who acts as guide and tormenter to Sam in 1973 is the personification of (at least British) television: the BBC test card girl (from BBC Test Card F) who turns to camera and actually "turns off" the picture at the series end. Indeed, even Sam's 2006 "modern law" idea of policing comes from the media, as he makes clear to Gene:

> Our definitions of policing may vary marginally (Sam)
>
> And yours is? (Gene)
>
> Serve the public trust, protect the innocent, uphold the law (Sam)
>
> Training college? (Gene)
>
> *Robocop*. You can't uphold the law by breaking it (Sam, referring to the film *Robocop*)

In this way, police procedurals reveal that the definition of law itself is contestable; there are different conceptions of law, followed by different institutions, often in conflict with one-another and often irreconcilable. Police procedurals are thereby positing a pre-modern challenge to modern law and in this way arguably represent the first in a series of challenges to modernity, providing an alternative way of thinking about law. This is an idea that continues to be teased out in the *Law & Order* spin-offs *Law & Order: SVU* and *Law & Order: Criminal Intent*, which frequently juxtapose the police officers' and lawyers' responses to crime to reveal their (often very different) ideas of law. Perhaps most importantly it reveals a schism at the heart of law that is exploited by the third signifier of law in popular culture—the vigilante.

7.6 The Vigilante as Signifier of Law

I have previously argued that since the September 11, 2001 attacks on the World Trade Center and the Pentagon, a new signifier of law has been appearing with increasing regularity in popular visual media—the government agent (Bainbridge 2006). Most prominently, the government agent features as a signifier of law in the American series *Alias, Without a Trace* and *24*, the English series *Spooks* (known as *MI5* in America) and, perhaps most famously, in the *James Bond, Mission Impossible* and *Jason Bourne* film franchises (commencing with *Dr No, Mission Impossible* and *The Bourne Identity* respectively). The government agent is a signifier of law that moves still further away from the modern ideal of law, towards a purely pre-modern one, not only because justice remains the perceived aim, but because it is pursued with even fewer limitations. Here, threats of death (as classically represented by James Bond's licence to kill) or torture (as evidenced by Jack Bauer's actions in *24*) are presented as justifiable ways of achieving substantive justice. The signifier of law has therefore moved from the intimidation and threats of the police procedural to actual physical torture, with the increasing prevalence of "the state" as the signifier of law in popular media paralleling the increasing intervention of "the state" in the real world, particularly post-September 11 and particularly in the area of *proactive* law.

However, since 2006 a new and wholly unique signifier of law has appeared in popular visual media—the vigilante serial killer Dexter Morgan in the television series *Dexter*. Dexter is a Miami blood-spatter expert who also operates as a serial killer, but who only kills "bad people", those who have escaped or otherwise operate outside the reach of the law. Of course, figures that operate outside the law have long been celebrated in folk culture, like the outlaw in America (e.g. Jesse James, John Dillinger), the highwayman in England (e.g. Dick Turpin) or the bushranger in Australia (e.g. Ned Kelly, Captain Thunderbolt). More recently the vigilante has been celebrated in popular visual culture, in films like the *Death Wish* series and *Taxi Driver* and with characters like Marvel Comics' Punisher.

Dexter unites this tradition with popular media's 1990s fascination with serial killers—in films like *Silence of the Lambs*, *Seven* and *Natural Born Killers*—and the 1900s interest in forensic signifiers of law—in television series like the *CSI* franchise, *Bones* and the UK's *Silent Witness*—to produce a completely new signifier of law, the vigilante serial killer. Extradiegetically Dexter is marketed and merchandised as a *hero* with action figures, bobbleheads and calendars bearing his image. His excesses are celebrated, advertisements picture him dancing with a scalpel, lying provocatively in a chalk outline, wearing a piece of crime scene tape as a tie and walking along a red carpet of blood. DVDs of the series are sold in evidence bags or with red blood pouches that stain Dexter's face with blood. Diegetically, Dexter is also equated with "the hero", perhaps most significantly in the Series Two episode "The Dark Defender".

Here, an investigation into a murder in a comic-book store leads Dexter to discover that the victim was producing a comic book based on the "Bay Harbour Butcher" (the name the media has given to the serial killer, in actuality Dexter, whose bodies have been discovered in the harbour). As one of the workers in the comic-book store describes it:

> [Denny called him] The Dark Defender... Denny had this great idea to put a spin on that vigilante serial killer we've got running around... Denny was trying to set up the Dark Defender as a graphic novel. Stalker of the night, his blade of vengeance turns wrong into right.

This leads Dexter to fantasise about himself being a superhero, rescuing his mother from her killers. "I never really got the whole superhero thing", Dexter admits to himself, "But lately it does seem we have a lot in common. Tragic beginnings. Secret identities. Part human, part mutant. Arch-enemies." This leads Dexter to question his own role as signifer of law: "Things aren't always what they appear to be. And what about me? Am I the twisted Bay Harbour Butcher? Or the valiant

Dark Defender? Only time will tell... [but] Isn't this what heroes do? Avenge lost loved ones?"

The comparison is apt, for like the superhero to which this episode refers (see Bainbridge 2007), the vigilante as signifier of law also functions as a way of thinking discursively about the relationship between law and justice. A vigilante like Dexter Morgan personifies the tension between a modern adherence to the rule of law and pre- (or even post-) modern explorations of Derrida's *aporia* in different *personae*: the modern secret identity on the one hand (e.g. the blood-splatter expert) and the pre-modern justice figure on the other (e.g. the serial killer or "dark defender") (with a postmodern exploration arguably arising from the continuing oscillation between these two personae). In this way the vigilante can personify the inherent tensions in law in a way that other crime-fighters, be they Perry Mason or Harry Callaghan, cannot.

Once again, the father as signifier of law is important to the narrative of *Dexter* too. Policeman Harry Morgan adopted Dexter, the child of one of his informants, Laura Moser, after she was killed (along with three others) by a drug-dealer for stealing his cocaine and Dexter was left "for days, starving, in blood two-inches thick". Harry quickly recognizes Dexter's penchant for killing. "You're different aren't you Dexter", he says, "The Phillips say Buddy [their dog] disappeared... I found the grave son... there were a lot of bones in there Dexter. They weren't just Buddy's" (Pilot). He encourages Dexter that "[w]henever you get an urge you come to me, you tell me and we deal with it together" (Pilot) but when he finds Dexter with a bloody knife realizes he needs to do something more:

> I'm afraid your urge to kill is only going to get stronger... you're a good kid Dex, you are, otherwise it would've been a lot worse than animals, okay? So we can't stop this. But maybe we can do something to channel it. Use it for good... Son, there are people out there who do really bad things, terrible people. And the police can't catch them all. Do you understand what I'm saying? [You're saying they deserve it—Dexter] That's right, but of course you have to learn how to spot them, how to cover your tracks. But I can teach you.... You can't help what happened to you but you can make the best of it. Remember this forever, you are my son, you are not alone and you are loved (Harry)

Harry thus becomes the *pater imporiosius,* simultaneously Dexter's father figure and signifier of law providing Dexter with a code to be followed, "a ritual" involving preparation, rubber sheets, duct tape. Even when Dexter's faith in Harry is tested—as in the Second Season episode "There's Something About Harry" where Dexter discovers Harry committed suicide, most likely, because of "... me. The idea of a code was one thing, a grand idea, a noble cause, but the reality of it? Harry walked in on what he created. And he couldn't live with himself... I killed my father"—Dexter ends up internalizing the code, becoming the signifier of law in place of his father:

> Not long ago I had a dream that people could see me for what I am and for a brief instant in time the world actually saw my bodies of work. Some even cheered. But as it turns out, nobody mourns the wicked... I think Harry knew that from the start. That's why he gave me a code. It cost him his life but it kept me alive through incredible trials. The code is mine now and mine alone. So too are the relationships I cultivate. They're not just disguises any

> more. I need them. Even if they make me vulnerable. My father might not approve but I'm no longer his disciple. I'm a master now. An idea transcended into life. And so this is my new path, which is a lot like the old one. Only mine. To stay on that path I need to work harder, explore new rituals, evolve. Am I evil? Am I good? I'm done asking those questions. I don't have the answers. Does anyone? (Season Two "The British Invasion")

In Season Three Dexter is offered another potential *pater imporiosius* in the form of ADA Miguel Prado (Jimmy Smits), someone who as ADA clearly signifies law, but who also sympathises with, and ultimately participates in, Dexter's murderous approach; when Miguel uses Dexter's teachings to kill a rival defence lawyer, Dexter realizes Harry was right. "I didn't teach you the code to share with your buddies" Harry says in a vision to Dexter, leading Dexter to kill Miguel because he is another "unchecked version of myself... what I would have become without Harry's code." Dexter concludes the season by becoming a father himself (Season Three "Finding Freebo"), confessing that "I don't know what's more complicated, having a father or being one" (Season Three "The Lion Sleeps Tonight"), a struggle that continues to play out in Season Four. As Dexter notes: "I have moved on from my father but I still need his code"; Dexter has become the signifier of a pre-modern law that privileges justice above everything else.

When looking into the details of his father's death Dexter questions Captain Tom Matthews, Harry's superior officer. Matthews describes being a policeman as "a tough job. It can wear on even the best of us... The system doesn't always work. Sometimes they get away, you know that. And that just got harder and harder for Harry to deal with" (Season Two, "There's something about Harry"). Dexter therefore exists at the very end of the pre-modern spectrum, ensuring justice is served even when the "system doesn't always work". For just as the police procedural constructs a *pre-modern* idea of law through its "direct line" to the truth and lack of accountability, this pre-modern, or sacred, ideal of law is even more powerfully signified by the vigilante. Dexter clearly embodies the notion of transcendent justice over equality ("it's just a matter of time before he becomes a drop of blood on my glass slide collection", says Dexter about his next victim, "Pilot") and ritual over rationality ("Life is ritual. Routine. Control", says Dexter, Season Three "Our Father"). But throughout he maintains a very modern sense of progress by "bringing villains to justice" and "cleaning up the streets", i.e. making society better, safer and therefore more efficient. In *Dexter* then it is the execution of the criminal, by Dexter, that provides narrative closure, bypassing the court system with the slice of a scalpel and thus replacing the delivery of the verdict as the moment of catharsis, offering both resolution and a sense of justice being done.

7.7 Female Signifiers of Law

This chapter has almost exclusively focused on male signifiers of law as the vigilante, the police officer and the lawyer are more often male than female in popular visual culture—and, of course, the most frequent signifier of law in popular visual media, the father, is always male. While gendering law—and modernity—in this way may seem unusual, Rita Felski (1995) notes that "the idea is not as strange as it may initially appear. If our sense of the past is inevitably shaped by the explanatory logic of narrative, then the stories that we create in turn reveal the inescapable presence and power of gender symbolism (Felski, p. 1)." While Felski herself argues for unraveling the "complexities of modernity's relationship to femininity" (Felski, p. 7) she admits that not only is the masculinity of modernity "wide-spread" in contemporary theories of modernity, "the identification of modernity with masculinity is not, of course, simply an invention of contemporary theorists (Felski, p. 16)." She goes on to explain that:

> Many of the key symbols of the modern in the nineteenth century—the public sphere, the man of the crowd, the stranger, the dandy, the flaneur—were indeed explicitly gendered. There could for example, be no direct female equivalent of the flaneur, given that any woman who loitered in the streets of the nineteenth-century metropolis was likely to be taken for a prostitute (Felski, p. 16).

Perhaps unsurprisingly in media forms that so often trade in dichotomies, I argue that *postmodern* legality is most often symbolised by the figure of the feminine, juxtaposed against the totemic father figure of modernity. In this way, the signifiers of law in popular visual culture remain resolutely gendered. Where female lawyers do appear they are either in the "daughter" role (literal or figurative as in *Class Action*), masculinised in some way (either in dress or manner) as in the case of *Damages* Patty Hewes (Glenn Close) or presenting an alternative and somewhat irrational approach to lawyering, as in the case of *Ally McBeal's* titular character (Calista Flockhart) where personal and public affairs, logic and emotion, rhetoric and dress all become parts of her legal argument.

We can also see these ideas of the postmodern feminine taken up in some predominantly "modern" signifiers of law as well, as where *Law and Order* introduced the character of DA Nora Lewin (Dianne Wiest), to replace the totemic DA Adam Schiff (Steven Hill). As Keetley notes in her analysis of the series, the earlier series of *Law & Order* are marked by a refusal to consider "contextual defences" (Keetley, p. 48) like the "black rage" defence in the episode "Rage". Keetley sees this as in part arising from the series' mission statement to "prosecute the offender" betraying a desire to "try *and* convict *someone*", "offender" implying an "individual" rather than societal cause (Keetley, p. 48). This resulted in a blind spot as regards contextual defences, an unwillingness by either McCoy or the other ADAs to even consider such an idea. *Law & Order's* debates revolved around applications of the law, never defences to it (which were often dimissed out of hand, especially during Michael Moriarty's era as Executive ADA Benjamin Stone). Wiest's character is defined as more liberal than McCoy and liberal in this sense intersects with postmodern ideas of *contextuality*. Lewin is more inclined to consider upbringing, race and all the contextual details—all the non-rational, alternative knowledges external to the practice and procedure of law—and remind McCoy of them when he prosecutes his cases. The difference is highlighted in the following seasons when Lewin is replaced by the more conservative, paternal, Southern DA Arthur Branch (Fred

Dalton Thompson)[12] and later Jack McCoy himself, reasserting the supremacy of the modern signifier of law.

As Tushnet (1996) notes in his consideration of *Class Action* (1991), a film classified above as reinforcing the modern approach to law, often in legal texts "law is associated with the Dominant, usually the white male, and justice with the Other" (p. 244). Here, Tushnet claims tension is derived from a clash between the two because, as has already been outlined above, "Western culture valorizes both law and justice" (p. 244). In defining the Other Tushnet explains:

> The Other may be an indigenous person, a woman, a man who somehow has escaped the bonds of the Dominant, an immigrant or older person as in *Twelve Angry Men* or, as in *The Caine Mutiny*, a man who would ordinarily *be* the Dominant (p. 247)

an idea Tushnet traces back to *The Leatherstocking Tales* with Natty Bumpo as the Other standing for justice against Judge Temple, as Dominant, standing for law.

Tushnet develops this idea through a consideration of *Adam's Rib* (1949) noting how when the Other—here Amanda Bonner (Katherine Hepburn)—is also a lawyer and therefore "at least an obstensible representative of the law, the association between justice and anarchy is weakened. Law's victory, and the preservation of male dominance, becomes more ambiguous" (p. 247). Here then, again at the risk of generalization, I would argue that femininity in popular visual media overwhelmingly signifies a *postmodern* approach to law, *postmodern* in the sense that Amanda, like Ally, Patty and Nora Lewin, suggests both the limits of traditional, modern law while offering a series of alternative knowledges (that can have the added effect of equalising the genders as well). While the ways in which differently gendered signifiers of law impact on the idea of law signified clearly falls outside the scope of this chapter, it is an area that clearly demands more research in the future.

7.8 Conclusion

Popular visual cultural texts are ideal sites for navigating different conceptions of law as shifting signifiers of law—fathers, police officers, lawyers and even vigilantes—set up different signifieds of law—what I have termed pre-modern, modern and (even) postmodern. As legal scholar John Denvir puts it, "'law' is no longer a concept limited to the law reports; it is a consciousness that permeates American—and by extension the world's—culture" (Denvir 1996, p. xiii).

But beyond simply representing law we can also read these popular visual cultural texts as being in a dialogic relationship with law, actively commenting upon the relationship between law and justice. Cultural theorist Douglas Rushkoff (1994), for example, has suggested that "popular cultural forums" (like film and television)

---

[12] In the spin-off series *Law and Order: SVU* which, as noted above is closer to having a premodern rather than modern ideal of law at its heart, alternative knowledge structures are introduced and maintained through the permanent cast addition of B.D. Wong's therapist character.

offer a "conceptual interface between the order of our laws and the chaos of our world" (p. 51) that makes them:

> the place for us to evaluate our rules and customs... because lawyers, unlike detectives or policemen, are well-suited for open discussion of such issues as they are nominated as our culture's best professional debaters (Rushkoff 1994, p. 52).

Certainly series like *Law & Order*, *Life on Mars* and *Dexter* promote debate around what law is, its limitations and the ease with which justice can be achieved. Helle Porsdam similarly suggests that cultural definitions of law also serve as an indication of national identity for:

> if the cultural life of the nation may in any way be considered a reliable gauge, a cursory look at the number of films, television series, and books currently being produced and written suffices to diagnose the United States as a thoroughly law-permeated country (Porsdam 1999, p. 4).

Popular cultural definitions of law thereby contribute to a wider understanding of both law's functioning and its limitations. Through the very process of representing law on-screen, popular visual media (quite literally) make visible how contestable law can be and puts these ideas out into the public sphere where they can be further debated and disseminated. Using semiotics to unpack how law is defined in popular visual culture is therefore a vitally important part of understanding how fluid law is and how very different law can become, in different contexts and for different institutions.

References

Agamben, Giorgio. 1998 [1995]. *Homo Sace: Sovereign Power and Bare Life*. Stanford, CA: Stanford University Press.

Atkinson, Maxine P. and Blackwelder, Stephen P. 1993. Fathering in the 20th Century. *Journal of Marriage and Family*, 55, 975–986.

Auerback, Jerold S. 1983. *Justice Without Law?* New York, NY: Oxford University Press.

Bainbridge, Jason. 2006. Lawyers, Justice and the State: The Sliding Signifier of Law in Popular Culture. *Griffith Law Review*, 15(1), 153–176.

Bainbridge, Jason. 2007. 'This Is The Authority. This Planet Is Under Our Protection' An Exegesis of Superheroes' Interrogations of Law. *Law, Culture and the Humanities*, 3, 455–476.

Balkin, Jack. 1994. Transcendental Deconstruction, Transcendental Justice. *Michigan Law Review*, 92, 1131.

Barry, Norman. 2000. *An Introduction to Modern Political Theory*, 4th edn. London: Macmillan.

Barthes, Roland. 1972. Myth Today. In *Mythologies*. New York, NY: Noonday Press.

Bennett, Tony and Woollacott, Janet. 1987. *Bond and Beyond: The Political Career of a Popular Hero*. London: Methuen.

Bruzzi, Stella. 2005. *Bringing Up Daddy: Fatherhood and Masculinity in Post-war Hollywood*. London: BFI.

Chase, Anthony. 2002. *Movies on Trial: The Legal System on the Silver Screen*. New York, NY: The New Press.

Clarke, Alan. 1986. In Bennett, Tony et al. (eds). *Popular Culture and Social Relations*. Milton Keynes: Open University.

Coltrane, Scott and Parke, Ross D. 1998. *Reinventing Fatherhood: Toward an Historical Understanding of Continuity and Change in Men's Family Lives*. Philadelphia, PA: National Center on Fathers and Families, December.

Coontz, Stephanie 1992. *The Way We Never Were: American Families and the Nostalgia Trip*. New York, NY: Basic Books.

Creeber, Glen. 2001. *The Television Genre Book*. London: British Film Institute.

Culler, Jonathan. 1976. *Saussure*. New York, NY: Fontana.

Denvir, John. 1996. *Legal Reelism: Movies as Legal Texts*. Chicago, IL: University of Illinois Press.

Derrida, Jacques. 1992. Force of Law: The 'Mystical Foundation of Authority'. In ed. Drucilla Cornell, Michael Rosenfield and David G. Carlson, *Deconstruction and the Possibility of Justice*. New York, NY and London: Routledge.

Derrida, Jacques. 1994. *Specters of Marx*, trans. Peggy Kamuf. New York, NY and London: Routledge.

de Saussure, Ferdinand. 1983 [1916]. *Course in General Linguistics*, trans. Roy Harris. London: Duckworth.

Feibleman, James K. 1985. *Justice, Law and Culture*. Dordrecht: Martinus Nijhoff.

Feldman, Stephen. 2000. *American Legal Through from Premodernism to Postmodernism: An Intellectual Voyage*. New York, NY: Oxford University Press.

Felski, Rita. 1995. *The Gender of Modernity*. Cambridge: Harvard University Press.

Fiske, John. 1982. *Introduction to Communication Studies*. London: Methuen.

Fitzpatrick, Peter. 1997. "In the Exigency of His Longing": Freud's Discovery of Law and Fiction in *Totem and Taboo*. *New Formations*, 32, 143–156.

Fitzpatrick, Peter. 2001. *Modernism and the Grounds of Law*. Cambridge: Cambridge University Press.

Frank, Jerome. 1949. *Courts on Trial: Myth and Reality in American Justice*. Princeton, NJ: Princeton University Press.

Freud, Sigmund. 1950. *Totem and Taboo*, trans. J. Strachey. New York, NY: Norton.

Friedman, Lawrence. 2000. Lexitainment: Legal Process as Theatre. *De Paul Law Review*, 50, 539.

Frow, John and Morris, Meaghan. 1993. Introduction. In *Australian Cultural Studies: A Reader*. Chicago, IL: University of Illinois Press.

Gillers, Steven. 1989. Taking *LA Law* More Seriously. *Yale Law Journal*, 98, 1608.

Goodrich, Peter. 1997. Maladies of the Legal Soul: Psychoanalysis and Interpretation in Law. *Washington & Lee Law Review*, 54, 1047.

Grant, Judith. 1992. Prime Time Crime: Television Portrayals of Law Enforcement. *Journal of American Culture*, 15, 58.

Hawkes, Terence. 1977. *Structuralism and Semiotics*. London: Methuen.

Fallon, Richard H., Jr.. 1997. "The Rule of Law" as a Concept in Constitutional Discourse. *Columbia Law Review*, 97, 1.

LaRossa, Ralph. 1997. *The Modernization of Fatherhood: A Social and Political History*. Chicago, IL: University of Chicago Press.

LaRossa, Ralph, Jaret, Charles, Gadgil, Malati, and Wynn, Robert G. 2004. The Changing Culture of Fatherhood in Comic-Strip Families: A Six-Decade Analysis. *Journal of Marriage and Family*, 62(2), 375–387.

Laster, Kathy. 2000. *The Drama of the Courtroom*. Sydney: Federation Press.

Litowitz, Douglas E. 1997. *Postmodern Philosophy and Law*. Lawrence, KS: University Press of Kansas.

Lyotard, Jean-Francois. 1985. *Just Gaming*, trans. Wlad Godzich and Jean-Loup Thebaud. Minneapolis, MN: University of Minnesota Press.

Menkel-Meadow, Carrie. 2001. Can They Do That? Legal Ethics in Popular Culture: Of Characters and Acts. *UCLA Law Review*, 48, 1305.

Meyrowitz, Joshua. 1985. *No Sense of Place*. Oxford: Oxford University Press.

Miller, Mark Crispin 1986. Dads Through the Decades: Thirty Years of TV Fathers. In ed. Todd Gitlin, *Watching Television*. London: Pantheon. Viewecd on 16 July 2009, http://www.medialit.org/reading_room/article38.html.

Mintz, Steven 1996. From Patriarchy to Androgyny and Other Myths: Placing Men's Family Roles in Historical Perspective. In eds. A. Booth and A. C. Crouter, *Men in Families*. Mahwah, NJ: Erlbaum, 3–30.

Moran, Albert. 1985. *Images and Industry: Television Drama Production in Australia*. Sydney: Currency Press.

O'Sullivan, Tim, Hartley, John, Saunders, Danny Montgomery, Martin, and Fiske, John. 1994. *Key Concepts in Communication and Cultural Studies*. New York, NY and London: Routledge.

Porsdam, Helle. 1999. *Legally Speaking: Contemporary American Culture and the Law*. Amherst, MA: University of Massachusetts Press.

Redhead, Steve. 1995. *Unpopular Cultures: The Birth of Law and Popular Culture*. Manchester: Manchester University Press.

Rushkoff, Douglas. 1994. *Media Virus: Hidden Agendas in Popular Culture*. New York, NY: Random House.

Sarat, Austin. 1999. Rethinking Law and Fatherhood: Male Subjectivity in the Film *A Perfect World*. *Genders*, 30. Accessed on 16 July 2009. http://www.genders.org/g30/g30_sarat.html

Sarup, Madan. 1996. *Identity, Culture and the Postmodern World*. Edinburgh: Edinburgh University Press.

Silverman, Kaja. 1992. *Male Subjectivity at the Margins*. New York, NY and London: Routledge.

Thomas, Jeffrey, E. 2001. Legal Culture and the practice: A postmodern depiction of the rule of law. *UCLA Law Review*, 48, 1495–1519.

Tushnet, Mark 1996. Class Action. In ed. John Denvir, *Legal Reelism: Movies as Legal Texts*. Chicago, IL: University of Illinois Press.

Weber, Max. 1991. *Protestant Ethic and the Spirit of Capitalism*, trans. Talcott Parsons. London: HarperCollins Academic.

Filmography

24, FOX Network, 2001–
Adam's Rib, Dir George Cukor, 1949
Alias, ABC Network, 2001–2006
Ally McBeal, Fox Network, 1997–2002
A Time to Kill, Dir Joel Schumacher, 1996
A Touch of Frost, ITV1, 1992–2009
The Bill, ITV1, 1983–
Blue Heelers, Seven Network (Aust), 1994–2006
Bones, Fox, 2005–
Boston Legal, ABC Network, 2004–2008
The Bourne Identity, Dir Doug Liman, 2002
Cagney and Lacey, CBS Network, 1982–1988
Class Action, Dir Michael Apted, 1991
Columbo, NBC Network, 1971–1977; ABC Network, 1989–1993
Compulsion, Dir Richard Fleischer, 1952
Cracker, ITV1, 1993–1996
CSI: Crime Scene Investigation, CBS Network, 2000–
Damages, FX, 2007–
Death Wish, Dir Michael Winner, 1974
The Defenders, CBS Network, 1961–1965
Devil's Advocate, Dir Taylor Hackford, 1997
Dexter, Showtime, 2006–
Dirty Harry, Dir Don Siegel, 1971

Dr No, Terence Young, 1962
The Firm, Dir Sydney Pollack, 1993
Hawaii Five-O, CBS Network, 1968–1980
Hill Street Blues, NBC Network, 1981–1987
Homicide: Life on the Street, NBC Network, 1993–1999
In the Name of the Father, Dir Jim Sheridan, 1993
Inspector Morse, ITV1, 1987–2000
Jagged Edge, Dir Richard Marquand, 1985
Kojak, CBS Network 1973–1978; ABC Network 1989–1990
LA Law, NBC Network, 1986–1994
Law & Order, NBC Network, 1990–
Law & Order: Criminal Intent, NBC Network, 2001–
Law & Order: SVU (Special Victims Unit), NBC Network, 1999–
Life on Mars, BBC One, 2006–2007
Mission Impossible, Dir Brian De Palma, 1996
Natural Born Killers, Dir Oliver Stone, 1994
North Square, BBC1, 2000
NYPD Blue, ABC Network, 1993–2005
Picket Fences, CBS Network, 1992–1996
The Paper Chase, CBS Network, Showtime,1979–1983
The Practice, ABC Network (USA), 1997–2004
Robocop, Dir Paul Verhoeven, 1987
Seven, Dir David Fincher, 1995
The Shakedown, Dir James Glickenhaus, 1988
The Shield, FX Network, 2002–2008
Silence of the Lambs, Dir Jonathan Demme, 1991
Silent Witness, BBC, 1996–
Spooks, BBC, 2002–
Taxi Driver, Dir Martin Scorsese, 1976
The Star Chamber, Dir Peter Hyams, 1983
The Sweeney, ITV1, 1975–1978
To Kill A Mockingbird, Dir Robert Mulligan, 1962
True Believer, Dir Joseph Ruben, 1988
The Verdict, Dir Sidney Lumet, 1982
Without a Trace, CBS Network, 2002–2009
Z Cars, BBC1, 1962–1971

Chapter 8
Legal Controversies About the Establishment of New Places of Worship in Multicultural Cities: A Semiogeographic Analysis

Massimo Leone

8.1 Précis of Semiogeography—Landscapes Versus Scenes

Large migratory phenomena usually modify the cultural demography of societies. Previously relatively homogenous, they begin to feature a dialectics between a cultural majority and one or more cultural minorities.[1] Tensions and even confrontations might ensue, some of which concern "semiotic landscapes". "Semiotic landscape" in this paper is meant as a pattern of perceptible elements that individuals come across in public space. By contrast, "semiotic scene" in this paper refers to a pattern of perceptible elements that individuals come across in private space.

The first difference between semiotic scenes and semiotic landscapes concerns agency (Leone 2009a). Whereas semiotic scenes can be altered by individual agencies, semiotic landscapes require individual agencies to merge into collective ones. However, the opposition between semiotic landscapes and semiotic scenes is not clear but gradual. Furthermore, the rigidity of boundaries between them varies across cultures. Incidentally, this can become an issue in multi-cultural societies.

The second difference between semiotic scenes and semiotic landscapes concerns stability. Whereas in semiotic scenes perceptible elements are relatively stable, for they mostly depend on individual agencies, in semiotic landscapes perceptible

M. Leone (✉)
University of Torino, Turin, Italy; Monash University, Melbourne, VIC, Australia
e-mail: massimo.leone@unito.it

[1]"Semiogeography" is a neologism. It is meant to designate a sub-discipline that studies patterns and processes that shape human interaction with various environments, within the theoretical framework of semiotics, the discipline that focuses on signification and communication. The term "semiogeography" is modelled after that of "psychogeography", first defined by Guy Débord as the study of the precise laws and specific effects of the geographical environment, consciously organized or not, on the emotions and behaviour of individuals (Debord 1955). Semiogeography shares some issues with psychogeography. However, it is not primarily meant as a field of artistic performance involving human emotions, but as a field of cultural analysis involving human patterns of signification and communication. On psychogeography, Stein (1987), Stein and Niederland (1989), Coverley (2006), and Self (2007).

A. Wagner, J.M. Broekman (eds.), *Prospects of Legal Semiotics*,
DOI 10.1007/978-90-481-9343-1_8, © Springer Science+Business Media B.V. 2010

elements are relatively unstable, for collective agencies change continuously. Large migratory phenomena usually entail a rapid reorganization of collective agencies and, therefore, conspicuous changes in semiotic landscapes.

The third difference between semiotic scenes and semiotic landscapes concerns transparency. According to Charles S. Peirce's semiotic theory, a sign is a triadic relation between an element that stands for another (the *representamen*) and a second element that is stood for by the first (the *object*) through a third sign that relates the first with the second (the *interpretant*). The interpretant is another sign, consisting, in its turn, of a further triadic relation between a representamen, an object, and an interpretant. Since every sign needs to be interpreted by another sign, the process of semiotic interpretation is virtually endless. Peirce called it "unlimited semiosis" (Peirce 1960–1966; Eco 1979).

For instance, when I perceive my Italian coffee maker in the kitchen, this perception is the result of a semiotic process in which something (e.g. a cluster of sensorial stimuli such as the shape, material, and colour of the coffee maker) stands for something else (e.g. the idea of a coffee maker) through an interpretant (e.g. the English word "coffee maker") that creates a relation between the cluster of sensorial stimuli and the idea it stands for. However, the English word "coffee maker" is also a sign, therefore consisting in a triadic relation between a representamen (the vocal or graphic stimuli that compose the word) and an object (the idea of a coffee maker), through further interpretants (e.g. "caffettiera", the Italian translation of "coffee maker", but also mental memories of coffee makers I saw in advertising, of what happened in my kitchen when my coffee maker once exploded, of the smell of coffee in my grandmother's house when I was a child, etc. etc.).

Another example of unlimited semiosis jurists are familiar with is when we use a dictionary in order to understand the meaning of a word: definitions are also composed by words, whose meaning is described by further definitions, and so on and so forth *ad infinitum*.

As each sign needs to be interpreted by another sign, then, in theory, human beings should be surrounded by permanently unstable meaning and paralysed by unlimited semiosis. However, as Peirce pointed out, human beings generally feature semiotic habits, that is, a tendency not to explore the semiotic chain of interpretants more than it is necessary in a given context. For instance, pondering on the infinite chain of interpretants stemming from the contemplation of my coffee maker might be an adaptive mental behaviour if I want to write a poem on my childhood, but it would be certainly unfit if my wife is waiting for me to prepare her morning coffee. Analogously, musing on the intricate web of relations between words in a dictionary might be acceptable for a lexicographer, but definitely inappropriate for a jurist who, for instance, seeks to define the meaning of the word "church" in a legal controversy.[2]

---

[2]See, for instance, *Bankstown City Council v House of Peace PTY LTD*, Land and Environment Court of New South Wales 1998.

Since semiotic scenes are arranged by individual agencies, they are not only relatively stable but also relatively transparent. Their meaning is determined by a series of semiotic habits. On the contrary, since semiotic landscapes are arranged by collective agencies (including the agency of nature), they are not only unstable but also opaque. Semiotic habits that determine their meaning are continuously challenged and must be reshaped accordingly.

And yet, the difference between transparency and opacity is gradual as well. Semiotic scenes are not always completely transparent, as semiotic landscapes are not always completely opaque. On the one hand, individuals often voluntarily change the semiotic scene on which they exert almost complete agency, and that are largely stable and transparent to them, in order to challenge their own semiotic habits. Inviting friends or contracting a decorator to re-arrange furniture are two examples of voluntary introduction of alternative agency, instability, and opaqueness in a domestic semiotic scene.

On the other hand, individuals always develop semiotic habits in order to limit the alternative agency, instability, and opaqueness of semiotic landscapes. Moving from home to workplace always through the same path or having lunch breaks always in the same restaurant are two examples of such limitations.[3] Sociological investigation has frequently called them the "comfort zone" of individuals in the public semiotic landscape (Bouma 1996, p. 90).

The extent to which an increase or a decrease in alternative agency, stability, and transparency of semiotic scenes and semiotic landscapes are considered as desirable varies a lot depending on both socio-cultural and psychological factors. Some individuals in certain socio-cultural contexts might wish to transform their semiotic scenes into semiotic landscapes, for example, by moving out or leaving their house constantly open to friends or friends of friends. Conversely, some individuals or groups in certain socio-cultural contexts might wish to turn their semiotic landscapes into semiotic scenes, for example, by contrasting any emergence of alternative agencies.

However, unpleasant emotions are generally attached to either a lack or an abundance of change in semiotic habits that are experienced as extreme. "Boredom" and "confusion" are the emotions that usually accompany these extremes. On the contrary, pleasant emotions such as "excitement" and "harmony" are generally attached to the limitation of these extremes, respectively.

The distribution and articulation of these emotional responses varies greatly, but a cross-cultural or even biological dimension might underlie them. It might be argued that, in an evolutionary explanatory scheme, individuals who do not seek the conditions to develop semiotic habits are as unfit as individuals who do not seek the conditions to have their semiotic habits challenged: the former cannot create the

[3] On the contrary, developing techniques to "get lost" in one's own city is meant to increase the opaqueness of familiar semiotic landscapes. A vast literature exists on this topic (Baudelaire, Benjamin, Simmel, Debord, Sebald, etc.). Cfr Mohr (2009).

conditions to exert agency on the environment, whereas the latter cannot recreate them after they have been challenged by some change in the environment.[4]

8.2 Semiogeographic Attitudes—Engagement Versus Disengagement

Massive migratory phenomena usually modify semiotic landscapes. New somatic features, new kinds of cloths, new gestures, postures, and movements, new feelings of distance and proximity, new music, new food, new sounds and smells, new buildings, new ways of experiencing the body in space and time, new conceptions of private and public, individuality and collectiveness become increasingly conspicuous to old residents. New residents too are surrounded by the unusual semiotic landscape created by old residents.[5]

Reactions to changes in the semiotic landscape may vary a lot. On the one end of the spectrum, "semiotic engagement": old and new residents seek to deconstruct their semiotic habits in order to shape new ones. They feel excited about the possibility of seeing or even befriending people from another culture, admiring or even wearing their cloths, smelling or even tasting their food, listening to their music, enjoying the different sound of their language or even learning it, seeking sexual or even marital relations with them, visiting their buildings or adopting their architectural style, learning about their religion or even converting to it, etc.

On the other end of the spectrum, "semiotic disengagement": faced with changes in the semiotic landscape, both old and new residents are not willing to change their semiotic habits accordingly. The instability and opaqueness introduced by alternative agencies in the semiotic landscape are experienced not as a source of further excitement, but rather as a source of confusion and lack of harmony. If the first attitude brings about aesthetic appreciation and even desire, the second one generates aesthetic derogation and even rejection: new bodies are ugly, new gestures are ungracious, new cloths are unfashionable, new smells are bad smells, new food is disgusting, new music is just noise, new buildings are ugly, "others" live too close to- or too far from-each other, they are too lazy or too active, they enjoy working or leisure too much, their buildings are ugly, their ways of living space and time are wrong, their sexuality is perverse, their religions are fake, etc. Total semiotic disengagement means that no semiotic habits are changed in order to respond to changes in the semiotic landscape. On the contrary, any change in the semiotic landscape must be eliminated so that old semiotic habits may not vary.

[4]Incidentally, one might even argue that if sciences have been developed in order to improve the human capacity to elaborate semiotic habits, arts have been developed in order to improve the human capacity to challenge existing semiotic habits.

[5]Actually, old residents who are puzzled by the changes the new ones introduce in the semiotic landscape often omit to think about how puzzled the new residents might be in the same situation, and vice versa.

Generally, total semiotic disengagement generates policies of both cultural assimilation (by the old residents) and cultural self-ghettoization (by the new ones). In both cases, the semiotic landscape is turned into a semiotic scene: old residents feel compelled to reject the new ones as if they had invaded their homes, and new residents feel compelled to create new semiotic scenes in the semiotic landscape where they can "feel at home".

Tendencies toward either semiotic engagement or semiotic disengagement vary according to the availability of material resources in a society, but do not strictly depending on it. History shows that rich societies are more likely to feature semiotic engagement, but history also shows that rich societies might incline toward semiotic disengagement as poor societies might show the opposite inclination.

Thanks to an Endeavour Research Award Fellowship by the Australian Government and thanks to the support of the Section of English, Communication, and Performance Studies at Monash University, I have been developing a research project aiming at comparing the current semiotic landscapes of Europe and Australia. The general hypothesis of this project is that societies, like the Italian one, where massive incoming migratory phenomena are relatively recent, might learn from both failures and successes of societies, like the Australian one, where such phenomena have been dealt with for a long time.

Politics, broadly construed, is the domain in which a society reaches a certain point of equilibrium between individuals and groups inclined toward either semiotic engagement or semiotic disengagement. Such point of equilibrium, and the processes that lead to its elaboration, are embodied in many manifestations of social life, which can be studied in order to understand the present trends of a society, foresee the future ones, and modify both—if considered unsuitable—through appropriate policies.

Legal documents are among the sources considered by my research project. An important part of it concerns the inclusion/exclusion of new religious minorities in/from the semiotic landscape of European/Australian cities. Legal controversies about the construction of new places of worship, for instance, are analysed as if they were the script of a performance where different agencies advocate for either a more inclusive or a more exclusive semiotic landscape. Judgements are therefore considered not only as legal statements but also as the narrative embodiment of the point of equilibrium reached by different actors of semiotic engagement/disengagement competing over the agency, stability, and transparency of a semiotic landscape.

8.3 Semiogeographic Tensions—Muslims Versus Koalas

The corpus of legal documents concerning controversies about the construction or institution of new mosques in Australia is particularly interesting. No religious community has been facing as many legal controversies in establishing new places of worship or related buildings in Australia as the Islamic ones. At the moment Islam is neither the biggest non-Christian minority in Australia nor the fastest growing nor the one in which the larger percentage of believers was not born in Australia.[6] However, it is quite probable that the current geo-political situation and the way in which its relation with Islam is represented by both the national and the international political and mediatic discourse fuel the adversity with which new Islamic settlements are considered in Australia.

These legal controversies show a recurrent structure (Dunn 2001)[7]: an Islamic community decides to build a new mosque or to convert an existing building (frequently a church that is no longer used by any Christian community) into a mosque. The community's representatives submit an application for a planning permit to the competent city council. The city council advertises for the application through letters to the adjoining property owners and occupiers, a public notice sign on the site of the application, and a notice in the local newspaper(s). Those who think that themselves or their property will be negatively affected by the plan submit objections, stating their reasons. In many circumstances, citizens also write to local newspapers, usually in order to express their adversity to the plan and the reasons for it. Urban planning consultation meetings are held in order to allow interested people to express their views on a planning permit application. The city council usually rejects the planning permit application under pressure from the local non-Islamic majority. In many circumstances, representatives of the Islamic communities submit an appeal to the competent planning and environment court, which normally upholds it. In some cases, such as 1983 *Moslem Alawy Society LTD v Canterbury Municipal Council*, the legal controversy goes on to the Court of Appeal and even to the High Court of Australia (Humphrey 1989).

From the point of view—adopted by the present paper—of the cultural semiotics of the legal discourse, several steps in this process deserve closer attention. First of all, the objections lodged by those who oppose the establishment of a new mosque, as well as the transcriptions of what they say in planning consultation meetings constitute a rich corpus of documents whose semantic analysis not only reveals the level of semiotic (dis)engagement in a certain socio-cultural context, but also the way in which such (dis)engagement is expressed through legal discourse. To this regard, the comparison with the way in which the same (dis)engagement is voiced through letters to the local newspapers is particularly interesting.

Second, the way in which the decisions of city councils—that usually yield to the objections of the majority—are systematically overturned by judgements of higher legal authorities is also worthy of consideration, mainly as regards the discrepancy that this phenomenon manifests between how the dialectics between religious majority and minority is perceived in Australia at the local and the national level.

---

[6]See the 2006 Australian Census of Population and Housing—Religious Affiliation; the bibliography on Islam in Australia is extensive; for an effective survey on the history of Islam in Australia up to 2004, Dunn (2004).

[7]Isin and Siemiatycki (1999) and Siemiatycki (2002) for a study of mosques development in Toronto; Feirabend and Rath (1996) for a study of the same topic in Rotterdam and Utrecht. For a general survey on Europe, Shadid and Koningsveld (1996). For a complete survey of the existent literature on this topic, Leone Forthcoming.

There have been numerous legal controversies in Australia concerning the establishment of new mosques.[8] The most interesting cases probably are, in chronological order: the already mentioned *Moslem Alawy Society LTD v Canterbury Municipal Council* (Land and Environment Court of New South Wales 1983; followed by *Canterbury Municipal Council v Moslem Alawy Society*, Supreme Court of New South Wales 1985; followed by *Canterbury Municipal Council v Moslem Alawy Society*, High Court of Australia 1986–1987); *Bankstown City Council v House of Peace PTY LTD* (Land and Environment Court of New South Wales 1998; followed by *House of Peace PTY LTD and Another v Bankstown City Council*, Supreme Court of New South Wales 1999–2000); *Designlink International v Auburn Council* (Land and Environment Court of New South Wales 1999–2000); New Century Developments PTY LTD v *Baulkham Hills Shire Council* (Land and Environment Court of New South Wales 2003); *Kotku Education and Welfare Society Inc. v Brisbane City Council* (Planning and Environment Court of Queensland 2004); *The Muslim League of New South Wales Inc. v Liverpool City Council* (Land and Environment Court of New South Wales 2005–2006); *Afghan Community Support Association v Blacktown City Council* (Land and Environment Court of New South Wales 2008); *Gelling & Ors v Cairns City Council and Anor* (Planning and Environment Court of Queensland 2008).

The present paper will propose a cultural-semiotic analysis of *Kotku Education and Welfare Society Inc. v Brisbane City Council* (Planning and Environment Court of Queensland 2004) (QPEC 068), an appeal against Brisbane City Council's rejection of the appellant's application for a material change of use permitting the construction of a mosque and a cultural centre on land at 1860 Mt Gravatt-Capalaba Road, Capalaba West.

The appellant is an Islamic religious organization taking its name from a twentieth-century Turkish Muslim scholar, Mehmed Zahid Kotku. It was first established in Australia in 1984 and in Brisbane a decade later. In order to establish a place of worship, the organization acquired two other properties in 1994 and 1996. It was forced to move from a house on the first property after the Council advised that it was not a proper place for religious activities. The second, at Capalaba (in Redland Shire) was purchased after extensive consultation with that Council's town planning staff but met strong local opposition and the Society's application was ultimately rejected. In the years 1997–2004 the Society rented five properties, mostly in shops and office premises and at the time of the appeal was operating in an office building in an industrial estate at Capalaba for which it had no town planning approval, and where it was limiting its activities to prayers.

The co-respondents were local residents. Almost all the immediate neighbours were adverse. For the purposes of the present paper, the semantics of the objections they submitted is particularly relevant. In this legal controversy, as well as in other

[8]The link between the number of these controversies and the way in which the relation between Islam and the geo-political international situation is represented by the mediatic and the political discourse at both the national and the international level deserves further investigation.

similar cases in the corpus, no objection to the establishment of a new mosque shows an overtly anti-Islamic content. Whereas such content is frequently present in anti-mosque letters sent to local newspapers, any reference to the fact that, for instance, "Australia should be a Christian nation", or that "a new mosque would give rise to ways of life that are against the Australian one", or even to Islamic terrorism, are accurately avoided in the objections lodged against a new mosque's planning permit.

However, it is not easy to determine whether religious discrimination is not in the mind of those who object to the establishment of a new mosque,[9] or it is just not in their language, an administrative and bureaucratic language that they learn from their legal advisors in order to coat their semiotic disengagement toward religious difference so that such semiotic disengagement might be acceptable, and hopefully successful, vis-à-vis the politico-legal establishment of Australian courts.

One of the central features of this language consists in translating religious intolerance, generally stigmatised by both the Australian political and legal discourse, into three different kinds of intolerance, still considered as a viable matter of debate both in the public arena and in courts: (1) logistic intolerance; (2) environmental intolerance; (3) aesthetic intolerance.

The legal rhetoric[10] of logistic intolerance is centred on the value of safety: those who object to the establishment of a new mosque claim that it would generate an intolerable increase in traffic and a consequent shortage of car parking. However, this rhetoric is not very powerful, for it can be overturned with quantitative arguments. In the Brisbane controversy, for instance, traffic engineers easily established that there were no traffic safety issues connected to the proposal, by also pointing out that these issues had not arisen in connection with other Christian places of worship already present in the area.

The legal rhetoric of environmental intolerance dislocates the rationale of the objections against the new mosque from human beings to nature. A report submitted along with the objections of the Brisbane controversy, for instance, contended that the new mosque would have " . . . net negative impact on the koala habitat values of the site" and be " . . . inconsistent with the conservation strategy intention and provisions for a property within the Koala Conservation Area" (QPEC 068: 13). The court later demonstrated that the site did not provide at the moment any koala habitat, and that, on the contrary, "the proposed landscaping and re-vegetation compelled the conclusion that any effect on koala habitat values was likely to be at worst neutral and, more probably, beneficial." (ibid., p. 14)

However, the symbolic value of the opposition between the needs of a religious minority and those of an archetypical Australian animal species probably goes

---

[9]Isin and Siemiatycki (1999, p. 18): "Explicit motivations behind neighbourhood opposition to a development like this are difficult to establish".

[10]Cfr Coombe and Herman (2004, p. 560): " . . . rhetoric is a social and material practice of the pragmatics of power that punctuates the world with meaning and thereby renders social action possible . . .".

beyond the mere environmental issue.[11] The desire of protecting koalas against the "invasion" of a Muslim community might be interpreted as sublimating, at an environmental level, the desire to protect the Anglo-Celtic culture considered as both native and in danger of extinction.

The third legal rhetoric, that of aesthetic intolerance, is probably the most common and also the most effective one in this kind of legal controversies. As Mr Enright, one of the co-respondents, pointed out in his objection against the new Brisbane mosque, the new building would be "just too big and out of character for the site that has been chosen. It will unduly impact on our lives in many ways, and on the environment and character of the area." (ibid., p. 3) Similarly, most of the other objections revolved around the belief that the new mosque would be out of character with the surrounding area, and that it would ruin its visual amenity through the impacts of associated noise and lighting. While experts called by the parties, Mr King and Mr Kamst, were in agreement that the acoustic barrier fence of the new mosque would achieve strict compliance with noise impact assessment criteria in the Brisbane city plan, Mr Kamst suggested, nevertheless, that noises associated with the mosque's religious services in the early morning, and the evening, may affect local residents because they were "entirely uncharacteristic" (ibid., p. 13). Mr Enright also declared that the Turkish-styled proposed mosque and annexed buildings,

> whilst of architectural interest, are out of character with other structures in the area—which are residential dwellings, many also having backyard sheds and chook houses in keeping with the nature of the area. Despite attempts to ultimately block views of the structures with planting of trees, the buildings will still be quite easily visible, particularly from Tinchborne Street. (ibid., p. 14)

A word recurs in all the objections: "character". Whereas the legal, administrative, and bureaucratic Australian arena would not accept objections against the settlement of a new religious minority on the basis of the fact that it contradicts the "religious character" of Australia, it accepts them on the basis of the fact that the presence of this religious minority in the Australian territory contradicts the "aesthetic character" of Australia, the way in which Australia "should appear/look". The focus of intolerance is therefore dislocated from the religious minority per se to the way in which the religious minority modifies the semiotic landscape of Australia.

For the legal purposes of the majority such dislocation is effective because, whereas the Australian philosophy of city planning generally promotes a conception of cultural (and religious) harmony based on the notion of cultural heterogeneity and even mix of cultures, the same philosophy also promotes a conception of aesthetic harmony based on the notion of aesthetic homogeneity and cultural characterisation (the philosophy of cultural precincts, one might call it). However, these two conceptions are often contradictory: if the coexistence of Christian Australians and

[11] Incidentally (speaking about nationalism and archetypical animals), if referring to themselves as an animal, Australians use the term "Skip" (he she is a Skip), and people become proper Skips. This is from the children's TV show (of the 1960s), *Skippy*. Skippy was a kangaroo. But cfr also the (boxing) kangaroo used as a sports flag—when supporting Australian teams.

Muslim Australians is a value, how can the coexistence of Christian and Islamic architectures be not a value?

In the Brisbane legal controversy, for instance, on the one hand the 2000 City Plan has as one of its Desired Environmental Outcomes "to promote social and cultural diversity, and non-discriminatory access to public and private development" (Brisbane City Council 2000, Section 3.2.2.8); on the other hand, the same City Plan has as one of its DEO "the protection of landscapes that enhance amenity and character in rural and semi rural areas, and sympathetic development which complements surrounding character and style in both urban and rural areas" (Brisbane City Council 2000, Section 3.2.2.4). According to the first DEO, the establishment of a new Turkish styled mosque in semi-rural Brisbane should be welcomed, while according to the second DEO it should be contrasted.

What is at stake here is much more than an issue of city planning; it is the problem of reaching an equilibrium between a concept of religious harmony based on the heterogeneity of private semiotic scenes and a concept of aesthetic harmony based on the homogeneity of the public semiotic landscape (Leone 2009b). The fact that permits for the establishment of religious minorities' new places of worship are refused at the local level of city councils but granted at the global level of state or federal courts is symptomatic of this opposition: whereas from the close point of view of residents the value of a monocultural public aesthetic sphere is more important than the value of a multicultural private religious sphere, from the distant point of view of jurists in state or federal courts this hierarchy of values is reversed.

In his judgement on the Brisbane controversy, Judge Alan Wilson dismisses the aesthetic objections of the future neighbours of the new mosque. He writes that "these buildings (and the formal garden) are in a 'Turkish' style, featuring colours and intricate patterns of Turkish origin, quite different from the nearby houses but on any view interesting and pleasing" (ibid., p. 4); that "it is undeniable that the buildings are exotic, and interesting" (ibid., p. 5); that "even the most jaundiced eye would concede it [the new mosque] is no less attractive than some of the residential development that has taken place, and the only fair conclusion is that, as Mr Riddell said, it will ultimately be, while different, nevertheless attractive and pleasing" (ibid., p. 14).

Analysing the documents of this legal controversy, someone who supports freedom of religious belief and the value of aesthetic multiculturalism should definitely endorse Judge Wilson's opinion. However, an unbiased semio-cultural analysis of this controversy should not neglect the following point: if we grant that the rhetoric of aesthetic intolerance is not just a disguise for religious intolerance or for the fear that the economic value of the local real estate might drop, and that therefore non-Muslim neighbours would be perfectly happy with the establishment of a new mosque—provided that it does not look conspicuously alien to the surrounding semiotic landscape—then the right to an aesthetically monocultural semiotic landscape that they seek to defend by objecting to the construction of a new "Turkish-styled" mosque in the territory of semi rural Brisbane is the same right that the Turkish Islamic community seeks to defend by establishing a Turkish-looking mosque in the same territory.

In fact, as it emerges from the documents of this legal controversy, the community wanted to establish a new mosque because it felt that its identity was not adequately represented by other mosques in the area. The Imam says that the mosque at Bald Hills is predominantly used by persons of Fijian background, and the one at Kuraby by South Africans, while the mosque at Buranda is predominantly attended by people with Pakistani, or Afghan connections. Some mosques provide food after the major services, usually with a national flavour, and Judge Wilson admits that this nationally flavoured food is not necessarily attractive to those of other cultures (ibid., p. 5).

In other words: Judge Wilson is sympathetic toward the local Turkish community and its desire to establish a Turkish mosque, designed by Turkish architects, "of particular interest (and pleasure) to persons with a Turkish background" (ibid.), and serving Turkish food after major services (the Turkish vocation of the mosque is even used as an argument against the objection that the mosque is going to attract non-Turkish Muslims too and generate traffic and parking problems). On the other hand, though, the same Judge is unsympathetic toward the non-Islamic neighbours of the new mosque when they want to preserve the Australian character of their semiotic landscape.

While Judge Wilson's judgement is commendable in the way it protects the religious rights of a minority, it also embodies a conception according to which the right of a minority to express its aesthetic identity by creating a semiotic scene—a sort of aesthetic enclave—within the semiotic landscape of the majority is worthier of projection than the right of the majority to achieve the same mono-cultural aesthetics by thwarting the aesthetic discourse of minorities. In other words, the judgement fails to acknowledge the fact that both attitudes are a manifestation of semiotic disengagement bringing about what could be called "architectures (and urban planning) of nostalgia": on the one hand, the nostalgia of predominantly Christian and Anglo-Celtic Australia; on the other hand, the nostalgia of a lost motherland.

Several points can be drawn from the semio-cultural analysis of this legal controversy. First of all, there seems to be a contradiction between the way in which multiculturalism is conceived as an abstract principle by the predominant discourse of the Australian legal, administrative, and bureaucratic system at both a state and a federal level, and the way in which the same multiculturalism is experienced in its concrete aesthetic embodiments at the local level.[12] At the state and federal level, the semiotic landscape of Australian cities is imagined as a place where citizens should "naturally" welcome, with a mixture of curiosity and excitement, changes introduced by new aesthetic cultures. At the local level, instead, there is a strong desire by both majorities and minorities to transform the semiotic landscape of Australian cities into semiotic scenes: the majority would like to minimize

[12]In 1997 Australian comedy film by Rob Sitch *The Castle*, one of the most acclaimed movies in the history of Australian cinema, represents a similar gap between the local aesthetics of Australian working-class citizens and the global interests of the state and federal elites. Cfr Turnball (2008).

the impact of minorities in the semiotic landscape, while minorities would like to minimize the impact of the majority in their "semiotic enclaves".

Second, there seems to be a discrepancy between the ways in which these local desires are acknowledged by the legal, administrative, and bureaucratic discourse at the state and the federal level, as if the desire to preserve the character of the Australian semiotic landscape was less understandable than the desire of minorities to create 'semiotic enclaves' reproducing the character of non-Australian semiotic landscapes. In many cases, as the semiotic analysis of judgements reveals, this seems to be caused by an optical illusion: Australian judges are unable to perceive the character of the Australian semiotic landscape, probably because it is too familiar,[13] while the character of minorities' "semiotic enclaves" appears to them as perfectly identifiable and, usually, exotic. This depends also on the fact that the creation of "semiotic enclaves" by minorities often entails an emphasis on signs of identity. However, such a paternalistic attitude of the Australian legal discourse toward the character of minorities' aesthetics is, after all, an expression of orientalism, favourable for short-term legal purposes, but probably unfavourable in long-term cultural terms.

8.4 Semiogeographic Policies—Multicultural Planning and Grass-Root Engagement

It is difficult to formulate suggestions about policies that might be able to contrast these two phenomena. Certainly, if local objections against changes in the semiotic landscape are simply dismissed as manifestations of the NIMBY syndrome, to be ignored in the grand framework of global multiculturalism, and if the burden of changing semiotic habits is bestowed exclusively on the majority, the contradictions and discrepancies analysed above are likely to create an increasing amount of micro-tensions, ultimately detrimental also to those minorities that the policies of multiculturalism is meant to protect. To this regard, the semio-cultural analysis of legal controversies about the establishment of new places of worship by minorities indicates the presence of some urgent needs.

First, while the Australian legal, administrative, and bureaucratic discourse at both the state and the federal level has fully embraced multiculturalism, local urban planning is, under many regards, still mono-cultural. In the 2000 City Plan of Brisbane, for instance, mosques and the like were not mentioned at all and it appears they were intended to be encompassed within the notion of "community facilities", which were defined as: "a use of premises for the provision of cultural, social or

[13]The intellectual trend of "suburbia bashing" initiated by Boyd (1960) might also be one of the reasons of the Australian legal discourse's inability to identify and cherish the aesthetics of semi rural Australia. The literature on the aesthetico-political contrast between urbanites and suburbanites in Australia is extensive; for an introduction, cfr Ferber et al. (1994) and Gleeson (2006).

community services e.g. community centre, community hall, youth sub, library, church or public building." (Brisbane City Council 2000, p. 67).

However, as the documents of this legal controversy reveal, urban planners cannot simply solve the problem of the location of a mosque, or a synagogue, or a Buddhist temple, by simply assimilating these places of worship to Christian churches, because each religion has a specific way of living the semiotic scene of a place of worship. Just to give an example, whereas in Brisbane the location of churches near retail or commercial centres benefits from the fact that the parking facilities of such centres are mostly empty on Sunday mornings, the location of a mosque in the same position would create an unpleasant competition for parking between Muslims attending the Friday prayer and non-Muslims attending the Friday shopping. In other words, urban planners should be more familiar with the ways in which different communities experience the semiotic landscape of the city in which they live, and possibly plan urban development so as to maximize the equilibrium among different needs.[14]

Second, citizens should be encouraged to reach a point of equilibrium between the way in which they treasure the character of a certain semiotic landscape and the way in which they accept that this character is changed by alternative agencies. However, the responsibility to elaborate such a point of equilibrium should be equally distributed: no minority should be obliged to entirely abandon its conception of the semiotic landscape, but no minority should be allowed to entirely impose its conception on the majority either. For instance, non-Muslim Australians should be encouraged to see a mosque not as a cradle of religious fundamentalism or—worse—terrorism, or as an alien building devastating the landscape of Australian cities, but as a site to be cherished as both a place of worship that embodies the freedom of belief of a minority and a building to be looked at with curiosity and even excitement, as an element of novelty in the architectural routine of the city. At the same time, Muslim Australians should be encouraged to see mosques not as non-Australian enclaves in the Australian semiotic landscape, but as places of worship that, exactly as many Australian churches, synagogues, and temples, would not lose their religious and cultural identity if they borrowed some elements from Australian non-Muslim architecture.

Fulfilling the first need (injecting multiculturalism in urban planning) will be sterile without fulfilling the second (creating a semiotically engaged citizenship). However, such a semiotically engaged citizenship cannot be imposed by state or federal legislation through abstract and distant legal, bureaucratic, and administrative declarations of multiculturalism, and cannot be planned either by multicultural urban planning, although it can be facilitated by both. On the contrary, grass-root initiatives, also encouraged by the state and the federal governments, are more likely to achieve this goal.

[14]The literature on multicultural planning is vast; for an introduction, Burayidi (2000), for a comparison with the Canadian practice, Qadeer (1997).

First of all, agencies that contribute to the creation and diffusion of cultural contents, and above all the educational and the mediatic system, should help citizens to attain a thicker knowledge of the semiotic landscape in which they live. By "thicker knowledge" here it is meant a greater familiarity with the variety of signs that weave the fabric of multicultural city landscapes. Faced with the relatively unfamiliar architecture of a mosque, for instance, non-Muslim citizens should be encouraged to perceive it not as a threatening mystery, but as a system of architectural signs whose cultural and religious meaning they partially know, and even want to explore further. Also cultural minorities, including religious minorities, can give an important contribution to the creation of this thick knowledge. For instance, many Islamic communities in Australia already organize open-days in which non-Muslims can visit their mosques and, with the help of members of the community, learn more about the way in which Muslim communities like to modify the semiotic landscape of Australian cities.

At the same time, cultural minorities should also acquire a thicker knowledge of both the cultural majority and the other minorities with which they share a semiotic landscape. It is only through this reciprocal effort of semiotic hospitality, in which each culture preserves its own identity but at the same time receives some elements from neighbouring cultures and offers some of its elements to them,[15] that a truthful multicultural planning is possible.

8.5 Semiogeographic Key-Factors—Cultural Frontier Mediators and the Body

Two factors, I believe, might be extremely effective in the establishment of this dynamic of semiotic engagement and hospitality: cultural mediators, and the body.

According to the semiotic theory of culture formulated by Russian semiotician Jurij M. Lotman (2001), each culture can be described as a semiosphere, as a semiotic biosphere that enables social life through the creation, circulation, and destruction of signs. Each semiosphere conceives its identity as opposed to what is outside of its frontiers. This "outside" can be conceived of as a "cultural void" (it is the typical attitude of cultural chauvinism) or as occupied by other semiospheres. In either case, the frontier of a semiosphere is fundamental not only in delimiting what is believed inside the semiosphere from what is believed outside of it (from either an internal or an external point of view), but also in determining the passage of cultural elements from the outside to the inside. No semiosphere, indeed, not even that representing the most conservative culture, is completely rigid. On the contrary, new elements from the outside of a semiosphere are continuously translated into the inside, and vice versa. Frontiers indeed work not only as delimitations between cultural semiospheres, but also as mechanisms of cultural translation.

[15]Cfr the concept of "ecumene" in Ulf Hannerz's works (1992, 1996), as well as the concept of "ecumeme" in Coombe and Herman's re-elaboration (2004).

This continuous dialectic between different cultural semiospheres can be observed in the semiotic landscape of contemporary multicultural cities: the signs through which citizens, groups, and communities manifest their identities create a frontier that divides what is characteristic of a certain culture from what is not. At the same time, transduction and translation processes constantly occur through a dialectics that is the more enriching the more it is reciprocal.

A key-role in determining a point of equilibrium between identity and communication in contemporary multi-cultural city landscapes can be played by cultural mediators. By "cultural mediators", here, it is not meant professionals contracted by private or public institutions in order to facilitate relations between different cultural communities. Professional cultural mediators are certainly fundamental, but perhaps even more fundamental are the people who, for one reason or another, find themselves at the frontier between two or more cultures. Singling out these people and giving them a primary role in building processes of mutual semiotic hospitality among the communities that live in multicultural cities might turn extremely effective, especially in potentially conflictive contexts such as the administration of public space (Jupp and Nieuwenhuysen 2007).

A second factor that is often neglected in multicultural policies is, paradoxically, the body. Multicultural policies are usually logocentric. They are based on the assumption that a suitable equilibrium among the cultural communities that share a certain semiotic landscape will be reached through words: by using the right words to describe cultures and their signs, by encouraging people to use these words, and by injecting words like "harmony" in the public discourse. In many cases, the way in which the Australian legal, administrative, and bureaucratic discourse seeks to protect and foster multiculturalism is the epitome of such a logocentric attitude.

Perhaps, a second factor multicultural policies should take into account, together with the centrality of grass-root cultural mediators, is the fact that no effective multicultural equilibrium can be reached if it does not affect the body of citizens as much as their verbal language. The fact that citizens use the appropriate words to describe fellow citizens from other cultures and pay lip service to an abstract formulation of multiculturalism is not relevant, and might even be counterproductive, if intercultural tensions keep simmering under the verbal surface of the society. On the contrary, the process of reciprocal semiotic hospitality mentioned above can take place only if citizens let their body be somehow affected by difference.

Eating the characteristic food of another cultural community, for instance, is a powerful symbolic process in which cultural difference is not merely acknowledged verbally, but also appropriated, literally ingested and transformed into part of one's own body and identity. Grass-root initiatives meant to encourage citizens to explore all the signs that constitute the identity of the different cultures that compose the semiotic landscape of a multicultural city are likely to create, in the long term, a more semiotically engaged citizenship, able to appreciate the musical interplay between identity and difference. The arts, meant as sources of alternative cultural agencies that deconstruct semiotic habits while inducing pleasant emotions (excitement, curiosity, etc.) can certainly play a major role in the institution of the multicultural body of contemporary citizenship.

To the credit of Australian institutions, it has to be said that enormous efforts and investments of economic and human resources are currently being made, at both local, state, and federal levels, to create a more favourable ground for multicultural planning.

8.6 The Semiogeography of New Mosques in Italy

The semio-cultural analysis of documents concerning Australian legal controversies about the establishment of new places of worship shows a need for both multicultural planning and initiatives to equitably spread grass-root and reciprocal attitudes of semiotic engagement and hospitality. However, although the Australian multicultural legal, administrative, and bureaucratic frameworks and the policies they have designed and implemented have not completely eliminated sources of tensions in multicultural cities, the results they have achieved thus far are incommensurably more advanced if compared with those of most present-day European societies.

In Italy, for instance—a relatively homogenous society that is still more used to the idea of Italians migrating to other societies rather than to the idea of individuals from other societies migrating to Italy—old residents are often extremely firm in rejecting modifications in the semiotic landscapes of Italian cities by alternative agencies, and in particular by relatively new religious minorities. Unlike the current Australian society, the present Italian society does not force the rejection of cultural and religious difference to be disguised behind bureaucratic language through logistic, environmental, or aesthetic rhetoric. On the contrary, the downright rejection of difference introduced by minorities is accepted as legitimate by the political, the legal, and the mediatic arena, and voiced—sometimes even encouraged—shamelessly at every level of the institutional system, from local city councils to the parliament. Furthermore, total semiotic disengagement, and the consequent willingness not to accept any change in the semiotic landscape of Italian cities, has become the centre of a vicious circle interlacing grass-root, political, and mediatic discourse. Both politicians and mediatic opinion-makers know that, in the context of the current Italian society, they can secure political and cultural leadership by voicing the arguments of aggressive monoculturalism, and at the same time contribute to spreading and reinforcing their presence at a grass-root level.

In their attempts to establish new mosques, the growing Italian Muslim communities have faced very aggressive opposition by both private citizens and institutions. *Lega*, a political party that has received increasing support by the Italian voters in the last elections—especially in the Centre and in the North of the country—and that presently integrates Silvio Berlusconi's coalition of government, has turned the rejection of cultural difference, and particularly of Islam, into one of its main propaganda arguments. Members of Lega have taken both spectacular mediatic and sophisticated legal initiatives in order to affirm this principle: on the one hand, high-ranking members of Lega—including European and Italian parliament deputies and ministers—alongside grass-root activists, have often used pigs or pigs' excrements to pre-emptively profane spaces that local administrations had conceded to Muslim communities for the construction of new mosques or Islamic centers (Fregonara 2007; Mangiarotti 2007a, b, etc.).

On the other hand, Lega deputies Andrea Gibelli and Roberto Cota on June 4, 2008 proposed to the Italian parliament an articulated bill (n. 1246) that, if approved, would introduce severe restrictions for Muslims wanting to build a new mosque or other Islamic place of worship in Italy (Cota and Gibelli 2008). Cultures of migrants are defined as "historically antithetic to ours" ["culture storicamente antitetiche alla nostra"] (ibid., p. 1); minorities are described as wanting to keep a cultural identity "by opposing ours" ["comunità ... che rivendicano ... il mantenimento di una loro identità culturale contrapponendosi alla nostra"] (ibid.).

Whereas art. 8 of the Constitution of the Italian Republic states that "all religion confessions are equally free before the Law" ["tutte le confessioni religiose sono egualmente libere davanti alla legge"], the bill proposes to introduce special hard and fast rules defining the activities of the Islamic community in "our" territory ["disposizioni normative che definiscano in maniera ferrea e precisa le loro attività sul nostro territorio"]. No genius in semiotic analysis is needed to understand that the language of this bill creates a net opposition between a non-Islamic "us" and an Islamic "them", as if Italian Muslims were not Italians and could not be represented by the "us" of Italian Parliament deputies as well as non-Muslim Italians.

The bill continues with the argument that mosques are not just places of worship, and that their establishment should therefore not be simply a matter of freedom of religious belief. The argument that mosques have been frequently associated with terrorist activities is used by the bill to underline its urgency. Mosques are actually defined by the bill as "military places" (ibid., p. 3), albeit between inverted commas. The overall strategy of the bill is clear: since mosques are not simply places of worship, but also and actually predominantly political and military centres, as well as places for trade and instruction of under-age individuals, their establishment cannot be ruled according to art. 8 of the Constitution of the Italian Republic but must be regulated by local political institutions, from the councils of Italian regions down to local city councils. In other words, the bill would like to entrust decisions about mosques to local institutions in order to eliminate the constitutional control of the higher levels of the legal system on these matters, the same control that enabled many Australian Islamic communities to overturn the unfair judgments of local councils.

Article 2 of the bill suggests that Muslim communities that want to establish a new place of worship should provide not only full information about the building plan and the origin of the financial resources to implement it, but also collect a number of signatures whose amount is to be determined by local authorities. Local authorities therefore prepare a building plan that is proportional to the number of Islamic citizens legally present in a certain area and submit it to the approval of a popular referendum by the citizens that live in that area. Decisions about religious minorities are therefore completely entrusted to the religious majority, with consequences that are not difficult to foresee.

Article 3, point 1/b of the bill states that no new Muslim places of worship should be established within a range of one kilometre from previously existing places of worship such as Christian churches or synagogues. The effect of such a norm is to ban any mosque from the semiotic landscape of Italian cities, and to ghettoize them in suburban or industrial areas. The rationale of such provision is evident also in point 1/c, which states that Muslim communities cannot broadcast sounds or display images in the public space. However, aesthetics is important to xenophobe Italian politicians too: according to point 1/d, Muslim places of worship must respect the typical (another word for "characteristic") building typologies of the local territory.

It is very unlikely that this bill will be approved as it is by the Italian parliament. Even if it was, it would be probably declared unconstitutional by the Constitutional Court of Italy, because it clearly contradicts, under many respects, art. 8 of the Constitution of the Italian Republic. However, this is not the point. Probably, the Italian deputies who wrote this bill and presented it to the Parliament know that it will never be approved as it is. The point is that such bill carries a propagandistic value, which can be used by the deputies and their political parties in order to strengthen their leadership vis-à-vis an increasing number of Italians. This bill therefore matters less for its legal consequences than for what it represents from the cultural point of view: a society where total semiotic disengagement toward cultural minorities, and especially the religious Islamic minority, can be presented as a useful argument to gain mediatic and political attention and control.

8.7 Conclusions

The comparative, semio-cultural analysis between legal sources concerning the establishment of new places of worship by minorities in the semiotic landscape of, respectively, Australian and Italian cities, which was outlined by the present paper, was too sketchy to produce any general conclusions about the level of semiotic (dis)engagement in the two societies. Furthermore, the different genre of the analysed documents undoubtedly influenced the comparison: on the one hand, as regards the Australian political, legal, administrative, and bureaucratic system, a judgment revealing both the relative semiotic disengagement represented by reactions of aesthetic intolerance at the Australian local level, and the relative semiotic engagement represented by abstract multicultural frameworks at the state and the federal level; on the other hand, as regards the Italian system, an evidently discriminatory bill presented to the Italian parliament by members of the current coalition of government.

Nevertheless, despite the inchoate character of both the analysis and the comparison, some conclusions can be drawn from both. On the one hand, in Australia multiculturalism seems to be already a predominant socio-cultural framework, generally endorsed by the political establishment (broadly construed) and by its decisions in terms of the legal, administrative, and bureaucratic system of the country. Action must be taken so that this framework might tally with local attitudes concerning semiotic (dis)engagement and hospitality, mainly in terms of finding a point of equilibrium between the particularistic aspirations of both the majority and the minorities and the need that they share a common semiotic landscape. The danger to address here is that tensions that do not find expression in the public arena might simmer privately until they give rise to sudden and unexpected explosions of violence (on the "landmark of Cronulla", see Collins 2007).

On the other hand, in Italy as well as in many other European societies the predominant socio-cultural framework is still monoculturalism. Alternative agencies—which introduce or are believed to introduce changes in the semiotic landscape of Italian cities—are strongly rejected, often through overtly discriminatory rhetoric, both at the local level of grass-root initiatives and at the regional and state level of political and legal discourse. Politicians and mediatic opinion-makers, with few exceptions, know that they can benefit from their role of mediators between local and national disengagement and voice and titillate the point of view of the majority over those of the minorities.

In other words, whereas it is quite evident that the Australian political and legal discourse emphasizes its pedagogic role in transmitting a certain model of society top-down—sometimes running the risk, as it was pointed out earlier, to neglect the point of view of local agencies in favour of the ambition of fitting them into a grander socio-cultural plan—the Italian political and legal discourse adopts an excessively bottom-up attitude, almost completely giving up any pedagogical role of the political and legal elites and, on the contrary, shaping their political and mediatic agendas so as to represent the interests of the most powerful local agencies. If the dangers of an excessively top-down political strategy have already been underlined (the creation of a hypocritical rhetoric of multiculturalism), the dangers of an excessively bottom-up strategy are explosive. If the vicious circle between local semiotic disengagement and its political and mediatic referents is not broken, minorities in Italy will be more and more disempowered, whereas the majority will be more and more able to thwart alternative agencies of any kind. Social tensions that might arise from this excessive disequilibrium of power will potentially disrupt the social fabric of Italian cities. It is also in order to avoid such potentially painful situation that Italy, as well as many other European countries, should start introducing at least some of the policies that have been proved successful in keeping a certain degree of social harmony in societies that, like the Australian one, have coped for a longer time with the issue of cultural diversity.

Acknowledgments This paper was written thanks to the support of an Endeavour Research Award Fellowship by the Australian Government.

References

Bouma, Gary. 1996. *Many Religions, All Australian: Religious Settlement, Identity and Cultural Diversity*. Melbourne: The Christian Research Association.
Boyd, Robin. 1960. *The Australian Ugliness*. Melbourne: Penguin Books.
Brisbane City Council. 2000. *Brisbane City Plan*. Brisbane: Brisbane City Council.
Burayidi, Michael A. 2000. *Urban Planning in a Multicultural Society*. Westport, CT and London: Praeger.

Collins, Jock. 2007. The Landmark of Cronulla. In eds. James Jupp and John Nieuwenhuysen, *Social Cohesion in Australia*. Cambridge: Cambridge University Press, 61–69.

Coombe, Rosemary J. and Herman, Andrew. 2004. Rhetorical Virtues: Property, Speech, and the Commons on the World-Wide Web. *Anthropological Quarterly*, 77(3), 559–574.

Cota, Roberto and Gibelli, Andrea. 2008. Project of Law n. 1246 proposed to the Italian Parliament on June 4, 2008: Disposizioni concernenti la realizzazione di nuovi edifici destinati all'esercizio dei culti ammessi.

Coverley, Merlin. 2006. *Psychogeography*. London: Pocket Essentials.

Debord, Guy. 1955. Introduction à une critique de la géographie urbaine. *Les Lèvres nues*, 6, 11–15.

Dunn, Kevin M. 2001. Representations of Islam in the Politics of Mosque Development in Sydney. *Tijdschrift voor Economische en Sociale Geografie*, 92(3), 291–308.

Dunn, Kevin M. 2004. Islam in Sydney: Contesting the Discourse of Absence. *Australian Geographer*, 35(3), 333–353.

Eco, Umberto. 1979. *A Theory of Semiotics*. Bloomington, IN: Indiana University Press.

Feirabend, Jeroen and Rath, Jan. 1996. Making a Place for Islam in Politics: Local Authorities Dealing with Islamic Associations. In eds. Wasif Shadid and Sjoerd van Koningsveld, *Muslims in the Margin: Political Responses to the Presence of Islam in Western Europe*. Kampen: Kok Pharos, 243–258.

Ferber, Sarah, Healy, Chris, and McAuliffe, Chris, eds. 1994. *Australian Suburbs*. Melbourne: Melbourne University Press.

Fregonara, Gianna. 2007. 'Maiale day anti moschea', sfida di Calderoli, *Corriere della Sera* (September 14)

Gleeson, Brendan. 2006. *The Australian Heartlands: Making Space for Hope in the Suburbs*. Sydney: Allen and Unwin.

Hannerz, Ulf. 1992. *Cultural Complexity*. New York, NY: Columbia University Press.

Hannerz, Ulf. 1996. *Transnational Connections: Culture, People, Places*. New York, NY: Routledge.

Humphrey, Michael T. 1989. Islam: A Test for Multiculturalism in Australia. *Asian Migrant*, 2(2), 48–56.

Isin, Engin F. and Siemiatycki, Myer. 1999. Fate and Faith: Claiming Urban Citizenship in Immigrant Toronto, *Working Papers of the Joint Centre of Excellence for Research on Immigration and Settlement – Toronto*, 8.

Jupp, James and Nieuwenhuysen, John. 2007. *Social Cohesion in Australia*. Cambridge: Cambridge University Press.

Leone, Massimo. Forthcoming. Citizens of a Lesser God – Religious Minorities and the Legal Discourse of Multi-Cultural Democracies: the Case of Canada, to be submitted for publication to the International Journal for the Semiotics of Law.

Leone, Massimo, ed. 2009a. *Actants, Actors, Agents. The Meaning of Action and the Action of Meaning – From Theories to Territories*. Special issue of *Lexia*, 3–4.

Leone, Massimo. 2009b. Sustainable Religions in Contemporary Cities – A Semiotic Approach. *International Journal of Environmental, Cultural, Economic, and Social Sustainability*, 5(3), 47–59.

Lotman, Iuri Mikhalovich. 2001. *Universe of the Mind – A Semiotic Theory of Culture*, Engl. trans. Ann Shukman. London: Tauris.

Mangiarotti, Alessandra. 2007a. Lega, iniziativa choc contro la moschea, *Corriere della Sera* (November 11).

Mangiarotti, Alessandra. 2007b. La Lega con un maiale contro la moschea, *Corriere della Sera* (November 11).

Mohr, Richard. 2009. 'Allontanarsi dalla linea gialla': Distance and Access to Urban Semiosis. In ed. Massimo Leone, "Actants, Actors, Agents. The Meaning of Action and the Action of Meaning – From Theories to Territories". Special issue of *Lexia*, 3–4.

Peirce, Charles S. 1960–1966. In eds. Charles Hartshorne and Paul Weiss, *Collected Papers*, 8 vols. Cambridge, MA: Belknap Press of Harvard University Press.

Planning and Environment Court of Queensland. 2004. QPEC 068: *Kotku Education and Welfare Society Inc. v Brisbane City Council.*

Qadeer, Mohammad A. 1997. Pluralistic Planning for Multicultural Cities – The Canadian Practice. *Journal of the American Planning Association*, 63(4), 481–494.

Self, Will. 2007. *Psychogeography*. London: Bloomsbury.

Shadid, Wasif and Koningsveld, Sjoerd van, eds. 1996. *Muslims in the Margin: Political Responses to the Presence of Islam in Western Europe*. Kampen: Kok Pharos.

Siemiatycki, Myer and Isin, Engin F. 2002. Making Space for Mosques: Struggles for Urban Citizenship in Diasporic Toronto. In ed. Sherene Razack, *Race, Space and the Law: Unmapping a White Settler Society*. Ottawa, ON: Between the Lines Press, 185–209.

Stein, Howard F. 1987. *Developmental Time, Cultural Space: Studies in Psychogeography*. Norman, OK: University of Oklahoma Press.

Stein, Howard F. and Niederland, William G. 1989. *Maps from the Mind: Readings in Psychogeography*. Norman, OK: University of Oklahoma Press.

Turnball, Sue. 2008. Mapping the Vast Suburban Tundra: Australian Comedy from Dame Edna to Kath and Kim. *International Journal of Cultural Studies*, 11(1), 15–32.

Index

A. Wagner, J.M. Broekman (eds.), *Prospects of Legal Semiotics*,
DOI 10.1007/978-90-481-9343-1, © Springer Science+Business Media B.V. 2010